Norbert Pohlmann | Helmut Reimer | Wolfgang Schneider (Eds.)

ISSE 2009 Securing Electronic Business Processes

Microsoft Dynamics NAV
by P. M. Diffenderfer and S. El-Assal

Microsoft Navision 4.0
by P. M. Diffenderfer and S. El-Assal

From Enterprise Architecture to IT Governance
by K. D. Niemann

Future of Trust in Computing
by D. Grawrock, H. Reimer, A.-R. Sadeghi and C. Vishik

Understanding MP3
by M. Ruckert

Process Modeling with ARIS
by H. Seidlmeier

The New PL/I
by E. Sturm

www.viewegteubner.de

Norbert Pohlmann | Helmut Reimer |
Wolfgang Schneider (Eds.)

ISSE 2009 Securing Electronic Business Processes

Highlights of the Information Security Solutions
Europe 2009 Conference

With 73 illustrations

**VIEWEG+
TEUBNER**

Bibliographic information published by the Deutsche Nationalbibliothek
The Deutsche Nationalbibliothek lists this publication in the Deutsche Nationalbibliografie;
detailed bibliographic data are available in the Internet at http://dnb.d-nb.de.

Many of designations used by manufacturers and sellers to distinguish their products are claimed as trademarks.

The editors are grateful to Professor Dr. Patrick Horster for granting permission to use his layout for the following contributions.

1st Edition 2010

All rights reserved
© Vieweg+Teubner | GWV Fachverlage GmbH, Wiesbaden 2010

Editorial Office: Christel Roß | Andrea Broßler

Vieweg+Teubner is part of the specialist publishing group Springer Science+Business Media.
www.viewegteubner.de

Cover design: KünkelLopka Medienentwicklung, Heidelberg
Typesetting: Oliver Reimer, Jena
Printing company: STRAUSS GMBH, Mörlenbach
Printed on acid-free paper
Printed in Germany

ISBN 978-3-8348-0958-2

Contents

Preface _____ xi

About this Book _____ xiii

Welcome _____ xv

Microsoft Sponsoring Contribution

    Claims and Identity: On-Premise and Cloud Solutions _____ 1
    Vittorio Bertocci

Economics of Security and Identity Management _____ 15

    Measuring Information Security: Guidelines to Build Metrics _____ 17
    Eberhard von Faber

    Demystifying SAP security _____ 27
    Marc Sel · Kristof Van Der Auwera

    The ISACA Business Model for Information Security _____ 37
    Rolf von Roessing

    ICT Systems Contributing to European Secure-by-Design
    Critical Infrastructures _____ 48
    Fabien Cavenne

    ROI, Pitfalls and Best Practices with an Enterprise Smart Card Deployment __ 63
    Philip Hoyer

    A General Quality Classification System for eIDs and e-Signatures _____ 72
    Jon Ølnes · Leif Buene · Anette Andresen · Håvard Grindheim
    Jörg Apitzsch · Adriano Rossi

    Second Wave of Biometric ID-documents in Europe:
    The Residence Permit for non-EU/EEA Nationals _____ 87
    Detlef Houdeau

Security Services and Large Scale Public Applications ___ 95

User and Access Management in Belgian e-Government_____ 97
Jos Dumortier · Frank Robben

PKI – Crawling Out of the Grave & Into the Arms of Government _____ 108
Phil D'Angio · Panos Vassilliadas · Phaidon Kaklamanis

Entitlement Management: Ready to Enter the IdM Mainstream _____116
Gerry Gebel · Alice Wang

**Secure E-Mail Communication across Company Boundaries
Experiences and Architectures** _____ 125
Markus Wichmann · Guido von der Heidt · Carsten Hille · Gunnar Jacobson

Voice Biometrics as a Way to Self-service Password Reset _____ 137
Bernd Hohgräfe · Sebastian Jacobi

**Security Requirements Specification in Process-aware
Information Systems**_____ 145
Michael Menzel · Ivonne Thomas · Benjamin Schüler · Maxim Schnjakin · Christoph Meinel

Privacy, Data Protection and Awareness _____ 155

Simple & Secure: Attitude and behaviour towards security and usability in internet products and services at home _____ 157
Reinder Wolthuis · Gerben Broenink · Frank Fransen Sven Schultz · Arnout de Vries

Social Engineering hits Social Commerce _____ 169
Werner Degenhardt · Johannes Wiele

How to Establish Security Awareness in Schools _____ 177
Anja Beyer · Christiane Westendorf

Privacy and Security – a Way to Manage the Dilemma _____ 187
Walter Peissl

Relative Anonymity: Measuring Degrees of Anonymity in Diverse Computing Environment _____ 197
Claire Vishik · Giusella Finocchiaro

User Privacy in RFID Networks _____ 206
Dave Singelée · Stefaan Seys

Web Sessions Anomaly Detection in Dynamic Environments _____ 216
Manuel Garcia-Cervigón Gutiérrez · Juan Vázquez Pongilupi · Manel Medina LLinàs

Standards and technical Solutions _____ 221

KryptoNAS: Open source based NAS encryption _____ 223
Martin Oczko

Secure Network Zones _____ 230
Peter Kai Wimmer

ETSI Specifications for Registered E-Mail REM _____ 242
Franco Ruggieri

Acceptance of Trust Domains in IT-Infrastructures _____ 255
Arno Fiedler · Selma Gralher

**Proposal for an IT Security Standard for Preventing Tax Fraud
in Cash Registers** _____ 262
Mathias Neuhaus · Jörg Wolff · Norbert Zisky

The Operational Manager – Enemy or Hero of Secure Business Practice? __ 270
Wendy Goucher

Secure Software, Trust and Assurance _____ 279

A Structured Approach to Software Security _____ 281
Ton van Opstal

Using Compilers to Enhance Cryptographic Product Development _____ 291
E. Bangerter · M. Barbosa · D. Bernstein · I. Damgård
D. Page · J. I. Pagter · A.-R. Sadeghi · S. Sovio

Why Secure Coding is not Enough: Professionals' Perspective _____ 302
John Colley

Proactive Security Testing and Fuzzing _____ 312
Ari Takanen

Protecting Long Term Validity of PDF documents with PAdES-LTV _____ 320
Nick Pope

RE-TRUST: Trustworthy Execution of SW on Remote Untrusted Platforms __ 328
Brecht Wyseur

Future of Assurance: Ensuring that a System is Trustworthy _____ 339
Ahmad-Reza Sadeghi · Ingrid Verbauwhede · Claire Vishik

**A Taxonomy of Cryptographic Techniques for Securing
Electronic Identity Documents** _____ 349
Klaus Schmeh

Index _____ 357

Preface

Dear Readers,

ENISA has once again co-organized the ISSE 2009, Information Security Solutions Europe Conference 2009 together with eema, TeleTrusT, the 'Identity 2009', and the city of The Hague.

The purpose of the ISSE has been to support the development of a European information security culture throughout the years. This goal is more than ever valid for the future of the Internet, with its ever increasing demand for cross-border framework of trustworthy IT applications for citizens, industry and administration.

The ISSE is designed to inform ICT professionals, key policy makers and industry leaders on the latest developments and trends in technology, as well as best practices. ENISA is highly committed to these targets, as the Agency is pursuing a strategy of mitigating risks through awareness, studies, reports and Position Papers on current NIS matters.

In this quest, we assist and advise the European Commission, Member States, and the business community in the field of Network and Information Security.

The security of communication networks and information systems is of increasing concern, in particular for the economy of Europe. Clearly, cooperation is key to address today's –and tomorrow's -complex information security challenges. Only by working more closely together, can we generate new strategies to manage these problems. In bringing together the wealth of industry knowledge, information and research in Europe (as well as worldwide) the ISSE 2009 has been an event that we could not miss.

The success of this event is based on the unique backgrounds of its 400 participants: governments, academia and other key stakeholders. This line up guarantees an impressive blend of ideas from actors in different sectors of society, thus generating new ways of thinking.

The ISSE is a platform for open, vivid policy and technical debates in a non commercial setting. Through new insights and sharing of different perspectives, experiences and solutions on current topics of IT security, the independent and vast nature of the event guarantees highly relevant results. This year, the main focus is cutting edge security and related issues, like Large Scale Public Applications, Security Management & Economics of Security, Cloud Computing and Awareness Raising, selected by worldwide security specialists.

This edition contains a selection of some key topics presented at this year's conference. As such, this compilation will serve as a valuable point of reference for IT security industry professionals. We hope that you will find it a useful, professional read.

Andrea Pirotti, Executive Director, ENISA

About this Book

The Information Security Solutions Europe Conference (ISSE) was started in 1999 by eema and TeleTrusT with the support of the European Commission and the German Federal Ministry of Technology and Economics. Today the annual conference is a fixed event in every IT security professional's calendar.

The integration of security in IT applications was initially driven only by the actual security issues considered important by experts in the field; currently, however, the economic aspects of the corresponding solutions are the most important factor in deciding their success. ISSE offers a suitable podium for the discussion of the relationship between these considerations and for the presentation of the practical implementation of concepts with their technical, organisational and economic parameters.

From the beginning ISSE has been carefully prepared. The organisers succeeded in giving the conference a profile that combines a scientifically sophisticated and interdisciplinary discussion of IT security solutions while presenting pragmatic approaches for overcoming current IT security problems.

An enduring documentation of the presentations given at the conference which is available to every interested person thus became important. This year sees the publication of the seventh ISSE book – another mark of the event's success – and with about 35 carefully edited papers it bears witness to the quality of the conference.

An international programme committee is responsible for the selection of the conference contributions and the composition of the programme:

- **Jeremy Beale, ENISA**
- **Gunter Bitz, SAP** (Germany)
- **Ronny Bjones, Microsoft** (Belgium)
- **Lucas Cardholm, Ernst&Young** (Sweden)
- **Roger Dean, eema** (United Kingdom)
- **Jan De Clercq, HP** (Belgium)
- **Marijke De Soete, Security4Biz** (Belgium)
- **Jos Dumortier, KU Leuven** (Belgium)
- **Walter Fumy, Bundesdruckerei** (Germany)
- **Robert Garskamp, Everett** (The Netherlands)
- **Riccardo Genghini, S.N.G.** (Italy)
- **John Hermans, KPMG** (The Netherlands)
- **Jeremy Hilton, Cardiff University** (United Kingdom)
- **Willem Jonkers, Philips Research** (The Netherlands)
- **Francisco Jordan, Safelayer** (Spain)

- **Frank Jorissen, McAfee** (Belgium)
- **Jaap Kuipers, DigiNotar** (The Netherlands)
- **Matt Landrock, Cryptomathic** (Denmark)
- **Madeleine McLaggan-van Roon, Dutch Data Protection Authority** (The Netherlands)
- **Norbert Pohlmann (Chairman), University of Applied Sciences Gelsenkirchen** (Germany)
- **Steve Purser, ENISA**
- **Bart Preneel, KU Leuven** (Belgium)
- **Helmut Reimer, TeleTrusT** (Germany)
- **Joachim Rieß, Daimler** (Germany)
- **Wolfgang Schneider, Fraunhofer Institute SIT** (Germany)
- **Jon Shamah, EJ Consultants** (United Kingdom)
- **Robert Temple, BT** (United Kingdom)

The editors have endeavoured to allocate the contributions in these proceedings – which differ from the structure of the conference programme – to topic areas which cover the interests of the readers.

Norbert Pohlmann　　　　　*Helmut Reimer*　　　　　*Wolfgang Schneider*

---

eema (www.eema.org)

For 22 years, eema has been Europe's leading independent, non-profit e-Identity & Security association, working with its European members, governmental bodies, standards organisations and interoperability initiatives throughout Europe to further e-Business and legislation.

eema's remit is to educate and inform over 1,500 Member contacts on the latest developments and technologies, at the same time enabling Members of the association to compare views and ideas. The work produced by the association with its Members (projects, papers, seminars, tutorials and reports etc) is funded by both membership subscriptions and revenue generated through fee-paying events. All of the information generated by eema and its members is available to other members free of charge.

Examples of recent EEMA events include The European e-ID interoperability conference in Brussels (Featuring STORK, PEPPOL & epSOS) and The European e-Identity Management Conference in London (Featuring the 2nd STORK Industry Group Meeting)

EEMA and its members are also involved in many European funded projects including STORK, ICEcom and ETICA

Any organisation involved in e-Identity or Security (usually of a global or European nature) can become a Member of eema, and any employee of that organisation is then able to participate in eema activities. Examples of organisations taking advantage of eema membership are Volvo, Hoffman la Roche, KPMG, Deloitte, ING, Novartis, Metropolitan Police, TOTAL, PGP, McAfee, Adobe, Magyar Telecom Rt, National Communications Authority, Hungary, Microsoft, HP, and the Norwegian Government Administration Services to name but a few.

Visit www.eema.org for more information or contact the association on +44 1386 793028 or at info@eema.org

TeleTrusT Deutschland e.V. (www.teletrust.de)

TeleTrusT Deutschland e.V. was founded in 1989 as a non profit association in Germany promoting the trustworthiness of information and communication technology in open systems environments.

Today, TeleTrusT counts 100 institutional members. Within the last 20 years TeleTrusT evolved to a well known and highly regarded competence network for applied cryptography and biometrics.

In various TeleTrusT working groups ICT-security experts, users and interested parties meet each other in frequent workshops, round-tables and expert talks. The activities focus on reliable and trustworthy solutions complying with international standards, laws and statutory requirements.

TeleTrusT is keen to promote the acceptance of solutions supporting identification, authentification and signature (IAS) schemes in the electronic business and its processes. TeleTrusT facilitates the information and knowledge exchange between vendors, users and authorities. Subsequently, innovative ICT-security solutions can enter the market more quickly and effectively. TeleTrusT aims on standard compliant solutions in an interoperable scheme. Keeping in mind the raising importance of the European security market, TeleTrusT seeks the co-operation with European and international organisations and authorities with similar objectives.

Thus, the European Security Conference ISSE is being organized in collaboration with eema, ENISA and the Municipality of The Hague this year.

Contact:
Dr. Holger Mühlbauer
Managing Director of TeleTrusT Deutschland e.V.
holger.muehlbauer@teletrust.de

Welcome

It is an honor for the city of The Hague and me to welcome the conference of ISSE in our International City of Peace and Justice. Tens of thousands of people in The Hague are working together towards making the world a better place. It is a unique concentration of international expertise and knowledge. The Hague is the city of the Peace Palace, the International Court of Justice, Eurojust, the International Criminal Court, the Organisation for the Prohibition of Chemical Weapons, the International Criminal Tribunal for the former Yugoslavia and Europol. And last nut not least we are making the dream of a sustainable city coming true in projects like the Seawater Power Station.

The Hague forms likewise the heart of Dutch democracy. The most striking building on 'Het Binnenhof' is the Knights' Hall, built in the 13th and 14th centuries as the castle for the Earls of Holland. It is the building where the decision was made to build the first modern republic! So history is in the air in this city, but the future also. On the The Hague historical grounds we will discuss modern developments.

And those contemporary developments are – as we all know – severe: the economical crisis grips us all to think about the coming weeks, months and years to develop new strategies. And that is why cities are important. Here the key-issues of the web 2.0 are developed and proven in the practice of all day living activities in the metropolitan areas. That is why in this conference we are discussing issues in a city like The Hague where security plays an important role in everyday life. The Knowledge Society will play a role in the sustainability of the society as a whole. And ICT-security of all the essential economic features is a sine-qua-non for the coming recovery and revival of the Information Society!

ISSE 2009 will in our view serve as the building stone of a scenario to re-establishment of a secure and sustainable society. We hope that the topics discussed during the event will serve as a reference for the work of the organisations involved in this interesting field.

Frits Huffnagel

Vice Mayor for Citymarketing, International Affaires and ICT

Microsoft Sponsoring Contribution

Claims and Identity: On-Premise and Cloud Solutions

Vittorio Bertocci

Microsoft Corp.,
http://blogs.msdn.com/vbertocci.

Abstract

Today's identity-management practices are often a patchwork of partial solutions, which somehow accommodate but never really integrate applications and entities separated by technology and organizational boundaries. The rise of Software as a Service (SaaS) and cloud computing, however, will force organizations to cross such boundaries so often that ad hoc solutions will simply be untenable. A new approach that tears down identity silos and supports a de-perimiterized IT *by design* is in order.This article will walk you through the principles of claims-based identity management, a model which addresses both traditional and cloud scenarios with the same efficacy. We will explore the most common token exchange patterns, highlighting the advantages and opportunities they offer when applied on cloud computing solutions and generic distributed systems.

1 The Sky Is the Limit

When you look at a cloudy sky, your inner child probably sees dragons and castles; don't be surprised if your inner architect, after having read this article, will see dollar signs. Cloud computing promises to bring radical advantages to the way in which we think of IT: Its basic idea is that companies can host assets outside of their own premises, reaping the benefits of those assets without the burden of maintaining the necessary infrastructure. This is somewhat similar to the idea of SaaS, where companies can avoid the burden of maintaining on-premise applications that are not specific to their core business, buying the corresponding functionality as a service. Cloud computing, however, pushes the bar further. Instead of buying complete applications provided by third parties, such as the classic CRM and HR packages, the cloud offers the possibility of *hosting your own resources* in data centers that are exposed to you as a *platform*. You have all the advantages of retaining control of the resource, without the pain of CPU and bandwidth usage, dealing with the hardware, cooling the room; you don't even need to worry about patching your system. If your Web application produces new data every day, using a data store in the cloud saves you from constantly buying hardware for accommodating growth. The best part is that you

N. Pohlmann, H. Reimer, W. Schneider (Editors): Securing Electronic Business Processes, Vieweg (2009), 1-13

can expect to be charged an amount proportional to the usage you actually make of the resource, instead of having to invest in hardware and infrastructure beforehand. This "pay-per-use" pattern is one of the reasons for you will often hear the term "utility computing" instead of "cloud computing," and it is even more evident in CPU-intensive tasks. Imagine if, instead of sizing your data center for handling its maximum forecasted peek and underutilizing it most of the time, you could deploy your most CPU-hungry processes in a data center of monstrous proportions: The CPU utilization could grow as much as requested, and you would pay your cloud provider in proportion. Those are some of the advantages that will light a sparkle in the eyes of your IT managers, but the Cloud holds even more interesting properties for architects. Since the cloud provider hosts resources on a common infrastructure, it is in the position of offering services that can be leveraged by every resource simplifying development and maintenance. Obvious candidates are naming, message dispatching, logging, and access control. Once a resource uses the cloud infrastructure, implementing those functionalities can be factored out from the resource itself.

The diligent architect, at this point, is likely to wonder, "Is my company ready for this?" Not surprisingly, answering this question is a complex task and requires considering many aspects of your architecture and your practices. In extreme simplification: If you run your business according to solid service orientation (SO) principles, you are in the ideal position to take advantage of the new wave. After all, if you respected autonomy, exposed policies, and used standards, who cares where your services run? If you are in that position, you have my congratulations. In my experience, however, nobody ever applies SO principles in excruciating detail. For example, services developed with the same technology offer special features when talking with each other, and there are situations in which it makes perfect sense to take advantage of those.

Identity management and access control are most likely to be affected by this phenomenon. Enterprises typically have their directory software, and they rightfully leverage that for many aspects of the resource access control; sometimes it works so well that developers are not exposed to identity concepts, which is actually a good thing, but that rarely happens. When faced with tasks involving some form of access control management, such as federating with partners outside the directory or using different credential types, you can expect developers to come out with the worst swivel chair integration solutions. If identity brings out the worst from development practices, why do we get away with it? The easy answer is that sometimes we don't. I am sure you have heard your share of horror stories of access control gone wrong. The subtler answer is that we get away with it because, until we own the majority of the infrastructure, if we exercise iron-fist governance, we can somehow handle it: We may use more resources than needed, we may deal with emergencies more often than needed, but somehow we go on. In fact, "we own the majority of the infrastructure" is a fact that is challenged by growing market pressure. When a lot of your business requires you to continuously connect and onboard new partners, where does your infrastructure end and theirs begin? Cloud computing is going to snowball this: Once the cloud is just another deployment option, crafting custom access code for every resource will simply be not sustainable.

The good news is that there is an architectural approach that can help manage identities and access control for generic distributed systems, and it works for on premise, cloud, and hybrid systems alike. The core idea is modeling almost everything as exchanges of claims, and model transactions in a much more natural fashion.

This article is an introduction to this new approach. Special attention will be given to the aspects that are especially relevant for the cloud, but the vast majority of the concepts and patterns presented can be applied regardless of the nature of the distributed systemWhile the principles laid down here apply to any system, hence also to simple cases, their expressive power is best utilized for scenarios including partnerships, complex access rules, and structured identity information.

2 Claims-Based Solutions

The issue with classic identity-management solutions can be summarized as follows: They presume too much.

The most common assumption is that every entity participating in a transaction is well known by some central, omnipresent authority that can decide who can access what, and it what terms. This is usually true in self-contained systems, such as enterprise networks managed via directories, but fails when business processes begin to require alien participant such as software packages with their own identity stores, partners and customers accessing your extranet, and consultants. Tactical solutions, like using shadow accounts, often have to do with pretending to be able to manage something we don't own; and as such, they are very brittle.

Another common assumption is that every participant in a transaction uses a consistent identity-management technology. Again, this is a fair assumption for self-contained systems (think network software), but it fails as soon as you let aliens in the process. The common practice in accommodating different technologies is treating those cases as exceptions. As a result, the resources themselves end up embedding a lot of identity-management plumbing code, written by developers that usually are all but identity experts. This is every bit as bad as the old taboo for embedding business logic in the presentation layer, perhaps even worse. Handling identity plumbing directly inside the resource not only makes the system brittle and hard to maintain, it also makes the life of system administrators miserable. How can you manage access control at deployment time if the logic is locked inside the resource itself?

The claims-based approach defuses these issues by assigning each task to the entities who are its natural owners, and avoiding introducing artificial dependencies and expectations by respecting the autonomy of all participants – nothing but good old SO architectural principles.

3 Basic Definitions

Here I will present a bestiary of the various concepts and constructs you will encounter while exploring claims-based approaches.

Claims

A claim is a fact about an entity (the "subject"), stated by another entity (the "authority").

A claim can be literally anything that describes one aspect of a subject, be it an actual person or an abstract resource. Classic examples of claims are "Bob is older than 21," "Bob is in the group "remote debuggers" for the domain Contoso.com", and "Bob is a Silver Elite member with one Star Alliance airline." A claim is endorsed by an authority; hence one observer can decide if the fact the claim represents should be considered true according to the authority's trustworthiness.

Trust

An entity A is said to trust an entity B if A will consider true the claims issued by B. While very simplistic, this definition serves our purposes here. Trusting what B says about a subject saves A from the hassle of verifying the claim directly. Entity A still needs to make sure that the claim is actually coming from B and not a forgery.

Tokens

A security token is an XML construct signed by an authority, containing claims and (possibly) credentials information.

Security tokens are artifacts, XML fragments described in (see Resources: WS-Security), which can fulfill two distinct functions:

- they provide a means to propagate claims
- they can support cryptographic operations and/or have a part in credentials authentication

Thanks to the properties of asymmetric cryptography, the fact that a token is signed makes it easy to verify the source of the claims it contains.

Tokens can also contain cryptographic material, such as keys and references to keys, which can be referenced in encryption and signatures in SOAP messages; those operations can be used as part of credentials verification processes. In this context, we consider a "credential" any material that can be used as part of some mechanism for verifying that the caller is a returning user: Passwords and certificates are good examples (for more details, see Resources: Vittorio Bertocci's blog, The Tao of Authentication).

Tokens can be "projections" of specific authentication technologies, such as X509 certificates, or they can be issued (SAML, a popular token format you may have heard mentioned in the context of Web services security, is one example of an issued token). The system is future-proof: As new technologies emerge, suitable token "projections" can be documented in profile specifications.

Security Token Services (STS)

A Security Token Service is a Web service that issues security tokens as described by WS-Trust (see Resources: WS-Trust).

An STS (see Figure 1) can process requests for security token (RST) messages and issue tokens via requests for security token responses (RSTR). Processing the RST usually entails authenticating the caller and issuing a token that contains claims describing the caller itself. In some cases, the STS will issue claims that are the result of transformations of claims it received in the RST. (For more details, see Resources: Vittorio Bertocci's blog, R-STS.)

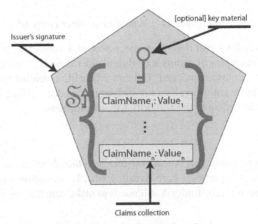

Fig. 1: Anatomy of a security token

The Identity Metasystem (IdM)

The Identity Metasystem (IdM) is a model that provides a technology agnostic abstraction layer for obtaining claims.

This is a very simplified definition that does not render justice to the model; for example, it does not mention policy distribution and systems management. (See Resources: WS-Security, WS-Trust.)

Every identity technology tends to accomplish the same tasks, following common patterns and dealing with more or less the same functional roles. The IdM describes those patterns and roles in an abstract fashion, modeling the behavior of any system in term of claims exchanges but leaving the details on how those are implemented to the specific technologies. The necessary level of abstraction is achieved by taking advantage of open, interoperable protocols such as the WS-* family of specifications.

The IdM describes three roles:

- **Subject.** The subject is the subject entity we mentioned in the claim definition. It is whoever (or whatever) needs to be identified in a transaction.
- **Relying party (RP).** The RP is the resource that requires authentication before being accessed. Examples of RPs include Web sites and Web services. RPs derive their name from the fact that they rely on IPs for obtaining claims about the subject they need to identify.
- **Identity provider (IP).** The IP is the authority entity we mentioned in the claim definition. An IP possesses knowledge about the subject, and can express it in the form of claims: Any RP that trusts that particular IP will be able to rely on those claims for making authentication and authorization decisions on subjects. Note: Often the IP will use an STS for issuing claims in the form of tokens; that does not mean that every STS is an IP. An STS is a tool that the IP uses to get its job done.

4 Architectural Patterns of Claims-Aware Solutions

The basic aforementioned concepts constitute the basis for a new physic of authentication, and as such they can be combined to describe any system and transaction. In this new world, we can finally separate two functions traditionally conflated into one: obtaining information about the caller (via claims) and verifying if it is a returning user (via credentials). Thanks to this separation, we can now choose which function fits best our scenario; for more details see Resources: Vittorio Bertocci's blog The TAO of Authentication.

There are certain patterns that are especially useful for describing common scenarios. To follow, I will describe the three most common of those patterns, along with some of the advantages that the claims-based approach brings to those scenarios with respect to traditional practices. All the patterns are suitable both for on premise and cloud architectures.

4.1 The Canonical Pattern: Subject-IP-RP

This pattern describes the minimal situation in authentication management: a subject wants to access a restricted resource (the RP). This happens when a Windows user tries to access a network share, when a smart client invokes a secure Web service, when a Web surfer wants to browse restricted content, you name it (see Figure 2).The key steps are as follow:

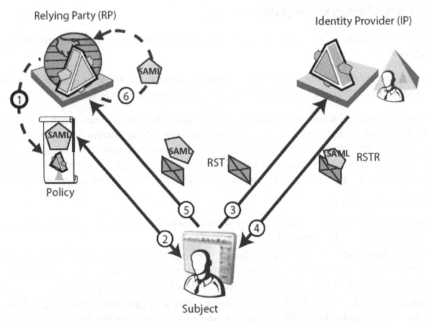

Fig. 2: The Subject-IP-RP canonical pattern. The numbers refer to the text.

1. (out of band) The RP publishes its requirements in the form of a policy. Those requirements include

    a. A list of claims

    b. The IPs that the RP trusts as sources of those claims

    c. Details about the specific authentication technologies that the RP can use; for example, the token formats that the RP understands

2. The subject reads the RP policy and verifies whether it can comply with it. In practice, it means verifying if the subject can obtain a suitable token from any of the IPs that RP trusts.

3. The subject invokes a suitable IP, requesting a token that complies with RP policies. In practice, it usually means sending an RST message to the IP's STS.

4. The IP receives the RST and authenticates the subject. If the subject is known, the IP will retrieve the required claim values, package it in a token, sign it, and send it back to the subject.

5. The subject receives the token and uses it for invoking RP.

6. RP extracts the token from the invocation message and examines it: Is it signed by one trusted IP? Does it contain the right claims? If the check is positive,

    a. the claims values are used for feeding some access control logic

    b. If the access control logic is satisfied, the claim values are made available to the resource itself and access is granted

For the purposes of this explanation, let's assume that the resource is a Web service. The pattern above exhibits many good properties.

Authentication Externalization

Using tokens and claims lifts from the resource the burden of writing any explicit identity-management code. The same infrastructure that takes care of publishing RP policies can also perform operations such as deserializing tokens, checking signatures, and making claims values readily available to the resource developer regardless of the token format that was actually used on the wire. The infrastructure can also perform some authorization decision based on claims values, reducing further the tasks that the developer needs to worry about.

This is an advantage that holds for any scenario, but especially for the cloud where the hosting technology is one of the variables. Using claims makes resources truly portable, by decoupling them from the details of the infrastructure that will host them and the authentication technology that will be available at runtime.

Resource-Level Policy

Being able to specify policies at the resource level allows for very agile deployments, fine-grained control, and dynamic negotiation of the authentication technology of choice. It allows for establishing a management strategy that will work regardless of the hosting environment, thanks to the use of interoperable standards. It decouples the resource itself from the execution environment, making it much easier to move the resource around (including to the cloud).

Autonomy

Every resource specifies its requirements in an autonomous fashion: It is the subject that matches those with its own capabilities. The interaction is an emergent property of the combination of the two. Both parties can change independently, and the set of subjects that can access the resource is defined solely by the ability to comply with the requirements as opposed to some out of band or infrastructural dependency. The system is very robust, since everybody needs to worry only about its own requirements and capabilities. Onboarding users is very easy, since it does not require any explicit negotiation or arrangement.

Centralization of Some Authentication and Authorization Logic

In this pattern, the IP performs all the attributes retrieval. The RP receives what it needs in the form of a token, without needing to query other systems. This is obviously an advantage for those attributes to which the RP would not have access (i.e., Airline A asks for the subject's frequent flyer status with partner Airline B), but it is also a great means of centralizing attribute retrieval logic in a single place. Not only does it reduce the number of endpoints that need access to attribute stores, with advantages for manageability and security, it can also reduce the number of accesses itself, since once the subject obtains a token it can cache and reuse it until it expires without getting back to the IP. The IP can also be used for authorization decisions, which can be expressed via claims as well; however, this can happen only when the IP has a tight relationship both with the subject and the resource. While this happens in important scenarios, such as when the IP represents a directory and the RP is one of the resources it manages, in the generic case no relationship can be assumed between RP and IP.

This is key to many cloud scenarios, in which resources need to rely on external IPs for verifying information about possible users; however, it is also very useful in more agile versions of classic federation, in which users of a partner organization can be represented by technology- and platform-agnostic tokens, and for crossing boundaries of any kind.

4.2 The Claims Transformer Variation: Subject-IP-Claims Transformer-RP

The pattern just described can be applied to a wide range of scenarios, from consumer (frequent flyer with Airline A accessing the Web site of partner Airline B) to enterprise (almost any Kerberos scenario can be modeled that way, with the added bonus of technology independence).

However, there are situations in which certain constraints may prevent the application of the pattern as it is:

1. **Indirect trust** – A RP may not directly trust the IPs that are in a relationship with the subject, but there could be a chain of intermediate authorities that can be traversed for brokering trust. If you want to board a plane, you won't be able to do so using just the documents already in your wallet; the employee at the gate will trust only a boarding pass issued by the proper airline. However, you can use the documents already in your possession (passport or driver's license, issued by the government) at the check-in counter to obtain the boarding pass (issued by the airline).

2. **Claims format** – The RP may not be able to understand the claims in the format issued by the IPs that are directly available to the subject. Sometimes it is a simple matter of format (my Italian ID says "nato il" instead of "birth date," a bartender in the U.S. would not be able to extract the information he needs even if it's there), other times the claims required by the RP are the results of some processing of the raw information received (the RP may need a "CanDrink?" claim, which may be the result of processing "age" and "Nationality").

The new constraints can be easily addressed by adding a new element, which we will call a claim transformer, that can process a token before it reaches the resource and can be leveraged by the RP to broker trust and convert the incoming claims in a more suitable format. Between the subject and the RP, there could be an arbitrarily long chain of claim transformers. Dynamic negotiation of policy can automatically "choose" a path, if available, without any need to plan it at a high level.

The best artifact for implementing a claim transformer is, again, the STS. Instead of populating the issued claims from its own data sources, the STS used by the claim transformer will mainly manipulate the incoming information. Since it is often run by the same entity that owns the RP, as in the classic federation case, this kind of STS is usually referred to as Resource STS, R-STS or RP-STS. I recommend reading my blog for more details (see Resources).

This variant presents some powerful advantages and, in our opinion, will emerge as the dominant pattern for identity management in distributed systems (see Figure 3).

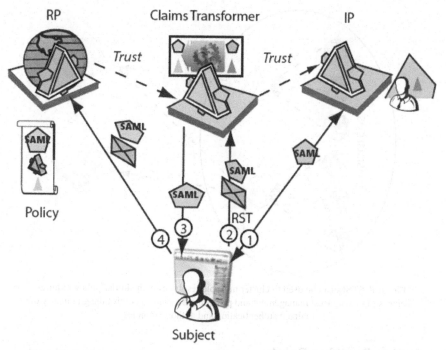

Fig. 3: Basic claims transformer pattern. The Subject (1) obtains a token from the IP and (2) uses it to get a token from the claims transformer. The R-STS of the claims transformer processes the incoming claims and (3) issues the subject a new token. The subject (4) uses the new token to invoke the resource.

Resource Clustering

Claims transformers can offer a granularity continuum between single resources and the directory at the enterprise level. An R-STS can be used for corralling multiple resources with similar requirements. It simplifies the policy management of single resources, moving the complexity of brokering trust and processing raw claims in a single point but without requiring it at the enterprise level. An R-STS can be a virtual boundary protecting legacy resources that may not play too well with the rest of the network. Those are just few examples of the expressive power of claims transformers (see Figure 4).

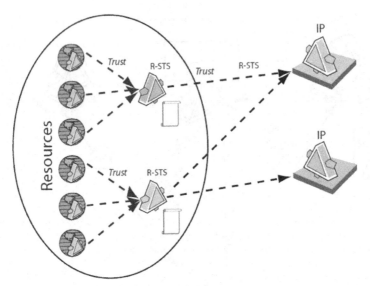

Fig. 4: R-STSes can be used to cluster multiple resources with similar policy requirements, simplifying trust management and providing a means to control the granularity of
externalized authentication and authorization logic.

Authorization Decision Point

While an IP is usually an independent entity, very often the R-STS has some knowledge of the resources
it fronts. Such knowledge may enable the R-STS to perform authorization decisions. The incoming
claims can be processed together with the requirements of the resource the subject is trying to access,
and the result may be a decision about whether the subject holds the necessary privileges. Such a decision can be expressed in different ways:

- If the subject does not hold any privileges, the R-STS may simply refuse to issue a token and
  block the invocation. In this case, it would enforce authorization.
- If the subject holds some privileges, the R-STS may formalize those authorization decisions in
  the form of claims. The RP is hence relieved from the need to run authorization logic, and will
  just enforce the directives it receives from the R-STS in the form of claims.

The use of tokens, claims, and IPs made authentication externalization possible; the R-STS can, in certain cases, help to do the same with authorization decisions.

Delegation

There are many resources that are not claims-aware: legacy systems, resources managed directly at the
directory level, and so on. Often some investments have been already made to manage access to those
resources, such as assigning ACLs and creating groups. The identity of a subject calling a front-end
application via claims-based security would not be suitable to leverage those investments; if the frontend application could obtain a directory identity on behalf of the caller, however, the problem would be
solved. In fact, the value of obtaining tokens on behalf of somebody else is clear even when the issued
tokens remain in the realm of claims.

5 Claims and Cloud

The beauty of what I've described so far is that it adapts to any loosely connected system; and what is the cloud, if not the ultimate distributed system? When you reason at cloud scale, you deal with a world where every entity is managed independently: claims, tokens, trust, and identity metasystem roles can help you make the best of whatever little information you may have about the relationships among the parties you deal with. By describing a claims-based solution, we killed two birds with one stone, giving you tools that can be applied on premise and on the cloud alike.

We still know too little of how things will evolve to give detailed guidance on cloud scenarios. However, with some working hypothesis, we can certainly highlight the aspects of claim aware identity management that are especially well suited for the cloud.

Access Control via Claims Transformation

We have seen that a cloud provider may offer services such as storage and compute, messaging, and integration. If you recall what we described in the claims transformer section, you will see that an obvious access control strategy for the cloud provider is to offer an R-STS and have the resources trust it. Every tenant would then be able to govern access control simply by manipulating the claim transformation rules of the R-STS.

Let's say that you are an ISV, and you want to deploy your services at a certain cloud provider. You decide on the set of claims your services will accept, and you set your services to trust the provider's R-STS. Your access control strategy is already in place, regardless of who calls your services! When onboarding a new customer, you simply have to define how to map his claims to yours, by setting some rules at the R-STS level. This can be incredibly agile and easy to maintain (see Figure 5).

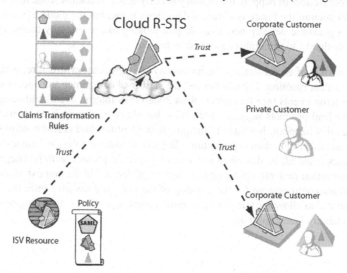

Fig. 5: An R-STS in the cloud is a very powerful tool for managing access control. The resource always handles tokens and claims in the right format, from the same trusted source; the R-STS takes care of handling trust management and credential verification from different sources, using rules to perform the necessary transformations and isolating the resource from changes and unnecessary complexity.

Externalizing Authorization

We have seen how a R-STS can conveniently externalize and aggregate authorization decisions; this is, of course, valid in cloud scenarios as well. In fact, there are cases in which this can be pushed further to include authorization enforcement. Getting back to the ISV example:

If the services are exposed by taking advantage of some messaging offering, the dispatch infrastructure itself can take care of enforcing authorization decisions by examining the authorization claims even before the message is routed to its destination. This relieves the ISV from yet another burden: If the services are not exposed using the provider's messaging infrastructure, the authorization decision claims have to be enforced by adding some processing pipeline in front of the resource

Managing Relationships

With the model described, an ISV can represent a customer relationship as a set of rules. This is much more agile than creating a federation relationship by traditional means, directory to directory. While coarser to manage, it also avoids the burden of extra management that is necessary in peer partners relations but would often be overkill for vendor-customer relationships.

The model also allows for accommodating individuals and customers without advanced identity capabilities. The ISV services will always see tokens issued by the R-STS, regardless of whether the customer authenticated with a token issued from his own IP or with simple, one-off username and password.

6 The Future

The shift toward the cloud will happen: the industry is fairly quick to acknowledge that it is not a matter of if, but when. Predicting the future is always a dangerous game, but the cloud is just too exciting for not venturing in a plausible development that, despite looking like an identity utopia today, is in fact perfectly plausible thanks to principles described so far.

Today, access control is often constrained in the railways of organization structure, with privileges reflecting rank rather than function. The number and the caliber of companies and open-source initiatives participating in interop events (see Resources: RSA 2008 OSIS Interop event) and integrating support for claims in their lead products suggests that claims-based programming is on its way to becoming mainstream. Once that happens, it is easy to imagine how identities and access control structures may be corralled around tasks rather than organizations. Subject, resources, roles, and authorities from many different companies could all be described in terms of a specific project, with privileges assigned not according to organization rank but reflecting the function performed in the context of the project itself. Virtual organizations could emerge for the duration of the task, and dissolve once the mission is performed. That would also allow for templating of cross companies efforts, enforcing best practices and improving predictability (see Figure 6).

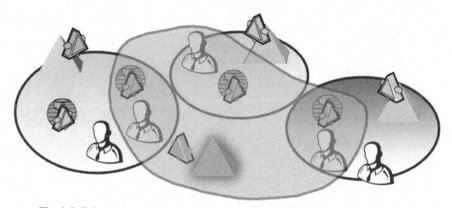

Fig. 6: Policies, claims exchanges, and virtual directory management make possible the semi-spontaneous emergence of virtual organizations (center).

For this to happen, claims are a necessary, but not sufficient, condition: Emerging technologies such as virtual directories will play a key role as well (see Kim Cameron's blog, www.identityblog.com, for more details).

Call to Action

The claims-based approach is great for traditional and cloud scenarios alike. The difference is that while in traditional scenarios you can sometimes use a great deal of extra resources to get away with bad strategies, once the cloud is upon us, it won't be that easy. If you want to prepare yourself and your organization for the upcoming wave, here there are some things you can do:

- Experiment with Web services and security, if you are not already doing it
- Experiment with claims-based programming, taking advantage of Windows Identity Foundation and Active Directory Federation Services 2.0
- Consider running pilots within your organizations. For example: create an IP for your employees

7 Conclusion

Here I could offer the proverbial "we barely scratched the surface of the topic," and that would be true. Instead, I will say that claims are the cornerstone of exciting developments in identity management for traditional and cloud scenarios alike. I invite the geeks among you to enjoy this special transition moment in which much of those interactions are still evident, and I reassure all the others by foreseeing that most of the details will likely sink in the infrastructure and be made invisible by new breeds of tools.

Economics of
Security and
Identity Management

Measuring Information Security: Guidelines to Build Metrics

Eberhard von Faber

T-Systems
Eberhard.Faber@t-systems.com

Brandenburg University of Applied Science
Eberhard.vonFaber@fh-brandenburg.de

Abstract

Measuring information security is a genuine interest of security managers. With metrics they can develop their security organization's visibility and standing within the enterprise or public authority as a whole. Organizations using information technology need to use security metrics. Despite the clear demands and advantages, security metrics are often poorly developed or ineffective parameters are collected and analysed. This paper describes best practices for the development of security metrics. First attention is drawn to motivation showing both requirements and benefits. The main body of this paper lists things which need to be observed (characteristic of metrics), things which can be measured (how measurements can be conducted) and steps for the development and implementation of metrics (procedures and planning). Analysis and communication is also key when using security metrics. Examples are also given in order to develop a better understanding. The author wants to resume, continue and develop the discussion about a topic which is or increasingly will be a critical factor of success for any security managers in larger organizations.

1 Intention and Scope

Enterprises need to determine the current status or quality of information security and the maturity of their security processes and practices. There are several reasons for that. (i) In order to be able to improve something in a targeted way, one first needs to be able to measure it. In this context, the measurement basically provides the information being required for any action. In the first place, problem areas can be identified and found. Then the measurement shows if the right actions are taken and if they are effective or not. (ii) Enterprises need to justify costs and any allocation of resources for information security. Here the measurement means comparison on a relative level. Information is given about the effectiveness of current information security efforts. (iii) Enterprises need to benchmark in order to find out if the effort or expenditure is appropriate. This allows enterprises to control and adapt overall costs for information security. The measurement need to use an absolute level since it provides information about the efficiency. In summary, enterprises need to know if they do the right things, in the right way with the right intensity.

A metric is a means to measure against a predefined target. As a result the enterprise or authority can determine the status of information security, check the effectivity of actions, and control the costs allocated to information security. The metric must define the method and procedure of the measurements but also the target level. (iv) Enterprises need to take decisions on a sound, negotiable basis. A metric is the basis for taking such decisions, more precisely business decisions. This means that the target

N. Pohlmann, H. Reimer, W. Schneider (Editors): Securing Electronic Business Processes, Vieweg (2009), 17-26

should be defined such that the impact on the enterprises' business or the authorities' mission is being determined. This is important and not self-evident. Security actions are designed and selected with the intention of a concrete effect. This assumption needs to be proven using metrics as an objective testing method. Simultaneously, a metric relates effects to causes. It removes uncertainty as well as chance and helps organizations to create, track and increase accountability. (v) Finally, measuring information security can be an efficient way or contribution towards demonstrating compliance with laws as well as external and internal regulations. Also the maturity [ISO21827] can be determined as an overall measure of information security practices.

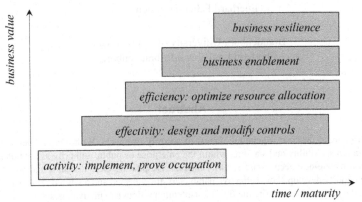

Fig. 1: Motivation for security metrics: evolvement of business value (schematic)

Each of the above objectives or targets contributes to the organization's success in a specific way as visualized in Fig. 1. The measurement also develops from tactical to being strategic as program maturity evolves. Note, however, that measuring security does not affect information security, it helps to understand and interpret reality and thereby to affect information security deliberately.

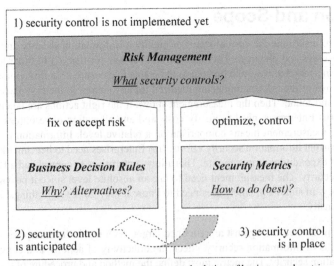

Fig. 2: The Risk Management Process and relation of business and metrics

Risk Management is vital for any organization. Though this process means rating and judgment, security metrics will not replace risk management as claimed in [Jaqu07]. *Security Metrics* as understood here are a mean supporting Risk Management (refer to Fig. 2). Metrics are (mostly) used when security controls are already implemented. Risk Management is the total process of identifying, assessing, and eliminating or controlling uncertain events that may affect valuated assets. The iteration starts (1) when some security control is not yet implemented and includes (2) planning and (3) control. Critical decisions are to be taken by the business unit not by IT or security people. This area with the underlying *Business Decision Rules* also supports Risk Management and is not superseded by metrics.

2 Required Characteristics

In order to deliver the above benefits, the metrics should have minimum characteristics (confer also [Wheat08]): (i) *consistent, reproducible,* as well as *reliable* since quantitative indicators are used, (ii) *relevant* because being correlated to security actions, (iii) *useful* or informative and functional, (iv) *high-piled* or sectional and at distinct level, and (v) *manageable* with low overhead and costs and *understandable*. These characteristics are discussed now.

The metric must first use quantitative (or at least quantifiable) indicators which can be obtained objectively and reproducibly. The latter characteristics mean that the result is independent from whom performed the measurement and that it can be repeatedly be obtained. The repeatability or reproducibility is important since one need to make comparisons of earlier and later values and to find trends. As a matter of course, the metric must provide consistent results (otherwise it is not reproducible). Note that this first requirement is often the reason for security managers to flinch from measuring security. But information security is not a feeling or notion. If risks are real, countermeasures must also be substantial which one should be able to demonstrate in some way.

Secondly, the rating produced by the metrics must allow to be attributed to a specific action or a group of actions for information security. Without such causality between measured data and information security action, the organization can not benefit from the metric because nothing can be learned. On the other hand this means that changing the action will effect the measurement. As a result, one can make improvements through controlling actions. Measuring parameters which are beyond the organization's control may provide quite interesting background information, mostly however the effort spent is for the birds.

This leads thirdly to the requirement that the metrics must provide enough information to enable the security managers to add or modify actions in a systematic manner. When designing a security metric it must at least be considered that the measured data can and will vary over time. But more over, the metric should be such that it provides benefit for the organization as described in Chapter 1. Specifically, the measurement should directly be aligned with the organizations' mission. Without a clear definition of the target the measurement will fail to accomplish anything real.

In practice, this requires a hierarchy. There are security measures on different levels. On each level transparency and the ability to control is required. Simultaneously, an aggregated rating with respect to security is required directly related to the organizations' mission.

Factor number five which should be considered when designing security metrics is rather pragmatic. The measurement should be manageable in every-day life. It should produce low overhead and costs. In addition, the results shall easily be communicated and clearly understandable – eventually, after some aggregation, also for the management board.

3 How to measure

Before any measurement is planned or done, there are some crucial questions which should be addressed. The starting point is to ask for the reason and the goal to be achieved. What is the purpose of the measurement? What shall be the benefit? Then it is important to know how the measurement will be used. Who will use it and how? What kind of result is expected and how should it look like? After having answers to such questions one can develop a suitable metric.

3.1 Approaching quantities

Fig. 3 provides further guidance. First one has to determine the *Purpose* (or goal) of the measurement. The figure shows three subjects (security controls, related processes and achievement of goals) and the five parameters from Fig. 1. So, one can aim to measure the effectivity of a security control for example. Second one needs an *Observable* (as the real-life source of information). Third a *Method* must be selected. One can count things, determine the coverage or density, meter length or durations, quantify frequencies or rates, determine a magnitude or degree, and find out costs or any effort. Fourth, one should consider the role of the information and decide if it directly evaluates towards the purpose (direct indicator), if more contextual information is being provided, or nothing of both. This is discussed in more detail in Chapter 3.2 below. Fifth, in most cases several measurements have to be *aggregated* and also be *interpreted* to obtain functional information.

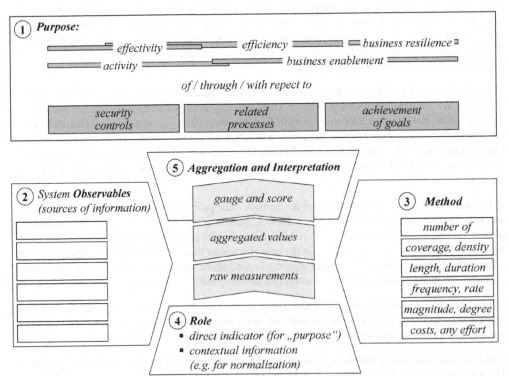

Fig. 3: Components and relations for the design of metrics (schematic)

A few very simplified examples demonstrate steps 2-5, each aggregate several measurements:

- effectivity of E-mail defense / usability: number of business E-mail blocked as "spam", number of spam delivered to the user, costs for manual cleanup after malware incidents, and number and severity of other security related E-mail communication incidents,
- effectivity of network and application defense (firewalls, IDS, DoS protection etc.): host and application downtimes (due to security incidents, security update or repair), number and severity of "attacker intrusions" (detected somewhere), costs for forensics and manual corrections (as respond to suspicious activities), number of and severity of incidents due to defective configurations,
- effectivity of processes: number of audited or evaluated systems, frequency of reviews and audits, loss of critical data or direct costs or number and severity of negative reports in the press due to incidents caused by inappropriate behavior of employees,
- effectivity of processes: time for password reset or user provisioning, time to fix and repair (e.g. vulnerabilities), coverage determining the completeness and accuracy of process documentation,
- achievement of "business process xyz is secure": percentage of sub-processes and related support processes being considered and actively covered by risk management, percentage of ISO27002 areas covered in that way, ratio of information assets for which a classification was carried out, ratio of information assets covered by security policies and deviated controls, number of wrong configurations, vulnerabilities and any other errors in policy enforcement, number and severity of policy violations (such as privacy and confidentiality incidents).

Note that there can be more levels of aggregation and usually much more measures are to be summed up at each level. And the measurement itself must be described more precisely.

3.2 Costs and contextual information

The vast majority of measurements recommended in the performance measurement guide [NIST08] pertain to actions for information security (or controls taken from [NIST09] which map to those in [ISO27002]). Typically, they measure "if there are activities or controls in place" which reads "X % of some things have something". Or the effort being spent is measured. It does in fact contribute to security "if 80% of the servers are equipped with a scanner". But what does this really mean? Primarily, however, it demonstrates that the security personnel were busy. There is no indication if the controls are effective. – Security organization shall use and maintain task lists and measure the degree of completion (as coverage). But from a global perspective *this is all about costs and effort*. Metrics in turn shall show effects of activities so that decisions about activities can be taken.

Similarly, it does not help much if the activity of a control is measured only. For example to measure how many packets are rejected by a firewall or count the viruses being found. This shows only that the security controls do something *with no indication if the function is appropriate and business related*.

Consequently, costs and operation are mostly context information required to understand the constraints or to be informed about boundary conditions. Costs are also used to normalize other measurements. For example, one can measure specific security incidents per Euro spent for countermeasures. This metric shows how efficient the countermeasure works.

Contextual information is generally important. Such information must be collected regardless of the concrete metrics since it describes the environment. Changes in the IT, in the number of users, in the application landscape or in business processes may affect information security. They may be required to appreciate the security people's work. Or the contextual information can help to interpret the results of measuring information security ex post. Sources for such information are mainly finance and controlling and the IT department.

It depends on the question raised with the metric if contextual information is contextual or security relevant. Moreover, contextual information may change its character. The number of security experts, for instance, is contextual information as long as it describes the resources being available. But if the organization wants to optimize the organization or change responsibilities, the number of security experts becomes a target figure or the like.

3.3 Sources, Pre- and Post-Implementation

There are several sources of information for the measurements. For each metric one should do the following [WBA04]:

- gather metrics before implementation,
- determine the expected change or effect on the metric if the security action is put in place; substantiate this in a document ("hypothesis"),
- gather metrics after implementation; analyze and communicate.

Security managers should always ensure that the reason for any action is documented. Afterwards it is often not easy to discover that because the context may have changed substantially. In addition, this transparency helps to control.

There are many sources of information. People can also look at

- log-data and alarms generated by intrusion detection and other systems,
- reports from SIM[1] systems including the output of scanners and collected log data,
- the outcome of penetration testing, the results of security evaluations,
- results from surveys and self-assessment questionnaires,
- employee's reports about security incidents and suspicious activities.

Processes, projects and actions provide other information. Here one can look at

- durations, delays, discrepancies, conflicts,
- budgets, people involved, policies, documents,
- organization, awareness etc.

It should be observed that an interpretation is required. Figures alone often do not provide any useful information. Is "a thousand events of type A" good or bad, high or low and where is it related to? If it is controllable by the security organization, a threshold often needs to be defined in order to interpret that data. Trends are often more useful than having absolute values because the latter are harder to interpret.

Any metric must be business relevant. First, one must identify the "purpose" (refer to Fig. 3). Information about security events or incidents can help to assess security controls, it can show the performance of processes, and it can measure if security goals are achieved.

---

1 SIM: Security Information Management

3.4 Maturity, Processes and Capabilities

The above metrics look at security controls, at related processes and at the security level by measuring the achievement of goals. Here one "looks back" onto "things that are done".

Another perspective is to look at *capabilities* to prove what an organization is able to do. Such measurements pertain to the organization as a whole or can be used to rate individual processes.

The maturity model described in [ISO21827] considers "base practices" along domains on the one hand side and "generic practices" that span the dimension of capabilities. The two are mapped demonstrating if an organization is capable of doing something in a specific domain. The measurement is made by evaluating if and to what extend pre-defined practices are in place. The result shows how the organization is capable of doing a specific activity. The generic practices are further grouped into 12 so called "common features" which in turn are associated to five hierarchical maturity levels.

A certain maturity level is achieved if the organization appears to have a set of "common features". Each "common feature" is an aggregation of several "generic practices". "Generic practices" are proven to be in place in "process areas" where each of the latter is associated with "base practices".

Tab. 1: Rating Achievement against Maturity Levels (atomic view onto one area)

References		Rating of "xyz"		
ISO21827-Level	**CMMI-Level**	**Interpretation (verbal for each level)**	**Achievement**	**Credits**
0: Not performed		example: "we don't have"		
1: Performed informally	1: Initial	example: "have some somewhere"	confirmation if achieved,	
2: Planned and tracked	2: Managed	example: "program to get, use and check"	description of controls	
3: Well defined	3: Defined	example: "program is compliant to..."	up to the last level where it applies.	example: 3 points
4: Qualitatively controlled	4: Quantitatively managed	example: "steering committee approved"		
5: Continuously improving	5: Optimizing	example: "integrated into overall QMS"		

An example how to utilize the maturity models for measuring a specific security action or realm is shown in Tab. 1. The standardized maturity model (as the one in [ISO21827]) provides the general scale. Then a specific security action or an area where information security needs to be measured is selected. Examples could be the user account provisioning for external workforce. In the next step, the maturity levels are interpreted for the area looked at. What needs to be in place to achieve the corresponding maturity level? For the sake of simplicity, lower level demands are automatically part of higher levels. In the last step the actual achievement is determined by comparing interpretation with reality. This rating should result in an appropriate figure to allow aggregation to a higher level.

4 Program for Development and Implementation

Most enterprises are expected to already have information security metrics. For a systematic approach the following steps can help to organize a procedure for development and implementation.

- The key question is: What shall be discovered and achieved? Or what kind of information shall be gathered to what purpose? Together with the purpose it helps a lot to consider the possible target audience.
- Then one can start to identify possible indicators or parameters. This is an analytical task since there must be a causal relation between the goal (what do I like to know) und the indicator (what I will measure).
- Then the data collection, aggregation and processing must be organized and performed. Here it is required to implement a process since mostly data need to be collected, aggregated and processed periodically on a regular basis.
- A defined process is also required for the subsequent examination, analysis and interpretation.
- Now the target audience must be determined. Different people require different information, view and forms of communication. So, one have to consider these issues and select the appropriate formats to present the results.
- Information is prepared now and formatted as required. For details about mathematical analysis and visualization refer to [Jaqu07].
- Not later than now the organization should consider the need of regular processes. The corresponding preparation should be carried out and maybe processes are installed.
- Finally, the results are communicated.
- Of course, there will be feedback and experience. The procedures and the metrics are to be analyzed, checked and adapted if necessary.

Note that not only the audience is important. The security managers need to incorporate major stakeholders and ensure support wherever necessary. This is important since metrics is a program which needs to be set-up and conducted continuously. Stakeholders include business units, employee representation, finance and control department as well as line manager and top management.

While doing all that it should be clear that metrics are about measurement only (Fig. 2). The actual security work is done within the framework of the Information Security Management Systems (ISMS as defined in [ISO27001]). For a description of program scope, processes and background or frameworks one can refer to [NIST08] and [ISO27004].

5 Communication

Nowadays the quality of communication is as important as accuracy [vFab08]. The security managers must also be experts in communication and promotion. In order to direct the general management's attention to security issues and in order to involve them as required, security people need to explain their methodology and metric in a descriptive way. Secondly, it is important to show the progress made together with remaining problems. Third, it is necessary to present all the information in an appropriate format. Examples are shown in Fig. 4. Possible formats which can be used on a management level include Harvey Balls, spider diagrams, targets, diagrams, trend charts, traffic lights, balanced scorecards as well as lists or even reports. If the format does not suit, the content may fail to be effective. One should also consider the manager's profession (engineer, lawyer, economist etc.).

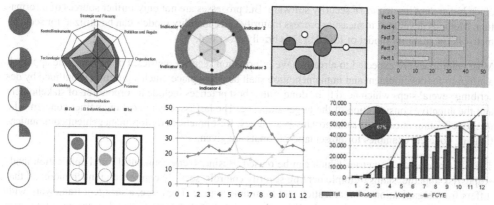

Fig. 4: Examples for presentation formats

6 Summary

A key question is still: How to justify all security related effort especially to the senior management, since information security is sometimes considered as a cost factor or overhead. Security metrics can help to demonstrate value and benefit for business. Metrics are also required to direct the work for information security. They are used to optimize resource allocation and to select, design and modify security controls. Metrics are an important supporting instrument for enterprise risk management. Despite the clear demands and advantages, security metrics are often poorly developed, or ineffective parameters are collected and analysed.

The paper describes best practices for the development of security metrics and their implementation and communication within enterprises and public authorities. The first part of the paper is to clear the way. Demands and advantages of metrics are summarized. Security metrics are a mean supporting Risk Management. They neither replace risk management processes nor taking business decisions. Metrics should be (i) consistent, reproducible, as well as reliable, (ii) relevant, (iii) useful or informative and functional, (iv) high-piled or sectional and at distinct level, and (v) manageable with low overhead as well as understandable.

The main body of the paper provides concrete rules and clauses, step-by-step procedures and a variety of tangible methods for the development of metrics. The first step is the determination of the purpose (or goal) of the measurement. This is based upon selecting a combination of one of three subjects (security controls, related processes and achievement of goals) with one out of five subject parameters. Then an observable (as the real-life source of information) is identified. Third a method is selected from a given set of six types. Fourth, one should consider the role of the information and decide if it directly evaluates towards the purpose (direct indicator) or if more contextual information is being provided. This issue and the selection and interpretation of information are discussed in great detail. Fifth, in most cases several measurements have to be aggregated and also be interpreted to obtain functional information. Simplified examples demonstrate the use of this procedure.

Understanding is key. The measurement shall be done before implementing any security control and the expected change or effect shall be identified as a hypothesis. The measurement is performed again after implementation which allows comparing hypothesis with reality on the one hand and trend analysis on the other. There are a lot of sources of information which can be used for measurement. Examples include but are not limited to IT security software. But processes are not only further sources of information. Methods developed to measure process maturity and capability models can be utilized for security metrics. The maturity model of ISO 21827 is briefly described.

Most enterprises are expected to already have information security metrics. For a systematic approach a program for development and implementation shall be put in place. Such a program is outlined by describing several steps which need to be done. Other best practices include incorporation of stakeholders and the attentive consideration of the target audience. The last issue is related to another concern. The quality of communication is as important as accuracy. Best practices for top-management communication and concrete examples for presentation formats are given.

There is not one set of metrics which can be reused. Business, environment, IT and application landscape, risk appetite, status of implementing security controls, security controls and much more: all that differs from organization to organization and from time to time. Therefore, a stringent framework with practical guidelines is required which allows the security management to develop and maintain their own set of security metrics. This paper provided a skeleton to accomplish the definition and implementation of metrics which allow to demonstrate progress and to justify allocation of resources as required in real-world business.

References

[ISO21827] ISO/IEC 21827 – Information Technology – Systems Engineering – Capability Maturity Model (SSE-CMM)

[ISO27001] ISO/IEC 27001 – Information technology – Security techniques – Information security management systems – Requirements

[ISO27002] ISO/IEC 27002 – Information technology – Security techniques – Code of practice for information security management

[ISO27004] Draft ISO/IEC 27004 – Information technology – Security techniques – Information security management – Measurements

[Jaqu07] Andrew Jaquith: Security metrics: replacing fear, uncertainty, and doubt; Addison Wesley, 2007

[NIST08] NIST Special Publication 800-55 Rev. 1: Performance Measurement Guide for Information Security

[NIST09] NIST Special Publication 800-53 Rev. 3: Recommended Security Controls for Federal Information Systems and Organizations

[vFab08] Eberhard von Faber: How Economy and Society affect Enterprise Security Management; in: N. Pohlmann, H. Reimer, W. Schneider (Editors): Securing Electronic Business Processes, Vieweg (2008), p. 77-83

[Wheat08] Jeffrey Wheatman: The Do's and Don'ts of Information Security Metrics; Gartner Research, 21 October 2008

[WBA04] Roberta J. Witty, Chris Brittain and Ant Allan: Justify Identity Management Investment with Metrics; Gartner Research, 23 February 2004

Demystifying SAP security

Marc Sel · Kristof Van Der Auwera

PricewaterhouseCoopers

marc.sel@pwc.be
kristof.van.der.auwera@pwc.be

Abstract

This article attempts to demystify the feature-rich SAP security functions, to demonstrate how they can cooperate to build a strong security posture, and how to avoid some classic pitfalls.

ERP systems continue to gain importance in the developed world, and while there are many alternatives to choose from (including competitive vendors as well as OpenSource projects such as Compierre), SAP is a major force in this field. Over the years SAP established a rich security model, including infrastructure aspects such as secure networking and separation of production and non-production environments , but more importantly they also included all relevant Identity and Access Management aspects, as well as electronic signature aspects. As a result, a SAP customer is today facing a wide range of potential safeguards to chose from, each with their own cost/benefit ratio. However, it is generally accepted that application level securty is in the end more important than infrastructure security. The SAP authorisation model is at the heart of application security in FI, CO, HR, MM etc. It evolved over the years from a fairly simple, profile-based model with capabilities towards today's model that includes identities, roles, profiles and fine-grained authorisation object management. Dedicated authorisation objects have been established for the different functional areas within SAP, and various additional software components both from SAP and from external vendors can assist with building and managing SAP authorisations. Those include e.g. Virsa FF/ SAP GRC, Axl & Trax (ex-CSI) and more recent CA's ERCM. PwC also still maintains their own ACE review tool.

Under the scrutiny of the ever increasing regulatory compliance, a company has to make the right options, or will face expensive mistakes. We will in this article address both the theoretical aspects of the SAP security model, including the authorisation model, and the more practical aspects as how to organise a SAP security project and how to tackle undesired side effects when implementing a real project.

1 Introduction

1.1 The scene

Common to many organisations is that they have a limited number of core value chains such as developing a product/service, selling it and collecting due compensation, and delivering the product/service. Often technology enables these value chains or is even fully embedded in the organisation's fabric. SAP's solutions grew from offering core business applications (Enterprise Resource Planning) to a wide spectrum of solutions, embedded in the economic ecosystem. These solutions play a role in accomplishing many different and challenging tasks, including for example managing the European Commission's budget.

N. Pohlmann, H. Reimer, W. Schneider (Editors): Securing Electronic Business Processes, Vieweg (2009), 27-36

1.2 Evolving functionality and technology

Originally SAP R/3 was introduced in 1992, based on a 3-tier (data, logic, presentation) architecture. It built on the concept of an enterprise model, supported by a data model, shared by all applications. The enterprise model is based on the 'Mandant' representing the highest organisational level of the enterprise. Within a 'Mandant', different organisational and legal entities can share data such as accounting ledgers, and can consolidate information. Across 'Mandanten', data is not shared. Through customization, SAP allows meeting the diverse compliance requirements for accounting and VAT, and supports most of the administrative business processes (Order2Cash, Procure2Pay, Treasury, HR, etc). .

Relational tables implement the data model, transactions are coded in the SAP-specific ABAP language through the ABAP workbench, screens are painted and chained with Dynpro, and end-user access is via the dedicated SAP-GUI. Transaction SE16 is the general purpose data browser, allowing you to browse all tables (assuming you have appropriate authorisations). The functional areas are structured into BC (Basis Components, client server technology, OS, DB and also security), CA (Cross-Application, euro support, document management, archiving), AC (Accounting, including FI – Finance and CO – Control, investment and treasury), HR (Human Resources), and LO (Logistics, including Materials Management, Plant Maintenance, Production Planning and Sales and Distribution). Specific modules such as APO for planning emerged. There are multiple alternatives for data exchange and integration. Within the Basis System, CTS, the Change and Transport System allows managing separate production and non-production environments.

As a next wave of integration, SAP introduced their Enterprise Portal solution, acquired from TopTier. The SAP GUI was complemented by the browser. This gave rise to the SAP login ticket, stored on the client-side as an HTTP-cookie to allow single-sign-on.

SAP introduced mySAP ERP in 2004. Under the complementary NetWeaver brandname, SAP embraced Java and Web Services technology. SAP R/3 expanded from applications on a basis system into an application core, enterprise and industry extensions and collaborative functions. These are all based on NetWeaver as application and integration foundation, with co-existing ABAP and J2EE logic. As such, the core financial functionality (FI-CO) migrated into mySAP ERP Financials, which included an enhanced GL. Further improvements addressed the Financial Supply Chain and its core processes (P2P, OTC, Treasury, etc), as well as reporting, planning, consolidation etc. HR enlarged into Human Capital Management.

Master Data Management was introduced to provide more integrated data views, eg producing a single view on all credits of a single debtor. Reporting was enhanced through the Business Integration functionality, and XI improved the data exchange and integration.

1.3 Fundamental safeguards

Originally, users were required to install the SAP GUI on their machine. Once authenticated with userid/password, they were provided a menu interface. Their run-time capabilities where constrained by the authorisation checks coded within the ABAP application programs. These checks verified that a user had the required authorisations in the form of Authorisation Objects (containing fields and values). This can include organisational checks (does the user belong to the appropriate part of the organisation), checks for the right to execute a particular transaction (does the user have the right to create a Purchase Order), and fine-grained checks (does the user not exceed e.g. a financial threshold). Such authorisations are granted via Profiles, which can be single or composite (composed of multiple single Profiles). This is typically referred to as a capability model, allowing fine-grained authorisation management.

For example, typical authorisation objects for transaction FB50 (GL Posting) includes the basic check for transactioncode: S_TCODE (with field TCD – transactioncode (which should then allow access to FB50)). Further objects are F_BKPF_BUK (with fields BUKRS (eg 0001) and ACTVT (01, 02, 03) – 'Buchungskreis' und 'Aktivität'), F_BKPF_BUP ('Buchungsperioden' – timeperiods), F_BKPF_GSB (with fields GSBER (eg 01, 02) and ACTVT – 'Geschäftsbereich' und 'Aktivität'), F_BKPF_KOA (with field KOART (D, K, A, S, M) and ACTVT – 'Kontoart' und 'Aktivität'). Note that modules may have their own additional complement to S_TCODE, eg the HR module has the additional P_TCODE object. SAP_ALL is probably the best-known composite profile, allowing virtually all accesses. Which authorisations are checked in which transaction is decided at customization time, and can later be managed via a.o. SU24.

It should be noted that in some situations, the model introduced undesired side-effects since AO's may be reused in different contexts. Furthermore, a complementary ACL (access control list) model was also implemented; its groups are managed via SUGR.

Management of identities and authorisations is via dedicated transactions such as SU01 (User management), SU02 (Profile management), SU03 (Authorisation management) and SUIM (InfoManagement). To find out which authorisation checks are used in transactions, you can make use of ST01 (trace) and SE38 (displays code source).

For larger landscapes SAP introduced the CUA (Central User Administration). For a good introduction refer to [SAPBRTW].

As specific applications required their own fine-grained access control, dedicated AO's such as for HR were introduced. And as the combinatory space of users, profiles, authorisation objects and authority checks increased, R/3 4.5 introduced the Profile Generator PFCG and activity groups (AGRs). It is then recommended to segregate administrative tasks into three distinct sets:

1. 'Authorisation data administrators' create activity groups and maintains authorisations;
2. 'Authorisation profile administrators' generate profiles;
3. 'User administrators' assign activity groups (or profiles) to users.

These administrators will be the only ones with the activity groups and authorisations that allow them to manage the accesses of the end user community.

As from R/3 4.6, there were approximately 900 authorisation objects, structured into some 40 object classes. Activity groups were replaced by the concept of roles, and template roles were introduced. These roles are translated into Profiles, linking the users to their authorisations.

Finally, all table updates/deletes can be logged at system level. The existing logs can be displayed with Transaction Table history (SCU3).

2 Enriching the model

2.1 SAP Basis security

SAP Basis contains the authorisation model with the authorisation objects (as introduced in the preceding section), as well as the Change and Transport System security, network security, and secure 'store and forwarding'.

2.2 Change and Transport System security

The Change and Transport System allows coordination of own developments, their migration across the SAP landscape, program upgrades, and copying of 'Mandanten'. It is mainly composed of the Transport Organiser and the Transport Management System.

TO manages customer developments created with the ABAP workbench. What development is actually allowed is fixed at the level of the 'Mandant'. The Transport Organiser safeguards the originals in a repository, and migrates copies through the SAP landscape. TMS allows to define which systems play a role in the landscape, and the transports between them. This allows to build a segregated production/ non-production landscape, and to control the transfer of software developments into production.

2.3 Network security – SNC and SAProuter

Secure Network Communications (SNC) was created to guarantee confidential data transfer between SAP GUI and an Application Server, particularly in an Internet and WAN setting. It relies on cryptography and is based on the well-known GSS API. Its usage was later expanded toward protection of network traffic between distributed SAP components. SNC relies on an external crypto product. In addition you can implement additional features offered by the external security product (Single Sign-On, or smart card authentication).

SAProuter is an Application Level Gateway, serving as an intermediate station (proxy) in a network connection between a SAP System and programs accessing that system. It complements traditional port and network level firewalls. SAProuter and SNC can be integrated, where the former will then decide which SNC connections can reach which applications.

Alternatively, non-SAP specific firewalls and VPNs can be used too for network security.

2.4 Http access and SSL

The ITS (Internet Transaction Server) opened access to browser-based clients. SAP also acquired Top-Tier and their portal solution, allowing access via iViews. This allowed standard browser access, with SSL/TLS possibilities where required.

2.5 Complementary smart card authentication

Furthermore, the basic userid/password authentication can be improved using third party smart card products. However, given the relative complexity of rolling out smart cards, readers and drivers, as well as a Card Management System of some form, this was not a very popular route for most customers.

3 Electronic signatures

3.1 Electronic signatures – TrustManager

Electronic signatures have been in use since the 1970's, but got a boost by the Internet. They are typically based on a combination of two complementary transformations, signing and verifying. Most systems are based on so-called public/private key solutions, where signing happens with the private key (safely stored in e.g. a smart card) and verifying relies on the public key (published in a certificate, and made available via e.g. a public directory). Management of public keys and their certificates is typically done via a PKI (public key infrastructure). SAP provides the TrustManager to manage keys & certificates. Underlying cryptographic libraries can be obtained from vendors such as IAIK.

3.2 Application level cryptography – SSF

SAP's SSF (Secure Store and Forwarding) offers signing/verifying as well as encrypting/decrypting features. The classical signature formats are supported such as PKCS#7, XML, S/MIME, PDF and more recently the various XML formats. SSF is provided for SAP Web Application Server, for the ABAP stack and for J2EE. Integration into applications is performed with Business Add-ins (BADI), customer exits, or own modifications. Alternatively you can use SAP's Business Connector.

If required, e-signatures can also be used to secure the output of e.g. payment programs such as SAPF110S via BADI's (Business Add-In). Key management is with SAP's TrustManager or an external PKI.

4 SAP GRC suite

For various reasons, the notion of Governance, Risk and Compliance increasingly gained importance. This confirmed the relevance of Internal Control models such as COSO, which relies on Segregation-of-Duty as a fundamental control principle.

The SAP GRC suite assists in addressing access control and segregation-of-duty matters in an ABAP-based system. It evolved from the 'Continuous Compliance' toolset acquired from Virsa (and originally developed by PwC as SAFE – Security Administrator for ERP). GRC Access Control can be considered an evolution of the Profile Generator, expanded by a segregation-of-duty matrix. The matrix is structured into domains, which map to transactions, authorisation objects and similar. Furthermore it includes much-sought after functions such as self-service password reset. The Access Control product is complemented by:

- Risk Analysis and Remediation (formerly 'Compliance Calibrator') which controls violations preventively at provisioning time. Its functions are callable via Web Services too;
- Superuser Privilege Management (formerly 'Firefighter'), enabling super-users emergency access to enterprise systems without committing regulatory violations by introducing mitigating controls.
- Toolset Configuration and Business Process Enhancements for User Access Management (Compliant User Provisioning) and role administration (Enterprise Role Management).

5 NetWeaver and Identity Management

5.1 NetWeaver

SAP introduced J2EE-based Web Application Servers with NetWeaver. In J2EE and Portal systems identities are typically based on LDAP or third party IAM systems. NetWeaver's user management is based on the UME (User Management Engine), comparable to SU01 for ABAP systems. In a J2EE environment, access control comes in two different approaches: declarative and programmative. Declarative corresponds to a coarse-grained check defined in the deployment descriptor of the program, while programmative means fine-grained with checks hardcoded inside the program. Obviously, declarative controls are faster to implement and the first way to go.

NetWeaver allows Web Services, program-to-program communication with service announcement, discovery, transport and all other WS features. Authentication and authorisation is now converging towards SAML and Ping Identity, with key management where required via XKMS. Key management is now receiving renewed attention, because SAML assertions about a subject may be signed too.

5.2 The identity federation challenge

Once an organisation wants to accept users from other entities with who they cooperate ('the federation'), they are facing federation challenges. In such a federation, the key roles are the producer and consumer of assertions. A producer makes statements about a subject such as 'authenticated by me (so if you trust me, you can let him in)', or 'in possession of attribute X (e.g. I confirm that he's older than 18 years of age)'. Note that these two assertions may come from independent providers. A consumer makes use of such assertions. Furthermore, the subject may wish to select which producer to use for a specific application service he wants to access. The service provider is the one 'consuming' the assertions. He is also said to be the relying party since he trusts the party that endorsed the assertion. Assertions are typically expressed in XML, and digitally signed to protect their integrity.

Where SAP originally relied on their own format for assertions ('tickets'), through cooperation with a.o. Ping Identity they moved into open federation standards such as SAML (Security Assertions Mark-up Language). Third parties such as IBM also started to offer federated identity management solutions for NetWeaver.

5.3 NetWeaver Identity Management

Acquiring MaxWare enabled SAP to further improve NetWeaver Identity Management. It aims at managing IDs across the entire SAP landscape, with or without any existing CUA. NetWeaver IM is based on the MaxWare directory concepts and services, on which provisioning scripts are based. This allows creation of high-level business roles, which can be mapped onto technical roles, containing the actual resources, which may include Profiles and other managed elements. Information available in SAP HR can either be leveraged via propagation of HR attributes into LDAP, or accessed more directly. The two core components of IM are the Identity Center (with workflow, the ID database, and event processors) and the Virtual Directory Server (creating a unified view over many physically different directory services via connectors and SPML).

Through integration, NetWeaver IM can make use of all controls defined in GRC, including segregation-of-duty, allowing capitalization on investments in prior control developments.

It can be observed that where many traditional IAM vendors started from non-SAP and gradually expanded their scope towards SAP, Netweaver Identity Manager started in the same way (due to its Max-Ware roots), but is obviously well placed to integrate tightly with all other existing and future SAP security safeguards. And due to its non-SAP specific roots, it can easily reach outwards, towards the non-SAP sphere too.

6 Complementary tooling

Besides the SAP-supplied solutions, there are numerous additional tools. We will only discuss a small subset of relevant tools and have no objective of being exhaustive.

6.1 CA ERCM

In 2008 Computer Associates acquired Eurekify, a player in the deployment of pattern matching technology which can be used to automatically generate roles across an entire organisation, including for SAP. Furthermore, business rules could be expressed and validated over the existing or envisioned authorisations. This can be done for off-the-shelve applications, as well as home-grown developments, greatly facilitating both compliance and IAM solutions. It is particularly well suited to express segregation-of-duty constraints over all possible authorisations, both coarse and fined grained. The Enterprise Role and Compliance Management solution is now integrating with the CA IAM solutions. This allows e.g. testing a business rule such as segregation-of-duty prior to granting an authorisation.

6.2 Other

There are numerous security add-ons available for SAP. These include Virtual Forge's ABAP scanner and CodeProfiler, which reveals security defects in custom programs.Other complementary products include the product suite from Axl & Trax (formerly CSI), BizRights' Approva, and Aveksa's suite. Furthermore, despite its name, Security Weaver offers functionality similar to the SAP GRC suite, i.e. focused on traditional authorisation objects and ABAPs. Swiss-based but in India developed Conteliga also offers such functionality.

7 Tying it all together

7.1 Organising your SAP security project

There is sufficient high-level guidance on how to organise security projects in general. However, before committing to a SAP security project, you may find it helpful to consider the various SAP safeguards from an ISO 27K perspective.

#	Security domain (aligned on ISO 27001)	Possible SAP safeguard
1	Policy 'Information Security'	May be referenced at SAP login time.
2	Organisational design, including roles & responsibilities, and horizontal and vertical segregations of power/control	'Mandant' and organisational structures reflected in Authorisation Objects SAP HR
3	Asset management	Can be handled via SAP functionality
4	Human Resources Security	SAP HR/HCM and EPP
5	Physical and environmental security	n/a
6	Communications and operations management	SAP router, SSF and SNC TrustManager (PKI) Platform hardening PUT (patches) management, SAP Notes
7	Access control	SU0x, SUIM, Role, Profiles, Authorisation Objects, Profile Generator, CUA SAP GRC suite and NetWeaver IM
8	Information systems acquisition, development and maintenance	Access to ABAP Workbench, NetWeaver Developer, developer key CTS – Change and Transport System
9	Information security incident management	SAP Logging – SCU3
10	Business continuity management	'High-availability' landscape
11	Compliance	SAP GRC suite
12	Independent audit and review	Various reports as well as SAP AIS

Finally, it is also relevant to consider accreditation (e.g. according to the Common Criteria) when selecting a safeguard.

7.2 SAP Authorizations

At the core of any SAP security project lies the development of an appropriate authorization concept.

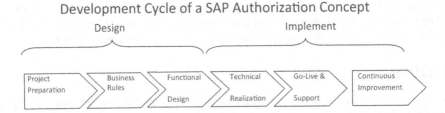

Development Cycle of a SAP Authorization Concept

Our approach is always based on a collaborative team comprising PwC and client staff. The most effective approach is to start from the business context and assess the actual situation compared to the required good practice situation (i.e. business rules based on the organisation and constraints stated in for example in regulations such as Sarbanes-Oxley). Next, we identify any discrepancies in the technical implementation, resulting from a historically grown combination / mix of SAP authorisations. The root cause of this 'inadvertent' access can either be poor role design & maintenance based on approved user access requests or ineffective approval procedures for requests. Conceptually:

	Business Rules	SAP Roles	SAP Authorizations Challenge
As-is	Actual functions performed by individuals Current segregation of duties and access rules in place	Actual roles assigned to individuals Degree of segregation of duties conflicts contained in current roles	Does the combination of roles lead to additional unintended access? Do the underlying SAP objects effectively support the role description?
To-be	The appropriate segregation of duties and access rules (in the form of a matrix) Required compensating controls where segregation of duties cannot be achieved	Roles required to support business rules Transactions required in each role Suitable role hierarchy and segregations	Changes required in the current authorizations of profiles? Creation of new authorisation profiles required?

We illustrate this as:

	Business Rules	SAP Roles	SAP Authorizations
As-is	Person A performs functions 1, 2 & 3 which have been approved by his manager	Person A has been granted roles which gives him access to functions 1, 2, 3, & 4	The combination of roles has allowed person A to have access to functions 1, 2, 3, 4 & 5
To-be	Person A should only be performing functions 1 & 2 Until a new resource is allocated for function 3, Person A's manager has to monitor the performance of function 3	Person A has roles assigned which will only allow him to perform functions 1 & 2	The combination of roles does not lead to any additional unintended access

To identify all important gaps, the project team will define the to-be situation and then compare the as-is situation for business rules, SAP roles and underlying SAP authorizations with it. To analyze 'as is' authorizations, PwC developed ACE ('Automated Controls Evaluator'). ACE first extracts configuration controls and security data from a client's SAP system and copies it into a customised MS Access environment for analysis. Profile designs and user allocations can then be analyzed against SAP administrative objects, critical module transactions and combinations of transactions. ACE allows the user to complete all test cases at the authorisation level, thus the results are more representative of the client's actual security design. Complementary, data from RBE (Reverse Business Engineer) can be used to match transaction usage to users, including frequency of usage. RBE is an ABAP program that extracts data from the Performance Management system (ST03). It helps to compare transaction and system usage between R/3 installations, clients and within organizational entities. Tools such as CA ERCM can be instrumental here, even more so because they work across all applications, not just SAP.

Through the gap analysis, we identify root causes for exceptions. These may be in the area of business rules, of SAP role definitions or underlying SAP authorizations. This information is critical to plan effective remediation efforts and develop a sustainable access and authorisation maintenance policy in future.

To close the gaps, it is suggested to work with role tiers. Tier 1 contains the general roles, accesses assigned to all end users across all functional areas. Tier 2 contains common reporting and display roles within functional areas. Tier 3 contains the functional roles, allowing users to make changes to both transactional and master data. There roles contain the typical create/change/delete/block/post functionality, and are grouped e.g. into tasks. Finally, tier 4 are referred to as the enabler roles, controlling the field-level accesses. These roles do not contain transactions, only authorisation object level definitions to various organizational level fields. Where Tier 2 and 3 provide access to transactions, tier 4 enabler roles permit the accesses required to specific organisational values that allow these transactions to be executed properly.

Testing for undesired side-effects via test suites and tracing remains a key activity throughout the project.

7.3 SAP GRC projects

Also here, our approach is based on a collaborative team comprising PwC and client staff. A typical SAP GRC project would include the following five phases:
- Scoping, Planning, SAP GRC & Controls Awareness Training and Roadmap;
- Toolset Configuration and Business Process Enhancements for sensitive access and SoD (Risk Analysis & Remediation and Super User Privilege Management) including initial remediation of 'quick win' segregation-of-duty conflicts;
- Toolset Configuration and Business Process Enhancements for User Access Management (Compliant User Provisioning) and role administration (Enterprise Role Management);
- Putting into practice Security Processes; and
- Remediation of Security Design (Role Design).

The client typically provides a senior level project manager to work as a dedicated member of the project team. The purpose of this arrangement is to assist with management of the project schedule and help to efficiently coordinate the various work sessions required. As a critical success factor in this process a business sponsor at the C-level (CFO, CEO, CIO) who can set the 'tone at the top' as to the importance and relevance of the project and ensure buy-in and commitment of the right business representatives who will act as decision makers and owners of the SoD rules to be enforced.

7.4 SAP NetWeaver IM projects

With NetWeaver IM, the scope of SAP-based Identity Management increases significantly. We are now likely to see IM and IAM projects that will make use of the foundation of SAP HR and corporate LDAPs. It will be possible to integrate SAP HR/HCM user attributes and organisational values and use them in the NetWeaver context. Most organisations start to make use of a 'business role mapped onto technical roles' model. The quality of the identities using these roles is under increasing scrutiny from regulators, as is the quality of the organisation-wide segregation-of-duty. NetWeaver IM has a great role to play here. This may well be in cooperation with partners such as Ping Identity, and their toolkit for federation ('PingFederate'). This technology is converging towards SAML, WS-Trust and WS-Federation. Hence an important part of the work will be defining the high-level roles with regard to identity and attribute providers, and the types of reliance that service providers can take from these assertions. And these roles have subsequently to be implemented across ABAP and J2EE stacks.

8 Conclusion

SAP-based solutions became commonplace in the 21st century, both in private and public sector. There is a well established body of best practices and possible safeguards that can be deployed to mitigate operational, security and internal control risks. It relies on balancing security at the levels of policy, management processes, applications, and infrastructure. Alignment on the ISO 27000 family [ISO27K1] is increasingly common, because it offers a solid structure to justify security investments. At the core of it lies a well-designed and managed authorisation concept. And SAP authorisation objects and SAML assertions will work side-by-side to get the job done. Just as breaks allow a car to go faster, safeguards in terms of security and controls allow better business.

References

[ISO27K1] ISO/IEC 27001 Information technology – Security techniques – Information security management systems – Requirements (available from www.iso.ch)

[SAPBRTW] SAP Berechtigungswesen, IBM Business Consulting Services, ISBN 3-89842-312-3, 2003

The ISACA Business Model
for Information Security:
An Integrative and Innovative
Approach

Rolf von Roessing

SCM Ltd
rvr@scmltd.com

ISACA

Abstract

In recent years, information security management has matured into a professional discipline that covers both technical and managerial aspects in an organisational environment. Information security is increasingly dependent on business-driven parameters and interfaces to a variety of organisational units and departments. In contrast, common security models and frameworks have remained largely technical. A review of extant models ranging from [LaBe73] to more recent models shows that technical aspects are covered in great detail, while the managerial aspects of security are often neglected.Likewise, the business view on organisational security is frequently at odds with the demands of information security personnel or information technology management. In practice, senior and executive level management remain comparatively distant from technical requirements. As a result, information security is generally regarded as a cost factor rather than a benefit to the organisation.

ISACA´s Business Model for Information Security (BMIS) has been developed to address the weaknesses in existing models. It addresses information security primarily from a management perspective, by placing it in the context of a functioning, profit-oriented organisation. The model further outlines approaches and key organisational factors influencing the success or failure of security. The paper presents the BMIS in its entirety, and reflects on the individual components and their significance for information security. It will be shown that the current framework for the BMIS can interface with existing models as well as common control frameworks and international standards. The paper will demonstrate that the complete integration of information security with business is an essential prerequisite to overcoming the technical restrictions and managerial disadvantages often experienced in the past. In relating some of the aspects of BMIS to typical incidents and security violations, the paper will conclude by presenting an outlook on practical BMIS use and addressing typical security risks by means of the BMIS.

1 Introduction

For a period of several years, information technology has been at the very top of many reports listing business-related challenges and so-called "hot topics". In accountancy [AICP06, AICP07, AICP08] and various other disciplines, the topic has been ranked as the highest managerial priority for many years. More often than not, information security in its widest sense is directly linked to general compliance, risk management and corporate governance [ISAC06, ISAC07]. Failure to comply with existing rules,

N. Pohlmann, H. Reimer, W. Schneider (Editors): Securing Electronic Business Processes, Vieweg (2009), 37-47

or weaknesses in governance, may easily lead to consequences that reach beyond the sphere of information technology or information management.

Conversely, the single obstacle most quoted in theoretical and practical work on the subject is the perceived (or observed) lack of "senior management support". The primary concern voiced by senior business managers is the lack of clear economic parameters and the lack of an unequivocal business case for information security. Concepts such as "return on security investment" (RoSI) and others have addressed this expectation gap, but they remain largely disconnected from the traditional models in security and information technology. In order to provide an answer to some of the well-known problems in information security, the Business Model for Information Security (BMIS) [ISAC09] presents a holistic view of security as one of the organisational goals. The following sections of this paper outline its foundations in theory and practice.

1.1 Business Imperatives in Information Security

Information security, or InfoSec in short, has been a largely technical discipline for many decades. Early information technology did not present any security-related challenges in the civilian context, With the advent of office-based information technology use and the increasingly commercial focus of the web, investments in information security increased over a long period of time. Today´s business imperatives in information security are therefore multi-dimensional and multi-faceted. The use of IT itself is subject to security requirements, as the profitability of business processes is often directly dependent on their technical support. As a secondary imperative, the interaction between business and the interaction with customers has brought a wide range of laws, regulations and contractual requirements. At the same time, organisations are seeking cost reductions and enhancements to efficiency. The cost of IT, and thus of information security, is a frequent target for reductions, particularly during economic downturns or in phases of intense economic competition.

As a result, there is a widening gap between the reality of information security and the notional demands of business. The long-range consequences of a decoupling between the business view and the technical view have been subject to extensive research. The results – dating back to the mid 1970s – form a picture of imminent danger and growing risk, regardless of the processes and technologies involved. Where [Turn76, Turn78, Perr84] and others found that an unrealistic business perspective on technology led to disaster, more recent authors such as [PaMi92] formulated the theory of "crisis-prone" organisations whose narrow view on reality will lead to erroneous conclusions, flawed actions and finally, disaster. It has been shown in earlier works on the subject that factors conducive to "crisis proneness" apparently do not change over time: they are in evidence both in a non-IT age and in the modern IT-dependent world [Roes06, Roes09].

1.2 Historical Context and Existing Models

The vast majority of extant models dealing with information security addresses technically descriptive or normative aspects. The former category may be traced back to the theory of data access and integrity, for instance in [BeLa73] and subsequent publications. The narrow system of reference adopted disqualifies these models for use in practical day-to-day business. The normative category, on the other hand, takes a wider view on security as a technical objective by setting control objectives and introducing various operational controls. Examples of this latter category are common frameworks such as COBIT, ITIL or the ISO 27000 series. In this historical context, existing models often lack the decisive business focus that is required for practical application. The business view is only found in secondary literature that is usually focused on narrow topics, as witnessed by somed illustrative examples. [SoSo05] argue for a more business-centric view, following their work on information security governance [Solm05]. Another interesting, if partial, perspective on the business impact of infosec is given in [CaMR04] who argue that the external perception of information security violations and failures will inevitably influence an organisation's market value. [GoSa02] make a clear case for a stronger emphasis on "people security" and human factors, thus illuminating another perennial problem in infosec that has been treated in many incidental papers. On another topic, early evidence of outsourcing and resulting security risks is presented in [Fink94], followed by a large body of literature on this aspect of security. Even this short synopsis of literature addressing aspects of security leads to the conclusion that "frameworks" and "models" alike are not as all-encompassing as infosec itself. It follows that there is a theoretical and practical justification for the ISACA BMIS as presented below.

2 The ISACA Business Model for Information Security

The recently published "Business Model for Information Security" was developed on the basis of earlier research by the University of Southern California [KiBe06], and subsequently extended to provide a holistic view on infosec. Figure 1 shows an overview of the model, depicting a dynamic framework of business-related elements and dynamic interconnections. The underlying assumption is that infosec as an operational reality will change rapidly, and that security concepts and actions must match this mode of constant change.

It should be noted that the model in itself is three-dimensional, although this is often difficult to visualise in printed matter. Both elements and dynamic interconnections are mobile and may change shape in accordance with the overall position that an organisation takes vis a vis information security.

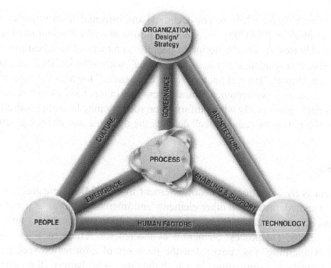

Fig. 1: BMIS Overview (Source: ISACA)

2.1 BMIS Fundamentals

The BMIS takes a holistic view on information security. It is grounded in systems theory, inasmuch as it regards the organisation, or the system of reference for infosec, as a tightly coupled and interactive area. The foundational view suggests that the model may be applied not just to infosec, but to other security-related tasks in any organisation. The BMIS provides the requisite tools to accommodate adaptive processes as well as linkages to well-known security frameworks. At this comparatively early stage, theoretical treatment of individual elements and dynamic interconnections is scarce, but it is likely that more in-depth work will follow in the near future.

2.2 BMIS Elements

2.2.1 Organisation Design and Strategy

The BMIS regards the organisation as a loosely-defined, wide-ranging basis for enacting information security in accordance with business needs [ISAC09]: *An organization is a network of people, assets and* processes interacting with each other in defined roles and working toward a common goal. Within the organisation element, business management and information security managers are required to build structures and to set strategic objectives in a way that provides an adequate level of security. The organisation element is connected to the other elements by "Culture", "Governing" and "Architecture". The cultural interconnection between organisation and people is well understood and researched, see for instance [Sche04]. The governance link to business processes may be interpreted as the corporate governance framework, the individual IT governance and security governance measures taken by the organisation itself. The "Architecture" interconnection follows from the presence of technology in any organisation, and the overarching frameworks and guidelines governing technology deployment and use.

2.2.2 People

The people element extends the BMIS to non-technical and informal security issues, as expressed by one of the key descriptors in [ISAC09]: *It represents a human collective and must take into account values, behaviors* and biases. Again, the notion of people as an element is at best loosely-defined. This element may therefore be regarded as the least "controlled" within the BMIS. It displays the interconnections "Culture" (as above), "Human Factors" and "Emergence" towards the other elements. Human factors, for instance usability, convenience, intuitiveness and others have been a central topic in information systems research, particularly where information security may be compromised or weakened by human behaviour. The notion of "emergence" denotes the dynamic and changing nature of processes through people.

2.2.3 Process

The process element is by definition the central element in the BMIS, comparable to an engine supporting the changes and adaptations in other elements and interconnections, as per [ISAC09]: Process includes formal and informal mechanisms [...] to get things done and provides a vital link to all of the dynamic interconnections. The process element is connected via "Emergence" (as above), "Enabling and Support" and "Governing" (as above). For the purposes of information security, emergence describes a series of adaptive transformations by which the process is changed (through people). In terms of technology, processes are usually defined as enablers for parts of information technology, whereas technology in turn supports processes.

2.2.4 Technology

The technology element symbolises the origins of IT as well as information security, as illustrated in [ISAC09]: Given the typical enterprise's dependence on technology, technology constitutes a core part of the enterprise's infrastructure and a critical component in accomplishing its mission. As a result, the interconnections "Architecture", "Enabling & Support" and "Human Factors" are more easily understood and placed in the context of traditional security. The emerging challenge for infosec is most likely in the rapid progress seen in technology, and the corresponding problems arising in human resources and processes. The interconnections originating from the technology element demonstrably extend the BMIS to link information security to non-technical factors of influence.

2.3 BMIS Interconnections

2.3.1 Governing

The "Governing" interconnection summarises the theory and practice of corporate governance [CDSL03] as applied to infosec. When combining it with the widely-accepted triad of "governance, risk compliance" (GRC), the organisation and the process alike should be governed by the notion of "doing the right things" rather than "doing things right" (compliance). The information security strategy defined by the organisation will provide for a corresponding structure, for instance in the person of an infosec manager. The "Governing" interconnection is designed as a repository for earlier research on information security governance and related subjects, thus integrating these works into the BMIS.

2.3.2 Culture

The "Culture" interconnection is the widest within the BMIS as it subsumes human behaviour, habits, actions and omissions alike. The overall culture observed in an organisation will in turn influence its outlook on information security, both from the senior management perspective and from the individual acceptance view. Where "security" as a concept is ingrained and culturally internalised, infosec is likely to be much stronger. The "Culture" interconnection incorporates the body of literature in organisational psychology, organisation design and related fields to the BMIS.

2.3.3 Architecture

The "Architecture" interconnection summarises interactions between organisation and technology, as there are various strategic and design issues to be resolved when using technology in a business setting. Both the overall IT architecture and the corresponding security architecture evolve as part of the organisational strategy and changes. This interconnection incorporates the body of literature on technical architectures and organisational design into the BMIS.

2.3.4 Enabling and Support

The "Enabling and Support" interconnection provides the necessary link between technology and organisational processes. It is this interconnection that integrates existing control frameworks, published standards and compliance-related topics into the BMIS. This interconnection closely links the business objectives, profit drivers and core business activities to the technological foundations and solutions. For information security purposes, it includes the typical security issues arising from process design and execution as well as technology weaknesses and vulnerabilities.

2.3.5 Human Factors

The "Human Factors" interconnection addresses both the presence of technology and its use by people. People's behaviour is subject to changes which are reflected in the underlying technology. From an infosec point of view, the use of technology may create challenges and vulnerabilities, particularly where users display unintentional or intentional behaviour that compromises security. This interconnection therefore expands the scope of technology use to questions of usability, convenience, intuitiveness and the underlying risks.

2.3.6 Emergence

The "Emergence" interconnection introduces both unpredictability, and the presence of emergent patterns into the BMIS. In an organisational setting, the well-defined processes driving core business will inevitably change over time, particularly where individuals or group re-interpret or innovate such processes. This interconnection is less well defined than the remainder of the model, due to the fact that it spans a wide range of business phenomena that may influence not only information technology or infosec. The "Emergence" interconnection incorporates general systems theory and related research into the BMIS.

2.4 Business Integration

Historically, information security has been widely regarded as a cost factor only. The presence of information technology, itself a cost factor, appears to self-propagate the need for security in the eyes of many managers. The BMIS propagates as one of its primary objectives the full integration of information security with the core business processes and functions of any organisation. Any benefit from enhanced information security, whether quantitative or qualitative, must be justified in terms of a clear business case. Similarly to traditional risk management, the value of infosec investments is usually seen in the avoidance of unfavourable situations, the containment of security violations, and the "non-events" that might have occurred had there been weaknesses and vulnerabilities. The BMIS may in turn be applied as a tool to test security-related investments in terms of their business value.

2.4.1 Technology-Based Perspective

Typically, infosec investments and funding are mainly technology-centric. While policies, standards and other influencing factors play a significant role in shaping the information security management function, the implementation and operational measures are normally manifest at the application level, or in the underlying infrastructure layers. Applying the BMIS to technology investment (or cost increase, used interchangeably below) assists in structuring the investment and its opportunity cost: The "Technology" element as the most common origin of investment proposals is therefore a good example to illustrate the BMIS logic. Once tested against other elements, the business rationale for investing in technology becomes apparent (or not).

2.4.2 Other Perspectives

The BMIS permits the use of other perspectives, regardless of any technology investments or planned cost increases. For instance, where the "Organisation" element is subject to a planned investment, testing the business cases in terms of "technology", "process" and "people" leads to comparatively simple deductive logic. For a quantitative approximation of potential financial impacts on the business, a discounted present value method may be applied [Roes04]. For a qualitative estimate of what the infosec investment might achieve, various methods are available, ranging from direct interviewing or questionnaires to industry benchmarking. The direct and indirect impact of an investment decision in information security is obtained by examining the interdependencies between information technology and supported business processes. Where information security weaknesses or incidents form the root cause of a business impact, a function of damage over time (in business terms) is obtained that takes into account cascading effects, or "long chains" of cause and effect relationships, see for instance [Roes03].

Depending on the situation, any infosec spending may be beneficial in any number of ways not directly attributable to the financial position of the firm, including but not limited to:

- PR-related success or necessity (e. g. analyst calls, rating agencies)
- competitive pressure in the short term (e. g. competitors marketing "security" in a B2C context)
- preventive / pre-emptive action (e. g. serious security incidents elsewhere in the sector or country, impending punitive regulation etc.)
- stakeholder preference (e. g. economically unclear, but influential decisions by various stakeholders)
- unexpected changes in risk exposure or threat scenarios (e. g. reactive investments to targeted attacks, unplanned investigative effort)

As with other issues in investment decision theory, the fundamental uncertainties do of course remain and cannot be remediated solely by means of applying the BMIS. However, the model represents a significant advance in systematic analysis of infosec-related investments or cost increases.

3 Integration with Governance, Risk and Control (GRC) Frameworks

In contrast to the purely business-driven view on information security, the discipline itself is subject to a multitude of legal and regulatory provisions that form part of strategic management and day-to-day operations. In most larger organisations, corporate governance covers, to a large extent, the design of policies and standards in infosec. It is shown below how the BMIS as an integrative and adaptive toolset incorporates these requirements and permits seamless integration with commonly used frameworks in GRC.

3.1 COSO Enterprise Risk Management

The COSO ERM framework describes risk management in the widest sense, using eight domains and a fairly large set of sub-domains and control objectives. It has been recognised as an adequate risk management framework under the Sarbanes-Oxley Act 2002 and others. COSO is therefore an important target model for alignment with the BMIS. In practice, information security management may be regarded as a subset of the wider information risk management within organisations. For corporate environments under the provisions of the Sarbanes-Oxley Act 2002, both the requirements and suggested control objectives have been defined in "IT Control Objectives for Sarbanes-Oxley" [ISAC06] – Table 1 shows a summary for the COBIT control objective related to information security.

- *Objective – Controls provide reasonable assurance that financial reporting systems and subsystems are appropriately secured to prevent unauthorized use, disclosure, modification, damage or loss of data.*

- *Rationale – Managing systems security includes both physical and logical controls that prevent unauthorized access. These controls typically support authorization, authentication, nonrepudiation, data classification and security monitoring. Deficiencies in this area could significantly impact financial reporting. For instance, insufficient controls over transaction authorization may result in inaccurate financial reporting.*

Table 1: BMIS and "IT Control Objectives for Sarbanes-Oxley": Security-related controls

[ISAC06]	COBIT	BMIS Elements / Interconnections
An information security policy exists and has been approved by an appropriate level of executive management	DS 5.2 (PO 6.3, PO 6.5)	Organisation, Processes / Governing
A framework of security standards has been developed that supports the objectives of the security policy	DS 5.2 (PO 8.2)	Organisation, Processes / Governing
An IT security plan exists that is aligned with overall IT strategic plans	DS 5.2	Organisation, Processes / Governing
The IT security plan is updated to reflect changes in the IT environment as well as security requirements of specific systems	DS 5.2	Processes, Technology / Enabling & Support
Procedures exist and are followed to authenticate all users of the system (both internal and external) to support the existence of transactions	DS 5.3, application level controls (AC)	Processes, People, Technology / Enabling & Support, Human Factors, Emergence
Procedures exist and are followed to maintain the effectiveness of authentication and access mechanisms (e. g. regular password changes)	DS 5.3, DS 5.4	People, Technology / Human Factors
Procedures exist and are followed related to timely action for requesting, establishing, issuing, suspending and closing user accounts (Include procedures for transactions originating outside the organization)	DS 5.4	People, Processes / Emergence
A control process exists and is followed to periodically review and confirm access rights	DS 5.4	People, Technology, Processes / Enabling & Support, Human Factors, Emergence
Where appropriate, controls exist so that neither party can deny transactions, and controls are implemented to provide nonrepudiation of origin or receipt, proof of submission, and receipt of transactions	DS 11.6, AC	People, Technology, Processes / Enabling & Support, Human Factors, Emergence
Appropriate controls, including firewalls, intrusion detection and vulnerability assessments, exist and are used to prevent unauthorized access via public networks	DS 5.10	Organisation, Technology / Architecture
IT security administration monitors and logs security activity at the operating system, application and database levels, and identified security violations are reported to senior management	DS 5.5	People, Processes, Technology / Human Factors, Emergence, Enabling & Support
Controls relating to appropriate segregation of duties over requesting and granting access to systems and data exist and are followed	DS 5.3, DS 5.4	Organisation, Processes, People / Governing, Emergence
Access to facilities is restricted to authorized personnel and requires appropriate identification and authentication.	DS 12.2, DS 12.3	Organisation, Technology / Architecture

For another typical GRC framework in financial services, the "Basel II" provisions have been mapped to information security in "IT Control Objectives for Basel II" [ISAC07]. Table 2 shows the mapping of information security risks to typical operational risks in business, again using COBIT as the common language:

Table 2: BMIS and "IT Control Objectives for Basel II": Security-related controls

[ISAC07]: Generic risk event types under Basel II	IT risk components encompassed by COBIT DS5	BMIS Elements / Interconnections
Internal fraud	Deliberate manipulations / changes to the IT environment	People, Technology / Human Factors
External fraud	as above	as above
Employment practices and workplace safety	Misuse of IT resources, lack of security responsiveness	People, Processes, Organisation / Governing, Emergence
Business disruption and system failures	Sabotage, theft of sensitive information, viruses, failure to backup, DDoS etc.	Processes, People, Technology / Enabling & Support, Emergence, Human Factors

It should be noted that both the SOx view and the Basel II view are closely related to the underlying COSO ERM framework for risk management. In this sense, Tables 1 and 2 are illustrative in breaking down the generic risk into defined information security risks and BMIS mappings. It is likely that further research will be needed to complete the detailed mappings on the BMIS side.

3.2 COBIT and Val IT

The COBIT framework in its version 4.1 is designed to provide a wide range of IT processes, control objectives and control activities which enable and inform the governance of IT in the corporate context. For information security purposes, the main control process is DS 5 (ensuring systems security), closely linked to a number of secondary processes. As COBIT itself is undergoing constant change, any future mapping is by definition a "fuzzy" one. For practical purposes, the security requirements and control objectives within COBIT are reasonably well defined and expressed through BMIS elements and interconnections. The ValIT framework addresses business value derived from information technology in the widest sense. It is therefore conducive to materialising the business cases and business rationale for information security investments / cost increases where such investments are part of a portfolio of other investment opportunities. ValIT is therefore a useful toolset to establish the link between BMIS and general business, although it does not directly address infosec issues or topics.

3.3 ISO 27000 Series

The ISO 27000 series is a growing set of security standards with broad international acceptance and coverage. At the time of releasing this paper, both ISO 27001 and 27002 are being revised. The following paragraphs outline a tentative alignment of the BMIS against the areas of infosec management now under consideration at ISO level. Table 3 outlines the suggested ISO clauses and the corresponding BMIS elements and interconnections.

Table 3: BMIS and ISO 27000 Series: High Level Alignment

ISO 27000 Series	BMIS Elements / Interconnections
Security Policy	Organisation, Processes / Governing
Organizing Information Security	Organisation, Processes / Governing
Asset Management	Processes, Technology / Enabling & Support
Human Resources Security	Processes, People, Organisation / Culture, Governing, Emergence
Physical and Environmental Security	Organisation, Processes, Technology / Architecture, Governing, Enabling & Support
Communications and Operations Management	People, Technology / Human Factors
Access Control	People, Technology / Human Factors
Information Systems Acquisition, Development and Maintenance	Organisation, Processes, Technology / Governing, Architecture, Enabling & Support
Information Security Incident Management	Organisation, Processes, People / Governing, Culture, Emergence
Business Continuity Management	Organisation, Processes, People / Culture, Governing, Emergence
Compliance	Organisation, Processes, People / Culture, Governing, Emergence

Given the structure of the ISO 27000 series, the bias towards the organisational, process and people elements is easily understood: the subsidiary standards to 27001 and 27002 address more specific issues and technical questions, thus complementing the information security management system defined in the high-level standards. Further research is needed to complete the alignment of the BMIS to these subsidiary standards.

4 Conclusions and Outlook

Historically, any extant security models have neglected the business and managerial aspects of a dynamically changing environment. While some models are more descriptive in nature, others are definitive and normative in their content without providing practical guidance to the organisation. The recently published business model for information security (BMIS) presents a synthesis of descriptive and normative models by integrating information security and business. It further incorporates existing frameworks and concepts in infosec and business (risk) management. This paper has provided a first outline based on existing BMIS publications, and it has attempted an outlook on further research based upon the BMIS. Some of the shortcomings in the current BMIS representation will undoubtedly be remedied in due course, and considerable bodies of research will need to be aligned and analysed with a view to underpinning the model with the requisite level of theory and empiricism.

Literature

[AICP06] American Institute of Certified Public Accountants (AICPA). Top Technologies Survey 2006.

[AICP07] American Institute of Certified Public Accountants (AICPA). Top Technologies Survey 2007.

[AICP08] American Institute of Certified Public Accountants (AICPA). Top Technologies Survey 2008.

[BeLa73] Bell, D. E., L. J. LaPadula. Secure Computer Systems: Mathematical Foundations. MITRE Technical Report 2547, vol. I. [https://wiki.cac.washington.edu/download/attachments/10000785/Bell73.pdf]

[CaMR04] Cavusoglu, H., B. Mishra, S. Ragunathan. The Effect of Internet Security Breach Announcements on Market Value: Capital Market Reactions for Breached Firms and Internet Security Developers, in International Journal of Electronic Commerce, vol. 9 no. 1, 2004. 69-104.

[CDSL03] Colley, J., J. L. Doyle, W. Stettinius, G. Logan. Corporate Governance, in The McGraw-Hill Executive MBA Series. New York: McGraw-Hill, 2003.

[Fink94] Fink, D. A Security Framework for Information Systems Outsourcing, in Information Management & Computer Security vol. 2 no. 4, 1994. 3-8.

[GoSa02] Gonzalez, J. J., A. Sawicka. A Framework for Human Factors in Information Security. Proceedings of WSEAS 2002, Rio de Janeiro.

[ISAC06] ISACA. IT Control Objectives for Sarbanes-Oxley, 2nd ed. Rolling Meadows IL: ISACA, 2006.

[ISAC07] ISACA. IT Control Objectives for Basel II. Rolling Meadows IL: ISACA, 2007.

[ISAC09] ISACA. An Introduction to the Business Model for Information Security. Rolling Meadows IL: ISACA, 2009.

[KiBe06] Kiely, L., T. Benzel. Systemic Security Management: A new conceptual framework for understanding the issues, inviting dialogue and debate, and identifying future research needs. White Paper, Institute for Critical Information Infrastructure Protection (ICIIP), University of Southern California 2006.

[PaMi92] Pauchant, T., I. I. Mitroff. Transforming the Crisis-Prone Organization. San Francisco: Jossey-Bass, 1992.

[Perr84] Perrow, C. Normal Accidents. New York: Basic Books, 1984.

[Roes03] von Roessing, R. Quantified Risk and Business Impact: A Strategic Decision Support Model for Security and Business Continuity Management. Proceedings of ISSE 2003.

[Roes04] von Roessing, R. IT-Sicherheit und Basel II: Security als operationelles Risiko [IT Security and Basel II: Security as Operational Risk]. Proceedings of D-A-CH Security 2004.

[Roes06] von Roessing, R. Sicherheit und Krisenanfälligkeit – Erfolgsfaktoren und Warnindikatoren [Security and Crisis Proneness – Success Factors and Warning Indicators]. Proceedings of D-A-CH Security 2006.

[Roes09] von Roessing, R. Business Resilience – Wege aus der Krisenanfälligkeit [Business Resilience – Ways Out of Crisis Proneness]. Proceedings of D-A-CH Security 2009.

[Sche04] Schein, E. H. Organizational Culture and Leadership. 3rd ed, Wiley 2004.

[Solm05] von Solms, S. H. Information security governance – compliance management versus operational management, in Computers & Security vol. 24, 2005. 443-447.

[SoSo05] von Solms, S. H., R. von Solms. From information security to... business security? in Computers & Security vol. 24, 2005. 271-273.

[Turn76] Turner, B. A. The Organizational and Interorganizational Development of Disasters. Administrative Science Quarterly, vol. 21, September 1976.

[Turn78] Turner, B. A. Man-Made Disasters. New York: Crane, Russak & Co., 1978.

ICT Systems Contributing to European Secure-by-Design Critical Infrastructures

Fabien Cavenne

THALES Information Systems Security
for European Organisation for Security – EOS
fabien.cavenne@thales-esecurity.com

Abstract

Over the last two decades, the world's landscape changed considerably, relying increasingly on the availability and exchange of information in all sectors to fuel economic growth and improved competitiveness. ICT systems, whether we speak of applications, telecommunications or integrated system solutions, are key components of many Critical Infrastructures, and, as such, their disruption, malfunction or compromise can seriously impact our societal and individual well being.

The objective of this paper is to understand what is the situation in terms of how these ICT systems can contribute to the security and resilience of the Critical Infrastructures both from the operators and ICT solution suppliers' points of view. It then provides an analysis of the gaps to be covered through a comprehensive approach including operational, regulatory and technical stand points detailing what should be the objectives of an approach aiming at building and maintaining Secure-by-Design systems. Indeed, an important element is to understand that security is not just a technological issue but is a complete mindset involving all organisations and individuals. Therefore, the Secure-by-Design approach advocated in this paper represents a process oriented strategy defining clearly identified roles within organisations and specific tools to support these roles. While we specialise it to ICT systems, its driving principles can be adopted for applied to all systems.

This paper concludes on possible actions to be undertaken at European level to improve the situation and therefore contribute to overall Critical Infrastructure protection.

This paper is presented by Fabien Cavenne from THALES Information Systems Security as a member of the European Organisation for Security (EOS). The European Organisation for Security – EOS – was created in July 2007 by European private sector suppliers and users from all domains of security solutions and services. Today, EOS has 34 members, representing 12 European Countries, and 30% of the 30 Billion Euro worldwide security market. EOS focuses on the market side, and seeks to develop a close relationship with the main public and private actors.

The main objective of EOS is the development of a consistent European Security Market, while sustaining the interests of its members and satisfying political, social and economic needs through the efficient use of budgets, and the implementation of available solutions in priority areas, in particular through the creation of a coherent EU Security strategy.

N. Pohlmann, H. Reimer, W. Schneider (Editors): Securing Electronic Business Processes, Vieweg (2009), 48-62

1 Introduction

Over the last two decades, the world's landscape changed considerably and became reliant on the availability and exchange of information in all sectors to fuel economic growth and improved competitiveness. This is leading to a new revolution with the emergence of widespread concepts such as cloud computing.

The common enablers of this revolution are the underlying networks enabling the information exchange and the vast storage capacity available where terabytes of digital data are now standard even for home computers. While initially such networks were often limited to a single enterprise, the entire world has since grown to rely on the pervasive use of large information networks, including the Internet.

The dependency of the economy on such networks is both a main driver for innovation and a major weakness of operations:

- A main driver because the increased outreach has led to exponential growth and the exchange of sensitive data and information is today vital to the protection of political or economic interests of all countries.

- A major weakness because the pervasiveness and connectivity of infrastructures have made it virtually impossible to unambiguously identify the main operators. Therefore, when failures occur, the chain of responsibility is unclear and structured emergency and recovery plans are difficult to define, while in parallel economic or even life-threatening impacts can reach dimensions that are often huge with respect to the initial cause of failure.

In addition to failures, the dependency of the economy on information networks has also given rise to the emergence of criminal activities that intentionally target them. We increasingly see attacks targeting public and private critical infrastructures as well as identity thefts affecting the privacy of citizens and the operations of businesses.

The US government has made important investments on intelligence and cyber security. In Europe, the approach and funding is more fragmented (often also at national level).

In this complex context, cyber security for national infrastructures has become a top priority in the vast majority of EU Member States. Unfortunately, as will be seen in the following, the protection of these essential assets is insufficient, and more remains to be done.

2 To which ICT Systems is this paper applicable?

To fully understand the objectives of this paper, the scope of the security principles proposed has to be clearly defined, both in terms of what – the systems – and to what extent – new and existing systems.

Therefore, the key elements clarified in this section include

- What does the word "system" mean?
- What is the scope of applicability of the approach?
- What is a system?

A Critical Infrastructure (CI) represents any environment, small and large, active in isolation or in connection, regional, national or trans-national, whose operations are critical to the everyday lives of citizens, administrations or industries, and whose failures can lead to large and / or catastrophic impacts.

The ICT systems we are addressing support such environments. In some cases, the ICT systems themselves constitute a CI.

From a theoretical point of view a system is a set of interacting or interdependent entities, real or abstract, forming an integrated whole. In the ICT world, these so-called entities can be incarnated by a vast variety of components at all levels of perspective. On the small side, a hardware component used in the control system of cars, airplanes and other transport means requires a high security level to avoid any outside tampering with its programming and operation. On the larger side, the information systems increasingly linked together to manage the electricity distribution and power balancing across European countries have to, collectively, reach a security level that protects them from accidental failures and criminal activities.

To ensure that systems are well understood, examples are developed in more details below.

2.1 SCADA environments

It is now well understood that the SCADA systems currently in operations and running many segments of our Critical Infrastructures in the field of electricity, water, oil & gas and transportation suffer from many security weaknesses. Only very recently in April 2009, the US government has admitted that the nation's power grid is vulnerable to cyber attack. According to reports, it had been infiltrated by foreign spies. This situation is sometimes aggravated as these often relatively old systems have been designed to satisfy drastic safety requirements but with little care devoted to security. In addition, they often rely on huge networks spanning across wide geographical areas with equipment located in very remote locations; security upgrades, often involving hardware upgrades, are made difficult, and consistent implementation of security is a true challenge. Unfortunately, the history is still running and "improvements" are applied to these environments often without a prior comprehensive security assessment when introducing either new IP based equipment, open Operating Systems or links with the standard IT of the corporate world. On the other hand, the situation is improving through a new emerging security culture, but the levels of maturity vary with the sectors which have been exposed earlier to these threats being more advanced. It is therefore necessary to support all sectors in reaching the necessary security level.

In these often large legacy systems, the goals of the Secure-by-Design approach are to

- improve the federated security through increased interoperability and collaborative management of the infrastructures;
- identify the local vulnerabilities of the environment and recommend targeted improvements to decrease the open-doors into the overall system.

2.2 Telecommunication networks

With the emergence of an increasingly interconnected world, the telecommunication networks have reached out and spanned across the globe. In the meantime, entire countries have and are moving their administration to computerised environments, with the goal of increasing the efficiency of their operations both within their own governments and in offering services to their citizens and industries.

Recent events have shown that while this approach represents positive advances in terms of accessibility to information, at the same time the vulnerability of these regions and countries has increased tenfold when attacks, such as repeated denial-of-services and organised botnets[1], come into play. In this

---

1   Collection of compromised computers (called Zombie computers) running malicious software under a common command-and-control infrastructure.

case, the vulnerability lies in the fact that the redundancy of the underlying networks is insufficient and therefore attacks can be achieved relatively easily by targeting a small number of identified nodes. In some cases, redundancy could have been implemented, but was simply not thought about in the initial design. In other cases, the existing telecommunication networks do not even allow such a redundancy to be implemented without going to expensive back-up solutions involving satellites, for instance.

In these environments, the goals of the Secure-by-Design approach are to

- decrease the risks of criminal activities by identifying the key entry points that have to be protected;
- identify the necessary redundancies in the underlying environments and optimising the cost of implementing the minimal level that is required;
- identify the potential collaborations that can span across the borders to effectively create redundancy through international operating plans that can be put quickly into force whenever necessary.

2.3 Hardware components

Hardware components are included in every element of our environment, from cars to infrastructure management systems, from household appliances to strategic control systems. As such, these hardware components can often, either in isolation or together, constitute major vulnerabilities.

Applied to hardware (i.e. dedicated hardware module with embedded software), a "Secure-by-Design" approach means verifying (expressing, formalizing, checking or better proving) that security features are (well) implemented in the solution at the design stage. For example, topographic properties (no wire transmitting cryptographic key data at the upper level of the Integrated Component), physical properties (no correlation between processed data and power consumption), functional properties (fault resistance during cryptographic computation), algorithmic properties (in situ integrity checking at every use of critical data) are security features efficient to counter classical attack methods. "Secure-by-Design" means expressing such properties and a tool-based verification.

Even the best component is subject to attack, this is just a question of competence, resources and time. A "Secure-By-Design" subsystem using hardware crypto components will take into account the efforts necessary to break it and implement adapted counter-measures. For example, limited key life time (in term of number of use), audit subsystem (counting the number of detected errors), recovery procedures (secure key update even if the previous configuration is compromised) are efficient measures which could be expressed, specified and checked at the design level.

The approach is generic and scalable: each subsystem level (or layer) is potentially able to express the potential weaknesses of the lower subsystem levels and implement dedicated measures. This implementation has to be verified, if possible in an automatic way.

3 The cost of security

The previous examples show that ICT systems are complex, ranging from small to large. If their value in contributing to the overall security of CIs is not fully taken into account, the corresponding security breaches can have huge impacts, both at operational and economical level.

This is not a theoretical approach, as previous incidents have shown the sheer size of these impacts.

Consider the following examples. As early as 2005, 1.2 million credit card accounts of the Bank of America were hacked – with a direct impact on 900,000 Pentagon employees[2]. In July 2009, hackers accessed company confidential information of Twitter that was stored on cloud based Google Apps– putting in jeopardy the 7 million $ plan by Los Angeles to also shift to cloud computing based applications.[3] In 2009, the UK Financial Services Authorities fined bank HSBC a total amount of 3 M£ for failing to put in place adequate security measures to protect data.[4]

Beyond these security breaches that are confined to the online world, incidents also impact the physical world – and the awareness of the cost and negative reputation is increasing. For instance, water utilities and other plants have become direct targets for such incidents, with both insiders and outsiders identified as the originators of the malfunctioning. The recent article "Is your plant secure"[5] on the Water & Wastes Digest portal highlighted the following examples.

In Europe, a group of Russian hackers recently took control of a municipality and turned off all of its lights from a remote location. The hackers then extorted more than $100,000 from the municipality in exchange for turning the lights back on. In Australia, a disgruntled employee of a municipal wastewater station used his knowledge of its control system to discharge large amounts of wastewater into the nearby environment. Consequences of these cyber attacks are that plants lose extremely valuable assets such as computer networks and actual equipment, environmental damage is caused, area security is threatened and monetary damage is most certainly done.

The picture that is emerging is complex; not only can security breaches originate from both internal and external sources, but security itself encompass a series of domains whose list is in constant evolution. For instance, the Annual Security Survey[6] organised for the financial world prioritises every year the topics included within the security domain. It also rates the security operations of financial institutions across the world in terms of governance, investment, risk, use of security technologies, quality of operations and privacy. Even within the list of security technologies, the list of domains is changing with access and identity management often high on the list, closely followed by privacy[7], resilience, data protection and other such topics. Overall, all these elements strongly support the fact that security requires a comprehensive approach, and while innovation is fuelling the technology to provide more and more advanced solutions, innovation is also helping criminal organisations to become increasingly devious in their attacks.

As a consequence, the expansion of security needs is exponential, and the CI operators are learning it the hard way – by taking the necessary actions and, sometimes, being fined large amounts, when security breaches occur. Therefore, this sheds a whole new light on the need for Secure-by-Design approaches.

Indeed, with respect to the economics of CI operations, security is perceived as a "must-have" feature, but not as a key contributor to the economics of the infrastructure, whereas on the contrary the financial impact of a non-functional infrastructure or even worse, the impact of malicious operations following the theft of information, the injection of wrongful processes, etc. can expand far beyond the original cost of implementing security.

In other words,
- the evolution of connectivity has led infrastructures to rely on pervasive networks

---

2 http://www.time.com/time/nation/article/0,8599,1032140,00.html
3 http://www.cio.com/article/498237/Twitter_Breach_Revives_Security_Issues_with_Cloud_Computing
4 http://www.fsa.gov.uk/pages/Library/Communication/PR/2009/099.shtml
5 http://www.wwdmag.com/Is-Your-Plant-Secure-article9171
6 « Protecting what matters - the Sixth Annual Global Security Survey » by Deloitte Touche Tohmatsu
7 "Privacy requires security, not abstinence » – MIT Technology Review – 2009 – July-August issue

- the accessibility of the Internet with 1.5 billion connected individuals has opened many more doors to intentional and unintentional errors
- security has moved from a feature to protect operations within known frontiers to a function to be managed in the whole cyber-space.

In this context, security is not a technological issue but is a complete mindset involving all organisations and individuals. Technology supports its implementation but does not guide its proper operation.

The real challenge facing operators is therefore to reach the best compromise in terms of cost / functionality at the level of security *implementations* and *processes*, taking advantage of the cyber-space that provides them on the one hand with accrued access to information, faster intervention capabilities and on the other with a giant leap in vulnerability.

Our goal in proposing the Secure-by-Design strategy that clearly identifies processes ranging from creation, implementation, operation and decommissioning supported by the most appropriate tools is to support the CI operators in facing the challenge.

4 Current Gaps and Needs

To face current challenges to ICT security, stakeholders can already benefit from technological elements such as existing standards, tools and guidelines to follow. The introduction to this section describes a subset of these elements.

These elements have different purposes and can prove indispensable in various fields of application (e.g. software coding, hardware development, Information System architecture design) or at various stages of system life cycle (design, development, operations and maintenance).

Among processes for secure software development, Microsoft's Security Development Life cycle (SDL), OWASP's[8] Comprehensive, Lightweight Application Security Process (CLASP[9]) and Mc-Graw's Touchpoints[10], are recognized as the major players in the field.

Regarding the security of the data itself, the set of standards and guidelines known as Federal Information Processing Standards (FIPS[11]) have been designed and are compulsory when compelling US Federal Government requirements such as security and interoperability are not met by existing standards.

Concerning methodologies for assurance, the Common Criteria[12] provides assurance that the process of specification, implementation and evaluation of a product has been conducted in a rigorous and standard manner. But while Common Criteria can deliver fully valid results, its applicability is realistically limited to dedicated sub-systems. The use of Common Criteria applied to the security architecture of a system of systems would be arduous. Similarly, the Systems Security Engineering Capability Maturity Model[13] (SSE-CMM) covers all phases of the development cycle and thus can be used to evaluate and improve an existing process.

---

8 OWASP – Open Web Application Security Project at http://www.owasp.org/index.php/Main_Page
9 CLASP – (Comprehensive, Lightweight Application Security Process) – http://www.owasp.org/index.php/Category:OWASP_CLASP_Project
10 "Software Security: Building Security in " – Gary McGraw – Publisher: Addison-Wesley, 2006 – ISBN – 0321356705, 9780321356703.
11 FIPS – Federal Information Processing Standards – http://www.itl.nist.gov/fipspubs/index.htm
12 Common Criteria methodology at http://www.commoncriteriaportal.org/
13 Systems Security Engineering – Capability Maturity Model – http://www.sse-cmm.org/index.html

These elements already demonstrate that there is no lack of technical standards, but none of them provides a complete answer to all the security issues. Indeed, as we highlighted in the previous sections, security cannot be addressed simply from the technical view point and in isolation.

On the contrary, the implementation of security design is fundamentally a governance issue, and the fact that ICT security is not sufficiently guaranteed can be attributed to the following gaps and unaddressed needs.

4.1 Operational issues

4.1.1 Lack of sufficient awareness and expertise on the importance of ICT security on part of most CI operators

To begin with, critical infrastructure (CI) operators do not necessarily have all the expertise or even sufficient awareness of security issues regarding the systems they procure or develop. Often, the business functionality remains the primary driver, while security is considered a possible constraint at best, or even managed as an afterthought. This state of affairs results in late implementation, patched-up solutions and leaves little room to address the needs at the required level. Moreover, at this late stage of implementation, the available options are usually much more expensive, a fact that often prohibits their correct implementation.

It is important to note that this factor varies significantly from one CI sector to another and from one class of system to another since the maturity level is not the same. For example, corporate information systems or transactional systems have been exposed to security considerations much earlier than SCADA environments.

4.1.2 No incentives for the implementation of ICT security measures

Today's reality is harsh: while security is always high on the wish list of Critical Infrastructure Operators, it is rarely designed into the systems from the beginning. Although the "Secure-by-Design" approach is not a new concept, it is still not applied yet. Indeed, if security is not expressed as a requirement by a customer, it is unlikely that suppliers will include it in their proposed solution since the extra cost will make them uncompetitive by comparison to a less secure option. Unfortunately, less security aware customers tend to work with less security orientated providers, thus creating "niches" of particularly exposed infrastructures.

In this approach, security is rarely perceived as an opportunity; however, when analysing the direct financial impact of security breaches, it is clear that the return on investment of security implementation and operations can be huge. In addition to the financial impact, the negative image generated by the often well-publicised malfunctions can be even more destructive to the operator than the direct financial cost.

Another factor is that security design capabilities require stakeholders both to have developed the associated internal project management processes, and to have recruited people with appropriate skills. These two factors make it challenging for most providers to be in a position to propose a robust security service as part of their general offer.

Security is considered as a constraint rather than as a compulsory feature, and no incentive is provided to CI operators and to IT suppliers to ensure that it is built-in from the start and managed during operations.

4.1.3 Lack of a common approach

Although this situation is certainly not the reality for all CI operators, the fact that Critical Infrastructures are largely interdependent propagates the issue of security and necessitates that the whole CI community stakeholders apply the appropriate security level to their infrastructure in order to ensure a collective level of resilience.

Indeed, failure of one particular CI has an impact not only on its own sector, but also on other sectors.

In addition to cross-sector interdependencies, the issue of propagation is further enhanced by the fact that the CI community nowadays expands far beyond national borders. This was recognized by The Future Group Report[14] which highlighted that "An EU Secure Management Information policy would help promoting a coordinated development of information technology, providing a coherent approach to the secure exchange of information, for a professional, business-oriented and cost-effective use of information technology and information networks."

The recent EC Communication, proposing the "Stockholm Programme[15]" for the JLS security policy for the next 5 years, underlines that security in the EU depends on effective mechanisms for exchanging information between national authorities and other European players. "To achieve this, the EU must develop a European information model based on a more powerful strategic analysis capacity and better gathering and processing of operational information. This model must take account of existing systems, including those in the customs field, and overcome the challenges of exchanging information with non-member countries."

4.2 Administrative, Regulatory, Governance and Procedural issues

4.2.1 Lack of a common EU Directives and regulations

The concept of Operator Security Plans (OSPs) as defined today by the European Critical Infrastructure Directive[16] and initially applied for Energy and Transport infrastructures (though at national level, without EU guidelines across countries and applications) is an example of practical progress already made towards collective resilience building based on an innovative approach that considers critical asset identification, risk assessment, the implementation of a risk mitigation strategy.

However, EU Member States are called to define a comprehensive concerted action, and interoperability has to form an integral part of federated security. For instance, an EU Secure Management Information policy, for example through OSPs for the ICT sector is in the making but will not be defined by the EU before 2012[17].

Also, the EC communication on Critical Information Infrastructure Protection (CIIP)[18], a welcome step forward in promoting the involvement of the private sector in supporting the definition of the CII Di-

---

14 Future Group, "Freedom, Security, Privacy – European Home Affairs in an open world", June 2008. Future Group publications can be viewed at http://www.statewatch.org/future-group.htm

15 COM (2009) 262 final "An area of freedom, security and justice serving the citizen".

16 COUNCIL DIRECTIVE 2008/114/EC of 8 December 2008 – "On the identification and designation of European critical infrastructures and the assessment of the need to improve their protection.

17 SEC(2009) 766 – JUSTICE, FREEDOM AND SECURITY IN EUROPE SINCE 2005: AN EVALUATION OF THE HAGUE PROGRAMME AND ACTION PLAN – An extended report on the evaluation of the Hague Programme.

18 COM(2009) 149 – on Critical Information Infrastructure Protection – "Protecting Europe from large scale cyber-attacks and disruptions: enhancing preparedness, security and resilience".

rective and proposing measures for the implementation of the foreseen activities, should consider all infrastructures connected via ICTs, Telecom, Scada, ATM (Air Traffic Management) etc. Otherwise all the different approaches selected for the implementation of ICT security measures persist, affecting the overall security and resilience of Europe's infrastructure.

Actually, the present situation is unsustainable both from a security point of view and from a macroeconomic perspective, as it contradicts the EU's vision of a common market, which requires that operators implement security to similar requirement levels across countries, responding to the needs of an open, global market without frontiers or other limitations. A truly common market will avoid contingencies that may lead to undesirable effects such as the distortion of market competition arising from uneven costs of security risk mitigation requirements.

Looking at traditional EU suppliers for ICT security solutions and services, we still see a low coordination and weak impact at EU / international level (though could be important at national level to protect sensitive MS networks). Europe has still to create a strong and competitive ICT security industry to propose its solutions and services across the world.

4.3 Technical and Services issues

Today, technical solutions exist that adequately address the security needs. However, while this third category is therefore less important than the two previous ones, we highlight the need to ensure a system approach and a coordinated strategy with a focus on the specific context of cyber-security.

4.3.1 Lack of a system approach to the implementation of security

Even when security is taken into account, it is often implemented as a security manager or, worse, through an assorted set of dedicated or add-on modules: a firewall for network security, a VPN for secure communications, a crypto circuit or boards for cryptography implementation, etc.

Such implementations often consider that these specialised subsystems are perfect, resistant and cannot be compromised. Sometimes, additional organisational measures are implemented, such as password policies, revocation, etc. However, experience has shown that there is no perfect system.

Even the most sophisticated hardware systems (smartcards or crypto modules) can be attacked and compromised.

Security issues, including attack possibilities and attack models, have to be taken into account in the early design phase of a system and be considered at its core. Redundant security is also a key element for complex and critical systems, as well as for ensuring the security of the security elements themselves. This subsystem approach does not take into account the system view, nor does it support the changes that are inherent to the dynamicity of real systems.

The implementation of security requires a global view from both the process and technology aspects, supporting a clearly defined governance model.

5 Proposals for Change: EOS recommendations

The ICT domain is critical in two different dimensions: as the underlying support to other critical infrastructures such as in the energy, transport, finance and other domains, as well as when the ICT systems themselves are considered critical. Both dimensions are fundamental in targeting the future.

If we want to face the growing and global threats to infrastructures leveraging on ICT (Information and Communication Technologies), not only do ICT security capabilities of national public and private users/operators need to be increased, but also the competitiveness and competence of the European ICT security providers have to be strongly supported.

Based on the previous analysis, we focus our recommendations to address the need of a common EU approach to enhance the security of ICT systems and ICT CIs, taking into account the cross-sectoral and cross-borders realities while at the same time moving from an approach of security as a constraint to security as an opportunity and a positive discriminator.

Such an approach would prove beneficial for the interoperability of security solutions and enhance the consistency of the critical infrastructure landscape.

Moreover, making an early move towards common requirements could give EU industries a competitive edge on the international market as being a step ahead on the security implementation.

Finally, implementing security in an integrated manner from the earlier stages of a project is more cost effective than late solutions.

Indeed, since the identification of risks is more accurate, it allows for more effective security budget allocation (i.e. implementation of the right security level at the right place), it aligns with security governance models and avoids expensive solutions which often provide limited efficiency in certain contexts.

In order to realise these benefits, thus remedying the above-mentioned gaps and needs, EOS proposes the following recommendations.

5.1 Recommendation 1 – Build a comprehensive public-private dialogue with all relevant stakeholders (telecom, energy, transport, finance etc.) on the issues at stake

An increased dialogue and cooperation between MS and EU Institutions as well as the private sector (operators and suppliers) could identify common issues across EU countries for cyber security and the protection of ICT networks, defining ways and means for the development of common tools and solutions (including: technical standards / procedures, sharing of best practices etc) to allow, when requested, a secure exchange of data or reinforced ICT network protection. This dialogue should also allow the EC to elaborate a common legislative framework to secure Europe's information systems.

The establishment of a Public-Private Dialogue to address the security and resilience of Information and Communication Networks and Critical Infrastructures based on ICT solutions (i.e. all infrastructure networks leveraging on ICTs: transport, energy, finance, supply chain, but also the Internet, Administrations, etc.) has been proposed in the recent EC communication on Critical Information Infrastructure Protection (CIIP) of March 2009 with the creation of EP3S (European Public Private Partnership on Security).

Such a dialogue on CIIP should lead to concrete actions for the development of common capabilities and processes, and facilitate the adoption of common solutions and/or procedures across different countries and their critical infrastructures for CIIP as an extension of the present EPCIP. It should be based on the following main principles: Representativeness, Participation and Trust.

5.2 Recommendation 2 – Define an EU legislative framework for secure European information systems on the basis of a "Secure-by-Design" system approach

The EC needs to elaborate a common legislative framework for secure European information systems that will:

- clearly target the overall cyber-security policies emerging at European and Member States levels;
- legally require security to form an integral part of all ICT systems from the initial design phases, and throughout all other stages, including the capture of requirements, procurement, design, development, technical Testing, user acceptance, "go live", operations and maintenance (evolution and interconnections), and the decommissioning phase;
- ensure a large adoption of the approaches as the Secure-by-Design approach by national administrations and the entire Critical Infrastructures community as the suitable framework for design and implementation of resilient systems for critical infrastructures, by incorporating this approach into the legislative framework, and by encompassing the complete cycle of operations from detection to reaction, recovery and resilience. A Secure-by-design approach is not in itself a technology approach, nor is it novel – but what is new is the policy support towards its adoption as a process oriented strategy that directly addresses the change in mindset required to fully implement security throughout system implementation and operations. Only in the latter stage does it become specific to its target domain of application.
- be consistently applied all over the EU, and possibly be extended beyond through internationally legally binding agreements;
- include a liability model to protect those operators that invest in security measures in the case of a natural disaster of or a man-made attack, such as an act of terrorism. The actual definition of this liability model and the estimate of the amount of the investment in security that is necessary should preferably result from the above-mentioned public-private dialogue.

Such a legislative framework could form the basis of and feed into the directive on critical information infrastructure protection which the directive (2008/114/EC) foresees to be elaborated by 2012.

6 Foundations for a "Secure-by-Design" framework

6.1 Objectives

A Secure-by-design approach should be designed in a way that:

- security requirements are captured from the earliest stages through for example the identification of use cases/ misuse cases, attack models, etc.;
- risk assessments are implemented in a continuous, iterative approach at each stage of a system lifecycle;

- the focus is not only given to isolated vulnerabilities but also considers cascading effects and the incorporation of interdependencies considerations by means of interoperability requirements;
- tools are identified to support the approach (e.g. list of attacks, threats, secure coding practices, existing standards);
- provisions are made to deal with conflicting requirements (e.g. business functionality vs. security requirement);
- autonomous, adaptive security is facilitated;
- the security level of the secure functionalities is continuously assessed, ensuring through an iterative approach that the security level is not assumed to be adequate but extensively monitored.

6.2 Synchronising and integrating security activities in the lifecycle of ICT systems

As mentioned earlier, our approach is not only to build resilience into Critical Infrastructures as a first line of defence, but also to support, monitor and address security throughout the entire operation of these infrastructures.

To ensure this comprehensive approach to security, security needs to be introduced at the earliest design & development stages of systems and to be maintained through the entire operational life including time of decommission. The complexity stems also from the inherently dynamic aspects introduced by

- the continuous appearance of new vulnerabilities and threats created by new attack strategies;
- the changes in the existing critical infrastructures implemented by the operators to address evolutions in usage and requirements, such as increasing number of users, changing partnerships etc;
- the additional requirements emerging from the interconnections of Critical Infrastructures;
- the technological evolution through which new innovations and regulations impact the security components and lead to their replacement or additions.

As a consequence, security needs to be addressed at all stages, including

- capture of requirements,
- procurement,
- design,
- development,
- technical Testing,
- user acceptance,
- go live,
- operations and maintenance, including evolution and interconnections,
- decommission.

At each of these steps, the associated security activities, responsibilities, inputs, outputs, supporting tools and methods need to be identified and typical security activities (like Security Risk Assessment, Security Objectives identification, Security specifications, Security Mechanisms development, penetration testing) need to be clearly synchronised with the system lifecycle. This encompasses:

- who is responsible to conduct the activity e.g. responsibility of the business, the security development team, a third party security assessor, etc?

- how should the activity be implemented, i.e. what specific available standards or tools should be applied?
- what should be covered by the activity?

The purpose is not to reinvent security standards but to make sure that all activities and responsibilities are identified, properly allocated and that their scope is clearly defined.

6.3 Expressing & communicating security

Standards of security evaluations (Common Criteria, FIPS, etc) are based on the idea of a clear description of the security of systems in terms of assets, security policies, security objectives, etc. However, attack strategies and weaknesses equally need to be understood and described and are currently often poorly expressed and therefore overlooked and underestimated. A really secure system needs to integrate various security components, ensuring that they are used in a best fit configuration, but also that the inherent and known security weaknesses of one component are compensated at the system level. In addition, the composition process of security components can introduce new weaknesses that need to be understood, managed and avoided.

The "Secure-by-Design" framework intends to address this lack and enhance the global security level of Critical Infrastructures by adding the identification and subsequent modelling of attack strategies, vulnerabilities and other weaknesses. While the unpredictable will always exist, our goal is to use governance and technology to reduce it as much as possible.

6.4 Contributing to the development of "Secure-by-Design" framework: mapping of security activities and operator survey

As described in section 6.2, security activities and responsibilities need to be clearly identified. In this context, EOS is currently building a map of these security activities against Critical Infrastructures and ICT systems lifecycle.

The essence of this work can be depicted on the following table which is actually being developed by EOS as part of the agenda of our ICT security working group.

In parallel to this activity, EOS is currently engaging with CI operators in order to discuss ICT security and the associated challenges (operational, technical, regulatory, etc.) and how a "Secure-by-Design" framework could provide appropriate answers to some of them.

The result of this work will then be published in a green paper that will be made public to contribute to the debate at European level.

Table 1: Building the high level foundations of a "Secure-by-Design" framework

System Life Cycle	Security activity	Responsibilities	Input	Output	Supporting tools and methods
Requirements Gatherings And Analysis	Security requirements analysis and specification – At the requirements gathering and analysis phase, security requirements should be considered at the earliest stage of the definition of business requirements for the information system. Depending on the value of the information assets involved, the nature of the IT system and its business purpose, an appropriate risk assessment process will define the security controls to be considered. System requirements for information security and processes for implementing security should beintegrated in the early stages of information system projects. Controls introduced at the design stage are significantly cheaper to implement and maintain than those included during or afterimplementation.				
Procurement	Introduction of clear, measurable, adapted security requirements				
	Raising security as a formal factor in the solution selection process				
Design (activities need to be iterated several times)	Technical risk analysis implementation				
	Validation of risk analysis				
	Choice of security controls				
Development	Development of security functions				
	Code security review				
Technical Testing	Security Assessment				
	Penetration testing				
User Acceptance	Security accreditation, approval of residual risks				
Go live	Initialisation of security functions (e.g. activation of crypto keys, secure migration of data, etc.)				
	Secure migration from test to operational environment				
Operations and Maintenance	Development and operation of an ISMS (Information Security Management System) covering: • Incident management, • Regular review s of Risks • Change management, • Business continuity, • Access control management, • Etc…				
Decommissioning	Secure disposal of sensitive materials				

7 Conclusion and benefits

The primary benefit of the "Secure-by-Design" framework proposed by EOS is to increase the security of Critical Infrastructures and therefore strengthen the protection of EU citizens against a wide variety of threats including terrorism or organised crime targeting cyber infrastructures. This approach clearly targets the overall cyber-security policies emerging at European and Member States levels.

The secondary benefit is to ensure that the underlying ICT networks of information and data contribute to enhancing and maintaining high security levels rather than bringing an additional weakness and creating back doors for criminal attacks. This is a preliminary step to contribute to the extension of the European Critical Infrastructures directive to the ICT domain, following its current applicability to energy and transport.

Moving to the next level of details, these benefits have a wide impact across many different aspects ranging from cost efficiency to competitiveness, including

- Adopting such an approach on a European basis will prove beneficial for the interoperability of security solutions and enhance consistency across a critical infrastructure landscape which does not stop at Member States' borders;
- Getting an early move towards a standard could give EU industries a competitive edge on the international market as being a step ahead on the security implementation;
- Implementing security in an integrated manner from the earlier stages of a project is more cost effective than late solutions. Since the identification of risks is more accurate, it allows for more effective security budget allocation (i.e. implementation of the right security level at the right place) and avoids expensive solutions which could prove to actually provide limited efficiency in given contexts;
- It allows for proactive security versus a reactive approach. Considering that security is a perpetual race between vulnerabilities discovery and countermeasure implementation, this constitutes a very valuable advantage;
- Integrating security as a core capability of the ICT systems also contributes to develop the awareness of the risks an organisation faces by identifying clearly the managed risks, and as importantly the residual risks. This awareness creates an associated security culture that although intangible in itself, is pervasive and a key asset for the resilience of Critical Infrastructures;
- Addressing security as a core feature of any system will also contribute to decreasing the huge economic impact of non-functional systems due to security breaches or accidents. Putting the cost of security in the perspective of the economic impact of security breaches.

For this approach to be effective and possible, Europe has a major role to act as a coordinator and enabler of the fundamental changes required in the governance of security in ICT. This role has to be undertaken in a way that:

- all the relevant stakeholders are engaged in a wide public-private dialogue in order to exchange on the issues at stakes and to prepare the objectives and approach for the creation of an EU Framework for security.
- an EU legislative framework is adopted for the implementation of secure European information systems on the basis of a "Secure-by-Design" system approach

ROI, Pitfalls and Best Practices with an Enterprise Smart Card Deployment

Philip Hoyer

Senior Architect – Office of CTO
ActivIdentity (UK)
117 Waterloo Road, London SE1 8UL
phoyer@actividentity.com

Abstract

This paper will describe the highlights of the ActivIdentity sponsored Datamonitor study into Return On Investment (ROI) when implementing smart cards in the enterprise in the following areas: physical and logical access convergence, remote access when replacing OTP tokens and Enterprise Single Sign-On. It also provides additional information about the pitfalls to avoid when implementing smart cards and describes best practices for deployment.

1 Introduction

This paper will first detail the ROI that can be achieved by fully embracing and deploying smart cards in a typical SMB enterprise of 2000 users. It will then give the reader a list of pitfalls commonly experienced and better avoided during deployment and hence gives advice on best practice on how to successfully turn the ROI suggestions to reality. It is mainly based on the study 'A New Look at the ROI for Enterprise Smart Cards', which was published by Datamonitor in January 2008. The study established that organizations with approximately 2000 users can save up to one million US dollars per year by deploying a fully converged smart card system.

It is highly recommended that interested readers wanting to deepen their understanding of the findings should read the referenced study itself. [Dmon08]

1.1 Market trends revealed – physical logical convergence

One of the main trends in the industry that is relevant to the ROI calculation of smart card deployments is the ongoing convergence between physical and logical access. Whereas in 2003 71% of people thought that physical and logical security were separate functions, that number had shrunk to 46% in 2007 [GSIS07]. Gartner highlighted in 2007, that the number of inquiries related to convergence of physical security and logical (IT security) has increased during the past 18 months and that the trend was continuing showing a year-by-year increase of over 17,2% [GAR07]. The findings from Datamonitor [Dmon08], confirmed this trend, since the majority of respondents to the study believe that enterprises in their industry are moving towards a single identity badge for both physical and logical access

Smart cards are currently the preferred form factor to consolidate credentials since they can contain either a single dual interface chip (contact interface for logical access) and contact-less (for physical access) allowing multiple credentials and applications to be hosted concurrently (for example the PKI

N. Pohlmann, H. Reimer, W. Schneider (Editors): Securing Electronic Business Processes, Vieweg (2009), 63-71

certificate for Microsoft Windows logon and the credential for physical access). Gartner confirmed this with a study of using 'One Card for Access Control' [GAR08], which recommended that enterprises should consider integrating cards to improve security, as well as long-term costs, using one card to promote the convergence of physical and IT security.

1.2 Current Ecosystem for ROI – the Password Problem

Enterprises are generally operating different password systems for applications and databases, networks and workstations, representing an inefficient means of employee identification.

The trend for multiple applications each with their own passwords is continuing despite some applications being able to potentially accept the Kerberos ticket generated by the original workstation login. The plethora of access credentials is additionally acerbated by the current trend to start using Software-as-a-Service (SAAS) hosted in the cloud.

All these passwords present a big problem as users either start using the same password for all systems, hence significantly lowering the security and risk of compromise, or – if following the policies of separate user passwords – forget them. Often users also share or borrow passwords from colleagues creating a governance nightmare.

The study revealed that 62% of enterprises have experienced problems relating to passwords being shared, borrowed or stolen from within their organizations and only 21% of enterprises are confident that passwords will provide sufficient user authentication over the next five years. One the other hand approximately 40 man hours per week could be saved by enterprises if identification credentials are replaced by a smart card and Enterprise Single Sign-On solution [Dmon08].

1.3 Current context findings

Let us look closer at what the study revealed in terms of what identifications systems are used today (e.g. smart badge, OTP tokens, PKI, etc) and how many hours are required to administer them

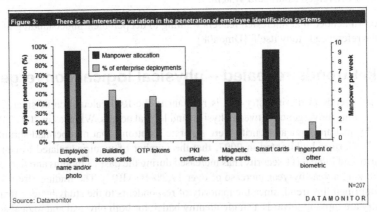

Fig. 1:

As expected there is a wide variety of systems deployed by today's enterprises. Of specific interest is the amount of manpower that is required to operate all the different systems. This is one of the main reasons why one can leverage credential consolidation to save cost:

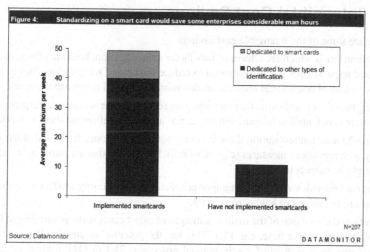

Fig. 2:

2 Return of Investment (ROI)

When looking at ROI it is important to identify the number of hard (tangible) and soft (intangible) cost savings that can stem from the deployment of a secure access smart card solution

2.1 Hard (Tangible) Cost Savings

The following are some of the tangible cost savings:

- When deploying smart cards there is almost always, as a direct consequence, a reduction in password-related help desk queries, stemming from reduction of the password problem of too many and too hard to remember.
- When moving to smart cards and embracing the use of two-factor authentication (something that you have: the card and something that you know: the card PIN), an enterprise can demonstrate higher security and hence have a potential reduction in cyber security insurance premiums.
- By using smart card management systems enterprises can manage the cards whilst in the field and hence can obtain a reduction in ongoing operational costs. One example would be the re-newal of the logical access or email signing certificate whilst in the field, reducing the cost of re-issuing the card and lost employee time to obtain a new card.
- When coupled with the use of Enterprise Single Sign-On technology, substantial time savings can be made for the employee related to the speeding up of authentication processes through simple sign-on.
- Smart cards are potentially less expensive than other two-factor solutions such as some One Time Password (OTP) tokens. This is especially true when considering physical and logical convergence where the combined smart card is cheaper than a proximity card and separate smart card for logical access (not even considering the cost of fulfilling one card instead of two).

2.2 Soft (Intangible) Cost Savings

The following are some of the intangible cost savings

- Using smart cards which are a form of two-factor authentication, because of heightened security compared to passwords has the potential to reduce the cost of security breaches in terms of loss of data, or loss of operational application downtime by locked password accounts.
- By using two-factor authentication and allowing secure remote access to enterprise networks via VPNs there is potential to increase employee productivity by allowing them to work from home.
- By using 2 factor authentication there is strong potential to reduce fraud and at the same time to comply with regulatory measures (e.g. PCI-DSS). Enterprises that are found in breach of compliance might be subject to fines.
- A smart card provides a accredited tamper-proof storage for security credentials reducing the risk of exposure to Trojans or keyboard sniffers.
- As mentioned above one of the main advantages of smart cards is the possibility to host multiple credentials at the same time, e.g. PKI. This has the potential to enable electronic signature in business processes instead of costly manual processes. PKI or OTP authentication would increase the confidence of outsourcing business processes (for example company confidential data hosted by in-cloud services).
- The use of advanced security mechanism such as smart cards will enhance the perception of the Enterprise among customers and partners, which in the current economic and trust climate might only transact with businesses of proven security integrity.

2.3 ROI Calculation

The ROI calculation considers the following three core areas where smart cards are being deployed in the enterprise:

1. Converged logical and physical access – Smart cards used for identification in the enterprise, both in terms of computer and network authentication as well as replacements for physical access and ID badges
2. Remote access – Smart cards used as a replacement for one-time password tokens
3. Enterprise Single Sign-On with smart card authentication – Smart cards used for strong authentication to secure a single sign-on session

2.3.1 ROI Analysed scenario

The Datamonitor ROI study is based on an assessment of an organization with 2000 employees, which is considering the deployment of smart cards instead of using OTP tokens. The organization recognizes that its users are overburdened with passwords and that this creates a general level of risk. Thus, the long-term strategy is to use strong authentication to secure access, and eliminate passwords through either strong authentication or Enterprise Single Sign-On.

2.4 ROI Results – Converged Logical and Physical Access

Based on the following premise and findings of the study:

- One smart card requires an average of 9.5 hours of manpower allocation per week, matching exactly the time spent on generic employee badges with name/photo.

- Enterprises can manage a smart card deployment using roughly the same manpower as an employee badge, and with a card management system it can manage all of the other credentials along with it.
- Enterprises operating a non converged smart card, dedicate an average of 39.8 man hours to other types of employee identification.

Converging these credentials results in the following net savings:

- 39.8 hours x 52 weeks = 2069.6 moan-hours/year
- Administration Savings over three years (assuming $75 / hour for IT staff) = (2069.6 man-hours / year) * three years * $75 / hour = $465,660 savings / three years

2.4.1 Physical Access Savings

The following figures, representing the savings in relation to physical access time savings, are based on findings in the Datamonitor study [Dmon04], which still hold true today.

Net savings:

- Time savings through quicker access to buildings and facilities = $347,569
- Reduction in staff costs through automation of physical access $125,000
- Total physical access savings over three years = $472,569 * 3 = $1,417,707

2.4.2 Logical Access Savings

The costs for logical access almost disappear when using smart cards because users are instantly logged on after typing a pin, and Enterprise Single Sign-On eliminates further password prompts. The log-off procedure works instantly because people need to carry their card with them due to company policy: smart card removal locks the workstation, and the user won't be able to use doors if they fail to carry it, in the ROI, productivity savings for logical access are excluded.

2.4.3 Remote Access Savings – Tokens versus Smart Card

This cost analysis follows the scenario outlined in Section 2.3.1 and is based on a cost of acquisition of 200 units.

Table 1: Comparison of Token vs smart card cost.

Token	Smart card
• Majority of token types expire over a fixed period of time, and require a repurchase. • MSRP for these tokens starts at $56/token for a three year period (basic model), meaning that two tokens must be purchased over three years • ($56 / three year token) x (2 token / user) x (2,000 users) = $224,000	• has no expiry date nor a battery • over three years users can continue to use the same card. • requires a reader on a computer or a standalone hand held reader • smart card costs an average of around $19/card, with readers costing $20/reader on average • ($19 / smart card) x (1 smart card / user) x (2,000 users) = $38,000 • ($20 / smart card reader) x (1 smart card reader / user) x (2,000 users) = $40,000
Total cost = $224,000	Total cost = $78,000

Savings over three years = $224,000 – $78,000 = $146,000

2.4.4 ROI Enterprise Single Sign-On

The number of passwords entered by employees per day is growing all the time, especially considering the rise of outsourced software as a service in the cloud. The Datamonitor study [Dmon08] indicates that 17.3 passwords may be entered per day on average by each employee in various areas of enterprise IT.

With 264 work days per year, the average employee is entering:

- = 17.3 passwords * 264 work days = 4,567 passwords annually
- A 2,000 employee organization is experiencing 9,134,000 password attempts annually

If a person forgets a password 0.25% of the time (one out of every 400 attempts), and requires a help desk call, this translates into 22,835 help desk calls annually

Considering an average help desk call costing $20-$50 per call, this translates into a cost of $456,700, using the conservative $20 cost per call

Over three years, the cost is therefore: =3 * $456,700 = $1,370,100

The cost of password resets can be virtually eliminated with a smart-card enabled Enterprise Single Sign-On solution for PC / workstation authentication

As authentication is consistent, and the PIN and card combination is the same and does not change every 30 days, users are unlikely to require further password services

2.4.5 ROI Calculation: Costs

Per Seat Cost

License costs estimate of $164 based on industry averages

- Card Management System $50
- Enterprise Single Sign-On $35
- Smart Card Reader $49
- Client Software $30

Total $164

Deployment Costs

Smart cards typically cost more to deploy than tokens primarily because a token is a standalone device, whereas a smart card management infrastructure integrates with directories, PKI, identity management, and desktop authentication. Conversations with a professional services team have established that the total cost of in-house staff and professional services for a deployment in a 2,000 user organization is typically around $120,000.

In order to build a conservative ROI estimate, a figure of $200,000 was used

Hence total cost of solution is 2,000*$164 + $200,000 = $528,000

2.4.6 Total Savings and ROI

Table 2: Total savings.

Converged logical and physical access	$465,660
Physical access	$1,417,707
Remote access savings	$146,000
Single Sign-On (help desk) savings	$1,370,100
Total	$3,399,467 over 3 years or $1,133,155 per year

Table 3: ROI calculation over 3 years.

	Year 1	Year 2	Year 3	Total
Cost	$528,000			$528,000
Savings	$1,133,155	$1,133,155	$1,133,155	$3,399,467

Over a three year period, a 2,000 user organization can experience an ROI of 644%

Assuming $1,133,155 savings each year with costs of $528,000, the study estimates that payback will be achieved in 5.6 months

3 Turning the Theory into Practice

After demonstrating the numbers it is time to analyse how a smart card deployment can turn into reality. The following two sections will give the reader an insight into the experience in what to avoid (pitfalls) and best practice when deploying smart cards in the enterprise.

3.1 Pitfalls when implementing a smart card strategy

The following is a list of pitfalls that are common in projects relating to smart cards and can invariably lead to a disastrous and unsuccessful outcome of the project.

Not having a business case to start with – The business must understand the value and there must be a business case for smart cards to start with. Sadly IT lead projects without buy-in form the business tend to fail.

Not educating the user why and what is happening – The end user is the one that is abusing the passwords to begin with and is your client. Unless the end user knows why smart cards are being deployed and what their benefit is they will hamper the delivery of the project.

Going for big bang approach – budgets for big bang approach are normally held by different people and departments on different cycles, making the delivery of cross departmental and cross budget line projects longer and prone to failure. As a result your project becomes an enterprise transformation program.

Not involving infrastructure team early enough – Long data-centre allocation planning and hardware procurement cycles are usually delaying project.

Choosing the wrong smart card technology – Choosing smart card technology too early based only on physical access requirements without taking into consideration logical access requirements. Additionally smart card technology is still evolving fast and is not always supported by all components in the solution

Misconception of not needing client middleware – Microsoft Mini-Driver out of the box functionality is very basic. One example is no PIN caching between CAPI and PKCS#11 frustrating the users that have to enter PINs continuously.

Not involving enough senior stakeholders – It cannot be stressed more that a smart card deployment that touches all parts of the organization, needs the buy in of as many senior stakeholders as you can get

Technical resources making business requirements decisions – It often can happen that technical resources make business decisions or assumptions that business processes cannot be changed with the introduction of smart card technology. It is recommended to always get signoff of business requirements from the business line owners.

3.2 Best Practices for a Successful Smart Card Deployment

The following is a list of advice based on years of experience deploying smart cards in Enterprises forma few hundred employees to Fortune 500 companies with over 100.000 employees:

Don't be technology centric – Deploy the cards based on your requirements and processes, don't base your requirements around what a specific card from a specific vendor is capable of. Smart card technologies are always short lived and go through the normal hype and discard cycle. It is important to understand the pros and cons of each function a smart card can enable and adopt those that are relevant to your Enterprise.

Smart card is the tip of the Identity Management iceberg and most challenges are organizational – Identify and refine the corporate security policy before embarking on a smartcard rollout. Clearly define roles and responsibility in relation to smartcard related processes.

Get executive support when planning physical / logical convergence – Executive support is crucial in terms of budgeting and funding and in terms of ownership, especially if current physical and logical functions are separate with separate ownership.

Keep business involved throughout the project -Make sure the business is in the loop in decision making. Make the business aware of all options and not just the ones satisfying current technical requirements.

Continually educate on the benefits of the strategy and develop user acceptance – end user adoption is never a given and should be planned and executed with care and method. Best buy-in from the end user can be achieved by single sign-on enable the most used applications first.

Fine tune end user interaction with the smartcard service(s) to provide tangible benefits to the day to day user – Provide fast access to workstation and applications, try to reduce or even eliminate the number of passwords to remember. By analysing the help desk calls in the first period of rollout fine tune the service that they can almost be reduced to zero.

Involve the infrastructure team early – The infrastructure team needs to be involved as early as possible with medium to large organisation the lead times for infrastructure and data centre space are the single most frequent cause for delays to projects. This is compounded by the fact that organisations are moving to outsourced IT, which might require additional legal and contract work to accommodate the new infrastructure required by the smart card deployment.

Learn from other people's mistakes and engage experts that have done successful roll-outs before – Speak to your peers about smart card deployments. Get experts in that have successfully delivered these projects before, (e.g. a vendor's professional services team).

4 Conclusion

As detailed above, there are some great tangible cost savings that can be achieved by implementing smart cards in an enterprise. The technology has matured to a point whereby the benefits by far outweigh the drawbacks and it appears that the time to implement smart cards is now. In the current climate, where trust in even established institutions has been seriously eroded, the intangible benefit of showing your customers and partners that your organisation takes security and accountability serious will become the cornerstone for ongoing company survival. By giving the reader additional guidance in what pitfalls to avoid and what best practices to follow, one hopes that your organisation will soon have a smart card strategy and a successful deployment with both happy end users and more secure and governance friendly converged physical and logical access.

References

[GSIS07]   CIO, CSO and PWC, In Global State of Information Security, 2007.

[GAR07]   Gartner: Let's get physical, In: www.gartner.com 2007.

[GAR08]   Gartner, Using One Card for Access Control, In: www.gartner.com, march 2008.

[Dmon08]   Datamonitor: A new look at the ROI for enterprise smart cards. In: www.datamonitor.com, 2008.

[Dmon04]   Datamonitor: The ROI case for smart cards in the Enterprise. In: www.datamonitor.com, 2004.

A General Quality Classification System for eIDs and e-Signatures

Jon Ølnes[1] · Leif Buene[2] · Anette Andresen[3] · Håvard Grindheim[4]
Jörg Apitzsch[5] · Adriano Rossi[6]

[1]Difi, P.O.Box 8115 Dep, N-0032 Oslo, Norway
jon.olnes@difi.no[1]

[2]DNV, Veritasveien 1, N-1322 Høvik, Norway
leif.buene@dnv.com

[3]BBS, N-0045 Oslo, Norway
anette.andresen@bbs.no

[4]Unibridge, P.O.Box 197 Kjelsås, N-0411 Oslo, Norway
havard.grindheim@unibridge.no

[5]Bremen Online Services GmbH, Am Fallturm 9, D-28359 Bremen, Germany
ja@bos-bremen.de

[6]CNIPA, viale Marx, 31/49, I-00137 Roma, Italy
rossi@cnipa.it

Abstract

The PEPPOL (Pan-European Public Procurement On-Line) project is a large scale pilot under the CIP programme of the EU, exploring electronic public procurement in a unified European market. Interoperability of electronic signatures across borders is identified as a major obstacle to cross-border procurement. PEPPOL suggests specifying signature acceptance criteria in the form of signature policies that must be transparent and non-discriminatory. Validation solutions must then not only assess signature correctness but also signature policy adherence. This paper addresses perhaps the most important topic of a signature policy: Quality of eIDs and e-signatures. Discrete levels are suggested for: eID quality, assurance level for this quality, and for cryptographic quality of signatures.

1 Introduction

Deliverable D1.1 [PEPPOL-D1.1] from the PEPPOL project[2] presents functional specifications for cross-border e-signatures. Although written in the context of public procurement, the specifications should be general enough to be used in many other application areas. The specifications address ar-

---

1 The work of Jon Ølnes, Anette Andresen and Håvard Grindheim on this paper was mainly carried out while they were employed at DNV (http://www.dnv.com).
2 Pan-European Public Procurement On-Line, http://www.peppol.eu Links referenced are valid by 17th July 2009.

N. Pohlmann, H. Reimer, W. Schneider (Editors): Securing Electronic Business Processes, Vieweg (2009), 72-86

eas such as trust models and architecture, validation service interfaces (profiles of the X-KISS part of XKMS v2 [XKMS] and the verifying protocol of OASIS DSS core [OASIS-DSS-Core]), signature policies, and quality classification. Quality classification, and to some extent the signature policy part, are the topics of this paper.

Technical interoperability of e-signatures is challenging. This means the ability to cryptographically process eIDs and signatures and check revocation status of eIDs from a large number of issuers (about 100 even when limiting the scope to qualified signatures in Europe). To relive the receiver of the resulting integration complexity, use of trusted validation services [Ølnes] is suggested. This approach is further refined by the EU Commission's action plan on e-signatures and eID [COMM03] into a system of federated validation services across Europe. PEPPOL is the Commission's suggested instrument for implementing this system, a task that PEPPOL has decided to accept.

The Commission's action plan [COMM03] limits scope to qualified signatures and advanced signatures using qualified eIDs. PEPPOL's view is that this scope has to be advanced in the future to be able to incorporate non-qualified solutions when such are acceptable, e.g. corporate eIDs and eIDs issued outside of Europe (the qualified concept is still mainly European).

To enable signature acceptance criteria that go beyond referral to the qualified term, PEPPOL suggests defining signature acceptance criteria as signature policies. The most important acceptance criteria are eID and e-signature quality, and in many case the formal approval status (e.g. nationally accredited) of the eID issuer. The latter can also be considered a quality aspect, and can be generalised to an assurance level for the eID quality. Thus this paper addresses three quality aspects:

- eID quality, as derived from certificate policy and possibly other information sources, referring to the QCP/QCP+ [ETSI-101-456] and NCP/NCP+/LCP [ETSI-102-042] policy requirements;
- eID assurance level and approval status (e.g. supervised issuer of qualified eID);
- cryptographic quality of signature: hash and public key algorithm and key length.

Chapter 2 provides background information on the need for signatures in public procurement. Chapter 3 describes signature policies as used by PEPPOL. Chapter 4 presents the suggested scheme for eID quality and assurance level. Chapter 5 is on cryptographic quality. Chapter 6 presents signature quality. Some additional issues are presented in 7, and the paper is concluded in 8.

2 Public Procurement and e-Signatures

2.1 Public Procurement Directives

The EU Directives on public procurement [EU02] [EU03] put electronic procurement processes on par with traditional means of communication. The directives cover only tendering (pre-award) processes. Equally important is electronic exchange of business documents according to existing contracts (post-award), e.g. orders and invoices.

Signatures play an important role in traditional procurement processes, and electronic signatures are in many cases deemed necessary for the corresponding electronic processes. Thus, electronic public procurement must rely on cross-border interoperability of signatures. This is identified by the EU Commission as a major obstacle [COMM01] and even mentioned as "the single most important blocking factor to cross-border e-procurement" [ICT-PSP].

2.2 The PEPPOL Project

PEPPOL (Pan-European Public Procurement On-Line) is a three-year (mid-2008 to mid-2011), large-scale pilot project under the EU's Competitiveness and Innovation Framework Programme (CIP). The project covers the following aspects of public procurement:

- Virtual company dossier (VCD) covers interoperable solutions for utilisation of company information that is already registered, in order to reuse this information in electronic tendering processes across Europe.
- E-catalogues for use in both tendering processes and for orders.
- E-ordering – order and order confirmation.
- E-invoicing – claims for payment for goods and services.
- E-signatures for business documents in procurement processes.
- Transport infrastructure[3] for exchange of business documents across Europe.

A VCD [PEPPOL-D2.1] is a structured collection of documents obtained from business registers and other sources (see for example [Siemens]). Documents will in the first run mainly be human readable but a gradual transition to structured information is envisaged. The VCD package can be automatically exchanged between systems, extending today's interactive, on-line solutions[4]. Results from the BRITE[5] project are utilised by PEPPOL. A VCD must be signed by its issuer and individual documents may be signed by their issuers.

While catalogue (see also [EDYN]), order, order confirmation, and invoice may also be electronic documents intended for human use, PEPPOL largely focuses on system to system processes using structured documents. Business processes and documents are standardised by the CEN BII Workshop[6]. PEPPOL is a main contributor to this work, which is based on the NES[7] profiles of UBL (Universal Business Language). According to the needs of the actors, such business documents may be signed. Specifications of business processes and documents should cover use of signatures.

PEPPOL has no overall pilot on e-tendering; only VCD and to some extent e-catalogues are covered. E-tendering today largely consists of manual processes for uploading of documents to e-sourcing services, considered to be out of scope of PEPPOL's system to system focus. However, due to the particular importance of e-signatures in the tendering phase [COMM01] [ICT-PSP], PEPPOL will run tendering pilots to demonstrate e-signature interoperability.

2.3 Present Signature Requirements for e-Procurement

End 2007, IDABC [IDABC] found 15 countries with e-procurement services (in this context covering e-tendering only) in operation, where 6 required qualified signatures, 7 required advanced signatures (sometimes with the additional requirement of a qualified eID), while two countries required only simple electronic signature implemented by authentication (log on with a mechanism of sufficient strength, upload documents, click "submit"). The services furthermore either listed one or a few eID issuers or were able to accept all domestic issuers and perhaps a few foreign issuers.

---

3 See http://www.peppolinfrastructure.com
4 As demonstrated by the European Business Register, http://www.ebr.org
5 Business Register Interoperability Throughout Europe, http://www.briteproject.net
6 http://www.cenbii.eu with specifications available at http://spec.cenbii.eu
7 Northern European Subset of UBL, http://www.nesubl.eu

Other signature requirements can be more or less explicit, such as statements about accepted signature formats, cryptographic algorithms, and use of time-stamps. In some countries, such aspects may be covered by regulation.

The aim of the signature policy work in PEPPOL is to replace this situation by one where buyers are able to select a transparent and non-discriminatory signature policy from a small set of alternatives.

3 Signature Policy

3.1 Signature Policy in PEPPOL

The concept of signature policy was introduced around the year 2000, and standards were published by ETSI in the years 2002-2003. It is fair to say that the idea of formalizing signature policies has not caught on. Standards are fairly old and not much referred to. Possible reasons, such as weaknesses in the approach, lack of market maturity etc. are not discussed here.

When developing specifications for e-signature interoperability in PEPPOL, it became clear that the concept of signature policy is exactly what is needed to describe the rules for signature acceptance. A signature policy according to ETSI must always be stated in humanly readable form (parts may be machine processable) and be assigned a unique reference in the form of an OID (Object Identifier). However, PEPPOL has taken a more pragmatic approach and does not (at least not at this stage) define complete, comprehensive signature policies. PEPPOL needs to define the policy parts that are required for the project's topics. At least some of these, like quality parameters, need to be machine processable since PEPPOL's scope is mainly automated system to system communication.

3.2 Definition and Content

A signature policy[8] defines a set of rules for the creation and validation of electronic signatures, under which a signature can be determined to be valid [ETSI-102-038]. Valid in this context means not only cryptographically and otherwise correct but also acceptable for the purpose at hand. The signature policy rules that apply to functionality are termed Signature Validation Policy [ETSI-102-038]. A signature validation policy includes:

- Rules to be followed by signer,
- Rules to be followed by verifier,
- Rules for use of CAs (Certificate Authority, i.e. eID issuer),
- Rules regarding use of TSAs (Time Stamping Authority),
- Rules on use of AAs (Attribute Authority) issuing attribute certificates (AAs are not in common use and this role is not discussed further in this paper),
- Rules on use of algorithms.

A signature validation policy essentially defines *quality and procedural requirements* for the aspects of the bullet list above. This is further described below. The receiver of a signed document is responsible for setting the signature policy and for making the policy available to interested parties, notably to senders.

---

8 Firstly defined in ETSI TS 101 733 Annex C, see also ETSI TR 102 038, ETSI TR 102 272, ETSI TR 102 045.

3.3 Protocols and Commitment Rules

In addition to the signature validation policy, a signature policy may express rules for protocols and commitment, originally introduced by [ETSI-102-045] as signature policies for "extended business model"; specifically:

- Which documents must be signed at which stages of the (business) protocol?
- What shall these signatures imply in terms of commitment, and/or what authorizations (roles) are implied by the signatures?

These parts of a signature policy (and their possible quality issues) are out of scope of this paper but are discussed in detail in [PEPPOL-D1.1] part 3.

3.4 Procedural Rules, PEPPOL Recommendations

Examples of procedural rules are requirements for certificate path processing, revocation grace period, signature format[9] to be used, and specification of information to be included in SDOs (signed data object) for both transfer and archival (such as time-stamps from local clocks or TSAs, eID information, revocation information and policy identifiers).

In the short term PEPPOL recommends flexibility with respect to signature formats used by the signer. This lowers the barrier to participation in cross-border public procurement since few requirements are placed on the signer's software. Later, the XAdES [ETSI-101-903] and CAdES [ETSI-101-733] standards should be used but PEPPOL still recommends to stick to the more basic variants (e.g. XAdES-BES) for the transfer SDOs and build more complex SDOs (e.g. for archival) under control of the verifier. Flexibility in signature formats comes at the expense of more complexity at the verifier side due to the need for handling many different formats.

The signer's certificate shall always be included in the SDO. Inclusion of the path should be optional and will ease path processing if required at the verifier side. However, the verifier should be able to build paths on his own or by use of validation services.

Use of basic SDO formats for transfer implies that revocation checking is the responsibility of the verifier. The signer is not required to supply OCSP responses in SDOs.

PEPPOL strongly discourages use of TSA time stamps at the signer's side. Introducing sending side TSA time stamps would result in an interoperability challenge with respect to mutual recognition of TSA services across Europe and validation of TSA signatures. Instead, the verifier is allowed to call a (locally) trusted TSA if required.

3.5 Quality Rules

With respect to a signature validation policy, quality is particularly relevant for the signer's and verifier's environments, quality of eIDs and the issuing CAs, and cryptographic quality. One could add quality of time-stamps and TSA services. PEPPOL recommends use of TSA time-stamps on receiving (verifier) side only, allowing the verifier to choose a well-known TSA of sufficient quality according to the verifier's requirements.

---

9 Examples are XAdES (ETSI TS 101 903), CAdES (ETSI TS 101 733), PKCS#7 (RFC2315), CMS (RFC2630), XML DSIG (RFC3275), and PDF signatures.

Thus, a signature validation policy should set objective, non-discriminatory rules for the quality of the signer's environment, the eID used, the issuing CA, and the cryptography. Additionally, the receiver must prove that his own environment is of sufficient quality. This is discussed further in 4.2 below.

4 Quality of eIDs

4.1 Previous Work on eID Quality

Quality rules are governed by two aspects: legal/regulatory requirements for specific levels or characteristics (such as qualified level), and requirements from risk management considerations. For a discussion on the latter and the resulting quality issues, see [Ølnes2]. Although [Lopez] observes that there is no unified or standardised classification scheme for PKI-based eID, quality classification is not a new topic. While quality is largely described through the certificate policy used by the CA (CPS (Certificate Practice Statement) and other documents may play a role), the aim is to define a relatively small, discrete number of levels. Examples are the five policy levels of the FBCA [FBCA] in the USA and the quality definitions used for the EBGCA pilot [EBGCA] in Europe. Industry bridge-CAs such as SAFE[10] and CertiPath[11] also impose quality requirements, usually at one level only.

ETSI defines policy requirements for the policy classes QCP/QCP+ (Qualified Certificate Policy) [ETSI-101-456] and NCP/NCP+/LCP (Normalised Certificate Policy, Lightweight Certificate Policy) [ETSI-102-042]. These are used for the classification scheme presented in this paper, as discussed below.

4.2 Objectively Verifiable Quality Aspects for Signatures

With respect to quality rules (see 3.5), the following observations can be made.

The signer's environment, and any claims made by the sender about this environment, cannot be assessed by the verifier, apart from those aspects that are covered by the CA's certificate policy. A CA may enforce use of an SSCD (Secure Signature Creation Device) for qualified signatures or other mandatory means of protection of private keys. For other aspects of the signing environment, the verifier must assume that the signer complies with the requirements of the certificate policy in force and otherwise ensures adequate security. Thus, *to the extent that assessment of the signer's environment is possible, this is indirectly covered by the CA's certificate policy.*

The verifier's environment is controlled by the verifier, who must ensure that requirements are met. If not, the verifier is in breach of his own signature validation policy. For this reason, assessment of quality of the verifier's environment is largely outside the scope of this paper.

The quality of an eID shall be precisely described by the certificate policy in force. In addition, one may need an assessment (assurance level) that the CA actually complies with the policy, and where relevant also Certificate Practice Statement (CPS) and other procedures. Quality aspects of the CA itself, such as financial standing and independence, may also be relevant (see 7.1). The assurance may be vouched for by some third party, including supervision or accreditation authorities for national approval.

---

10 eID and signature for the pharmaceutical industry, see http://www.safe-biopharma.org
11 eID and signature for the defence and aerospace sector, see http://www.certipath.com

Cryptographic quality of eIDs is controlled by the CA and covered by the certificate policy. This applies to the CA's own signatures (public key algorithm and hash) on certificates and status information (CRL, OCSP responses), and to the keys of certificate holders. Either the CA controls key generation for certificate holders, or the CA must enforce quality of keys generated under user control. However, the hash algorithm used for signing of documents is controlled by the signing software, which in general is outside of the CA's control. One may add requirements for implementation and environment, such as key generation, correct operation and adequate security, but apart from the aspects enforced by the CA through the certificate policy, reliable assessment of such properties is difficult. Assessment report or certifications by independent parties could be useful but requiring this in general for the signing software is probably a too strict requirement.

Assuming that all allowed signature formats are sufficiently secure, i.e. if a format is allowed, its quality does not need to be assessed, and leaving implementation failures out of scope, the conclusion is that the objectively verifiable quality aspects of e-signatures per se are:

- Claimed eID quality as described by certificate policy and possibly CPS and other documentation; this should also describe requirements imposed on the signer.
- Assurance level for the CA's policy adherence, i.e. that quality is as claimed.
- Cryptographic quality.

4.3 Granularity of Quality Scheme

This paper suggests using the three objectively verifiable aspects of e-signature quality as separate parameters of the classification scheme and defining some discrete levels for each of them. It is suggested that this is a necessary and sufficient granularity.

The simplest approach would be to just define one parameter for quality and aggregate all three aspects. We argue that this is not sufficient since CAs using the same policy may then get different rating based on lack of assurance for one of them, and furthermore two signatures produced using the same eID should be allowed to yield different signature quality depending on the quality of the crypto used by the signing software.

At the other extreme, [Ølnes2] shows how a quality structure may be constructed by defining discrete levels for the major components of a certificate policy according to [RFC3647]. The entire structure may be used to define fine-grained quality. We suggest that defining signature policies according to such a system will be too complex.

4.4 eID Quality Profile

Analysing existing approaches, and given PEPPOL's European starting point, a "PEPPOL profile" for eID quality is defined according to the ETSI policy levels as an extension of the quality classification scheme described in [Ølnes]. Two independent parameters are defined:

- one parameter for the certificate quality level as claimed by the CA through its Certificate Policy and CPS, and
- one parameter for the level of independent assurance that can be associated with the claimed quality level.

eID quality is represented by a pair of numbers (x, y) where x is the certificate quality level (0-6; see 4.4.1) and y is the independent assurance level (0-7; see 4.4.2).

4.4.1 Certificate Quality Parameter (Claimed Quality)

The following levels are defined:

0. **Very low or non-determined level:** Very low confidence or assessment not possible, usually because a certificate policy does not exist.

1. **Low level**: Low confidence in certificate but certificate policy exists or quality assessment is possible by other means.

2. **Medium level:** Certificates governed by a Certificate Policy in compliance with the ETSI TS 102 042 standard for LCP or a similar standard.

3. **High level:** Certificates governed by a Certificate Policy in compliance with the ETSI TS 102 042 standard for NCP or a similar standard.

4. **High level +:** Certificates governed by a Certificate Policy in compliance with the ETSI TS 102 042 standard for NCP+ or a similar standard. (Use of a SSCD is mandated in the CP.)

5. **Very high level:** Certificates governed by a Certificate Policy in compliance with the ETSI TS 101 456 standard for QCP or a similar standard.

6. **Very high level +:** Certificates governed by a Certificate Policy in compliance with the ETSI TS 101 456 standard for QCP+ or a similar standard. (Use of a SSCD is mandated in the CP. Thus, this level supports qualified signatures according to the EU Directive on electronic signatures.)

Note:
LCP = Lightweight Certificate Policy
NCP = Normalized Certificate Policy
QCP = Qualified Certificate Policy
SSCD = Secure Signature Creation Device

[ETSI-101-456] sets policy requirements to CAs issuing qualified certificates in accordance with the European e-signatures Directive [EU01]; this is the reference certificate policy QCP in the classification above. Annex I of this Directive specifies requirements for qualified certificates, and Annex II specifies requirements to CAs issuing qualified certificates. Additional requirements to use the qualified certificate with a secure signature creation device, as required by Annex III of the Directive, give the reference policy QCP+.

[ETSI-102-042] sets policy requirements to CAs issuing certificates at the same quality level as that of qualified certificates, but without the legal constraints implied by the e-signature Directive and without requiring use of an SSCD; this is the reference certificate policy NCP. Additional requirements to use the certificate with an SSCD give the reference policy NCP+.

The reference certificate policy LCP incorporates less demanding requirements as specified in [ETSI-102-042].

The assessment of certificate quality in accordance with the classification defined above can be illustrated as in Figure 1 below.

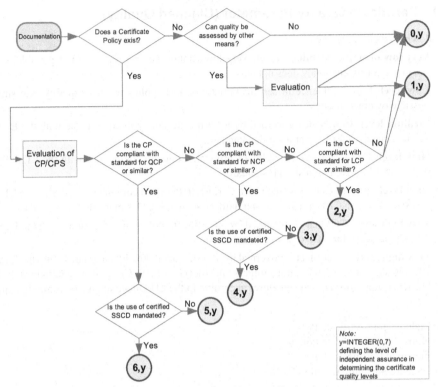

Fig. 1: Assessment of certificate quality level

One may argue that per definition NCP/NCP+ are of equal quality to QCP/QCP+ and thus should have the same quality value. However, QCP has the extra requirements for fulfilment of the e-signatures Directive [EU01]. Additionally, for legal reasons there is a need to identify qualified signatures and qualified eIDs. An eID issued according to NCP can also have a (national) supervision or accreditation status, and if it is assigned the same quality as QCP, the separation is not possible. Thus, there are good reasons for assigning a lower quality to NCP.

Since the QCP/NCP levels are almost the same, one may argue that more levels could be needed for lower quality, where only LCP is defined today. This is a valid argument that could be considered in future work, e.g. by bringing in [FBCA] levels.

4.4.2 Independent Assurance Parameter

The following levels are defined:

0. **No independent assurance:** self assessment only.

1. **Independent document review**: Statement of compliance issued by an independent, external unit based on document review only.

2. **Internal compliance audit:** Internal audit carried out periodically concludes compliance to applicable requirements.

3. **Supervision without compliance audit:** CA is supervised by a public, national or international authority according to applicable law to the CA.

4. **External compliance audit:** Audit carried out periodically by external, independent auditor concludes compliance to applicable requirements.

5. **External compliance audit and certification:** Audit carried out periodically by external, independent auditor concludes compliance to applicable requirements. CA operations are certified in accordance with a relevant standard; OR cross certification with a relevant bridge CA has been made; OR the CA has obtained membership in a PKI hierarchy as a result of appropriate assessment.

Note: Relevant standards include ETSI TS 101 456, ETSI TS 102 042, WebTrust Program for CAs, tScheme Approval Profile for CAs, ISO9001, ISO27001.

6. **Supervision with external compliance audit:** Audit carried out periodically by external, independent auditor concludes compliance to applicable requirements. CA is supervised by a public, national or international authority according to applicable law to the CA.

7. **Accreditation with external compliance audit:** Audit carried out periodically by external, independent auditor concludes compliance to applicable requirements. CA is accredited by a public, national or international authority according to applicable law to the CA.

Comment: Supervision and/or accreditation by a public, *international* authority (levels 3, 6 and 7) is not relevant at present, but will become relevant in the future if international schemes for such supervision/accreditation are established, e.g. by the EU Commission.

The assessment of independent assurance in accordance with this classification can be illustrated as in Figure 2.

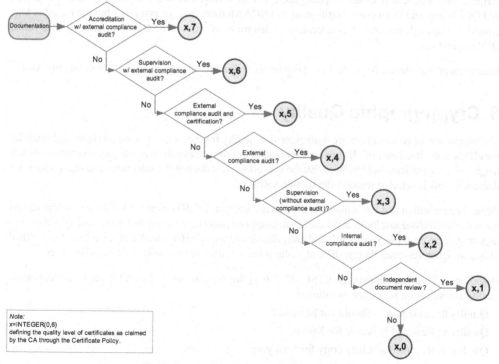

Fig. 2: Assessment of independent assurance level

Supervision and accreditation are the two models described for issuers of qualified certificates according to the e-signature Directive. In the supervision model, an issuer declares conformance to requirements in order to be listed as issuer of QC and accepts (later) inspections from the authority. In the accreditation model, the authority must assess conformance before listing the issuer. Note that discrimination between the two models supervision and accreditation for qualified certificates shall not take place; both shall be accepted as qualified. However, for other certificates (non-European, regarded as equivalent to qualified) the distinction may be relevant.

4.5 Assessment of non-European Certificates

The assessment criteria for certificate quality and independent assurance levels defined above can be applied to non-European certificates as well, even if the term "qualified certificate" is not defined outside of Europe.

If the CP of such a certificate does not make any claims as to compliance with one of the (European) ETSI standards or any other standard judged to be similar, the assessment of (claimed) certificate quality can be made by evaluation of the CP through document reviews.

A case of particular interest is that of CAs that have been cross certified to one of the US Federal Bridge Certification Authority (FBCA) certificate policies [FBCA]. A mapping between the quality levels (termed "assurance levels") of FBCA and the PEPPOL quality profile is shown in [PEPPOL-D1.1], part 7, appendix 1. As an example, it is suggested to map FBCA Medium level of assurance to eID quality 3 (NCP equivalent) and independent assurance level 5 (external compliance audit and certification). The results of the mapping are coherent with [ETSI-102-458], which states essentially that QCP is acceptable for cross-certification to FBCA Medium level of assurance but not the other way around. A thorough assessment is necessary to determine if a CA at FBCA Medium level also fulfils QCP requirements.

Similar mappings should be made for quality levels defined in other parts of the world, notably Asia.

5 Cryptographic Quality

The parameters of concern here are hash algorithm quality for the signed document (hash algorithm for the eID is considered part of eID quality), and quality of the combination public key algorithm and key length for the certificate holder. Note that the eID does not influence the selection of hash algorithm for document; this is selected through the signing software.

Public key algorithm and key length could be considered part of eID quality. A reason for separating this out is that even if one just looks at the qualified status, one may still be interested in the quality of the cryptography. As an example, Germany has already abandoned use of SHA-1 hash and RSA-1024 for qualified eIDs and signatures, even though these algorithms are still used in most other European countries.

Based on ETSI recommendations [ETSI-102-176-1] that are also aligned with US recommendations, a quality classification is defined as follows:

Quality 0: Inadequate – should not be trusted.

Quality 1: Reasonably secure for 3 years.

Quality 2: Regarded as trustworthy for 5-10 years.

Quality 3-5: Increasing levels of security.

Examples of hash algorithms (2009): MD5 = 0, SHA-1 = 1, SHA-224/256/384/512 = 2/3/4/5.

Examples of public key algorithms with key lengths (2009): RSA-1024 = 1; RSA-2048 = 2; RSA-4096 = 4.

Note that this classification assumes that key generation, random number generation, padding and other basic aspects are handled in an appropriate way, and that there is no inherent (undetected) weakness in the algorithms and no implementation flaws.

6 Signature Quality

Excluding implementation issues of signing software and hardware, the quality of a signature consists of the three parameters: eID quality (in the scheme described in this paper consisting of the two parameters quality and assurance level), hash quality, public key quality.

Each of these parameters should be above a certain level for the signature to be accepted; this level should be defined in the signature policy. The signature policy should normally not refer to specific CAs or algorithms, only to quality parameters.

The PEPPOL profile for digital signatures is then defined by the following parameters:

eID quality, ranging from 0 to 6

eID assurance level, ranging from 0 to 7.

Hash quality, ranging from 0 to 5.

Public key quality, ranging from 0 to 5.

PEPPOL suggests a notation for the signature quality as follows

Signature quality = {eID quality, eID assurance level, hash quality, public key quality}

A number of examples of use of this scheme is given in [PEPPOL-D1.1] part 7.

7 Other Issues

7.1 Quality of the Actor Issuing an eID

Some quality aspects cannot be derived from the CP alone. If desired, quality requirements may be imposed on the actor in charge of a CA, such as:

- Financial strength (will it survive and can it face liability claims),
- Insurance coverage,
- Owners and organization structure (may include judgements about independence with respect to third party roles),
- Market penetration (number of eIDs and their usage frequency),
- Company reputation,
- Competence and knowledge,
- Infrastructure.

Such requirements are at present not considered by PEPPOL.

7.2 Classification over Time

Cryptographic quality is reduced over time, a CA may change its service offering, or its supervision status may change. Thus, although frequent changes are not envisaged, quality is not static. When assessing the quality of an old signature, one essentially has two options:

- Assess quality rating at time of signing (or time of initial verification): was the signature acceptable at that time?
- Assess present quality rating: to what degree is the signature still secure and acceptable?

Which option to choose is a policy decision. Validation services may be prepared to handle both. Note that the first option depends on storing either enough old status information on classification ratings or a quality rating securely recorded at the time in question.

7.3 Who Shall Perform Quality Classification?

PEPPOL suggests that validation services [PEPPOL-D1.1] shall mediate quality rating. Setting values for the rating can then be done by the validation service provider or by some independent certification body; the latter is preferred. There is a possibility that different ratings will be reported from different validation services for the same eID, notably for independent assurance level for CAs without accreditations/supervision/certification. However, for cryptographic quality and the QCP levels, this should not be a problem.

[COMM03] suggests use of a common template for Trust Status Lists (TSL) [ETSI-102-231] of supervised and/or accredited issuers of qualified eIDs and work is in progress on this topic. Such TSLs will significantly ease the assessment of qualified eIDs.

8 Conclusion

The criteria for accepting an e-signature for a particular purpose are determined by legislative and risk management decisions. The quality and (national) approval status of eIDs and the cryptographic quality of the signatures are the most important aspects. This paper suggest a quality classification scheme where eID quality consists of two parameters: (claimed) quality from certificate policy, independent assurance level. For e-signatures, one additionally adds hash quality and public key quality, obtaining the classification:

Signature quality = {eID quality, eID assurance level, hash quality, public key quality}

eID quality has levels 0-6 where levels 2-6 are defined according to ETSI policy requirements for LCP/NCP/NCP+/QCP/QCP+. Independent assurance level is 0-7 ranging from self assessment to national supervision and accreditation. Cryptographic quality levels are defined according to [ETSI-102-176-1].

A signature acceptance policy will define minimum levels for the signature quality parameters, and validation services as specified by [PEPPOL-D1.1] shall be configured to answer not only for validity, but also for signature policy fulfilment of a particular eID/e-signature. The validation interfaces defined by [PEPPOL-D1.1] can convey this information, and [PEPPOL-D1.1] defines the necessary XML structures.

The proposed scheme should be viewed as a starting point for a European or international standard in the area. Comments and suggestions are highly welcome.

References

[COMM01] EU Commission: Action Plan for the Implementation of the Legal Framework for Electronic Public Procurement. Communication from the Commission to the Council, the European Parliament, the European Economic and Social Committee and the European Committee of the Regions, 2004.

[COMM02] EU Commission: Requirements for Conducting Public Procurement Using Electronic Means under the New Public Procurement Directives 2004/18/EC and 2004/17/EC. Commission staff working document, 2005.

[COMM03] EU Commission: Action-Plan on e-Signatures and e-Identification to Facilitate the Provision of Cross-Border Public Services in the Single Market, Communication from the Commission to the Council, the European Parliament, the European Economic and Social Committee and the Committee of the Regions, 2008.

[EBGCA] Certipost: Certification Practice Statement, European IDABC Bridge/Gateway CA for Public Administrations v2.0. EBGCA-DEL-015, 2005.

[ETSI-101-456] ETSI: Electronic Signatures and Infrastructures (ESI); Policy Requirements for Certification Authorities issuing Qualified Certificates. ETSI TS 101 456 v1.4.1, 2006.

[ETSI-101-733] ETSI: Electronic Signature and Infrastructure (ESI) – CMS Advanced Electronic Signature (CAdES). ETSI TS 101 733 v1.7.4, 2008.

[ETSI-101-903] ETSI: XML Advanced Electronic Signatures (XAdES). ETSI TS 101 903 v1.3.2, 2006.

[ETSI-102-038] ETSI: Electronic Signature and Infrastructure (ESI) – XML Format for Signature Policies. ETSI TR 102 038 v1.1.1, 2002.

[ETSI-102-042] ETSI: Electronic Signatures and Infrastructures (ESI); Policy Requirements for Certification Authorities issuing Public Key Certificates. ETSI TS 102 042 v1.2.2, 2005.

[ETSI-102-045] ETSI: Electronic Signature and Infrastructure (ESI) – Signature Policy for Extended Business Model. ETSI TR 102 045 v1.1.1, 2003.

[ETSI-102-176-1] ETSI: Electronic Signatures and Infrastructures; Algorithms and Parameters for Secure Electronic Signatures; Part 1: Hash Functions and Asymmetric Algorithms. ETSI TS 102 176-1 v2.0.0, 2007.

[ETSI-102-231] ETSI: Electronic Signatures and Infrastructures; Provision of Harmonized Trust Service Provider Information. ETSI TS 102 231 v2.1.1, 2006.

[EU01]   EU: Community Framework for Electronic Signatures. Directive 1999/93/EC of the European Parliament and of the Council, 1999.

[EU02]   EU: Coordination of Procedures for the Award of Public Works Contracts, Public Supply Contracts and Public Service Contracts. Directive 2004/18/EC of the European Parliament and of the Council, 2004.

[EU03]   EU: Coordinating the Procurement Procedures of Entities Operating in the Water, Energy, Transport and Postal Services Sectors. Directive 2004/17/EC of the European Parliament and of the Council, 2004.

[EDYN]   European Dynamics. Electronic Catalogues in Electronic Public Procurement. DG Internal Markets report, 2007.

[FBCA]   Federal PKI Policy Authority: X.509 Certificate Policy for the Federal Bridge Certification Authority (FBCA) Version 2.1. 2006.

[ICT-PSP] ICT Policy Support Programme (PSP): Guidelines to Common Specifications for Cross-border Use of Public Procurement. ICT PSP Programme note, 2007.

[IDABC] Siemens, Time.lex: Preliminary Study on Mutual Recognition of eSignatures for eGovernment Applications (Final Study and 29 Country Profiles). IDABC, 2007.

[Lopez] Lopez, J., Oppliger, R., Pernul, G.: Classifying Public Key Certificates. EuroPKI 2005 – 2nd European PKI Workshop, 2005.

[OASIS-DSS-Core] OASIS: Digital Signature Service Core Protocols and Elements. 2007.

[PEPPOL-D1.1] PEPPOL project: Requirements for Use of Signatures in Public Procurement Processes. http://www.peppol.eu, 2009.

[PEPPOL-D2.1] PEPPOL project: Functional and Non-Functional Requirements Specification for the VCD, Including Critical Synthesis, Comparison and Assessment of National vs. Pan-European Needs. http://www.peppol.eu, 2009.

[RFC3647] Chokani, C., Ford, W., Sabett, R., Merrill, C., Wu, S.: Internet X.509 Public Key Infrastructure Certificae Policy and Certification Practices Framework. RFC3647, 2003.

[Siemens] Siemens: Preliminary Study on the Electronic Provision of Certificates and Attestations Usually Required in Public Procurement Procedures. DG Internal Market report, 2007.

[XKMS] W3C: XML Key Management Specification (XKMS 2.0). 2005.

[Ølnes] Ølnes, J., Andresen, A., Buene, L., Cerrato, O., Grindheim, H.: Making Digital Signatures Work across National Borders. ISSE Conference, Warszawa, 2007.

[Ølnes2] Ølnes, J., Buene, L.: Use of a Validation Authority to Provide Risk Management for the PKI Relying Party. EuroPKI 2006 – 3rd European PKI Workshop, 2006.

Second Wave of Biometric ID-documents in Europe: The Residence Permit for non-EU/EEA Nationals

Detlef Houdeau

Infineon Technologies AG, Munich, Germany
Detlef.Houdeau@Infineon.com

Abstract

The first implementation of biometric documents, called biometric passports, based on a regulation is running, the second implementation since end of CY 2008 is coming to Europe. The focus is on persons staying for business, study or leisure for more than 3 months in Europe and coming from a state outside Europe and not being a member of the Visa-Waiver-Program of the EU. This second wave increases the demand for the security industry for certified security microcontroller chips, secure smart cards, readers and supporting infrastructure on top of the biometric Passport business. It underlines the continuing advance of contactless identification technology in the public sector. The article gives an overview on the application, the technology, the EU regulation, the EU roadmap and the implementations.

1 EU policy on biometric ID-documents

Back in June 20th, 2003 the European Council decided in the "Thessaloniki Declaration" on a coherent approach in the EU to biometric identifiers and biometric data for all EU citizens´ passports, for non-EU / European Economic Area (EEA) nationals and for the back office information system [1]. In the Council Regulation (EC) No 2252/2004 of 13th of December 2004 the roadmap for the security features and biometrics in passports and travel documents, issued by the EU Member States (EU-MS) was published. Since June 2006 all 27 EU-MS have switched to this new technology and issued only passports with an embedded security microcontroller with a contactless RF interface (ISO/IEC 14443) combined with at least one biometric feature: The facial image of the holder. Currently the two EU-Member States Latvia and Germany also store two fingerprint images in the chip. The deadline for implementation of two fingerprint images by all EU-MS in passports is June, 28th, 2009. These data are protected by the Basic Access Control (BAC) and Extended Access Control (EAC) security protocols defined by International Civil Aviation Organization (ICAO) and Brussels Interoperability Group (BIG).

About four years later the Council of the European Union published the regulation on the Residence Permits for third country nationals (EU 13502/2/07), on March, 7th, 2008 [2]. The following key purposes have been addressed with this regulation:

- harmonised immigration policy
- uniform format in the EU
- very high technical standard, in particular as regarding safeguards against counterfeiting and falsification

N. Pohlmann, H. Reimer, W. Schneider (Editors): Securing Electronic Business Processes, Vieweg (2009), 87-93

2 Technology of the Residence Permit for non-EU/ EEA nationals

With the decision to select the technical standard for travel documents, according to ICAO document 9303, part 3 on size 1 and 2 (ID1 and ID2 format) the link between the holder and the residence permit is achievable. This approach supports the authenticity of the document and the identity of the holder.

Two biometric data sets of the holder are defined, with face image and two fingerprint images, according to ISO/IEC 19794 stored on the Residence Permit card and protected with the EAC security protocol. The Residence Permit has the ICAO "chip inside" symbol printed on the card (top left corner of Figure 1) for machine readable travel documents with a contactless security microcontroller chip (e-MRTP, RF-chip) The front- and rear side layout of the card is also defined by the EU [2].

Data content printed are as follow:

- Name
- Given Name
- Validity of the Document
- Place and Date of Issuing
- Type of Permit
- Place and Date of Birth
- Sex
- Nationality
- MRZ (3-lines)
- Photo of the card holder

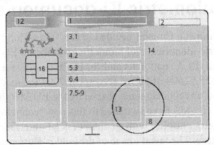

Fig. 1: Front-Side of the Residence Permit for ID1 documents; source [2].

1: type of document; 2: unique number of permit document; 3.1: name of the card holder; 4.2 valid date of permit document; 5.3: type of permit; 7.5-9: remarks; 8: document code; 9: issuing state; 12: additional information; 14: photo of the card holder; 16: biometric chip holds MRZ, photo and (optional) two fingerprints of the card holder;

The additional use of new technologies, such as e-Government and digital signature for access to e-Services should be facilitated by the EU Member States. For this application, the Residence Permit card could have a contact-based interface (ISO/IEC 7816) in addition to the contactless interface (ISO/IEC 14443).

3 Processing, Lifetime and Biometrics

Non-EU/EEA nationals, who are coming from a state outside Europe, which is not being a member of the Visa-Waiver-Program of the EU, needs a SCHENGEN Visa according the EU regulation (EC) 0269/2009, to travel to Europe. This SCHENGEN Visa has a maximum validity of 90 days. This SCHENGEN Visa is in a harmonized ID2-format, with printed photo, MRZ and name, given name, birth day and validity day. It must be pasted in the passport booklet of the visitor for travelling into SCHENGEN. European Commission has decided, that all immigrants must give there face photo and the ten fingerprints to the embassy of an EU-MS before travelling into SCHENGEN. Face photo and fingerprint data, name, given name, birthday and visa number move in a central data bank system and should be available cross border in Europe. The data of the holder and the face photo are printed on this self adhesive sticker. A huge data bank system, called VISA INFORMATION SYSTEM (VIS) must be placed on this.

Persons, which would stay longer than 90 days, like students, need a residence permit card. To capture such residence permit card, the person must go to a local immigration registration office in the EU-MS, for example in which this person would stay longer.

The validity of the residence permit card is up to 5 years.

With the new European Regulation such electronic ID document migrates from a pure visible ID document to a visible and electronically ID document, include digital and biometric data of the card holder. The person needs a frontal photo and the immigration office could have fingerprint scanner for data capturing.

The biometric passports have shown in the last three years two trends on biometrics data in opposite direction according the data quality, which are stored on the contactless chip: mainstream for face image data is to use data compression modes like JPEG or JPEG 2000. With this approach, the data frame size cut down from 18k byte (image) to 16k (JPEG compressed) respectively to 12k (JPEG 2000 compressed). Mainstream for fingerprint data goes in the other direction, high resolution image photos are requested. Examples are:

- USA with the FBI specification EFTS/F (Electronic Fingerprint Transmission Specification 7.1, Appendix F)
- Germany with the BSI technical guideline TR 03104 (Technische Richtlinie zur Produktionsdatenerfassung, -qualitätsprüfung und -übermittlung)
- High resolution photos need 16k to 18k byte. The specification of the EU has defined 12k to 15k byte.

4 EU Roadmap and Outlook

As same as for the electronic passport with biometric data, the EU Commission plan a two step implementation program [1]. The deadline for the first generation (face / BAC) implement would be 24 months after publication of the specification and the second generation (face and fingerprint / BAC and EAC) after 36 month. EU-MS are free to decide an earlier implementation date, as shown in for the e-Passport and the e-Residence Permit Card.

Deadline for the first implementation of the e-Passport was August 2006. Frontrunner was Belgium with start the issuing in November 2004, followed by Sweden in October 2005, Germany in November 2005, United Kingdom March 2006, France April 2006, Iceland May 2006, Austria June 2006 and Portugal July 2006. Deadline for the second implementation was July 2009. Frontrunners are Germany with November 2007 and Latvia with March 2009. For the second implementation are finger scanners in the document issuing offices requested as well as the managing of digital data via a secure channel to the office of the personalizing place of the booklet.

The specification of the Residence Permit Card was decided at an article-6-committee meeting in April 2009. Based on this, the EU-MS have the official deadline May 2011 for the implementation of the first generation (face / BAC) and May 2012 for the implementation of the second generation.

In case of the Residence Permit program all person data and all fingerprints of all non-EU/EEA nationals should be stored centralized on EU-MS-level and should be needed for exchange of information cross border. This approach is similar to the SCHENGEN Visa policy.

The annual run rate of all Residence Permit Cards in all 27 MS is expected in the quantity window of 15 to 18 Million cards.

It is expected, that this program could be bridged in future with the European Asylum-Seeker Program, called EURODAC [6]. This program was created in the context of the "Dublin Convention" and is in place since January 2003, according the EU regulation 2725/2000. It is based on a harmonized registration and approval process and needs 10 fingerprints, collected with an AFIS system. All EU-MS have access to this central data bank system EURODAC to avoid double bookings and to reduce time for the approval processing of the Asylum-Seekers.

4.1 Early Adopters

4.1.1 Case UK

The first implementation in Europe has already taken place. The UK has started the roll out on November 25, 2008. One example of the use-case: around 300,000 people apply every year for studies in the UK *The London School of Economics* alone take 66% of its students from overseas [3]. UK Border Agency (UKBA) issues Residence Permit in an ID1-format, smart card (Figure 2). This "Identity Card for Foreign Nationals" includes two biometrics data sets (face and two finger images) and is the first UK mandatory electronic ID document. The UK immigration and police officers now have the possibility to quickly, easily and securely check people. On-street-checking is also conceivable with one of the new generation of mobile contactless card readers with integrated MRZ (Machine-Readable Zone)-scanner now available from several reader providers.

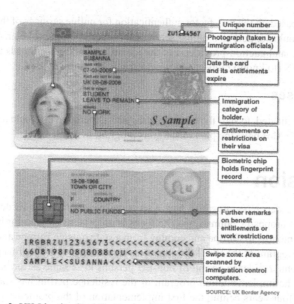

Fig. 2: UK Identity Card for Foreign Nationals, front- and rear side [3].

4.1.2 Case Sweden

The second implementation of a Residence Permit Card in Europe has already taken place. Sweden has started the roll out in June 6th, 2009. This project was driven by the Swedish Tax Agency [4]. The government have decided to store the face image in the contactless chip. The card body have also the "chip inside" symbol printed (top right corner on Figure 3). It is a hybrid card.

Fig. 3: Swedish Identity Card for Foreign Nationals, front side; source [4].

The residence permit card in Sweden support e-Government Services as same as for Swedish Nationals. The smart card has a second interface, contact-based, according ISO/IEC 7816. With this approach the selected technology, the government services and the used infrastructure (e.g. national PKI) is similar to the national eID-Card in Sweden. This project is in place since October 2005, as a voluntary document. In Sweden is no disclosure for a national ID card in place. The e-Government Service is along the new European Standard CEN 15480 and CEN 14980, called European Citizen Card (ECC). The application has three main pillars:

- Identification (I)
- Authentication (A)
- Signature (S)

This IAS concept is based on the two-factor authentication for online services of the government, called e-Government and could support also online services for other internet provider, like banks, insurance organization, trading- and auction-provider. For the identification the user needs the card (to have) for authentication is a PIN (to know) request and for electronic signature as well.

4.1.3 Other cases

France ANTS have indicated, to start the issuing for the new generation e-Residence Permit until spring-time 2010 [5]. Spain's MoI have the plan to start this program first half 2010.

5 Conclusion

With the electronic residence permit card comes a second wave of biometric ID documents over Europe by regulation of the European Commission. The focus is on persons staying for business, study or lei-sure for more than 3 months in Europe and coming from a state outside Europe and not being a member of the Visa-Waiver-Program of the EU. The biometrics technology, with face image and two fingerprint image for the electronic residence permit of non-EU persons is as same as for biometric passports for European citizens. The implementation program of the residence permit has started with UK in No-vember 2008 and is four years behind the first implementation of the biometric passports, which have started in Belgium in November 2004. It underlines the continuing advance of contactless identification technology in the public sector.

Literature

[1]   http://ue.eu.int/ueDocs/cms_Data/docs/pressdata/en/ec/76279.pdf

[2]   http://register.consilium.europa.eu/pdf/en/07/st13/st13502-re02.en07.pdf

[3]   http://news.bbc.co.uk/2/hi/uk_news/education/7747784.stm

[4]   http://www.icenews.is/index.php/2009/06/06/immigrants-to-sweden-now-able-to-get-id-cards/

[5]   speech from Philip Melchior, head of ANTS on a security conference in April 2009 in Berlin; See http://www.e-identify-df.de/

[6]   http://ec.europa.eu/justice_home/fsj/asylum/identification/fsj_asylum_identification_en.htm

Glossary

AFIS	Automated Fingerprint Identification Systems
ANTS	France national secure credentials agency
BAC	Basic Access Control; a security standard for travel documents
BIG	Brussels Interoperability Group; sub-group under the article-6-committee
BSI	Federal Ministry of Security in the Information Technology
CY	Calendar Year
CEN	European Committee for Standardization
EAC	Extended Access Control, a security standard for travel documents
EC	European Commission
ECC	European Citizen Card
EFTS/F	Electronic Fingerprint Transmission Specification 7.1, Appendix F
EU	European Union

EEA	European Economic Area
FBI	Federal Bureau of Investigation
IAS	Identification, Authentication, Signature
ICAO	International Civil Aviation Organization
IEC	International Electrotechnical Commission
ISO	International Standardization Organization
MRTP	Machine-readable Travel Passport
MRZ	Machine-readable Zone
MS	Member States
PIN	Personal Identification Number
PKI	Public Key Infrastructure
RF	Radio Frequency
TR	Technical Guideline; documents from BSI
UK	United Kingdom
UKBA	United Kingdom Border Agency
USA	United States of America

Security Services and Large Scale Public Applications

User and Access Management in Belgian e-Government

Jos Dumortier · Frank Robben

Interdisciplinary Centre for Law and ICT (ICRI), K.U.Leuven
Sint-Michielsstraat 6, B 3443
BE – 3000 LEUVEN
jos.dumortier@law.kuleuven.be
frank.robben@ksz.fgov.be

Abstract

Efficient e-government is not possible without integrated information management. From a privacy protection perspective systems integration has to be preferred over data integration. A well-accepted model for the organisation of user and access management in this perspective is a federation based on circles of trust. The following pages describe how this model is implemented in Belgium, using five building blocks: unique identification numbers, the electronic identity card, validated authentic sources, service integrators and sector committees for data protection. Using these building blocks user and access management is organised following a generic policy decision model. The objective is to illustrate that integrated e-government is not necessarily incompatible with optimal protection of privacy.

1 E-Government Requires Integration

Information management in the context of e-government has to ensure that the government can provide effective services to citizens, companies and other organisations. This is not possible without far-reaching integration. Citizens and companies assume that the government as a whole will only request the necessary information once and, after checking for accuracy, will then reuse the information whenever it needs to do so. With this in mind, agreements must be reached between government echelons and agencies. Which agencies gather which information, check it for accuracy, store it and make it available for other echelons and agencies?

Everyone expects services from the government aligned to specific situations and also offered as far as possible in personalised form.[1] The alignment of services to specific situations can be achieved by offering services from the perspective of the user. Citizens and companies no longer have to find their own way through the labyrinth of government institutions and competences, but receive integrated services relating to events taking place throughout their lives: birth, work, housing, illness, retirement, death, starting a business, etc. However, this presupposes that these services are offered across all government echelons, government agencies and private bodies.

Citizens, companies and their service providers must be able to find all the relevant information and services using one electronic access portal of their choice. This electronic access portal must not be

---

1 The Belgian OECD report on e-Government (2008) reads (p. 19): "Belgian citizens are more interested in accessing relevant, personalised services online, rather than learning the complexities of Belgian governments' competences". The full study is available from http://www.fedict.belgium.be/nl/downloads/.

N. Pohlmann, H. Reimer, W. Schneider (Editors): Securing Electronic Business Processes, Vieweg (2009), 97-107

unique in the sense that there can only be one, but users must be able to find everything they want regarding a given event on the electronic access portal of their choice. This requires that electronic services from different government echelons and agencies can easily be integrated into electronic access portals by all those who develop them.

Automation today is generally being developed by governments according to a Service Oriented Architecture (SOA). SOA is essentially an architecture for distributed development, management and use of ICT components, which call upon each other as services. It allows all those involved in electronic government service delivery to work together but still to maintain their individual autonomy and specific working methods. Local administrations and associations, health insurance funds, trade unions, banks, accountants, employment agencies, etc., can integrate the electronic services provided by the government – whether or not supplemented by their own services – and then offer them in a manner that is ideally suited to their target group. Companies or other end users can also have their internal company applications interact directly with electronic government services.

Where possible, users want services to be provided automatically. The government can, for example, relieve them of the burden of applying for tax deductions or exemptions, reduced rates for utility services, free public transport or other benefits that are allocated to them based on a social situation previously known to the government. At the same time, however, active contribution and a high level of self-service and self-steering are also appreciated. Services have to be offered in an efficient and user-friendly way, through various channels depending on the user's choice, as well as being reliably, securely and permanently available.

Government policy is expected to be based on objective and updated data. Citizens rightly demand that the government takes a proactive stance and that policy anticipates new trends. Everyone also wants the government to combat all forms of fraud in an efficient manner and to apply the most modern data mining techniques to do so.

All these requirements have to be reconciled with maximum protection of privacy. Of course, that does not happen automatically. In the quest for efficiency, it is easy to fall into the trap of a higher level of data concentration and centralised processing.

The Belgian approach demonstrates how the latter can be avoided, in particular by implementing a federated user and access management. Below we broadly describe how this approach has been conceived in Belgium.

2 Definitions

User and access management consists, as the term itself indicates, of two parts: user management and access management. User management itself covers five aspects: 1) identity registration, 2) user identification, 3) identity authentication, 4) registration of attributes and mandates and 5) verification of attributes and mandates. Access management covers the registration of authorisations and the verification of authorisations.

Within the context of this paper, the following definitions of the above terms are used: [2]

- The *identity* of the user is a unique number or a series of attributes of a user (natural person, company, branch of a company, etc.) enabling the user to be unequivocally identified. This im-

---

2 These definitions are also used by the Belgian Privacy Commission in a Recommendation regarding access and user management in the public sector (SE/2008/028) of 24 September 2008 (www.privacycommission.be)

plies that a user has one and only one identity. The fact that a pseudonym can be used in certain situations does not alter this fact.

- An *attribute* is any user characteristic, other than the attributes that determine the identity of the user, such as a specific quality, a position in a certain organisation, a professional qualification, etc. A user can have several attributes.

- A *mandate* is a right granted by an identified user to another identified user to perform a number of well-defined (legal) transactions in his name and on his behalf. A user can grant one or more mandates to one or more users.

- *Registration* is the process used to establish the identity of a user, a user attribute or a mandate with sufficient certainty before resources are made available and that is used to authenticate or verify an identity, an attribute or a mandate.

- *Authentication* of identity is the process of checking that the identity a user claims to hold does indeed belong to him. This can be carried out by checking: a) knowledge (e.g. a password), b) possession (e.g. a certificate on an electronically readable card), c) (a) biometric trait(s), or d) a combination of two or more of these means.

- *Verification of* an attribute or a mandate is the process of checking whether an attribute or a mandate that a user claims to have in order to be able to use an electronic service is actually a characteristic or mandate of this particular user. This can be carried out: a) based on the same type of means as those used for identity authentication, or b) after authentication of a user's identity, by consulting a database (authentic source) in which characteristics or mandates regarding an identified user are stored.

- *Authorisation* is the permission for a user to perform a certain transaction or to use a certain service.

3 Federated user and access management

Theoretically, it would be possible to achieve the objectives of e-government information management outlined in the introduction by centralising all the data concerning natural persons, legal persons and other entities as much as possible. Some years ago, there was a discussion in the Netherlands about a proposal to create a "digital vault" for every citizen. This would be controlled by the data subject and would combine all the data about this data subject that need to be available for use by the government. Ultimately, this idea was abandoned because of privacy and security concerns.

For this reason data protection supervisory authorities are often of the opinion that e-government data exchange should be organised as far as possible based on a distributed and decentralised storage of personal data.[3] A model that is frequently used for this purpose by the private sector is the model of a federation based on circles of trust.[4] Such a model implies that clear agreements are reached among the bodies involved in the electronic service delivery in order to organise user and access management together. Among other things, these agreements establish who performs which authentication, verification and checks, using which means, and who is responsible and liable for them. Agreements are also needed to determine how the results of the authentications, verifications and checks performed can be

---

3 In its Working Document on Online Authentication Systems, adopted on 29/01/2003 (WP 68) the Article 29 Working Party writes (p.15): „The adoption of software architecture that minimises the centralisation of personal data of the Internet users would be appreciated and encouraged as a means of increasing the fault-tolerance properties of the authentication system, and of avoiding the creation of high added-value databases owned and managed by a single company or by a small set of companies and organisations."

4 The model is based on the results of the "Liberty Alliance" project: http://www.projectliberty.org/.

electronically exchanged in a secure way between the relevant bodies. Who maintains which log files and how is it possible to ensure that an investigation – on the initiative of an inspection body or following a complaint – can perfectly reconstruct who has used which service for which transaction involving which citizen or company, when, via which channel and for what purposes?

Data protection supervisory authorities have emphasised that a federated system avoids unnecessary centralisation and the associated threats to privacy. For example, no copies of the validated authentic sources will be circulated. Moreover, multiple identical checks and the redundant storage of log data are avoided. Furthermore, this model also guarantees that every administration is working with the most up-to-date information. For example, if a user loses a characteristic, this will be dealt with in an appropriate way by the system at the time of registration. Finally, the system will liberate users from repeatedly having to provide proof of the same attributes or mandates.

A federated approach however assumes that everyone is singing from the same hymn sheet, so that all the components fit perfectly together. This is important, because administrative processes take place through various government echelons, institutions and agencies. For this reason, the same building blocks must be used everywhere.

4 Main Building Blocks

The most important building blocks used in Belgium in user and access management for e-government are the unique identification numbers, the electronic identity card, validated authentic sources, service integrators and sector committees for data protection. Each of these five building blocks will be briefly discussed below.

4.1 Unique Identifiers

In Belgium, unique identification numbers are used for natural persons and other entities (companies, associations, etc.) throughout the entire e-government data flow, at all levels and by all government institutions and agencies. Belgian citizens and foreigners living in Belgium are identified by their National Number. For other persons, not living in Belgium but who have contact with the Belgian authorities, the Social Security Identification Number (SSIN) is used. Legal persons and other entities are identified by the company number under which the entity is registered with the Enterprise Register (the so-called "Crossroads Bank for Enterprises").

Sector-specific identification numbers – sometimes presented as more privacy-friendly – are not used in Belgium. There has been some hesitation about using sector-specific identification numbers in the health sector and in field of e-justice, but this idea has finally been abandoned. The Belgian Privacy Commission has explicitly expressed its support to the decision to make use of the National Number (or the SSIN) instead of using a specific patient number in the health sector.

Many applications exceed the boundaries of one particular public sector domain. Working with sector-specific identification numbers can therefore lead to considerable complexity. Experiences in Austria, where sector numbers are used, demonstrate that in practice organisations tend to avoid separate identification numbers in order to work more rapidly and more securely.

The protection of privacy when using unique identification numbers can be guaranteed in various other ways. Use of the number can be restricted or recourse can be sought to strict control on the exchange of personal data that are linked to the unique number.[5] Belgium has opted for a combination of both of these methods.

4.2 Electronic Identity Card

The preferred method of electronic identity authentication in Belgium is the use of an electronic identity card (EID). However, depending on the required security level, use is also made of either a combination of user name, password and citizen token[6], or a combination of user name and password alone. The EID does, however, offer a range of advantages. It combines possession of a specific document with the availability of particular knowledge (PIN code). In addition, a number of factual and legal factors limit the risk of abuse in the event of possible loss or theft of the card.[7]

Verification of the attributes and/or mandates is not performed using the EID. In addition to a device for creating a qualified electronic signature, the EID is exclusively an instrument for identification and authentication. The information on the card therefore remains confined to the data that are necessary to identify the holder, the certificate that allows the holder to authenticate himself and the certificate that enables the holder to place a secure electronic signature. Data that have nothing to do with the identification or authentication of a physical person or the electronic signature, such as characteristics and/or mandates, do not belong on the EID.[8]

4.3 Validated Authentic Sources

The fact that the identity of a user has been authenticated is not always enough to grant the person concerned automatic access to an electronic service. A user's access rights to an electronic service (authorisation) can be linked to his attributes and/or mandates. Integrated user and access management therefore requires that unambiguous checks can be performed on the relevant attributes of a person or the existence of a mandate given by a legal person or a natural person to which an electronic service relates and the person who is using this service.

The verification of attributes and/or mandates (for example, is the user a qualified physician? Is the user a lawful representative of the legal person?) takes place via channels other than the EID. In this context it is not recommendable to rely on non-validated information that is simply provided by the user himself. These elements have to be checked against a source that offers the required guarantees in terms of accuracy and up datedness of the information it contains. In Belgium such sources are called "validated authentic sources". The government agency in charge of a validated authentic source is responsible for the availability and quality of the information it contains and made available for other agencies and echelons. The State Health Insurance Fund, for example, will be in charge of a validated authentic source of qualified physicians, the Royal Federation of Notaries will keep the validated authentic source of notaries, etc.

---

5 The Hungarian Constitutional Court (http://www.ceecprivacy.org/htm/91-15.htm) aptly formulated this alternative as follows: "(...) the use of PINs (Personal Identification Numbers) shall be restricted by security regulations. This can be done in two ways: either the use of the PINs is to be restricted to precisely defined data-processing operations or strict conditions or controlling measures are to be imposed on the availability of information connected to PINs and on the link-up of record-keeping systems using PINs".

6 A citizen token is a card (with the same dimensions as a credit card) that contains 24 numbered personal codes and that is sent to the person in question by post following verification of certain credentials (National Registration Number, SIS (social insurance number) card number and identity card number). When access to an application is requested (e.g. Tax-on-Web), the user is asked for one of the codes at random.

7 Danny De Cock, Christopher Wolf and Bart Preneel, The Belgian Electronic Identity Card (Overview), http://www.cosic.esat. kuleuven.be/publications/article-769.pdf

8 The Belgian Privacy Commission issued an opinion (no. 1/2005 of 7 September 2005) arguing against the inclusion of aspects such as blood group or the consent for organ donation on the electronic identity card.

The extent to which feedback is possible to validated authentic sources is a crucial factor in the success of a reliable electronic user and access management. It is therefore obvious that anyone wishing to expand this type of management system has to know on which sources they can rely. This requires the availability of an inventory of validated authentic sources. For this reason, at every level, government and related services must be identified that provide reliable information with regard to, for example, attributes or mandates of a person. The authentic information must be mapped out and the elements that demonstrate its quality must be indicated. Finally, a validated authentic source is only useful if the information is organised in such a way that it can be easily retrieved.

4.4 Service Integrators

Integration does not happen spontaneously. Process optimisation that transcends services, coordination of back offices, an integrated and personalised range of electronic services in the front office, coordination of semantics, interoperable electronic platforms developed according to a service-oriented architecture and reliable security and protection of privacy demand close, multidisciplinary cooperation among the various government echelons and agencies. This cooperation is needed in various fields: at the level of vision and strategy building, process re-engineering, the development of information and communication technology, the implementation of the measures regarding information security, the organisation of the required electronic data exchange, the adjustment of legislation, project management, services management, etc.. Moreover, within every government echelon and sector, the required level of consistency must be guaranteed among all these fields.

In various government sectors or echelons in Belgium, bodies have already been successfully designated for this purpose. They are the driving forces behind cooperation and coordination at the aforementioned levels in the relevant sectors or echelons. In this respect, they are responsible for organising the required electronic data exchange and act as "trusted third party", monitoring the correct application of the legislation regarding information security and privacy protection and the exchange of personal data performed within that context. These bodies are known as "crossroads banks" or, better and more up to date, "service integrators".

Examples of already existing service integrators include the Crossroads Bank for Social Security (CBSS) in the social sector[9], the Flemish eGovernment Coordination Unit (CORVE) [10] in Flanders, Easi-Wal[11] in Wallonia and the eHealth-Platform[12] in the health sector.

Service integration has to be distinguished from data integration. The latter involves merging data from various authentic sources and their storage in an integrated database, with a view to their communication to third parties. By contrast, service integration refers to integrating electronic sub-services into integrated electronic services with a view to offering them to third parties. Service integration is also not the same as infrastructure integration (the pure use of a shared infrastructure for separate data processing operations) or presentation integration (purely making data or services accessible in an integrated manner via one electronic point of contact, such as a portal).

When processing personal data, data integration is only acceptable if this is necessary and if the same functionality *cannot* reasonably be provided via service integration. This is a consequence of the proportionality rule. Personal data must not be pooled if this is not necessary for the intended objective. In other words, where service integration offers a solution, it should be given preference.

---

9 http://www.ksz-bcss.fgov.be/Nl/index.asp
10 http://www.corve.be/
11 http://easi.wallonie.be/xml/
12 https://www.ehealth.fgov.be/nl/homepage/index.html

Ideally, at least if justified by the volume and level of complexity, a service integrator should be designated (such as health, social security, justice or finance) within each government echelon and sector. In the sectors of the federal administration for which an individual service integrator is not justified – for example because the sector is too small – a federal government service for ICT (called FEDICT) takes over. FEDICT act as a service integrator for all government sectors that don't have their own service integrator. In addition, a service integrator exists in each of the three regions: Flanders, Wallonia and Brussels.

The sphere of activity and the tasks of each service integrator is laid down in a legal text. In this respect, a clear demarcation of the fields of application among service integrators is of the utmost importance. A vague demarcation of the sphere of activity of the different service integrators would lead to undesirable competition among service integrators in the public sector. Every service integrator further acts under the control of a Sector Committee of the Privacy Commission. This Sector Committee authorises service integration after testing it against the principles of the data protection legislation.

Experience with service integration has also demonstrated that every service integrator can best be managed by representatives of the various stakeholders in the relevant sector. In addition, the persons involved (patients, tax payers, etc.) must also be represented. This is important not only to enjoy the necessary trust, but also to guarantee a user-oriented operation. The service integrator may on no account detract from the responsibility and autonomy of the federal or regional government agencies themselves.

Explicit care is taken to ensure that each (federal) government agency only falls within the coordination of one service integrator. As a result, for each government agency, a coordination unit and the necessary link to only one electronic data exchange platform is ensured and a different approach to the same government agency by various service integrators is avoided. The various service integrators must ensure, in a consultation platform, the necessary mutual coordination and interoperability so that the various government agencies served by each of them can also use the electronic services of government agencies that are served by another service integrator. For example, in order to grant study allowances, the ministry of education will need a service from the service integrator of the public finance sector, in order to check the income of the applicant or his parents.

At the level of the ICT architecture, the cooperation model among the service integrators can be represented as follows:[13]

---

13 Key: FPS: Federal Public Service
ASS: Agency for Social Security (health insurance fund, employment agency, etc.)
RPS: Regional Public Service
VPN: Virtual Private Network

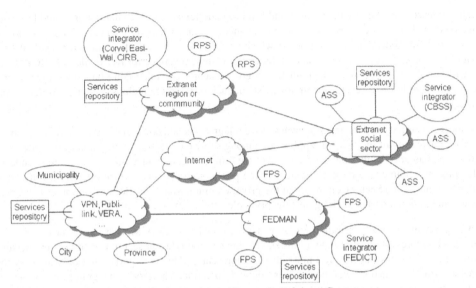

Fig. 1: Service integration architecture in Belgian e-Government

For each government echelon or sector, the relevant service integrator encourages cooperation at the aforementioned levels and coordinates the development of electronic services within its echelon or sector. The available electronic services are published in a services repository. These electronic services can be called upon by third parties and can be further used as building blocks for their own electronic service delivery.

Every service integrator manages a (virtual) network, and the various networks are linked. In this context, each service integrator acts as an independent trusted party, which does not itself fulfil any substantive tasks regarding data processing or storage and which ensures that the measures regarding information security and privacy protection are applied in practice within the government echelon or sector within which it operates and in the communication of personal data to other service integrators.

One important tool in service integration is the reference repertory. This repertory has a three-fold structure:

- who/where/how/when table (personal repertory): which people hold files in what capacities for which players regarding which periods?
- what/where table (data availability table): which types of personal data are available from which types of actor in the various types of file?
- who-gets-what table (access authorisation table): which personal data can which types of actor obtain regarding the various types of file and regarding which periods? Which personal data are automatically communicated regarding the various types of file and under what circumstances?

For example, the reference repertory of the service integrator in the health sector (the eHealth-Platform) will contain e.g. information on which physician or hospital contains which data with regard to a particular patient, identified by his/her Social Security Identification Number, and who has been granted which rights related to these data. The (medical) data themselves remain in the hands (computers) of the physicians and hospitals involved.

The reference repertory is in particular necessary for routing information, preventive access control and automatic communication of changes. Most importantly it avoids large-scale central storage of personal data.

4.5 Sector Committees for Data Protection

Within the Privacy Commission a number of so-called "Sector Committees have been created.[14] These committees are composed on the one hand of representatives from the Privacy Commission itself and, on the other hand, of independent experts in the relevant fields (e.g. social security, health care, etc.). The members are appointed by the federal or regional Parliament.

The most important task of a Sector Committee is granting authorisations for the (electronic) exchange of personal data, apart from the cases where this is explicitly permitted by law. For example, imagine that a regional public transport company wishes to automatically check whether a person is officially registered as a person with a handicap by the relevant social security institution. In order to obtain these data via a service offered by the service integrator of the social security sector, the regional public transport company will need to apply for an authorisation of the competent Sector Committee. The Committee will examine the application e.g. from a proportionality and security point of view. The authorisation will often include recommendations on how to organise the data exchange in the most privacy-friendly way.

Other tasks include establishing the organisation and policies, providing opinions and recommendations and dealing with complaints regarding infringements. Finally, the Sector Committee also exercises preventive control over the lawfulness of the exchange of personal data by a service integrator.

The authorisations of the Sector Committees are public and are published on the web site of the Privacy Commission. Over the years they constitute a authoritative body of jurisprudence with regard to personal data protection in the domain of e-government.

5 Generic Policy Application Model

How are the building blocks described above actually used for user and access management in the Belgian e-Government context?

The authorisation to use a service is given by the provider of the service, if necessary subject to prior authorisation by the competent Sector Committee. For this purpose, the identity and attributes and/ or mandates of the user need to be checked. The authentication of the user's identity takes place – depending on the required security level – by means of the electronic identity card, a combination of user number, password and citizen token or a combination of user number and password. Next, verification of attributes and mandates is carried out via access to one or more validated authentic sources.

Conformity of a specific request for access with access authorisations (does the user, identified as a qualified physician, have access to this patient's file?) is preventively validated by the competent independent service integrator, for instance using the reference repertory. All accesses are electronically logged at the level of the user so that, in the event of complaints, it is possible to check subsequently

---

14 The Law of 26 March 2003 introduced an Article 31bis into the Belgian law regarding the protection of privacy with respect to the processing of personal data, § 1 of which reads as follows, "Within the Commission, the law creates sector committees that are competent to examine and to assess requests relating to the processing or communication of data to which special legislation applies, within the confines established by the law".

whether access was legitimate (only who/what/when, not content). Access to the log files is strictly protected.

This is all developed using a generic policy application model that is summarised in the following diagram:

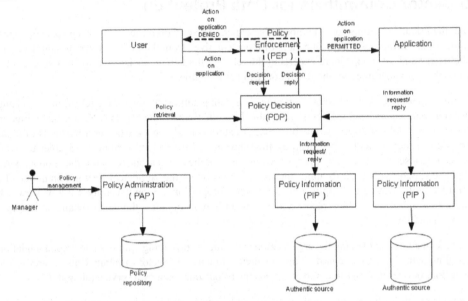

Fig. 2: Generic Policy Application Model

- The process begins with an authorisation request (application action) on behalf of a user. This request reaches the Policy Enforcement Point (PEP), together with all the available information about the user, the requested action, the resources and the environment. Following initial validation, the authorisation request is then forwarded to the Policy Decision Point (PDP) to obtain an authorisation decision (decision request). Based on the response (decision response), access is granted to the application, with forwarding of relevant credentials (application action permitted) or this access is denied (application action denied).

- Based on the authorisation request received, the appropriate authorisation policy is looked up in the Policy Administration Point(s) (PAP). This policy is evaluated and, if necessary, the relevant information for it is retrieved from the policy information point (PIP). Depending on the result, an authorisation decision (permit/deny/not applicable) is taken and forwarded to the PEP.

- The "Policy Administration Point"(PAP) is the environment for storing and managing the authorisation policies by the competent person(s) designated by the party who is responsible for the application. This information is stored in a "policy repository". The PAP ensures that the authorisation policies are made available to the PDP for making a policy decision.

- The function of the PIP (Policy Information Point) is to make information available to the PDP for evaluating the authorisation policies. The information comes from authentic sources with information about qualities, mandates, etc.

6 Conclusion and European Outlook

As in all other Member States of the European Union, user and access management in Belgium is conceived primarily on the basis of persons and entities that are registered in Belgium, whether as Belgians or as foreigners with residence in Belgium. Of course, for persons and entities wishing to use electronic government services for the first time from other countries, user and access management is highly problematic. How can a building contractor in Poland electronically declare the employment of his employees on a Belgian building site using the Belgian social security portal? Or how can an Italian manufacturer of office furniture submit his tender on the Belgian portal for public procurement?[15]

Interoperability is the goal at European level between the systems that are used for user and access management in the Member States.[16] With a view to implementation of the Services Directive and, in particular, the obligation regarding the central electronic help desk which every Member State must provide for, this aspect is also very important.[17] For the time being, Belgium is working with pragmatic solutions. For identity registration, the data are provided by the foreign user. For applications with a lower risk of fraud, such as the declaration of employees to the social security administration, this method is acceptable for the time being.[18] For the future serious efforts are needed to enhance interoperability between the user and access management systems put in place by the European Member States.

---

15 https://enot.publicprocurement.be/home.do
16 See http://ec.europa.eu/idabc/en/document/6484/5644
17 For more details: Report on the State of Pan-European e-ID Initiatives (ENISA), 2008: http://www.enisa.europa.eu/doc/pdf/deliverables/enisa_eID_management.pdf
18 Example: the web site www.limosa.be where foreign employers who employ staff in Belgium can electronically fulfil the obligation to submit a prior declaration of employment to the Belgian social security administration.

PKI – Crawling Out of the Grave & Into the Arms of Government

Phil D'Angio[1] · Panos Vassilliadas[2] · Phaidon Kaklamanis[3]

[1]Director Of Business Development, VeriSign – EMEA
2nd Floor, Chancellors Road, London W6 9RU, U.K.
pdangio@verisign.com

[2]General Manager, ADACOM S.A.
p.vassilliadis@adacom.com

[3]e-Government Actions Supervisor – Greek Ministry of Interior
f.kaklamanis@ypesdda.gov.gr

Abstract

This paper will analyze the characteristics of successful PKI projects lead by Government organizations. The paper will examine a recent E-Government project based on PKI credentials as well as suggest the approach for Government PKI programs emphasize strong collaboration with non-government use cases. It also examines the characteristics of PKI projects that were not successful in the past, and their role in creating the industry analyst perception that PKI was dead.

1 PKI – Crawling out of the Grave and into the Arms of Government

In October of 2004 analysts from Gartner published a research note titled, "Time Is Running out to Prove the Value of Government PKI", and they were absolutely right to say this at the time. In the United States the Federal Bridge had all but died because it proved to be incredibly complex and expensive for Federal Agencies to participate. In Europe the verdict was very much out on what the future of electronic signatures would be, and practical use cases were few and far between. Other parts of the world had started looking at PKI, but they weren't ready to invest in the infrastructure. Identrus was unable to bring the banking community together in a PKI community, and this didn't help the overall welfare of the market either. Broadly speaking the combination of technical shortcomings and poorly developed business cases contributed to the failure of large scale adoption of PKI based credentials. As a result, PKI entered what could be described as a "dead zone" for a period of time.

So what has brought PKI crawling back to life....practical and cost effective programs that enhance citizen-to-government transactions, bridge trust between government and non-government interactions, and the basic need to provide strong security for a set of sensitive documents or transactions. Governments across the globe are evaluating their requirements to build trusted platforms in their identity card, passport, and e-government programs. In many cases PKI is identified as a stable, secure, and scalable technology that satisfies the security requirement for multiple projects. In some cases Governments

N. Pohlmann, H. Reimer, W. Schneider (Editors): Securing Electronic Business Processes, Vieweg (2009), 108-115

have made PKI a mandatory technology for identity cards or e-government applications due to security requirements. These are practical and well defined requirements that PKI responds well to.

This paper reviews how successful National PKI programs have evolved out of a number of projects, highlighting the practical use cases, identifiable return on investment, and the need to partner with industry. This will include a review of the successful implementation of a PKI capability for the Greek Ministry of Interior's E-Government program.

2 Case Study: Greek Ministry Of Interior Optimizes E-Government With PKI Credentials

VeriSign and Adacom have been partners for nearly 10 years now, providing security services to customers in the Greek and Balkan regions. When the Hellenic Ministry of Interior developed its E-Government plans it awarded to the VeriSign-Adacom team the implementation of its PKI infrastructure in order to be able to provide secure e-Government Services. Today, Hermes e-Gateway is a fully enabled PKI based identity, electronic signature, and encryption solution used across a series of applications that are critical to deliver hundreds of Government to Citizens e-Services.

2.1 The Problem:

Greek citizens were required to visit multiple offices, often long distances apart, in order to complete all transactions with public administration services. These transactions could range from submitting a simple request for a public document (e.g. a certificate on insurance time), to death certificate claims, even documents required for creating a new company. Private sector companies were also required to enter into cumbersome and labor intensive processes to conduct business with the public sector. The issue became an ideal target for Greece's E-Government initiative, and the Hermes team was formed. The primary goal of the project was to improve the level of service and reduce the cost of these transactions.

As the Hermes team evaluated its business requirements to quickly offer improved services electronically, the need for confidentiality, non-repudiation and integrity became more apparent, while the need for interoperability between heterogeneous systems of agencies of the public sector was more than critical for the success of the project.

From a security perspective, the requirements of electronic transactions were also extremely demanding, especially for the authentication of the Hermes portal users. These requirements were a mixture of existing Greek and EU legal framework, technical dependencies, best practices, and different technical, legal and organization needs and they had to be met in a unified and interoperable way, in order for all agencies to be able to use the Hermes portal as a point of service for the citizens.

2.2 The Solution:

VeriSign and Adacom provide the PKI Root for E-Government in Greece, and also manage the implementation of PKI credentials for five other ministries within the E-Government framework. The Hermes team leveraged this existing experience to implement a customized infrastructure for their program; one that achieves scalability and compliance with the current Government PKI hierarchy. The implementation consists of the VeriSign Certificate Lifecycle Platform (CLP), integrated with a Card Management System, ORACLE Single Sign On, and a number of token solutions that enable citizens, businesses, and government users to optimize their interactions with the Hermes portal.

Through this infrastructure the Hellenic Ministry of Interior provides a central point of contact to all citizens and enterprises with regard to all their transactions with the Public Administration (natural or electronic), in a secure, friendly and interoperable manner. As part of the Hermes project, vast quantities of information were collected, organized and published, essential infrastructure was developed to support all services provided through the portal and secure mechanisms for the digital authentication of all citizens / enterprises were introduced.

Citizens and enterprises now have a central point of contact with the public administration, through which they can find information that a few years ago would not have access to and complete transactions which would normally take hours or days. Additionally, through the Hermes portal, agencies of the Public Administration can make available new services to the citizens, and have a single point of publishing information in a categorized and structured manner.

Throughout the design and development of the Hermes project, the issue of solving or taking care of existing or future interoperability problems was of great importance. As a result, alongside with the Hermes portal, the Greek e-Government Interoperability Framework was developed to be the guide to implementation of interoperable and secure electronic public services. The Greek e-Government Interoperability Framework contained specific and demanding requirements related explicitly to the organizational, procedural and technological aspect of digital authentication of citizens, enterprises and users, based on the information that each transaction contains. The Greek government's e-Gateway uses PKI and digital certificates to authenticate citizens and secure certain electronic transactions. By leveraging PKI functionality, offered by ADACOM, the Hermes Portal ensures that the security of the personal and sensitive data of citizens that are exchanged are protected, either by raising the security level of authentication procedures, or by encrypting and time stamping transactions.

Except from the technological perspective, Adacom team was called to design and implement workflows and procedures for the completion of the authentication and authorization processes. In the development of these workflows and procedures, Adacom team had to correlate all above mentioned organizational, legal and technical requirements, originated from laws, framework documents, security best practices and their experience, and try to develop and deploy the best matching solution to ensure both user friendliness of the offered service and operational security of the portal and the supported services.

After dealing with all challenges faced, the Hermes has gone live, supported by a robust and secure infrastructure, and a complete detailed set of easy to complete procedures, offering benefits to citizens, enterprises and agencies of the public administration.

3 National PKI: The Foundation of Trust in Government Programs

3.1 Introduction:

Governments around the world are gearing up to deliver the next generation of services to citizens. They want to accept digitally signed tax returns. Execute electronic transactions securely. Tighten border control. They want to do all this while maintaining the utmost security, streamlining administration, and containing operational costs. The challenge is significant. To provide such services, governments need robust and scalable technologies and policies to execute trusted transactions and establish trusted identities. And these technologies must be capable of being leveraged for identity-sensitive services provided by businesses and other non-governmental organizations, such as e-commerce and online banking.

Many governments have taken first steps toward implementing security technologies and policies. They've created digitally enhanced travel and identity documents, issued "smart" healthcare and tax ID cards, and implemented business authentication services. But governments have an obligation to move beyond implementing merely "adequate" protection mechanisms to deploying the strongest possible safeguards against transaction fraud, ID theft, duplication, and/or spoofing.

Strong credentials based on public key infrastructure (PKI) are the answer. By employing the right mix of authentication, encryption, and digital signatures, governments can significantly reduce the risk of forgery, theft, or abuse of identification credentials. This in turn allows them to secure their borders, protect and allocate public assets and resources, meet their fiduciary responsibilities, and boost overall citizen satisfaction.

Additionally, the trust that PKI engenders leads directly to significant cost savings. Because PKI enables them to immediately and definitively authenticate any person, organization, or device, governments can streamline processes and complete transactions in a fraction of the time and for a fraction of the cost of what it would take using other, less advanced, security mechanisms. PKI also opens up opportunities for joint efforts by governments and businesses to make citizens' lives more convenient, productive, and secure.

3.2 Why Governments Urgently Need PKI

Traditional identification credentials are neither robust enough to protect against modern fraud, nor can they enable the next generation of applications such as digitally signed tax returns, electronic tenders, and seamless border control. Instead, governments require the strong authentication, encryption, and digital signatures that are part of a comprehensive and scalable PKI platform.

PKI is the foundation on which governments can execute secure and trusted transactions. Whether between individuals and governments; businesses and governments; or intergovernment relationships, PKI allows public entities to securely authenticate all participants in a transaction. A combination of hardware, software, facilities, people, policies, and processes, PKI can be leveraged to create, manage, store, distribute, and revoke the digital certificates that lie at the heart of a trusted identity system.

PKI ensures the security and trustworthiness of transactions and identities in three ways: through authentication, encryption, and digital signatures.

- **Authentication.** Authentication is achieved by binding public and private keys to user identities through a certificate authority (CA). Each user identity issued by a CA is unique, ensuring that any credential issued that is based on PKI can be trusted to be reliable and credible.
- **Encryption.** Another way that PKI promotes trust is through encryption. The CA simultaneously creates public and private keys for an individual. The private key is kept private by that individual, and never shared with anyone or sent over the Internet. The public key is stored in a directory as part of a digital certificate. Anyone who wants to send a secure message uses the public key of the recipient to encrypt it. The recipient is the only one who can decrypt it, using his or her private key.
- **Digital signatures.** By far the biggest impact that PKI is expected to have in both public and private sectors is its ability to create and validate digital signatures to ensure the non-repudiation of transactions. A digital signature is created with an algorithm that combines an individual's private key with the electronic document that is being signed. Since only the person who owns

the private key can create the digital signature, that signature can be trusted. This can be verified by anyone possessing the public key for that individual.

3.3 PKI: The Path to a More Secure State

PKI has emerged as the trusted technology of choice for ensuring the trustworthiness of identity credentials in three key areas: e-government, national identity programs, and e-passport programs.

3.3.1 Facilitate the growth of e-government

E-government is the cornerstone of the next-generation of government. Citizens, businesses, and government agencies are already benefiting from their ability to access services and conduct transactions online. E-government programs allow government organizations to deliver services, distribute resources, and administer programs more efficiently, which drives operational costs down.

PKI plays a critical role in e-government by allowing governments to leverage authentication, encryption, and digital signature technologies when issuing identity certificates, business certificates, and device certificates.

The trust enabled by these certificates helps governments:

- **Streamline operations.** Day-to-day activities such as procurement, tax processing, and benefits administration are all executed much more efficiently.
- **Minimize the risk of fraud and waste.** This allows governments to protect public assets and conserve funds at a time when tax revenues are dropping precipitously around the globe.
- **Disseminate information more easily and securely.** By giving citizens convenient online access to such private information as tax and land records and other sensitive data that previously existed only in paper form, governments increase citizen satisfaction even as they reduce costs.
- **Partner with industry.** Whether issuing an identity credential in the form of a smart card, token, or other kind of "soft" certificate, governments must ensure that this credential can be leveraged in non-government applications. This is easily achieved by choosing the right partner and by building interoperability and scalability into the PKI program design.

3.3.2 Implement effective national ID programs

As part of a global trend toward issuing more secure identity documents, an increasingly large number of countries have started issuing national ID cards. These smart cards can be used to access healthcare services, verify employment, and complete online transactions. The countries of Belgium, Spain, and, most recently, Germany have already implemented highly successful national identification programs. Indeed, global shipment of smart cards surpassed an estimated five billion units in 2008..[1]

PKI provides a common framework for issuing verifiable identities through a natural trust hierarchy. These identities can then be used to electronically sign and encrypt documents for transactions such as filing taxes, redeeming benefits, or applying for jobs. By implementing national ID programs using PKI, governments can improve the security of the data stored on an ID card, and promote greater use of the card in non-government applications such as e-commerce, banking, and social networking.

---

1   "Smart Card Market Forecast to 2012," RNCOS, March 2009

National ID programs with PKI enable governments to:

- **More effectively allocate public resources.** As the costs associated with healthcare, pensions, and other public entitlements escalate, it has become critical to ensure that these resources are being distributed fairly and efficiently.

- **Secure virtual as well as physical facilities.** Ensuring that only authorized persons gain access to sensitive information and secure areas has never been more important.

- **Secure non-government relationships.** PKI credentials can be used to authenticate users who wish to access commercial online services or sign e-commerce transactions digitally. This makes PKI an invaluable element of any successful ID program.

- **Meet international compliance standards for data security and privacy.** Standards such as those established by the Euro Banking Association and International Standards Organization (ISO) as well as the myriad individual privacy acts passed by individual countries mandate strong authentication and data integrity.

- **Participate in interoperability programs.** Several projects have been launched by the European Union to promote standards and collaboration for interoperability in e-procurement, identity, and electronic signatures. PKI is the foundation for trust in all of these programs, including Secure IdenTity AcrOss BoRders LinKed (STORK), Pan-European Public Procurement Online (PEPPOL), and European Patient Smart Open Services (epSOS).

3.3.3 Administer secure e-passport programs

An e-passport is a combination paper and electronic document with an embedded chip that holds digital signature-confirmed data. A broad range of governments and industries – including the European Union (EU), Gulf Country Communities (GCC), and International Civil Aviation Authority (ICAO) – have collaborated to establish global standards that ensure travelers can quickly authenticate themselves as they move from country to country. E-passports are already being used by a growing list of countries, including the United States, Belgium, Austria, Australia, Norway, Spain, and the United Kingdom.

PKI is essential to e-passport programs, as it is used to create the digital certificates used by governments to digitally sign an e-passport at the time it is issued. Additionally, PKI is the foundation for the ICAO Public Key Directory (PKD), which facilitates a trust hierarchy that is leveraged to verify the authenticity of travel documents.

PKI-based e-passport programs allow governments to:

- **Streamline border crossings and customs processes.** Moving from one country to another is fraught with paperwork and delays. E-passports make these transitions easy and painless for citizens through standards created by ICAO.

- **Reduce the risk of forgery and fraud.** Traditional paper passports are notoriously easy to forge and/or steal and repackage. The digital signatures capability of PKI mitigates the risk of this type of activity being successfully implemented.

- **Maintain detailed information on citizens' movements in and out of the country.** Because this information can be sensitive – and subject to strict privacy laws – strong security mechanisms are needed to protect the rights of individual citizens.

- **Work with other governments on cross-border law enforcement initiatives.** Particularly after 9/11, governments have been attempting to collaborate more closely on anti-terrorist, anti-drug, and other law enforcement activities. E-passports enable more effective tracking of individuals traveling from one country to another.

4 What to Look for in a PKI Provider

The benefits of PKI are substantial. But implementing PKI is notoriously difficult due to the large number of components and the degree of integration required. The difference between success and failure lies in your partner selection. The right PKI platform from the right partner enables governments to:

- **Comply with standards.** Many international standards are very specific about the ways that PKI-based systems must implement certificate profiles and modify policies. They also require a deep understanding of complex hierarchies. As standards for PKI interoperability continue to evolve, it is important that a government's PKI partner supports technological advancements in a way that enables them to comply with these mandates.

- **Future-proof their investments in PKI.** If implemented correctly, a PKI platform is not just the foundation for building robust e-passports, national ID, or e-government programs. It also gives governments the ability to continue enhancing and expanding citizen services in the future. Rather than having to re-architect a completely new platform for new initiatives, a successful PKI deployment will set the stage for future successes.

- **Scale the platform as their needs grow.** Many national identification programs begin small, with pilot tests or for limited use such as drivers' license or healthcare programs. A PKI vendor must deliver a solution that enables governments to expand these programs without worrying about outgrowing their capacity or capabilities.

- **Integrate all identity programs onto a single PKI platform.** A successful PKI deployment establishes a single platform that can be used for all identity-related programs, including, but not limited to, national ID, e-passports, and e-government. This requires the use of open standards that make these programs interoperable with each other and with legacy systems.

- **Tap into a broad ecosystem of supporting technology vendors and integrators.** No one vendor can do it all. Open standards are a cornerstone of interoperability. In addition, your PKI partner should have strong relationships with other technology providers and integrators that enable seamless deployment of the plethora of technologies and services required to make a PKI implementation a success.

- **Support non-government organizations' PKI efforts.** A strong PKI partner for government programs will be able to co-develop services for commercial partners across a broad range of industries.

- **Minimize the costs of PKI deployment.** PKI is a complex technology. It takes highly experienced professionals dedicated to PKI deployments to implement successfully. Without such experience, implementations can take much longer than anticipated, resulting in significant cost overruns.

- **Implement policy, training, and knowledge transfer programs.** The policies and the trusted personnel that support PKI are as important as the technology. A PKI partner should have a strong background in developing PKI policies, an in-depth PKI training program, and an understanding of the importance of knowledge transfer for any PKI initiative to succeed.

5 Conclusion: Now is the Time for PKI

PKI implementations have reached critical mass. Today, all SSL servers use PKI; all Web browsers support PKI; in a number of countries, citizens can fill in tax returns using PKI certificates; countless commercial banks use PKI for online banking; and the scientific Grid community requires PKI. Today, thousands of organizations – in both the public and private sectors – depend upon PKI to ensure that identity-sensitive services are delivered in a safe and secure manner.

Most significantly, partnerships between government PKI-based programs and commercial entities mean that PKI investments can be leveraged across both public and commercial applications. With interoperability between national ID cards, commercial smart cards, e-passports, e-commerce trans-actions and other forms of identity-sensitive services, governments, industry, and individuals can all benefit equally from the world's accelerating adoption of PKI.

References

[GARTNER] Gartner Research Note, "Time's Running Out To Prove The Value Of Government PKI", 27 October, 2004

Entitlement Management: Ready to Enter the IdM Mainstream

Gerry Gebel · Alice Wang

Burton Group, Inc.
7090 Union Park Center Suite 200, Midvale, UT 84047 USA.
{ggebel | awang}@burtongroup.com

Abstract

Externalizing authorization processing from business applications has been a goal for architects and developers for many years. Recent compliance demands for more granular access control and policy transparency have increased the urgency to adopt an architectural model where authorization and entitlement management are consumed as a service rather than embedded within business applications. Major software vendors, such as Microsoft, Oracle, and SAP, are making significant steps to separate IdM functionality, including entitlement management from application logic. The market has also responded with a plethora of products that provide entitlement management and authorization functionality for commercial or custom-built application environments. Finally, the Extensible Access Control Markup Language (XACML) has emerged as the consensus authorization standard being supported by a growing number of IT and application vendors. Collectively, these forces form the basis of a nascent IdM market segment referred to as entitlement management.

This new entitlement management market continues to evolve over time as the industry's understanding of capabilities matures and enterprise requirements expand. In this paper we will discuss several dynamics currently at play, review the product landscape, cover recent standards advancements, and mention some issues that early adopters are addressing.

1 Overview

Seemingly overnight, the entitlement management market has expanded greatly from where it was just a couple of years ago. At one point, entitlement management was just the province of a few boutique vendors (i.e., Bayshore Networks, Securent [now Cisco], and Jericho Systems), CA's software development kit offering, or the neglected offering of a large platform provider (i.e., BEA). No more. The market is now awash in entitlement management products with offerings from across the identity management (IdM) vendor spectrum – at least 15 commercial and open source products are available, and more are on the way.

Consensus around Extensible Access Control Markup Language (XACML) has spared the entitlement management market from some of the agita endured by other technology areas, such as identity federation. XACML is the primary standard supported in entitlement management products, but other standards are likely to be part of a complete solution. Therefore, solutions will need to also support standards such as Web Services Security (WS-Security), WS-Trust, Security Assertion Markup Language (particularly the SAML 2.0 Profile for XACML 2.0), and Web Services Policy (WS-Policy) in addition to XACML. Despite the consensus, all is not perfect on the standards front. Among other issues, business application vendors remain slow to natively adopt XACML and a security architecture that externalizes authorization from business logic. In addition, there is no independent certification program for

N. Pohlmann, H. Reimer, W. Schneider (Editors): Securing Electronic Business Processes, Vieweg (2009), 116-124

XACML compliance and interoperability – although there have been multiple interoperability demonstrations at industry events.

When first introduced, entitlement management products were considered appropriate primarily for custom-built applications because source code was accessible to perform the necessary integration. Broader ranges of applications are now considered appropriate candidates because the technology has matured and attitudes have evolved. J2EE application platforms are also a prime candidate for integration with entitlement management systems because vendors have focused on building policy enforcement point (PEP) agents that handle authorization processing with little to no application changes. Web services style applications are also candidates for integration – consuming entitlement management functionality as a service for authorization. Finally, Microsoft SharePoint has emerged as a significant pull to spur demand for entitlement management products to protect SharePoint installations that have outgrown the application's native authorization capabilities.

In this report, Burton Group examines the current state of the entitlement management market through surveying available vendor products, the state of standards, business application trends, and emerging conventions for the use of this technology. This report also addresses unanswered questions that indicate where entitlement management technology must further mature to realize its full potential and accelerate adoption in the enterprise.

2 The Many Definitions of Entitlement Management

In talking with enterprises and vendors during research, Burton Group discovered many different understandings of the entitlement management term. This confusion has persisted in part because the marketplace and the business process both have the same name. Historically, this segment of the IdM market was referred to as "fine-grained authorization" because that was the focus of many early adopters. At this stage, fine-grained authorization is just one of a broader range of capabilities that current entitlement management products can offer. As such, entitlement management technologies and approaches resist a concise definition, but Burton Group uses the following definitions to distinguish between the business process and the market:

- Business Process: The process of (i) collection of information about individuals' job functions, authorities, and resource requirements, (ii) derivation of resource access entitlement information from that metadata, (iii) association of entitlement information to the appropriate people or roles, and (iv) periodic review of the association of entitlements to people or roles.
- Market: Products which implement fine-grained authorization using XACML (or proprietary interfaces) but do NOT implement the entitlement management business process.

3 Importance of Role Management

It became clear during research for this report that many enterprises are placing a premium on role management as it relates to an entitlement management deployment. Architects and others considering entitlement management products were not eager to launch into an implementation that perpetuates the excess complexity within existing application policy domains. Rather, these architects viewed a role abstraction layer as a valuable construct to rationalize the policy environment by bringing structure and organization to the view of system users as well as to the privileges and entitlements within the application. In the absence of roles, policy rules must replicate the intricacies of each application. With a role abstraction layer, it is expected that roles can compress the policy model and make it more manageable.

Of all the vendors in the entitlement management market, only Oracle and Sun Microsystems and CA have a role management product in their identity management suite portfolios. Discussions to date with these three vendors have not revealed concrete plans for how the two technologies can be joined to meet entitlement management market expectations. Of course the Sun product roadmap remains undetermined since Oracle announced an acquisition of Sun in April 2009. Given the lack of clarity in the industry, there is an opportunity, particularly for the smaller role management and entitlement management vendors to team up and address an important market requirement.

Role management continues to evolve as a concept with broad applicability and context. This technology has moved well beyond the confines of provisioning deployments and is viewed to be important for access certification, personalization, and now entitlement management. The outcome of a role discovery exercise is revealing in many other aspects as well. Organizations will have greater insight into relationships across the business areas with resulting impacts to areas such as human resources (HR) integration and business-continuity planning.

4 Policy Modeling Considerations

Industry conventions for policy modeling, and other aspects of entitlement management, are relatively sparse at this time. Deploying this technology still requires a heavy dose of engineering acumen, and it is not the intention of this report to clarify all unanswered questions – but to highlight areas where enterprise implementers need some additional assistance because of lack of best practices or common conventions. The previous section discussed the importance of role management in the overall policy-modeling context. Here, we explore the concept of applying policy rules at the data or application level. Proponents of data-level policies accentuate that security and business rules are enforced, regardless of what application consumes the data. In addition, data-level policies may reduce the number of policies under management – reducing complexity, cost, and overhead of the system. However, data-level policies may not address application-specific context, constraints, or obligations.

Application-level policies have the advantage of incorporating the additional context of the application that is presenting data to users or services. But administrators may have to deal with a multiplying effect on the number of policies managed, resulting in the burdens of extra cost and complexity. Ultimately, architects and developers must work through policy-modeling exercises with the input of business analysts, security specialists, and possibly others in order to develop a suitable outcome. Policy modeling and maintenance in today's frequently changing IT environments (e.g., agile SOA) is particularly costly and challenging. "Model-driven security" as a technology approach, as advocated by ObjectSecurity, tackles this policy management challenge by adding a policy management layer on top of entitlement management. Model-driven security can significantly simplify policy creation and maintenance. It can automatically generate and update policy enforcement rules when used alongside other model-driven software development/orchestration approaches such as Business Process Management (BPM), Model Driven Development (MDD), and Model Driven Integration (MDI).

5 Business or Security Decision

An extension to the policy-modeling exercise is the process of determining what decisions to extract from the business application. Under the surface, entitlement management products have rule engines that make decisions based on a policy and specific inputs. This equation works for security or business decisions – how do you tell them apart in your organization? For example, a security rule may state that updates to the general ledger system can only occur during normal business hours by authorized users from a secure network location. A business rule may state that currency traders can trade their normal limit until the firm's exposure reaches a certain threshold for a particular currency. Entitlement management systems can handle both instances, but an enterprise has to decide where to draw the line between security and business decisions. Once you begin to extract policy decisions from an application, you have to decide how far to go so that implementers in your organization have the guidelines to follow. In the absence of clear guidelines, there is the prospect of endless debates – and limited deployment progress.

6 Comments on XACML

XACML has emerged as the consensus choice to be the core standard for entitlement management products. It may not address every use case and detractors will find faults with the standard, but the vendor community is clearly behind XACML in the absence of better alternatives. Every vendor product reviewed in this report supports XACML, plus Microsoft and SAP have made public statements that they are evaluating the standard for potential inclusion in future products. XACML should not be considered the complete solution for all, or even most, entitlement scenarios because vendors incorporate other standards as well as proprietary capabilities to meet customer needs.

Interestingly enough, enterprise customers don't always rate policy standards as a high priority for their entitlement management deployments. Number one is the goal to remove authorization processing from applications and implement it in a shared infrastructure service. This may explain the fact that vendors and the Organization for the Advancement of Structured Information Standards (OASIS) have a laissez faire attitude toward formal XACML compliance and interoperability testing. There have been three informal interoperability demonstrations to date; the first one is summarized in the Identity and Privacy Strategies Methodologies and Best Practices (MBP) document "XACML Interoperability Demonstration." Burton Group expects enterprise customer attitudes to change over time as adoption of entitlement management technology increases, particularly in situations where PDPs and PEPs from multiple vendors may be deployed. Another contributing factor is that the entitlement management market now consists of approximately 15 vendors – many more than at any time in the recent past, making interoperability and XACML compliance a potential competitive differentiator. To balance expectations, achieving technical interoperability is one thing but realizing semantic interoperability is another matter. Therefore, enterprises should have realistic expectations for policy interoperability in business scenarios. Another caveat is that XACML as such helps solve policy interoperability, policy externalization and policy centralization, but does not automatically solve the significant policy manageability problem. Specifying complex policies for larger environments in XACML is a challenge, and model-driven security is being advocated by some as a potential part-solution to this problem.

7 Market Analysis

Although entitlement management products have been available for a few years, the market remains relatively immature as enterprise adoption has lagged behind other IdM technologies such as user provisioning, web access management, federation, and stronger authentication. That said, the past year has been very active on the supply, or vendor, side of the equation. When Burton Group first published a report on entitlement management in 2006, enterprise customers could choose from among BEA (acquired by Oracle in 2008), CA, Bayshore Networks, Jericho Systems, and Securent (acquired by Cisco in 2007). Now, the market participants also include Axiomatics, BiTKOO, IBM, NextLabs, ObjectSecurity, OpenIAM, Rohati Systems, RSA, Siemens, and Symlabs. Products from Novell, SAP, and Sun are also currently under development. The notable exception to this list is, of course, Microsoft, which has announced a new access platform called Geneva that doesn't contain anything that looks like an entitlement management service.

Microsoft's lack of an entitlement management vision certainly stands in stark contrast to the long list of IdM vendors that have committed to this space – including business application vendors Oracle and SAP. To date, Microsoft has not revealed specific plans for the entitlement management market except to say it is evaluating standards such as XACML and that its claims-based security model lays the foundation for future entitlement management capabilities. In the meantime, Microsoft is suddenly way behind the curve once again, leaving its customers to come up with alternative solutions from third-party providers – particularly for securing complex SharePoint environments.

7.1 Market Drivers

According to discussions with enterprises and vendors, the demand for entitlement management technology is spurred primarily by two motivating factors: compliance and security or business agility. Other issues also come into play, including externalizing authorization from business applications and fostering secure collaboration with partners.

In the compliance and security realm, entitlement management products implement access controls at a level of granularity far more specific than the application- or URL-level authorization that is possible with products such as web access management systems. Auditor demands and compliance requirements mean that more specific controls must be implemented for discrete functions within regulated applications to ensure that critical functions are properly secured – or that toxic combinations of access that result in separation of duty violations are eliminated. Additionally, entitlement management systems assist in the audit and certification of business applications by providing a central audit log for access activity and a shared policy enforcement apparatus that is a more visible authorization mechanism than is possible when security processing is concealed within application logic. This supports the trend that organizations are now not only looking at what users have access to, but also what they are doing with those access rights.

When considering business agility, entitlement management products assist in several instances. The first is during the application-development phase by offering a reusable service that multiple applications can integrate with. The historical approach is for developers to incorporate security decisions into their application logic. However, developer bandwidth and productivity are negatively impacted, developers may not have the expertise to perform security coding, and authorization is more difficult to manage across multiple applications when each application has its own embedded policy model and authorization process. One financial institution estimated that nearly 30% of its application development budget was consumed by building and maintaining code that should be instantiated within shared infrastructure services. Every enterprise won't experience the same level of redundancy, but suffice it to say that development time can be shortened by implementing shared services such as entitlement management, which will enable development teams to bring new products and services to market faster.

Once applications are built and implemented, policies must change from time to time in response to business changes or modifications to regulations. In this case, it is much faster to change policies that are managed in a shared service than to open up the application source code, change the code, perform quality assurance testing, pre-production testing, and production implementation – a process that could take weeks in most large enterprises.

7.2 Demand for Entitlement Management on the Rise

Burton Group sees demand for entitlement management growing steadily, based primarily on the market drivers discussed in the previous section. However, rapid adoption is not happening, nor is it expected in the near term for various reasons. Chief among them is the inherent complexity of the authorization problem – plus the fact that most applications do not support authorization standards or the clean architectural separation of authorization from the application. We referred to this as a "stateless" identity model for applications on the Burton Group identity blog. Instead, enterprises are left with the messy and intricately complex work of re-engineering custom applications to utilize entitlement management products or implementing vendor-developed PEPs to intercept access requests to legacy, ERP, or other commercial business applications.

Demand for entitlement management will increase over time as more field experience with products produces industry conventions for application integration, implementation, policy modeling, and so on. The real tipping point, however, occurs when major business application vendors extract authorization processing from applications via industry standards. Early signs of this tendency toward authorization standards have been sighted. IBM included support for XACML in their WebSphere middleware before introducing Tivoli Security Policy Manager. Oracle continues to build its IdM middleware stack, which now contains an XACML-based service, and has stated that business applications will leverage this capability over time. Oracle was also instrumental in the creation of the identity governance framework and building an authorization API specification to supplement what is already defined in XACML. SAP released a version of Business by Design in September 2007 that utilized a new role-based access management (RBAM) service that extracted authorization from the application. As a next step, SAP plans to extend the RBAM service into a more complete entitlement management system that will be part of the NetWeaver IdM platform released in late 2009 – though at the time of this report's publication, SAP had only confirmed that it is evaluating XACML for the new platform service. In addition, Microsoft's Geneva announcement details how applications can be developed using a claims-based model that externalizes authentication and attribute management from applications. Many enterprise customers have called for these progressive steps in the past, but they must remain patient because complex applications take a long time to re-architect and re-engineer. Also, application-development teams at major software vendors have to buy into the XACML-based authorization model – just like the application developers in your shops. Furthermore, many vendors and enterprise customers find limitations in XACML that will slow its adoption. Therefore, Burton Group doesn't expect Oracle or SAP business applications to natively support XACML interfaces for another two to three years because of the long development lead times and release schedules.

7.3 Accelerated Market Consolidation Expected

Although demand for entitlement management is growing, it may not be fast enough to support vendors through an expected tight IT budget cycles through 2010. There just does not appear to be enough buying customers to suport so many vendors in this market. Fifteen plus vendors were never viable anyway, so the tough economic environment is expected to accelerate the typical market consolidation cycle. Some vendors may go out of business and larger vendors seeking to solidify their offerings will acquire others. Examples of possible outcomes include the possibility that SAP will acquire a startup vendor to enter the market faster than possible via internal development and Microsoft may choose to make an acquisition to fill an obvious authorization hole in its IdM strategy. As an alternative, Microsoft could build on the claims-based model to expand into the entitlements management market. In another possible move, CA could choose to make an acquisition to bolster its EEM product, since EEM functionality as a stand-alone entity is now far behind other products on the market. In the meantime, CA is moving forward with plans to enhance its SiteMinder product by integrating EEM's functionality into SiteMinder.

7.4 Early Market Leaders

Current market demand has resulted in approximately 250 customers among all the vendors reporting this market, with a subset of that total in production implementations. Most customers have deployed entitlement management for a small number of custom-built applications or for J2EE applications and a growing number are addressing SharePoint access-control limitations. Few enterprises are considering company-wide implementations because of the cost and risk of opening up existing applications. Adopters of entitlement management generally apply the technology to new applications, applications that are in the development shop for major renovations, or applications that have commercially available PEPs – such as SharePoint. The early lead in market share goes to Cisco and Oracle, but the ultimate winner in this market is far from permanently established. Table 1 illustrates which application types entitlement management vendors are currently focusing on. Accordingly, customer growth will result mostly from demand to secure custom and web services applications, portal-based applications, and SharePoint.

Table 1: Vendor Focus for Entitlement Management

Vendor	Custom/web services apps	Portal apps	SharePoint	Network access	Database access
Axiomatics	X	X			
Bayshore Networks		X	X	X	
BiTKOO	X	X	X		X
CA	X	X			
Cisco	X	X	X	X	X
IBM	X	X	X		X
Jericho Systems	X	X	X		
NextLabs	X	X	X		
ObjectSecurity	X	X			X
Oracle	X	X	X		X
OpenIAM	X	X			
RSA	X	X	X		
Rohati	X	X	X	X	
Siemens	X	X			

8 Recommendations

As the entitlement management market grows more mature, there are certain items to consider when contemplating an investment in this technology. The following are topics that enterprise customers should investigate.

8.1 Application Selection

The current maturity of the technology in the entitlement management market has grown tremendously in the past 12 to 18 months. Choosing a viable phased approach in implementing an entitlement management component requires careful thought and analysis as to the business issues that a customer is truly attempting to solve. This analysis will in turn allow the customer to determine what applications should externalize fine-grained authorization and utilize an entitlement management service. From service oriented architecture (SOA) or custom-built applications to commercial off-the-shelf (COTS) applications such as SharePoint, choosing which applications to secure is just as important as choosing the mechanism for how to secure it.

8.2 Pressure Application Vendors to Support Standards

The popularity and viability of any standard boils down to the support and adoption of that standard. As with economics, it is all about supply and demand. Burton Group has observed an influx of suite and boutique vendors putting a stake into this market as well as customers clamouring for the ability to support externalizing fine-grained authorization of their resources via a service. The dilemma that customers are facing today is that even though they have voiced a need for the capabilities provided by this technology space, commercial application vendors are still lagging behind in architecting their COTS applications to support this. In order to balance out the supply and demand, Burton Group feels that customers should take into consideration which vendors support the standards prevalent in the entitlement management market and to encourage application vendors to support those same standards. Customer demand for externalizing the authorization component of an application will place added pressure for application vendors to re-architect their COTS applications, which in turn will allow the entitlement management vendors to provide additional capabilities. This dilemma is cyclical in nature, but only then will the entitlement management market truly take off.

8.3 Beware of Performance Issues

With the advent of multiple form factors to support the deployment of an entitlement management solution, performance has become an important factor in the overall picture. From policy management to policy enforcement to configuration of performance sensitive applications, the question of how a vendor's entitlement management component will perform in a production environment is difficult to predict. Burton Group recommends that customers be cognizant of the fact that performance-related issues are still very much at the forefront of each entitlement management deployment and to do their due diligence when it comes to product selection. Even if the entitlement management component is functionally capable, it still needs to scale and handle the hundreds of thousands of potential policy enforcement, determination, and administration transactions within the production environment, both offline and online. To not take this into consideration would be a detriment to an organization as a whole.

Once Oracle and SAP fully embrace (if they do) entitlement management model, it will be a huge signal to other independent software vendors and application developers. At that point, one could expect to see broader adoption of and native support for entitlement management systems.

Microsoft is also well positioned to have a huge impact on the entitlement management market. Although this report has been critical of Microsoft, the Geneva claims-based model gives Microsoft a path to be very influential in the entitlement management market as well as providing clear guidance to its vast developer community on how to build applications that externalize security functionality.

9 Conclusion

Externalizing authorization processing from business applications has been a goal for architects and developers for many years. Recent compliance demands for more granular access control and policy transparency have increased urgency to adopt an architectural model where authorization and entitlement management are consumed as a service rather than embedded within business applications. The market has responded with more than 15 products available by the end of 2009, with Microsoft the notable bystander. Demand and adoption, however, have not kept pace, which causes immediate pressure for consolidation. Enterprises with needs in this area should proceed cautiously as many products have limited field-testing.

References

Gerry Gebel and Alice Wang, "Entitlement Management: Ready to Enter the IdM Mainstream," 16 December, 2008, Burton Group Identity and Privacy Strategies Report, (www.burtongroup.com)

Gerry Gebel, "XACML Interoperability Demonstration," 3 December 2007, Burton Group Identity and Privacy Strategies Report, (www.burtongroup.com)

Secure E-Mail Communication across Company Boundaries Experiences and Architectures

Markus Wichmann[1] · Guido von der Heidt[1] · Carsten Hille[1]
Gunnar Jacobson[2]

[1]Siemens AG, Corporate Information Technology
{markus.wichmann | guido.von_der_heidt | carsten.hille}@siemens.com

[2]Secardeo GmbH
gunnar.jacobson@secardeo.com

Abstract

The important role of e-mail in business communication demands a protection of the transmitted information, not only within one company, but in particular across company borders. E-mail encryption using digital certificates provides means to fulfill this demand. The article discusses the obstacles organizations are faced with during the set up and operation of e-mail encryption between companies. Based on the case study of Siemens, experiences made as well as organizational and infrastructural solutions are outlined.

1 Introduction

Today, the communication between organizations takes place to a large extent electronically in which e-mail covers a main part of the correspondence and business processes.

E-mails are used to communicate all kind of information including highly confidential information while the standard e-mail itself does not offer any protection against espionage, fraud and disclosure of company-owned information when sent via public networks, as this will be the case for inter-organizational communication.

To counter this risk, to be compliant with legal regulations, e.g. data protection, and to meet internal security policies, confidentiality and data integrity can be ensured with encryption and digital signing of e-mails. Despite an increasing demand can be observed for such solutions, we still notice a limited knowledge on the topic and practical implementation issues.

This paper discusses the general problems organizations are facing to exchange encrypted e-mails and outlines how these issues can be met by an appropriate IT security infrastructure. The focus lies on the S/MIME e-mail encryption standard.

The article is based on the case study of Siemens and the experiences made when setting up e-mail encryption with business partners. It will give an insight on the respective infrastructure at Siemens.

N. Pohlmann, H. Reimer, W. Schneider (Editors): Securing Electronic Business Processes, Vieweg (2009), 125-136

2 The Way to encrypted E-Mail Communication

Using the S/MIME e-mail encryption standard, the interoperability between different e-mail clients and infrastructures, which used to be troublesome still some years ago, turned out to be not a major problem any more and its integration became a widely available standard functionality.

But despite this positive development, establishing encryption capabilities between business partners needs to be well prepared, implemented and introduced.

The following questions are describing the main obstacles and will be further discussed in the subsequent paragraphs of this article:

1. How can we ensure sufficient know-how at all partners?
   To establish encrypted communication and to ensure its operability, it turned out to be necessary to define "caretakers" who keep the contact between the different partners and who can support the users in case of problems. As most communication partners will not be IT personnel, this role is very important for the acceptance of e-mail encryption.

2. Are digital certificates available to both communication partners?
   Still, many organizations either do not have their own Public Key Infrastructure (PKI) or did not equip all of their employees with digital certificates. Thus, prior to any encrypted communication, it must be ensured that all communication partners do have PKI certificates in place. If needed, certificates must be issued and installed aligned with the corresponding IT infrastructure.

3. How do we establish „Trust" between PKIs and can we do so?
   As Trust is the start point on which the later encrypted communication is based on, PKI policy mapping as well as acceptance and secure exchange of Root certificates must be carefully organized.

4. How can we access each other's certificates and validate them?
   For the set up and the daily operation of encryption between organizations, this is the most crucial question. As the exchange of single user certificates is fast and easy when very few people are exchanging encrypted e-mails, it becomes very quickly unpractical and very different to manage when larger and changing numbers of communication partners are involved. Thus, to keep a high standard in usability, automated access to user certificates must be supported by the IT infrastructure. Furthermore, to ensure a correct validation of certificates, the corresponding certificate revocation status checking mechanisms must be supported in an organization's infrastructure.

3 Implementing Encryption across Companies

3.1 Provision of Knowledge and Support

It turned out that end users do not have the knowledge to set up e-mail encryption with their partners outside of the own organization. Especially when larger groups need to communicate encrypted, further support is needed.

To achieve and keep a high acceptance for e-mail encryption, it is essential that a company ensures the distribution of the necessary knowledge and provides support to the affected users and also to their partners.

The information to the users should describe the own infrastructure regarding e-mail encryption. In general, users do need to know which processes they have to follow, to which persons they need to speak and which technical possibilities their own company offers. They also need to know which steps they have to perform on their own clients, e.g. how to access their partners' certificates.

Unfortunately, many partner organizations do lack own expertise in this field. Therefore, it is helpful to provide also descriptions for the partners and offer complementary information as to the internal users.

Often experienced "caretakers" are needed to organize the collaboration with the external partner and to manage the issues described in the subsequent paragraphs. This aspect can be described as "taking by one's hand", often time consuming but quite crucial to ensure the successful set up and the ongoing operation.

Without the caretakers, problems between internal and external users might be very difficult to solve for a normal helpdesk which does only have knowledge about one infrastructure and was not involved during the set up between the partners.

3.2 Availability of Certificates

Preferably, the communication partner has access to an own PKI within his organization respectively there is a process in place how to get certificates. In that case no additional efforts need to be taken for certificate issuing, but the processes already in place can be used.

Unfortunately and despite their already broad use, digital certificates are yet not common to every user, as encryption and PKI is not common in every company.

If this is the case, certificates need to be issued to the users on the partner's side.

One possibility is to procure these certificates at a public Trust Center. The partner might be advised at which Trust Center to procure the certificates, depending on the own business relations or on technical circumstances, e.g. availability within the own infrastructure.

Another possibility is to issue certificates from the own PKI to the partner's users. Usually, such business partner certificates contain different information in their properties, clearly identifying the owner of the certificate as business partner. Also, the certificates might be issued from a different certification authority as certificates for the own employees. In general, the advantage of this way would be the direct integration of these certificates into the own IT infrastructure, such as certificate directories.

3.3 Establishing Trust

Establishing "Trust" between the PKIs of different organizations means
  • mutual acceptance of the policies and practices for operating the PKIs and
  • ensuring certificate validation across different IT infrastructures.

Depending on the business use reliance on digital certificates from an external PKI requires a proper assessment of the processes for issuing and managing the certificates including secure registration of PKI users and secure operations of the PKI system. Not only the acceptance of digital signatures but also the use of certificates for exchanging sensitive information (via encrypted e-mail) requires an appropriate security level of the business partner's PKI.

Certificate Policies (CP) and Certificate Practice Statements (CPS) build the basis of a PKI. In order to determine the security and trust level of a PKI an assessment of the CP and/or CPS is needed. Although RFC 3647 [IETF03] is a widely adopted standard for writing a CP or CPS, policy assessment and policy mapping are complex processes requiring deep expertise.

Ensuring certificate validation across different IT infrastructures is based on a reliable distribution of the Root CA certificates. While the root certificates of most public Trust Centers are preconfigured in current web browsers and operating systems the root certificates of private PKIs are not instantly available. Furthermore, for encryption purposes the respective intermediate Issuing CA certificates of the partner PKIs must be also available to validate end-entity certificates.

In order to manage trust relationships different trust models and trust communities exist. The main common trust models are compared below:

- Bilateral trust
- "Brigde CA" model
- Hierarchical PKIs

3.3.1 Bilateral Trust

Bilateral trust means establishing individual trust between two organizations, i.e. assessment of policies, (manual) secure exchange of the root certificates and distribution of Root CA and intermediate Issuing CA certificates on client and server systems in both IT infrastructures.

Managing bilateral trust relationships becomes quickly unwieldy with the number of partners involved and bears the risk that policy mapping is not properly processed. However, bilateral trust is a viable option for local business processes and smaller partners where a global trust on corporate level is not suitable. This process should be supported by experienced caretakers as discussed in 3.1.

Alternatively to exchanging and distributing the root certificates cross-certification of both root certificates is possible, see 3.3.2. However, for one-to-one trust relationships we do not see an advantage due to complexity of cross-certification and potential certificate chain validation problems.

3.3.2 Bridge CA Model

A Bridge CA is a trust community where the bridge acts as a trust hub and central point for the interaction of the member organizations. Each member organization enters into a trust relationship with the Bridge CA and thus, an indirect trust is established between all member PKIs.

The Bridge CA defines policy requirements the member PKIs have to comply with and performs the mapping between the member policies and the central Bridge CA policy. In this way the members can rely on a defined security level and do not have to deal with individual policy mappings.

In order to establish the (technical) recognition of the root certificates there are two main approaches by

- managing "Certificate Trust Lists" or
- cross-certification of the member CAs with the Bridge CA.

A Certificate Trust List (CTL) is a list with the root certificates of the member PKIs. It needs to be distributed within the IT infrastructures of the member organizations. The CTL is digitally signed by the Brigde CA and can be verified against the Bridge CA root which acts as trust anchor for this model. Thereby, the Bridge CA root and the member root certificate are exchanged securely during the registration of the member organization. Unfortunately, CTLs are not standardized and product-specific implementations have to be used.

In the cross-certification scenario each member CA is cross-certified with the Bridge CA, i.e. the Bridge CA certifies the public key of the member root and vice versa. Thus, all end-entity certificates chain up to each member root. The main disadvantage is that certificate chain validation becomes more complex since multiple validation paths are possible and have to be supported by the respective PKI applications.

Known examples of Bridge CA based trust communities are the US 4 Bridges Forum [4BF] and the European Bridge CA [EBCA]. The 4BF combines four leading US bridges and its member organizations, the US Federal Bridge CA / government, CertiPath / aerospace and defence industry, the SAFE-BioPharma Association and the Higher Education Bridge Certification Authority.

While the [4BF] is based on cross-certifications the European Bridge CA deploys Certificate Trust Lists. The European Bridge CA is a public-private-partnership integrating several governmental PKIs, enterprise PKIs and public Trust Centers. Besides trust management the European Bridge CA promotes secure e-mail communication by interoperability testing and certificate directory services.

3.3.3 Hierarchical PKI

In a hierarchical PKI system all member PKIs are either subordinated to a common Root CA or unilaterally cross-signed by the common root. Thereby, all members have to comply with the CP of the central Root CA similar to the Bridge CA model.

The hierarchical PKI simplifies the certificate validation since only the common root certificate needs to be trusted and to be deployed.

Main examples of hierarchical PKI systems arise from managed PKI and root-signing services offered by commercial PKI service providers such as the "VeriSign Trust Network" or the "OmniRoot" root-signing program. Since the root certificates are preconfigured in current web browsers and operating systems a separate distribution is not necessary. Furthermore, also partners who are not member of the hierarchical PKI system can easily rely on end-entity certificates from those PKIs.

However, commercial hierarchical PKI systems seem to be not suitable to act as policy authority across public and private PKI organizations and usually do not address the other interoperability issues for secure communication explained in this paper. Thus, we see a neutral bridge instance acting as a policy and interoperability authority combined with (commercial) root- and/or cross-signing services to simplify certificate validation as the right solution.

An example for such a trust community is the "Trans Global Secure Collaboration Program (TSCP)" [TSCP] which engenders a common framework for secure collaboration for the defence and aerospace industry.

3.4 Supporting Encryption by dedicated Infrastructure

In the following, a dedicated infrastructure supporting e-mail encryption across company borders is described. For similar reference architecture see the "Secure E-Mail Specification" of TSCP [TSCP08].

3.4.1 Sending encrypted email

E-mail encryption can be done end-to-end between mail user agents (UAs, email clients) or server-to server between mail transfer agents (MTAs, mail servers) or border-to-border on the transport layer. A variant of the server-to-server approach is the use of secure mail gateways (SMGW) at the network border of enterprises. Also mixed scenarios for end-to-gateway or gateway-to-end encryption are possible with email gateways. For end-to-end security, the complete message including attachments will be protected by encrypting the message with a symmetric content-encryption key at the client. The content-encryption key will be encrypted with the public keys of each of the recipients. In the case of a secure e-mail gateway, the message is transferred in plaintext between the gateway and internal clients. At a gateway sometimes one organization public key is used commonly for all internal e-mail users. Only the intended recipients (or gateways) may decrypt the content-encryption key and the message itself using their private keys. If the private key is kept at the mail client, the decrypted message will only temporarily exist when viewing the message on the client computer. If the private key is used for decryption at an e-mail gateway, the message will be transferred in plaintext from the gateway to the client. Encryption of e-mail messages is done using the S/MIME standard, which is supported by all major e-mail clients and secure e-mail gateways [RFC3851]. Using PGP as an alternative requires licensing of additional software. Alternatively, encryption on the transport layer between network boundaries may be done using SSL/TLS. This however, will neither support mixed scenarios like end-to-border or border-to-end encryption and requires remarkable efforts for the installation and management of static and inflexible connections. E-mail signatures are not supported with the SSL/TLS approach.

3.4.2 Retrieving Certificates using LDAP

When sending an encrypted e-mail, the sender's e-mail client will send an LDAP search request to the configured certificate directory and will encrypt the e-mail using the recipient's public key of the X.509 certificate that was retrieved from the certificate directory [X.509]. Almost every PKI today uses a directory service as a certificate repository for storing and retrieving certificates and Certificate Revocation Lists [RFC5280]. Standard applications like MS Outlook, Lotus Notes, Thunderbird or Adobe Acrobat search and retrieve these certificates using LDAP [RFC2251].

In a typical enterprise PKI, the issued certificates will be provided in a company internal certificate repository. Accessing an internal directory from an external client using LDAP will fail in most cases due to request blocking by firewalls. The same happens to access attempts from an internal client to an external directory. Encrypting an e-mail in the manner described above by an internal sender to an external recipient will be prevented by this. Thus, a solution is required, that enables LDAP searches for external certificates from internal clients and that provides internal certificates to external clients in a secure and reliable manner.

3.4.3 Publishing Certificates securely

If an organization wants to provide its certificates to the public, adequate security measures should be implemented for this. A directory containing names, e-mail addresses and telephone numbers etc. is an ideal target for address dealers, industry spies, headhunters or spammers. Even the structure or the Distinguished Name (DN) provides enough information for unexpected investigations by an attacker. A strict policy would require that the directory responds only to qualified searches where an exact e-mail address is given. And the response would only contain the certificate that belongs to that e-mail address. Identifiers, distinguished names or other structure information should be hidden.

One solution approach is the implementation of an "Inbound LDAP Proxy" that resides in the DMZ and which analyzes and forwards LDAP search requests to the internal directory and returns back the response to the external client. The proxy will only forward requests containing valid e-mail addresses from sources that are not on a "black list". The policy defines how many failed searches will be allowed in a time frame. The proxy will encrypt the DN, which will be used by the client for further protocol messages. Only the proxy may decrypt and use this DN. In an alternative approach, a dedicated external (border) certificate directory is used which is synchronized with the internal directory. This external directory will also be protected by the LDAP proxy.

As an alternative to LDAP, an HTTP service can be integrated which serves for manual requests that are submitted by a user in an HTML search dialog. This provides also an easy-to-use option for ad-hoc certificate retrieval without any prior clarification and configuration.

3.4.4 Searching for External Certificates

1. An e-mail client will search for certificates in the locally configured LDAP server. As mentioned before, external LDAP servers may not be connected in most cases. Therefore, the task of searching for external certificates is passed to an "Outbound LDAP Broker", which is configured as a default LDAP server on the client. The broker resides in the DMZ, receives search requests from the internal network and forwards them to the corresponding external repository. It returns received LDAP responses to the internal client. In a first step the certificate repository which will contain the certificate for a given e-mail address has to be localized. For this, several approaches exiRepository Lists:
    The addresses and access parameters of known repositories may be configured and managed manually by an administrator using repository lists.

2. Virtual Repositories:
    A centralized, virtual repository may be used, which forwards the received search requests to the connected real repositories. Such a virtual repository, like the European Bridge CA, provides access to the certificate repositories of their members.

3. PKIXREP:
    The localization may be done using the DNS-based Repository Locator Services. However, this approach has not been adopted in the PKI community and its flexibility is limited.

Fig. 1 shows an infrastructure as described before.

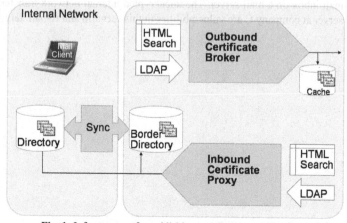

Fig. 1: Infrastructure for publishing and finding certificates

3.4.5 Retrieving Revocation Information

In order to validate the certificate chain, fresh revocation information has to be retrieved from the client. Clients like MS Windows will store revocation data in local caches until the validity period has passed. Today's standard applications will support the handling of Certificate Revocation Lists (CRLs) or the Online Certificate Status Protocol (OCSP). CRLs or OCSP messages are usually transferred using HTTP or LDAP. CRLs may be retrieved using the an LDAP proxy. For this, adequate IP routing rules have to be deployed in the network. Outbound HTTP messages for CRL download will usually be transferred via a HTTP proxy. In a Windows system, WinHTTP has to be configured to access HTTP and HTTPS servers through a proxy server.

3.4.6 A proven Architecture for PKI Interworking

In fig. 2 an architecture is shown that illustrates the discussed mechanisms: User Alice prepares an e-mail to be encrypted for her business partners bob@company-b.com and cathy@company-c.com. When pressing the „send" button, the following three steps are performed:

1. Certificate Retrieval: The LDAP search requests for the certificates of Bob and Cathy are passed to the corporate Outbound LDAP Broker, which is configured as the default LDAP search directory. The broker determines the LDAP repositories that are responsible for the given e-mail domains of Cathy and Bob. It forwards the search requests and returns the certificates of both (1b, 1c).

2. Certificate Validation: The client validates the certificate chain of each received user certificate. For this, explicit trust in the root certificates has to be configured previously, cf. 3.3. In a Windows client, this is done using the local root certificate store. The validity is typically determined through a CRL. If the required CRLs are not locally cached or if the cache is expired, the CRL will be downloaded from the URL that is given in the certificate's CRL distribution point. In the case of a HTTP CDP, the CRL is downloaded via the configured HTTP proxy (2b, 2c).

3. E-mail Encryption: The e-mail client encrypts the e-mail with a symmetric content-encryption key and encrypts the content-encryption key with the public keys from the retrieved and validated certificates. The e-mail is passed to the e-mail server and transferred to Bob's mail server and Cathy's secure mail gateway (SMGW) (3b, 3c). Bob receives the encrypted e-mail in his inbox and may decrypt it locally, e.g. by using his smart card. Cathy's e-mail is automatically decrypted on the SMGW, where her private key resides. The plaintext e-mail is then transferred to her e-mail inbox on a mail server. The unencrypted internal network transfer and storage on the mail server at company C are vulnerabilities in this scenario and remain targets for attackers.

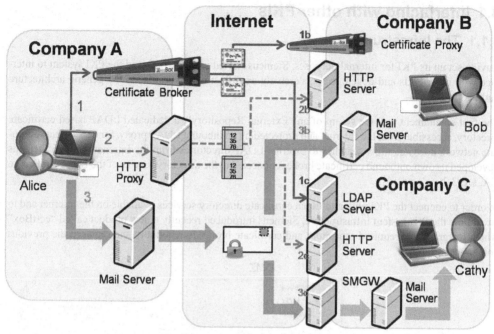

Fig. 2: Architecture for PKI interworking

4 Implementation at Siemens

As one of the first companies, Siemens has been developing successively and demand orientated a global corporate PKI, starting at the end of the 90s.

Today more than 320.000 employees and contractors worldwide are provisioned with digital certificates stored on smart cards by the central Siemens Trust Center. Additionally, digital certificates are provided for a number of various specific scenarios by the Siemens Trust Center, e.g. SSL server certificates, certificates for Windows Encrypting File System and Code Signing certificates. Many internal IT processes, such as HR-processes or electronic workflows given in Account Management or Quality- and Release Management, rely today on the functionalities of encryption and strong two-factor authentication provided by the Siemens PKI.

Business, legal and compliance requirements for a secure communication with partners require the opening up of the Siemens PKI by means of standard solutions. Besides the above discussed challenges to interfacing with other PKIs, Siemens had to address the need to equip individual business partners with digital certificates.

4.1 Interfacing with other PKIs

4.1.1 The Infrastructure

Having set up its PKI for internal purposes, Siemens started in 2004 to extend the PKI system to interface with other PKIs and developed successively an infrastructure similar to the generic architecture outlined in 3.4.

The first amendment was the set up of an "External Repository", a dedicated LDAP based certificate directory, accessible from the Internet and protected by an inbound LDAP proxy. Since Siemens' corporate network does not allow searches to external LDAP directories from the Intranet, in 2006 Siemens developed its own outbound certificate broker connected to the directory service of the European Bridge CA, s. 3.3.2

In order to connect the PKI with additional certificate directory services available on the Internet and to streamline the PKI system infrastructure, Siemens introduced recently a new product called "certBox" which integrates the required repository and certificate broker functionality and replaced the previous components, s. fig. 3.

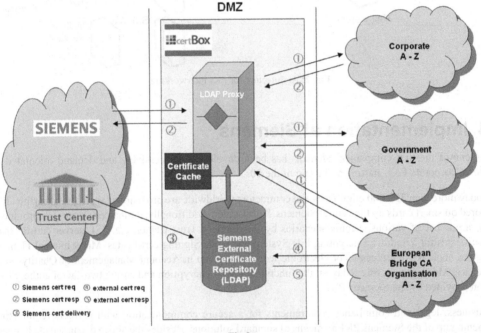

Fig 3:

The solution is based on a PKI appliance which provides the necessary outbound certificate broker functions for interconnecting the Siemens PKI with other certificate directories as well as the provision of the Siemens internal digital certificates for usage by external communication partners (i.e. inbound certificate proxy and border directory, as outlined in fig. 1). Additionally, the appliance provides Siemens with a web-interface for ad-hoc certificate retrieval.

To access the outbound broker the respective client configuration is currently being rolled out within Siemens.

One remaining infrastructural issue within Siemens is the validation of external CRLs. The standard mechanism for their verification is HTTP, however, Windows-based applications require configuration of WinHTTP and a separate proxy for Internet access, cf. 3.4.5. Siemens is currently evaluating solutions to provide this function.

4.1.2 Organizational Measures

Parallel with the initial rollout of the Siemens PKI, a network of experts was build up in the Siemens business units worldwide to support their users in all PKI aspects. This organization of so-called "PKI Coordinators" serves as knowledge multiplicator and as a pool of potential caretakers for their business units to address the issues of encryption with external business partners. Additionally, together with the PKI Coordinators instructions were developed for internal and external partners describing the options and possibilities to establish e-mail encryption between organizations. Besides addressing the topic to the PKI Coordinators, discussions took place with Siemens internal IT service providers to provide additional support for specific projects.

4.1.3 Trust

Complementing the technical infrastructure, Siemens takes organizational means to support the encryption with business partners. Being a member of the European Bridge CA since 2001, Siemens regularly distributes the CTL to its users, as the partner organizations do so. Siemens also connected its external certificate repository with the Bridge CA's repository. This enables business partner to access Siemens certificate also via the hub certificate repository of the Bridge CA.

Additionally, Siemens conducted bilateral agreements with other companies on different levels, from sole (local) root certificate exchange to dedicated contracts (on corporate level).

Supporting these actions, Siemens defined a set of Root and Issuing CA certificates to be considered as trustworthy and set up the technical means to distribute these certificates to the users' client systems. Unfortunately, it turned out to be technically complex to remove "unwanted" preconfigured certificates from the client systems.

4.2 Business Partner Integration

Based on the experience that in many cases companies do not have their own digital certificates in place and do not have the expertise and experience how to handle this issue, Siemens decided to develop a process to equip such business partners with certificates issued by the internal Siemens PKI.

These certificates are multipurpose soft certificates which are primarily intended to be used for secure e-mail encryption with Siemens. The challenge is to set up convenient processes connecting arbitrary business partners from outside the company with the internal PKI infrastructure and procedures.

5 Conclusion

Driven by the need for inter-company e-mail encryption, deficiencies in the interoperability of different platform regarding e-mail encryption were eliminated in the last years.

Today, several organizational and technical solutions do exist to facilitate e-mail encryption across company borders. Still, the knowledge how to do so and the availability of such solutions are yet not a common functionality, but their degree of implementation varies very much from company to company.

Very often e-mail encryption is not or only rudimentary available and additional support is required. Even if PKI is in place, many organizations do not publish their certificates on the Internet, complicating the certificate exchange with their business partners and preventing an automatic exchange.

With this article we would like to encourage other organizations to meet the demand for encrypted e-mail communication with partners, to create the knowledge, to join the trust communities and to set up the respective IT infrastructure.

References

[4BF]   Four Bridges Forum, http://www.the4bf.com.

[EBCA]   European Bridge-CA, https://www.bridge-ca.org.

[RFC2251] Internet Engineering Task Force: RFC2251, Lightweight Directory Access Protocol v3, 1997, http://www.ietf.org/rfc/rfc2251.txt.

[RFC3647] Internet Engineering Task Force: RFC3647, Internet X.509 Public Key Infrastructure Certificate Policy and Certification Practices Framework, 2003, http://www.ietf.org/rfc/rfc3647.txt.

[RFC3851] Internet Engineering Task Force: RFC2633, Secure/Multipurpose Internet Mail Extensions (S/MIME) v3.1, 2004, http://www.ietf.org/rfc/rfc3851.txt.

[RFC5280] Internet X.509 Public Key Infrastructure Certificate and Certificate Revocation List (CRL) Profile, 2008, http://www.ietf.org/rfc/rfc5280.txt

[TSCP]   Transglobal Secure Collaboration Program, http://tscp.org.

[TSCP08] Transglobal Secure Collaboration Program: Secure E-Mail Specification, 2008, http://tscp.org/pdfs/SecEmlTechSpecv2-1GR.pdf.

[X.509]   International Organization for Standardization: Information technology – Open Systems Interconnection – The Directory: Public-key and attribute certificate frameworks, ISO/IEC 9594-8, 200.

Voice Biometrics as a Way to Self-service Password Reset

Bernd Hohgräfe · Sebastian Jacobi

Siemens Enterprise Communications GmbH & Co. KG
SEN SER PS CNS IAM
{bernd.hohgraefe | sebastian.jacobi}@siemens-enterprise.com

Abstract

Password resets are time consuming. Especially when urgent jobs need to be done, it is cumbersome to inform the user helpdesk, to identify oneself and then to wait for response. It is easy to enter a wrong password multiple times, which leads to the blocking of the application. Voice biometrics is an easy and secure way for individuals to reset their own password. Read more about how you can ease the burden of your user helpdesk and how voice biometric password resets benefit your expense situation without harming your security.

1 Passwords and Related Problems

Today, passwords are both a blessing and a curse: They allow easy and secure access to almost all applications independent from special hardware. The consequence: The number of passwords, which employees use for private and job-related purposes, is constantly growing – so is the chance that users occasionally forget these passwords. Occasionally from a users' point of view, (too) frequently from a company's viewpoint, whose user helpdesk has to reset the passwords. For example users tend to forget their passwords more often when they needed to change it because of a password policy. This is also critical from the business perspective, when employees absolutely need to complete time-critical work as to comply with deadlines for tenders or offers. The service hours of the user helpdesks often only cover the regular working hours for financial reasons. The consequences for the business can be serious.

Nevertheless, costs for the business also arise during normal working hours: Depending on the scope of duties, the employee cannot be productive during this time; in addition to the costs arising from this, the business also faces the user helpdesk costs arising from the password reset itself. Yet equally important is the subjectively biased effort of the employees. Who has experienced the cumbersome procedure of password reset, will be tempted to choose easier passwords or to write them down in order to avoid this process in the future. This is shown in different surveys and studies like [SN05], [UN06] and [RS06].

Certainly, this leads to the question why companies use passwords for authentication at all. After all, there are numerous alternatives in the market today ranging from password synchronization over single sign-on and smartcard solutions to different biometric methods (cp. [AB07]). However, there are several reasons for using passwords for authentication, but only a few should be named here:

- On the one hand it is generally not possible to log on to all existing business applications with any of the above mentioned solutions. Many companies still use legacy applications, in which the authentication via user name and password is a fixed programmed component of the application and difficult to replace.

N. Pohlmann, H. Reimer, W. Schneider (Editors): Securing Electronic Business Processes, Vieweg (2009), 137-144

- Further, many smartcard and biometric based solutions require special hardware on the computer like smartcard readers or fingerprint sensors, which generate costs and are not always practical for notebooks.
- In addition the potential damage on single sign-on and password synchronization systems is higher in case the wrong people get hold of the central "master password", since the master password grants access to all computer applications.
- On the other hand these solutions do not function without a password or PIN, used as a master password or as fall-back solution in case of a defective scanner.

This shows that there is no way around passwords for a conceivable time, even if alternatives such as single sign-on systems for frequently used applications will be implemented. Even then passwords will retain their right as cost-effective alternative for remaining applications. Therefore, it is necessary to implement mechanisms and processes to reset forgotten passwords easily, quickly, cost-effectively and securely.

2 Today's Password Reset Methods

These days security is one of the most important aspects, because companies are bound to adopt adequate IT security measures, due to numerous regulations dictated by law (cp. [BD07]). The catchword "regulatory compliance" can be mentioned in this context. This includes that only entitled and appropriately authenticated users have access to IT resources. Therefore, the password reset method must be at least as secure as the most secure authentication system of any application in order to avoid weak spots. Otherwise an attacker could gain access to the application and its data through a password reset. Companies have to provide documentation of the compliance with these security measures within the scope of audits. Hence, solutions which are already certified by neutral institutions are better than others.

Users like their password resets to be quick, straightforward and independent from time and place. For this reason paper based solutions such as faxing the copy of the identity card to a helpdesk employee are not working, because a fax machine is not always available. Corporate web portals for password resets also have a serious disadvantage: They assume a working desktop PC. In case the user has forgotten the password for his Windows login and consequently has no access to his computer, a password reset is not possible. But using a colleagues' computer is not possible during lunch break, at night or at weekends either. A user who can log on to his computer but has forgotten the password for the remote access to the corporate web is also confronted with a problem. Again, a password reset portal is not of any help in this case. In addition challenge-response queries (e.g. the common question "what is your mother's birth name?") are not really secure. It is pretty easy for attackers to find the answers to almost all of these questions with the help of person search engines and maybe a little bit of social engineering as could be seen in the 2008 presidential election in the United States. Moreover, these questions are generally predetermined, which means that they are the least common denominator. Sending pieces of information about the new password to the user via email is also not secure.

Companies like the used methods to be quick and cost-effective. The costs involved include costs for the password reset process, which means costs for the needed infrastructure and licenses, the user helpdesk rate per case and possibly the user's time off. This is the reason why companies prefer automated solutions which decrease the helpdesk labor costs but still guarantee availability around the clock. This leads to the elimination of phone calls and faxes reaching the helpdesk, which have to be answered manually. Phones, on the other hand, are a pretty good medium for a password reset, just because phones are always available – even independent from computers. Furthermore, it is also a relatively secure communication channel, because the tapping of ISDN, GSM and UMTS telephone calls is rather complex.

Therefore, password reset methods based on automatic voice recognition over the telephone have achieved acceptance lately. The latest proceedings in digital signal processing, which have primary enabled a reliable voice recognition, have set the stage for this trend.

3 Biometric Speech and Voice Recognition

Though, biometric speech and voice recognition are two different methods, which can be differentiated as follows (cp. [SE08]): speech recognition has established itself in the market years ago and can be found in many every day applications. No matter if it is about the voice commands using a cell phone or using a navigation system, it is always about handling a system with the help of your voice. Only the content of the spoken words is important; it is not important how it is said assuming that the system "understands" the commands.

Voice recognition is rather new and works in a different way. Here it is more important how something is said than what is being said. This means that the voice recognizing system tries to find out – on the basis of certain characteristics – to whom a voice can be explicitly assigned. The content of what is being said is only a means to analyze the voice. The importance of the voice for the voice recognition is therefore exactly the same as the importance of the fingerprint for the fingerprint method – it is only a means to an end.

But how does the biometric voice recognition work? There are two main processes: The system becomes acquainted with the voice of a person through the "enrollment" process saving the generated "voiceprint" at a secure spot. During this process the voice biometric system extracts approximately 1.200 out of 2000.000 characteristics, which explicitly identify each voice.

Fig. 1: Individual voiceprint diagram of two different persons

Characteristic parameters of the voice are the size of the oral cavity, the throat, the nose and the mouth as well as the order of the muscles in the tongue, jaw, lips and palate, which is responsible for the articulation. Disguising one's voice, no matter if done intentionally or for example due to a cold, has no influence on the typical pattern of personal anatomy, way of speaking, wave-bands, energy levels and chronological structure.

The enrollment process works as follows: At first the user gets a link to a website, where he can log on with his user ID and password (for example Windows user name and password). The user obtains a PIN through this website for a limited time and is asked to call the stated telephone number. In fact, the real enrollment starts with this call: The user is asked to state his user ID and his PIN and afterwards has to repeat a few phrases. After a few minutes the user has introduced himself to the system and has created his personal voiceprint, which will be used for verification later on.

The process following enrollment is the verification. During this process, the user has to prove his identity with the help of the user ID and his voice in order to reset the password for the chosen IT system (such as Windows, SAP or others). After the user has stated his user ID, he will be asked to repeat a few words. In case the user is successfully verified, the system resets the relevant password and announces the new initial password. The whole verification process lasts less than a minute and can be carried out anywhere.

The human voice is unique with regard to its complexity and dynamic. This is also true for twins and voice imitators; even a voice imitator only speaks similarly. This allows voice biometric systems to identify a user clearly and reliably through the evaluation of numerous data points and parameters. The reliability of the method was proven through extensive, reproducible, TÜV-IT reviewed tests with more than a million verification calls. Significantly responsible for the reliability of the method is the combination of speech and voice recognition. A user only gets verified if he can tell who he is (speech recognition) and if he can then prove it through the repetition of given words (voice recognition). For this reason voice recognition is already used today when it comes to telephone banking and access control systems for buildings. In addition, access to confidential telephone conferences can be gained through voice recognition – access to other applications is only a matter of time.

The use of voice biometric systems is based on the use of telephones or cell phones. These devices are generally available and users are normally familiar with them. Furthermore, their use is independent of time and place. This makes voice biometric password reset cost-effective and much more flexible than traditional methods. The straightforwardness of the verification as well as the permanent availability of the system leads to a high acceptance on the part of the users increasing the security level of password resets significantly.

The high level of automation of the voice biometric password reset method leads to a significant cost advantage as a result of a noticeable reduction of user helpdesk utilization. This results from the fact that – according to analysts – 20 to 40 % of all helpdesk calls deal with password resets. The business case below shows as an example the resulting financial savings of a company per year; the costs of a password reset are purposely estimated low (13 €). Other sources assume costs up to 25 dollars and four resets per year instead of only two. The example also includes an overflow of 5 % of not identified callers. All mentioned figures are based on miscellaneous studies and analysis. More information can be found in [IS05], [IN02] and [IN03].

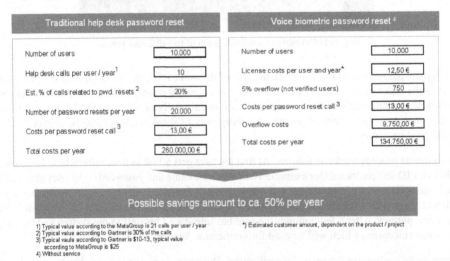

Fig. 2: Business case example

The costs of implementing the system (special hard and software components, consulting) and the operating costs (among others software licenses per user, support) are very moderate because of low infrastructure costs. This is the reason why a short amortization period can be expected. The amortization period generally depends on factors such as the size of the company and frequency of automatic password resets.

4 Biometric Password Reset

In principle, a voice biometric system can be implemented in different ways depending on the requirements. This chapter describes the most relevant implementation setups of [VT06] and [VT07] based on project experience. The figure below gives a simplified review of necessary components.

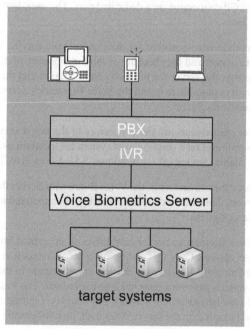

Fig. 3: Simplified system architecture

Absolutely necessary, but generally available in every company are devices for voice entry, which means telephones (fixed line network, VoIP) or cell phones as well as a telephone system (PBX) which assigns one or more telephone numbers to the Password Reset System.

The PBX is connected to the IVR (Interactive Voice Response) via ISDN or VoIP. The IVR and the voice recognition software are responsible for the acceptance and handling of the incoming calls. Here it is also possible to fall back on an already existing IVR provided that it works with the VXML 2.0 standard.

The Voice Biometrics Server, which is connected to the IVR via LAN, is the core component of the entire system. It is responsible for the whole operation of the password reset process and controls the voice dialogue and the authentication. The server includes the voice recognition module for the recognition of spoken words, the authentication module for the caller authentication through the comparison of a caller's voiceprint with stored voiceprints as well as the .NET application server and the Microsoft IIS web server for the creation and supply of VoiceXML data sets for the IVR. The Voice Biometrics Server communicates with the IVR via http respectively https providing the IVR with VoiceXML data sets for processing. The Voice Biometrics Server receives voice data in return, which it uses for the control of the voice dialogues and for the authentication. The parameters of the voice profiles of all users are stored in the file system of the server. The parameters are derived from the analysis of the users' enrollment words or phrases. These parameters are stored in coded form because of security and data protection reasons. The assignment of the parameters to the respective user is solely carried out through the user data base, which is assigned to the client. The recreation of the voice or the creation of a person's reference is not possible.

The user data base can be installed either on the Voice Biometrics Server or on an independent server and is addressed through a TCP connection on a dedicated port. The user data is normally imported via CSV file into the user data base.

A so-called Data Server module is responsible for the maintenance service including the creation of statistics, the daily user data import and the checking of the functionality of different components. Furthermore this module is used as the server for the web administration and the creation of the PINs for the PIN enrollments. Again, it is possible to install the Voice Biometrics Server both on an independent server and on the Voice Biometrics Server.

The last fundamental server components are the connectors to the target system. After all, these connectors carry out the password reset on a certain target system for a certain user. Currently a number of standard connectors are available (among others Windows, SAP, Lotus, RACF).

It is also possible to outsource the connectors of the Voice Biometrics Server through the use of optional Password Reset Proxy Servers. This architecture is especially recommended in case of multiple tenants that share one Password Reset System.

In this case, the central Voice Biometrics Server establishes an encrypted https connection to the relevant Password Reset Proxy Server. Only this one point to point connection on one port is necessary between both servers. The Password Reset Proxy Servers communicate in the client net with the individual target systems, on which a password reset shall be carried out. The Password Reset Proxy Servers are responsible for the translations on the network protocol level during the password reset. Work related data is not stored or recorded on the server. Moreover, no configuration data is stored.

Besides the possibility of outsourcing a few modules of the Voice Biometrics Server, it is also possible to connect a couple of Voice Biometrics Server in parallel. This is especially useful for the load sharing in case of high utilization of the system respectively high availability demands.

Before integrating the voice biometric Password Reset Service into the existing IT infrastructure, it is beneficial for companies to check which of the required components already exist within the business. Generally, devices for voice entries, a telephone system as well as several target systems are already in place. In addition, it is necessary to clarify the allocation of user data for the Password Reset Service through an existing business entity. Normally, the relevant user data will be extracted from the central Meta Directory, the Microsoft Active Directory or systems belonging to human resources (such as SAP HR). The recommended architecture for the construction of the service depends on the customer requirements. Important factors are the number of users, the level of system availability, the form and amount of the target system and the corporate structure (e.g. the corporate language, the number of different tenants, etc.).

A gradual implementation is advisable because of the relevance of the Password Reset Service for users. Therefore, a user acceptance test should be carried out before the company-wide rollout. This user acceptance test should be carried out for a defined period of time and for a small group of people. The company-wide rollout should only be continued after the successful completion of the test. On the other hand, it is also possible to install the service for a restricted amount of target systems. Suitable systems for this are systems like Microsoft Windows, which are used by many employees.

Special synergistic effects arise from the establishment of the Password Reset Service in combination with an Identity Management System. In general all important target systems are integrated in a complete Identity Management solution and therefore, it is reasonable not to integrate every target system additionally into a Password Reset Service. It is easier and more cost-effective to integrate the Identity Management System as the only target system into the Password Reset Service. After the password reset in the Identity Management System, the new password will be transferred into the respective target system via the relevant synchronization workflow. The figure below shows the described solution.

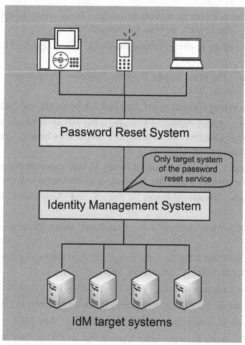

Fig. 4: System architecture in combination with an Identity Management (IdM) System

Many companies which use Identity Management Systems already have a password synchronization mechanism in place, so that there will be no further implementation costs. The Identity Management System is also beneficial for the allocation of user data, because it stores all relevant current data and can provide it in a very flexible way. As described, the Password Reset Service can be directly provisioned with user data from an Identity Management System.

5 Conclusion

While most of the other biometric methods presume extensive investments into the infrastructure (fingerprint scanner, iris scanner etc.), the voice biometric system is generally based on already existing hardware: telephones or cell phones. Users are familiar with these devices and their use is independent of time and place. This is what makes the voice biometric password reset comparatively cost-effective and flexible. Furthermore, the high level of maturity of this technology leads to a significant increase in the password reset security level.

References

[AB07]　Arslan Brömme, „Mehrerlei Maß – Leistungsfähigkeit biometrischer Personenerkennung", 2007

[BD07]　Bitcom / DIN, „Kompass der IT-Sicherheitsstandards – Leitfaden und Nachschlagewerk", Version 3.0, October 2007

[BR04]　Bundesamt für Sicherheit in der Informationstechnik, „Evaluierung biometrischer Systeme – Fingerabdrucktechnologien – BioFinger", Version 1.1, August 2004

[BR09]　Bundesamt für Sicherheit in der Informationstechnik, „Die Lage der IT-Sicherheit in Deutschland", 2009

[CS08]　Robert Richardson, „The latest results from the longest-running project of its kind", CSI Computer Crime & Security Survey, 2008

[IN01]　Wikipedia, "Self-service password reset", http://en.wikipedia.org/wiki/Self-service_password_reset

[IN02]　Belsoft IT Solutions, „Citrix Password Manager – Die effiziente Single-Sign-On Lösung für den Zugang zu passwortgeschützten Anwendungen", http://www.belsoft-security.ch/webseite/web.nsf/id/SEC_DE_CitrixPasswordManager

[IN03]　Psylock authentication, „Psylock Password Reset: Sichere Passwort-Neuvergabe im Self-Service Verfahren", http://www.psylock.com/index.php/lang-de/produkte/psylock-password-reset

[IN04]　Bromba Biometrics, „Bioidentifikation – Fragen und Antworten", http://www.bromba.com/faq/biofaqd.htm

[IS05]　IT-Sicherheit 5/2005, "Automatisiertes Passwort-Reset: Vattenfall reduziert Helpdesk-Kosten", October 2005

[RS06]　RSA Security, "Studie von RSA Security belegt: Zu viele Passwörter überfordern den Anwender und sind somit ein Sicherheitsrisiko", September 2006

[SE08]　Siemens Enterprise Communications, "Voice Biometrics – Trust Your Voice", 2008

[SN05]　SafeNet, „Weltweite Umfrage belegt mangelnde Passwortsicherheit in Unternehmen", 2005

[SS02]　Dirk Fox, „Editorial: Eine Schneise in die Informationsflut", July 2002

[UN06]　Shannon Riley, „Password Security: What Users Know and What They Actually Do",February 2006

[VT06]　VOICE.TRUST, "VOICE.TRUST Administration Guide", Release 5.2, 2006

[VT07]　VOICE.TRUST, "VOICE.TRUST Server – A Technical Description", 2007

[ZF06]　Bassen / Klein / Zöllner, „Ratingsysteme der Corporate Governance: Eine kritische Bestandsanalyse", zfo Wissen, 2006

Security Requirements Specification in Process-aware Information Systems

Michael Menzel · Ivonne Thomas · Benjamin Schüler
Maxim Schnjakin · Christoph Meinel

Hasso-Plattner-Institute
University of Potsdam
{michael.menzel | ivonne.thomas | benjamin.schueler |
maxim.schnjakin | meinel}@hpi.uni-potsdam.de

Abstract

Service-oriented Architectures deliver a flexible infrastructure to allow independently developed software components to communicate in a seamless manner. In the scope of organisational workflows, SOA provides a suitable foundation to execute business processes as an orchestration of multiple independent services. In order to secure services, requirements are usually defined on a technical level, rather than on an organisational level that would provide a comprehensive view on the participants, the assets and their relationships regarding security.

In this paper, we present a compilation of security requirements for Service-oriented Architectures and propose an approach to express these security requirements at the business process layer. An enhancement for BPMN is introduced to model these security requirements and illustrated in an example process that is deployed on a cross-organisational SOA infrastructure. Our aim is to facilitate the generation of security configurations on a technical level based on the modelled requirements. For this purpose, we foster a model-driven approach that is described as a suitable approach for future development.

1 Introduction

Business Process Modelling gains more and more attention, as it is the foundation to describe, standardise and optimise organisational workflows. A business process model can describe orchestrations of activities within an organisation and complex interactions with business partners. In addition, related business requirements can be indicated on an abstract level.

To support nowadays business processes, IT-infrastructures evolved into distributed and loosely coupled enterprise system landscapes such as Service-oriented Architectures, which expose a company's assets and resources as business services. These services can be orchestrated and modelled as business processes in order to enable a faster adoption to market changes and business demands.

In the domain of process-aware information systems, security and privacy intentions, legal regulations, and risk assessments define the requirements that specify how company assets such as systems, services and information should be protected. Especially the cooperation with business partners – demanding the utilisation of services across organisational boundaries – constitutes a key aspect regarding security in Service-oriented Architectures, since the seamless and straightforward integration of cross-organisational services conflicts with the need to secure and control access. A broad range of access control

N. Pohlmann, H. Reimer, W. Schneider (Editors): Securing Electronic Business Processes, Vieweg (2009), 145-154

models, security protocols and related implementations have emerged over the last decades and have been adapted in the scope of SOA to enforce security goals.

While some attributes of business processes, such as control- and data-flows, are directly expressed in the scope of the process models itself, related security goals are not expressed in this context. Currently available process modelling notations do not have the ability to capture security intentions or to evaluate risks.

In fact, while the engineering of service based systems starts with the consideration of processes and focuses on human and service interactions, security is typically not considered in the first place. Processes can be modelled and described on an abstract level (e.g. BPMN) and automatically translated to an executable service composition (e.g. BPEL). However, security mechanisms have to be implemented by security experts subsequently and can neither be modelled in the scope of process notations nor be applied automatically.

In order to have a comprehensive view on security, it is evident that business domain experts need to be able to define and verify their security requirements at a business process level, while the corresponding access control and security mechanisms need to be created and enforced at the service and resource level in a Service-oriented Architecture.

This paper presents a compilation of security requirements in SOA and discusses approaches to describe these requirements at the business process layer. A use case is presented that is based on a cross-organisational scenario to illustrate associated security requirements. This example is used as a basis to introduce an enhancement for BPMN that enables the integration of security requirements.

Our aim is to support the generation of security configurations based on the modelled requirements. For this purpose, we foster a model-driven approach: Information at the modelling layer is gathered and translated to a domain-independent security model. Our security model enables a straight mapping from the business process layer. The security layer is designed to reveal security aspects concerning messaging in an SOA landscape and the relationship among affected entities. Therefore, our model describes basic security goals and outlines the relationship to specific security attributes and mechanisms.

Altogether, we foster a model-driven approach in which security intentions are annotated in business process models and translated to consistent security polices. In this paper we provide

- a compilation of security requirements in Service-oriented Architectures that emphasis the relationship between security requirements and entities in a Web Service environment.
- an approach to enhance business processes description by properties and annotations to integrate requirements regarding SOA security concepts.
- a model-driven approach to generate policies based on the gathering of security information modelled at the process layer and the usage of security pattern to resolve appropriate security protocols.

This paper is structured as follows. Section 2 provides an overview about SOA security concepts concerning identity management and Web Service security specification. Based on these concepts, a scenario is introduced in Section 3. Section 4 provides a compilation of security requirements in SOA, while the next section discusses approaches to integrate these requirements in business process modelling. Our model-driven approach to generate security policies is described in Section 6. Section 7 discusses related work, while the final Section concludes the paper.

2 Background

This section introduces selected security concepts which underlie our example scenario in Section 3. This includes a user-centric approach to manage digital identities, which is based on the notion of claims, the so-called claim-based identity management. Afterwards Section 2.2 will give an overview about the Web Service specifications that provide the technical foundation to realize such concepts.

2.1 Claim-Based Identity Management

For years, the closed domain was at the heart of most identity management solutions. Within this domain user attributes were stored in a fixed data model and format by the identity management system and exchanged in a fixed format between the identity management system and the applications. While every participant within the domain would understand this format, someone outside the domain would not. Claim-based identity management on the contrary facilitates an open identity management model. It abstracts from concrete formats and protocols of identity systems and provides a platform-independent way to present identity information.

In the center of this approach is the notion of *claims*. A *claim* is a statement about a subject made by another subject and can relate to any type of an identity attribute, such as a name, address, etc. Claims are identified by an abstract identifier (e.g. a URI) and are used by applications to specify the identity attributes they require to perform certain business functions.

Using the notion of claims, the concept of an Identity Metasystem, as e.g. proposed by Microsoft in [Micros05], adds an identity management layer on top of existing identity management systems. This layer abstracts from concrete technologies and provides the necessary mechanisms to describe exchange and distribute identity information across identity management solutions.

The Identity Metasystem distinguishes three different types of participants as denoted in Figure 1: the consumer of identity information (Relying Parties), authorities who manage and provide users' digital identities (Identity Provider) as well as a component to choose a digital identity, called Identity Selector, and the user.

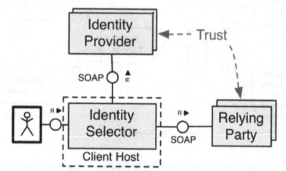

Fig. 1: Entities of the Identity Metasystem (FMC Block Diagram [Knoepf05])

The *Relying Party* is a service or Web site, which requires a certain set of user attributes / claims to perform a certain action. Instead of managing this information itself, it allows users to authenticate themselves at a federated Identity Provider and then relies on the assertion issued by this *Identity Provider*.

The *Identity Selector* is a piece of software on the user's system which handles the communication between the Relying Party and the Identity Provider and provides a consistent user interface to the user.

2.2 SOA Security Specifications

The Identity Metasystem takes care of the whole process of communicating required claims, find an authority to assert claims and transport asserted claims in specific containers, so called security tokens, to the applications that needs them.

The *Security Assertion Markup Language* (SAML) is an XML standard for exchanging identity information as security tokens. The essence of the SAML specification is the expression of identity information through SAML assertions about subjects such as the user. SAML-Tokens can be issued by the identity provider and consumed by the relying party.

The interface of an identity provider is defined by the *WS-Trust* specification that introduces a Web Service interface to issue, renew, validate and cancel security tokens. It introduces the concept of a Security Token Service (STS), which is acting as a trust broker between several parties.

The required identity information of a relying party can be expressed using a security policy. *WS-SecurityPolicy* specifies the security related policy assertions that can be used to express the security requirements of Web Services. The specification defines assertions to use *WS-Security*, *WS-Trust* and *WS-SecureConversation* at endpoint-level, per operation or at message-level.

3 The Order Scenario

The following section introduces a common claim-based service composition scenario as shown in Figure 2. It represents a scenario, which can be transferred to similar scenarios and is used as a reference use case to propose solutions and explain implementation decisions.

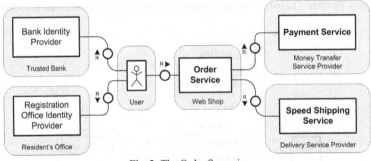

Fig. 2: The Order Scenario

The order scenario contains an order process, in which a user is requesting goods using an order application. The order service is running on a different location/site, so that the order application has to request all operations at the remote service. The order service denotes a service composition which uses two external services; a payment and a shipping service. Both services can be seen as local or remote services. This means that these services could also be run by third parties. A payment service run by a financial institute and a corporate shipping service by a logistic company are popular outsourced divisions. The payment service represents a service which handles the payment of the order process. In order to do so, the service needs payment information including a payment amount and credit card information like card type, card holder, card number, expiration date and a security code. The shipping service initiates the shipping of the goods using the recipients address. The process that is executed by the order service to orchestrate the money transfer service and the delivery service is shown in Figure 3.

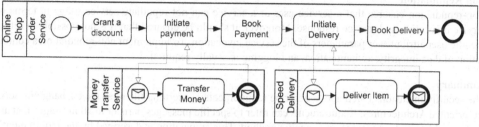

Fig. 3: The Order Process

In addition, the user has an account at his trusted bank and at the registration office, who act as identity providers managing the user's digital identity. The user can authenticate at the identity providers to request a security token that can be used to access a specific service. In particular, the payment service has established a trust relationship with the trusted bank, while the shipping service trusts information from the registration office.

4 Security Requirements in SOA

To identify security requirements in the order scenario, we will present a compilation of security intentions in this section. These intentions can be declared in security policies and refer to the internal functioning of a service or state requirements concerning the interaction with services. Since the interaction in terms of messaging constitutes the foundation in SOA, we will focus on these requirements in this paper. In particular, these requirements are related to the usage of identity information (identification, authentication, trust), transferred, processed or stored information (data confidentiality and data integrity) and the liability of service usage (non-repudiation).

Identification, Authentication, Trust
Authentication ensures the credibility of identity information by verifying that a claimed identity is authentic, while authorisation is the process of granting rights to participants to perform a task, for instance to access a service. These goals presume a secure management and trustworthy provision of identity information. With regard to a Service-oriented Architecture, the underlying trust relationships must be considered, since the usage and provision of services might not be limited to one trust domain. Trust can be defined as "the extent to which one party is willing to depend on the other party in a given situation with a feeling of relative security, even though negative consequences are possible." (McKnight and Chervany [McKni96]) Therefore, the trust relationships between actors in a SOA must be predefined to enable a trustworthy authentication and authorisation process.

Data Confidentiality and Data Integrity
Confidentiality provides protection against the unauthorised notice of transferred, processed, or stored information, while data integrity ensures the properness (intactness, correctness, and completeness) of information. Since the enforcement of these security goals might involve the application of complex security mechanisms, there is always the trade-off between the desired level of security and performance. The required security level depends on the information's value that influences the implementation (type of protocols, algorithms, etc.) of these goals. Moreover, these goals can refer to transferred, processed,

or stored data. Data should be secured if it is transferred over unsecured connections or if it is processed or stored by untrustworthy participants. Compliance requirements might be an additional reason that requires the application of data confidentiality.

Non Repudiation

Non-repudiation ensures that a service user or a service can not repudiate service usage in terms of service invocation and service response. Moreover, it should be ensured that it is not possible to refute specific user attributes or parameters of the service invocation. To implement non-repudiation a combination of data integrity, authentication, and logging is usually required.

Summary

The security intensions listed above describe requirements concerning the message exchange in Service-oriented Architectures. Requirements can refer to specific messages parts or to all messages that are exchanged to invoke a service or a specific method. This association is described by the requirement's subject as listed in Table 1. While the requirements integrity and confidentiality require the encryption and signature of specific information that are conveyed in a message, a requirement such as authentication is associated with a Web Method since all incoming messages must include an authentication information. The message-based provisioning of authentication information requires a trust relationship to enable a service to rely on this information. By default, a service will trust all identity providers in his own trust domain. However, the service might trust an additional third party such as the bank in the order scenario. Based on authentication and established trust relationships, a service or a method can require the provisioning of specific identity information that is expressed as claims as described in Section 2.1. This is described by the requirements trustworthy identity provisioning.

In addition, each requirement is associated with parameters. Authentication, integrity and confidentiality for instance are associated with a profile that describes the strength of the desired security methods. For example, the profile for authentication could identify concrete technologies such as SAML or refer to an authentication trust level that describes the strength of the authentication method using a numeric value as described in [Thom08]. Moreover, additional information is required for integrity and confidentiality to describe the entity that should sign a message part or should be able to decrypt it.

Table 1: Compilation of Security Requirements in SOA

Security Requirements	Requirement Subject	Parameters
Authentication	Web Service , Web Method	security profile
Trust	Trust domain, Web Service	Trusted Identity Providers, Trust domain
Trustworthy Identity Provisioning	Web Service, Web Method	Required identity information (Claims)
Integrity	Message Part	security profile, Issuer of the message part
Confidentiality	Message Part	security profile, Target of the message part
Non-Repudiation	Message Part, Web Method	-

5 Modelling security in business processes

The previous section provided an overview about organisational security concepts that address various security threats in SOA. We outlined that the required level of security in a process-aware information system depends on metrics that determine the value of enterprise assets and assign trust level to each participant. These values determine the risk that is associated with each asset. Appropriate security measures can be applied for each asset to reduce risks. A process-aware information system can be considered as secure, if the asset's risk complies with its business value. To facilitate a specification of security requirements and the determination of risks at the business process layer, we propose a set of security modelling enhancements for BPMN. BPMN provides a graphical notation to describe business processes in a diagram and has been designed to facilitate the development and design of those processes by domain experts. Graphical elements in BPMN can be classified in the following groups. *Flow Objects* such as *Activities* define the nodes in a business process diagram, while *Connecting Objects* specify the edges. *Swimlanes* represents participants in a process and *Artifacts* express specific situations and have no effect on the control flow. In BPMN Artifacts are *Data Objects* that can be used to associate data with flows or activities, *Groups* combine several activities and *Text Annotations* provide additional information.

Our security modelling enhancement for BPMN is based on the security requirements defined in Table 1. As described above, these requirements refer to specific subjects such as Web Services, Web Methods, trust domains and data. These subjects can be mapped directly to BPMN. In a process, activities are executed by Web Services and, therefore, it can be mapped to a specific Web Method. A trust domain can be represented using a pool, since all activities in this pool would be executed in the scope of this participant with the same trust requirements. Finally, data can be modelled using data objects as aforementioned.

In general, there are two possibilities to model these security requirements in BPMN. The first option is to express a requirement as a property of the subject of the requirement. For example, the BPMN element activity could be extended to contain an additional property 'identification'. This property would offer the possibility to specify a set of claim types that is required by an activity. The definition of required claims in an activity could be shown as small symbol in the corner of the activity. The second option to express security requirements is the definition of artifacts that can be used to annotate elements. Figure 4 illustrates the order process that has been extended with security requirements as annotations to express requirements regarding the management of identities. Annotation can be defined for each security goal and attached to the subject of the requirement.

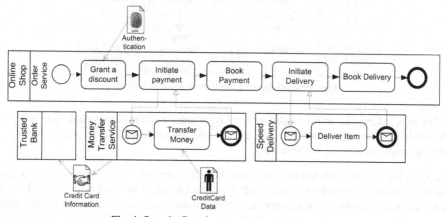

Fig. 4: Security Requirements in the Order Process

In Figure 4, there are three requirements specified. First of all, users have to be authenticated in the order process, since a discount is granted to registered business customers. Therefore, the authentication artifact is attached to the activity ‚grant a discount'. We assume that the profiles low, medium and high have been specified referring to concrete authentication technologies. In our example, the authentication artifact contains a single property that specifies the profile *low*. To perform the payment, the money transfer service is used in our scenario that requires credit card information from a trust worthy source to complete this task. The required claims are specified in the artifact that annotates the transfer money activity. Since the credit card data must be asserted by a trustworthy third party, the underlying trust relationship between the money transfer service and the trusted bank is annotated as well.

The advantage of annotating security requirements as artifacts is that the requirements are emphasised in the process model. In addition, these annotations could be integrated in a special security view for security experts that could unhide the annotations. A combined approach is possible as well that integrates security requirements as properties of the requirements subjects such as activities and that are visualised as annotations.

6 Model-Driven Generation of Security Policies

In the previous section, we have introduced an approach to model security requirements in business process. It supports business analysts and business process experts to analyse and improve processes concerning security requirements in a SOA. The specification of these requirements constitutes the foundation of our model driven approach to generate security policies that has been introduced in [Menzel09b] and is illustrated in Figure 5.

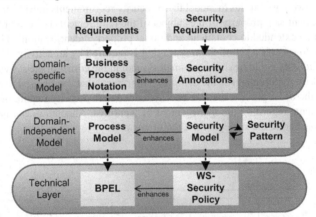

Fig. 5: Model-driven generation of security Policies

In the first step, information at the modelling layer is gathered and translated to a domain independent security model. This security model relates to a formal process model (e.g. a Petri net) that can be used to verify the modelled security configurations.

However, the information gathered from the modelling layer does not have to be sufficient to generate enforceable security configurations, since further knowledge might be needed. Expertise knowledge might be required to determine an appropriate strategy to secure services and resource, since multiple solutions might exists to satisfy a security goal. For example, confidentiality can be implemented by securing a channel using SSL or by securing parts of transferred messages. To describe these strategies and their preconditions in a standardised way, we foster the usage of security patterns as described in [Menzel09]. Security patterns have been introduced by Yoder and Barcalow in 1997 [Yoder97] and are based on the idea of design patterns as described by Christopher Alexander [Alex77]. Based on this work, we defined a pattern system that describes formalised patterns for each security goal and that is used to resolve appropriate security protocols and mechanisms. A security model has been defined

[Menzel09b] and is used to express the preconditions and relations in a pattern system. The final step in our model-driven approach is the transformation of security configuration into enforceable security policy languages, depending on the capabilities of the target environment.

7 Related Work

The domain of model-driven security in the context of business processes is an emerging research area. The need to describe security policies referring to an application scenario an abstract level is discussed in [Tats04]. Recent work done by Rodrguez et al. [Rodr06], [Rodr07] discusses an approach to express security requirements in the context of business processes by defining a meta-model that links security requirement stereotypes to activity elements of a business process and proposed graphical annotation elements to visually enrich the process model with related security requirements. Although they support several security intentions, they do not provide a comprehensive security model based on the evaluation of assets considering authentication and trust. A model-driven scenario based on their annotations is considered as future work.

Enforcing authorisation constraint in workflows is addressed in [Wei-ku99]. SecureFlow implements a Workflow Authorisation Model to define and enforce authorisations at runtime for users, roles, and workflow tasks. In [Crook03], Crook et al. proposed a framework to model and verify access control policies based on the derivation of roles from their organisational context. In contrast to our general security modelling concept these approaches focus on authorisation, without considering the relation to other security requirements.

Model-driven security and the automated generation of security enhanced software artefacts and security configurations have been a topic of interest in recent years. For instance SecureUML [Basin03] is a model-driven security approach for process-oriented systems focusing on access control. Similar to SecureUML, Jürjens presented the UMLSec extension for UML [Juerje02] in order to express security relevant information within a system specification diagram. One focus of UMLSec lies on the modelling of communication-based security goals, such as confidentiality, for software artefacts, while SecureUML describes desired state transitions and access control configurations for server-based applications, both do not leap for establishing the link between business processes and model-driven generation of related security requirements.

8 Conclusion and Future Work

Process modelling notations provide a suitable abstract perspective to specific security goals on a more accessible level, as we have shown in [Wolter08]. In this paper, we presented a compilation of security requirements in SOA and discussed approaches to enhance business process models to visualize these requirements. Moreover, we introduced an order service scenario that was the basis to illustrate the expression of security requirements in BPMN concerning authentication, trust relationship and identity provisioning.

The specification of security requirements on an abstract level is the basis for our model-driven approach that addresses the difficulty to generate security configurations for a process-aware information system. The foundation constitutes our generic security model that specifies security goals, policies, and constraints based on a set of basic entities as described in [Menzel09]. Security intentions and related requirements defined at the process layer can be mapped to this model. To resolve concrete security protocols and mechanisms, a security pattern-driven approach has been introduced in [Menzel09] that resolves appropriate security protocols with regard to specific preconditions. The gathered information can be mapped to policy specifications such as WS-SecurityPolicy.

Altogether, our proposed modelling enhancement constitutes a suitable foundation to describe and implement a model-driven transformation of abstract security intentions to enforceable security configurations in different application domains. As described in [Menzel09], security patterns are a promising approach to resolve additional information needed in the transformation process. In the next step we will use our security model and the pattern system to enable an automated reasoning on the modelled security intensions.

References

[Alex77]   C. Alexander, S. Ishikawa, M. Silverstein, M. Jacobsen, I. Fiksdahl-King, and S. Angel: A Pattern Lanuage: Towns – Buildings – Construction. In: Oxford University Press, 1977.

[Basin03]   D. Basin, J. Doser, and T. Lodderstedt: Model Driven Security for Process-Oriented Systems. In: SACMAT '03: Proceedings of the 8th ACM symposium on Access control models and technologies, 2003, pp. 100–109.

[Crook03]   R. Crook, D. C. Ince, and B. Nuseibeh. Modelling access policies using roles in requirements engineering. Information & Software Technology,vol. 45, no. 14, pp. 979–991, 2003.

[Juerje02]   J. Juerjens: UMLsec: Extending UML for Secure Systems Development. In UML '02: Proceedings of the 5th International Conference on The Unified Modeling Language, 2002, pp. 412–425.

[Knoepf05]   A. Knoepfel, B.Groene and P.Tabeling: Fundamental Modeling Concepts. John Wiley & Sons Ltd, 2005.

[Lamb06]   J. H. Lambert, R. K. Jennings, and N. N. Joshi: Integration of risk identification with business process models. In: Syst. Eng., vol. 9, no. 3, pp. 187–198, 2006.

[McKni96]   D. H. McKnight and N. L. Chervany: The meanings of trust. Technical Report, University of Minnesota, 1996. http://misrc.umn.edu/wpaper/Working-Papers/9604.pdf

[Menzel08]   M. Menzel, C. Wolter, and C. Meinel: Towards the aggregation of security requirements in cross-organisational service compositions. In: Proc. 11th BIS, no. ISBN: 978-3-540-79396-3. Springer LNCS, Innsbruck, Austria, May 2008.

[Menzel09]   M. Menzel, I. Thomas, and C. Meinel: Security requirements specification in service-oriented business process management. In: ARES, 2009.

[Menzel09b] M. Menzel, and C. Meinel: A Security Meta-Model for Service-oriented Architectures. In: SCC, 2009.

[Micros05]   Microsoft Corp.: Microsofts Vision for an Identity Metasystem, May 2005.

[Rodr06]   A. Rodríguez, E. Fernández-Medina, and M. Piattini: Towards a uml 2.0 extension for the modeling of security requirements in business processes. In: TrustBus, 2006, pp. 51–61.

[Rodr07]   A. Rodríguez, E. Fernández-Medina: Towards cim to pim transformation: From secure business processes defined in bpmn to use-cases. In: BPM, 2007, pp. 408–415.

[Tats04]   M. Tatsubori, T. Imamura, and Y. Nakamura. Best-practice patterns and tool support for configuring secure web services messaging. In ICWS, 2004, pp. 244–251.

[Thom08]   I. Thomas, M. Menzel, and C. Meinel: Using Quantified Trust Levels to Describe Authentication Requirements in Federated Identity Management. In SWS, 2008

[Wei-ku99]   Wei-kuang Huang and V. Atluri: Secureflow: A secure web enabled workflow management system. In: ACM Workshop on Role-Based Access Control, 1999, pp. 83–94. http://citeseer.ist.psu.edu/huang99secureflow.html

[Wolter08]   C. Wolter, M. Menzel, A. Schaad, P. Miseldine, and C. Meinel: Model-driven business process security requireme specification. In: Journal of Systems Architecture Special Issue on Secure Web Services, 2008.

[Yoder97]   J. Yoder and J. Barcalow: Architectural patterns for enabling application security. In: PLoP, 1997.

Privacy, Data Protection and Awareness

Simple & Secure:
Attitude and behaviour towards security and usability in internet products and services at home

Reinder Wolthuis[1] · Gerben Broenink[1] · Frank Fransen[1]
Sven Schultz[2] · Arnout de Vries[2]

[1]Security
[2]Innovation and User Experience Management
TNO Information and Communication Technology
Groningen, The Netherlands

{Reinder.Wolthuis | Gerben.Broenink | Frank.Fransen | Sven.Schultz | Arnout.deVries}@tno.nl

Abstract

This paper is the result of research on the security perception of users in ICT services and equipment. We analyze the rationale of users to have an interest in security and to decide to change security parameters of equipment and services. We focus on the home environment, where more and more devices are (inter)connected to form a complex end-to-end chain in using online services. In our research, we constructed a model to determine the delta between the perceived overall security and the real security in home networks. To achieve an understanding of perception and how to identify the delta between perceived and real security, our work forms the basis for examining how perception relates to behaviour. Since humans are referred to as the weakest link in security, there are also differences in behaviour and desired behaviour from a security perspective.

1 Introduction

More and more equipment enters the home environment that interacts with each other and is connected to the Internet. Examples that are already common are set-top boxes, PC's, game consoles and smart phones. New networked devices are emerging, such as the heating system, home surveillance systems, smart energy meters and many will follow. With the introduction of these (inter)connected devices all kinds of new services are enabled.

The main reason that these kind of devices emerge is ease of use and efficiency. But with increasingly connected equipment and services, the technical complexity in these chains of hardware and software increases.

When technology gets more complex, security also gets more complex. Often too complex for the average user to comprehend, let alone configure the security functions correctly. Of course we do not want others to have access to our home surveillance system or to our home banking account details, but the average user is not able to configure the technology in a secure way [BrMS08].

N. Pohlmann, H. Reimer, W. Schneider (Editors): Securing Electronic Business Processes, Vieweg (2009), 157-168

The complexity of the security configuration is shown when we take a look at the security warnings and notifications. One we are all familiar with is: "This certificate is not valid. Do you want to continue?". This is too difficult to interpret and therefore unfit to make a reasoned decision on what to do. The perception of security and trustworthiness by the user often doesn't match reality as they will under- or over estimate the risks and they may even lose faith in technology in some areas. This is caused by incorrect assumptions, bad security and trustworthiness decisions. Because of these issues, the user is commonly referred to as the weakest link in the security of a system. In order to create easy to use and efficient security solutions we need to know how users experience current solutions, what their perception of security in home networks is and how this perception is formed.

We will state the problem that we tackle in this paper in section 2. In section 3, we will describe the methodology that we used. In section 4 we present a model on attitude and perception and section 5 will expand on some theory on user experience and behaviour. In section 6 we describe a few commonly used security techniques and their user acceptance. Section 7 summarizes the key findings and conclusions and section 8 contains our plans for future research.

1.1 Trends

User education
Current solutions (used by e.g. banks) tend to educate the user how they should behave and how they should react on certain events. Examples in the Netherlands are:

- www.digibewust.nl   (make people conscious of threats)
- www.waarschuwingsdienst.nl   (warning service for security threats)
- www.surfwijzer.nl   (hints to safely surf the net)
- www.driekeerkloppen.nl   (only do online banking after three checks)

Although security awareness should always be part of the solution, this paper states that the burden should not be put one-sidedly on the user alone.

Fading network boundaries
Just like in the corporate world, the boundaries of the home network tend to fade. Wireless LAN networks are sometimes open to users outside the home environment, and some applications enable remote access to content stored in the home network.

Interconnection
More and more equipment and services are interconnected and connected to the internet. In this way, a chain of devices is created, each running their own software or service. On installation usually a default security configuration is used to make things easier for the end-user. This is not always a good thing to do (e.g. default passwords are easy to guess). Because there are many services and equipment that behave like this, the user looses track of the actual security situation in the home environment.

1.2 Scope

The focus of this paper lies on user perception and human-machine interaction with respect to security. Although Privacy and Trust aspect are important factors in security user experience, this will be out of scope for this paper.

2 The problem

This paper deals with the attitude of users to security in ICT services and equipment. We try to analyze the rationale of users to have an interest in security and to decide to change security parameters of equipment and services. We put the focus on the home environment. Private users of online ICT services, with part of the equipment installed at home. The central question we try to answer is:

How can a user be optimally supported to make the right decisions in security interaction between user and ICT service?

We analyze this both from a human (psychological) perspective and a technical (security) perspective. We use a Human Centred Design (HCD) approach.

3 Methodology

For the advancement of knowledge and theoretical understanding of security in relation to user perception various activities were conducted in this exploratory research.

We have started with a literature search, to develop knowledge about the user experience field, and the security field. To gain more insight in how people configured their home environment, some workshops have been held, where people with a different field of expertise were invited to explain how they configured their home environment, and how they perceived the security of their home environment.

With this knowledge, we analyzed the rationale of users to have an interest in security and to decide to change security parameters of equipment and services. In our research we developed a model to determine the delta between the perceived security and the real security in home networks and describe how user perception relates to user behaviour. Because there are differences in humans and their activities, there are also differences in behaviour and desired behaviour from a security perspective. Our analysis resulted in the conceptual model which is presented in this paper.

4 Attitude and perception

Attaining awareness or understanding of sensory information is one of the oldest fields of psychology called perception. By evaluating this information or experiences a user forms a consistent and predictable (positive or negative) judgement also called attitude. Insight in perception and attitude of users is key in offering security solutions that match user's expectations. Research of Furnell e.a. [FuBP07], on the perception of security among users of Internet, shows that there is a possible mismatch between the perceived security and the real security. To be able to measure the delta between perceived security and the actual security, the perception needs to be measured and more insight in the perception and the factors which form perception is needed.

A rational view on perception of security is about perception of risks and probability, accompanied by perception of the effectiveness of counter measures. In "The Psychology of Security" Schneier [Schn08] and Glassner [Glas00] add psychological factors in trying to understand how the brain processes risks and fear, where emotion plays a large role. In our current work we try to assess how this perception is influenced. First of all, perception can be based on the interaction of the user with the product, and the service which is provided with the product. Turner e.a. [TuZY01] conclude that the perception of security is also influenced in several other ways, like the brand, recommendations and the participant's own experience. Our current model, shown below in **Figure 1**, combines these influences to form the basis for perception of security. Aspects such as attitude, knowledge and predispositions are placed in individual characteristics, while influence of social networks and general media are placed in context and environment.

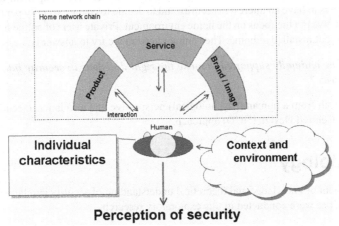

Fig. 1: Model for user perception of security

One approach in measuring perception and identifying the delta between perceived security and real security is to define how the desired security level from a user's perspective differs from the actual security in a home network. Another approach to define the desired security level is to define this based upon an impact analysis, as is common in businesses (known as business impact analysis). In this case you could call it a Personal Impact Analysis. In our opinion these perspectives can lead to two directions for solutions:

- Change the security of the product to match the perception of the user
- Change the perception of the user to match the real security level

We propose a model for not only identifying the difference in perceived security and real security, but also take into account that there is a vast diversity in perception between users. This is important when solutions are offered that try to close these gaps.

Perception of security is not only personal, but also differs per technology. In a home environment it can be applied to specific elements, such as services or devices or be applied to home network security as a whole. This is further elaborated in chapter 6.

5 User security experience and behaviour

5.1 Difference between target groups

In the home domain ICT services and products are used by people with a large variety of personal characteristics. In a typical household the age and gender are basic characteristics. Other basic characteristics are the knowledge, experiences and awareness of a person. When we look more closely to the activities and roles of the household members, more and more differences come to light. These differences play an important role in the perception of security. When for example the knowledge or expertise of a person is insufficient we cannot expect them to configure complex security settings without any support. A lot of characteristics potentially determine the attitude of a person to security, these are for example; Dependence, Altruism, Obedience, Impulsiveness, Integrity, Intellectual autonomy, Intelligence, Uncertainty, Self efficacy, Independence, Self confidence and Carefulness. To structuralize these personal characteristics, the 'Big Five' personality traits [JoSr99] and the Myers-Briggs Type Indicator [MyBr95] can be used to describe a person's character or to determine what a user will do in a certain situation. The 'Big Five' personality characteristics are accepted scientifically as five stable dimensions. The characteristics are:

1. Openness
2. **Conscientiousness**
3. Extraversion
4. Agreeableness
5. **Neuroticism**

In relation to security the two most important factors of the 'Big Five' in our opinion are Conscientiousness (*tendency to show self-discipline, act dutifully*) and Neuroticism (*tendency to experience unpleasant emotions easily*).

The activities of a person in a household are a very interesting and important aspect of security. Beside personal characteristics these activities determine the degree of vulnerability. Activities can predict to which extent a person is informed of current developments in the field of security or security risks. The security risk of for example someone downloading or sharing of files using Internet are different than when someone is blogging only once or twice a week. The more experience a person has in using computer and internet, the more familiar a person is with security messages and interaction. Of course, too much experience with simple tasks implies routine and routine does not always have a positive effect on security. For example, when a user is confronted with popups, containing useless information, every now and then he will get used to clicking ′ok′ for every popup without reading it. When an important popup appears, it will be useless, because the user will not read it, and click ′ok′.

5.2 Behaviour

As a second step we will look at behaviour. Perception and the knowledge that influences perception is an important factor, but insufficient to explain behaviour. Research of Abrahamse [ASVR07] indicates that the overall provisioning of information appears to lead to changes in knowledge about the issue at hand, but not necessarily to behavioural changes. Tailored information is potentially a more effective way to encourage behavioural change, but is still no guarantee. This is because behaviour is influenced by two other main factors: (i) motivation and what we call (ii) "the ability to engage" (see **Figure 2**).

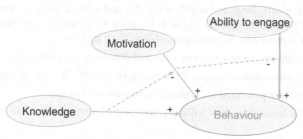

Fig. 2: Preliminary behaviour model

(i) Motivation comprises of aspects such as personal values, social approval, attitude and commitment. For example attitude is an important factor in motivation towards ICT security at home and strongly depends on the valuability and benefits suggested by Morville [Morv05], which are based on the model of Garret [Garr00]. A good example of this is a botnet as a security risk. A computer user rarely suffers from the damage he causes by being infected with a botnet. And as a result other users and companies are the victims (e.g. SPAM) of the lack of benefits for home users and their security choices.

(ii) The ability to engage include the necessary skill set, income and other factors that define if a user is capable to use a certain security solution. Furnell e.a. [FuBP07] state that there is a large number of novice users that know they have to deal with security somehow, but lack the confidence and skills to do so. Asgharpour e.a. [AsLC07] show that the computer skills or computer experience of a user have a clear link with the mental model concerning security risks. In current security configurations and functionalities the computer skills or computer experience of a user is not taken into account.

These models are still work in progress, and are primarily based on research of Stern [Ster00] where he states that behaviour is a function of the organism and its environment. His so called ABC model puts Behaviour (B) as an 'interactive product' of personal sphere attitudinal variables (A) and contextual factors (C).

5.3 Delta between perception of security and reality

As Bruce Schneier states in his psychology work on security [Schn08]: security is both a feeling and a reality. And they're not the same. The reality of security is mathematical, based on the probability of different risks and the effectiveness of different countermeasures. But security is also a feeling, based not on probabilities and mathematical calculations, but on your psychological perception to both risks and countermeasures. You might feel terribly afraid of terrorism, or you might feel like it's not something worth worrying about. Schneier comes up with five areas where perception can diverge from reality:

- The severity of the risk
- The probability of the risk
- The magnitude of the costs
- How effective the countermeasure is at mitigating the risk
- The trade-off itself (how well disparate risks and costs can be compared)

There's no such thing as absolute security, and any gain in security always involves some sort of trade-off. Costs in this sense has a broader meaning than money, it is also about costs in time, convenience, capabilities, liberties, and so on

We make security trade-offs, large and small, every day and a lot of them are made intuitively. And yet, at the same time we seem hopelessly bad at it. We get it wrong all the time. Here are some reasons Schneier proposes to explain why risk perception differs from real risk:

- People exaggerate spectacular, but rare risks and downplay common risks
- People have trouble estimating risks for anything not exactly like their normal situation
- Personified risks are perceived to be greater than anonymous risks
- People underestimate risks they willingly take and overestimate risks in situations they can't control
- Last, people overestimate risks that are being talked about and remain an object of public scrutiny

To make these assessments people have shortcuts, rules of thumb, stereotypes, and biases; generally known as "heuristics." These heuristics affect how we think about risks, how we evaluate the probability of future events, how we consider costs, and how we make trade-offs. We have ways of generating close-to-optimal answers quickly with limited cognitive capabilities. Donald Norman's [Norm98] essay "Being Analog" provides a great background for all this. He recognizes several biases and heuristics, which explain why humans are over or underestimating risks. In our opinion his work is relevant to gain insight in user behaviour towards security.

Most of the work of Schneier relates to strong fear reactions, which will often not be related to the ICT domain. In this domain the amygdala part of the brain, responsible for base emotion processing and immediate reactions, is expected to play a small role, since usually no lifes are at stake. However the analytic part of the brain, the neocortex, plays a more important role and that's where complex processes take place to form the (ir)rational perceptions. Evolutionary speaking the neocortex of the human brain is so new, it still has a lot of rough edges where these biases and heuristcs come into place. Psychologist Daniel Gilbert [Gilb06] even quotes that this part of the brain is still in beta testing.

6 Security techniques in the home environment and user acceptance

The conceptual model in section 4 tries to capture how a user precipitates the security of his home environment. To be able to estimate the real level of security, we look at the security methods and techniques that are used. In this section, the home environment will be described, and the different domains that play a role in it. We also compare some security techniques that are used regularly. We identify the parameters which play a role in the user acceptance of the security techniques. We also estimate the user acceptance of the security techniques. We will conclude this chapter by comparing the different security techniques on user acceptance and complexity parameters.

6.1 Home environment

There is a chain of devices between the user of a service, and the provider of the service. To be able to analyze the security of a service, it is necessary to know all the links in the chain, to determine who is responsible for the security, and what the weakest link is.

In **Figure 3** all the links in the chain are showed. First of all there is the web service; this is inside the domain of the service provider, so the service provider is responsible for the security at this link. The service provider offers a service for a user. To be able to use the service, data has to be sent over the internet, the second link in the chain. The internet is in the public domain, so nobody is responsible for the security inside this domain. Therefore, we make the assumption that the internet is a hostile environment. The third link is the network provider of the user, this is the company which gives the user access to the internet. And because all the communication between the internet and the user will travel via the network provider, the network provider is able to implement some security measures, e.g. a spam filter. The fourth link is the home gateway of the user. Together with the home network, the home gateway is placed in the home domain of the user. Configuration of the modem and network is the responsibility of the user. Connected to the network, there is the device which is used to get access to the web service. To ensure the security, some security measures have to be taken, e.g. installing a firewall. The final link in the chain is the user that uses the service.

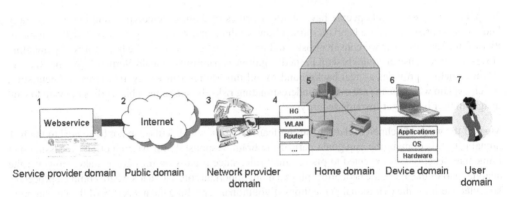

Fig. 3: End-to-end chain for use of online services in home networks

The chain explained in **Figure 3** assumes that the user is using a web service from a home environment. However, there are other environments too, for example the office environment, mobile environment and public environment. Another fact is that these environments increasingly integrate, e.g. a user could use his office laptop and a VPN connection to enter the office environment at home. This also means responsibilities will be mixed up too, so it is unclear who's mistake it is when something goes wrong.

6.2 Security techniques

To protect the home environment against different types of attacks, several security techniques are used. In this section, a small survey of these techniques is given. The focus of this small survey is the home environment, only techniques that can be encountered in the home environment are included. We will look at the following techniques:

- Username and password,
- File Encryption
- SSL.

6.2.1 Username and password

The most used security technique is a username and a password. It is used as login mechanism in al kinds of systems, e.g.: a computer system, an e-mail service, instant messenger, social network website, configuration tool of a modem or router.

The username and password mechanism is easy to implement, and all users are familiar with the concept. However, a secure password is often difficult to remember; this is the reason why many people use easy-to-guess passwords, or write their password down. This will cause the system to be less secure, because when a password can be guessed, or is written down, it will not guarantee the level of security it is supposed to.

Another problem with passwords is the amount of passwords a user has to remember, this will cause a user to use the same password for many services. And if one password is used for different services, one compromised password can potentially be used to compromise many services.

6.2.2 File encryption

To protect confidential data on a hard disk, it is possible to encrypt the data before it is stored. This means that even when the computer or hard disk is stolen, only the people who know the password can access the data.

Encryption can be used to easily protect data. However, decryption needs some kind of authentication, to ensure that only people who are allowed to decrypt the data, can decrypt it. And because most of the encryption tools use a password to authenticate a user, all these tools have the same disadvantages which are mentioned in section 6.2.1.

6.2.3 SSL

To make connections between servers en clients secure, all the communication can be encrypted. A commonly used protocol for this is Secure Socket Layer (SSL), and is standardised by the IETF as Transport Layer Security (TLS). SSL requires the server the authenticate himself, using a certificate. Once the certificate has been checked, an encryption key is negotiated, and the server and client can start communicating encrypted.

Several other protocols use SSL to secure their connection. Examples are https and smtp, these are normal (unsecure) protocols, which are secure because they use SSL. When these protocols are used, it is a lot more difficult for hackers to view or manipulate the communication.

6.3 Complexity and user acceptance

6.3.1 Complexity

To measure the complexity of the different security techniques, there are several important parameters to look at. The following parameters are recognized:
- Does the user have to remember something
- Does the user have to install something
- How much time is required for installation
- How many actions are necessary for installation
- Does the user have to possess specific knowledge to install or use the technique
- How many actions are necessary to log-on
- Does the user have options in using the security techniques?

We matched the security techniques to the different parameters. Overall, in our opinion SSL is a user friendly technique for the user because the user has security but does not have to remember anything, know anything, or install anything. Username and password are a bit more complex, because the user has to register his password, and remember it. The file encryption technique is most complex, because the user will need specific knowledge to install it correctly. However, once the tool is correctly installed, it is easy to use.

6.3.2 User acceptance

To measure the user acceptance, we estimated the frequency of use of the techniques. In Table 1, for each technique the usage is showed. In our opinion, username and passwords are the most used security mechanism in the home environment, because they are used by almost all systems, applications and websites. Secondly there is SSL, this technique is used on websites, to authenticate the server or to encrypt the communication. The technique which is used least is the file encryption, because only people with enough knowledge will use it.

Table 1: Usage of security technique

Technique	Used
Username + password	To login on systems, websites, and applications
File encryption	Some users use it to keep data confidential
SSL	Websites with confidential data use it to prove their identity, and encrypt the communication.

6.3.3 Correlation between complexity of security techniques and user acceptance

Insight in the real security by determining the security technique and the user acceptance is needed to determine the delta with the security perception of the user. We found that the level of complexity has a big influence on the user acceptance and consequences of the security level in the home network. The user acceptance can be measured in several different aspects; adoption of the solution, efficiency or effectiveness (ease of use) of the solution. In this paper we analysed the user acceptance by estimating the frequency of use.

File encryption seems to be a more complex technique, and also one of the less accepted techniques. When a security technique gets more complex, it will probable be less accepted. It is however not clear how the different parameters of complexity correlate with each other. It is not clear whether file encryption is less accepted because it is not required, or because it requires extra knowledge.

Another conclusion is that username and password (and SSL) are mostly used on initiative of the service provider and are used most often. However, further research should show how much effort users put in using secure, but complex passwords.

7 Key findings and conclusions

Individual characteristics and user experiences influence the attitude and user perception towards security. The activities of users in a home environment also influence the risks.

The perception of security is influenced in several ways. First of all, this perception can be based on the interaction of the user with the product, and the service which is given with the product. But we conclude that the perception of security is also influenced in several other ways, like the brand, recommendations of others and the participant's own experience and skills.

We presented a model which combines all those influences in combination with personal characteristics.

By looking at security from a user experience perspective, security measures can be implemented more secure and efficient. But to be able to look at security from a user experience perspective, in depth insight and knowledge is needed about human perception and behaviour and how these are influenced by the characteristics of security techniques.

Suppliers of products and services usually do not look at security form a user experience perspective. They should change that and also look at the whole picture and not focus just on their own product or service; a user with no interest or knowledge in security must be able to securely use services and products with minimal understanding of security.

We inventoried some of the more common security techniques, which a user can encounter in the home environment. The large number of combined devices with individual security techniques, configuration settings and userinterfaces creates a too complex environment to evaluate the security of the whole chain. Even for an experienced user it is difficult to evaluate the security of a home network. As a result users can have the perception to be secure, but are unknowingly vulnerable to different kinds of security threats.

8 Future work

The work presented in this paper is in a starting phase. We aim at improving the knowledge about the gap between perception and reality. Our work will therefore continue with improving the perception model by measuring perceptions through questionnaires and interviews in different households. We will also look at the social aspects of security. How does the social environment influence the security behaviour of an individual user. These assessments could help to provide insight in the risk perception, the trade-offs that a user is willing to make.

On the security side, we will identify the reality of the risk for each specific user in the home domain through probability figures, impact assessment and product specifications. Also we will investigate more thoroughly the usability of security techniques; what are the key parameters for this, how do they relate to user perception and how can we optimize the human-computer interaction of security techniques to ensure ease of use and a good match between security perception and reality.

This insight could lead to better support for users in understanding security and making the right decisions in interaction with security solutions of services or devices. Better understanding of perception of individual users could lead to various solutions and improvements such as automated adaption of security mechanisms or adaption in offering security features. Key is that they match the mental model of users and understand their perception.

References

[BrMS08] S. Bratus, C. Masone, S.W. Smith, "Why do street-smart people do stupid things online", 2008

[FuBP07] S.M. Furnell, P. Bryant, A.D. Phippen, "Assessing the security perceptions of personal internet users", 2007

[Schn08] B. Schneier; The psychology of security, Essay, http://www.schneier.com/essay-155.html, 2008

[Glas00] B. Glassner; The Culture of Fear: Why Americans Are Afraid of the Wrong Things, 2000.

[TuZY01] C.W. Turner, M. Zavod, W. Yurcik, "Factors that affect the perception of security and privacy of e-commerce websites", 2001

[JoSr99] John, O. P., & Srivastava, S. The Big-Five trait taxonomy: History, measurement, and theoretical perspectives. In L. A. Pervin & O. P. John (Eds.), *Handbook of personality: Theory and research*, New York: Guilford Press., 1999, Vol. 2, pp. 102–138.

[MyBr95] *Peter B. Myers with Myers, Isabel Briggs (1980, 1995). Gifts Differing: Understanding Personality Type. Mountain View, CA: Davies-Black Publishing. ISBN 0-89106-074-X*

[ASVR07] W. Abrahamse, L.Steg, C.Vlek and T.Rothengatter. The effect of tailored information, goal setting, and tailored feedback on household energy use, energy-related behaviours, and behavioural antecedents. Journal of Environmental Psychology 27 (2007) 265-276.

[Morv05] Morville, P. Ambient Findability: What We Find Changes Who We Become, User Experience Honeycomb, O'Reilly 2005

[Garr00] 'The Elements of User Experience' model by Jesse James Garret available at http://www.jjg.net/elements/pdf/elements.pdf, 2000

[AsLC07] Asgharpour, Liu, Camp, "Mental Models of Computer Security Risks", WEIS 2007.

[Ster00] P. Stern; Toward a Coherent Theory of Envrionmentally Significant Behavior. Journal of Social Issues, 2000, 56(3), 407-424

[Norm98] Donald A. Norman, "Being Analog," http://www.jnd.org/dn.mss/being_analog.html. Originally published as Chapter 7 of The Invisible Computer, MIT Press, 1998.

[Gilb06] Daniel Gilbert, "If only gay sex caused global warming," Los Angeles Times, July 2, 2006

Social Engineering hits Social Commerce

Werner Degenhardt[1] · Johannes Wiele[2]

[1]Ludwig-Maximilians-Universität München
degenhardt@lmu.de

[2]Defense AG Ismaning
johannes.wiele@defense-ag.de

Abstract

Looking at social commerce, a bunch of bewildering phenomena attracts the attention of social psychologists. The way customers participate today shows attitudes and ethical behavior which cannot be explained from the inherent conditions of Web 2.0 environments alone. Fraud often succeeds, when you do not expect it, and honesty can be found under circumstances that do not support honesty at all. The current situation seems to result from customers assigning experience and ethics from real world business to virtual business environments. But there are indications that this situation may change. Social commerce could suffer as soon as customers would use its inherent weaknesses to their own advantage. The following article outlines first approaches to research into this topic.

1 Introduction

There is much FUD-throwing out there about the looming dangers in cyberspace, the imminent collapse of the uncontrollable network infrastructure of less than perfect electronic devices and humans as the eternal weak link in socio-technical systems that are used by people.

In fact, our infrastructure of networked computers is inherently fallible and insecure as Bruce Schneier [Schn07] continues to show and there is a well-oiled, extremely efficient and growing black economy behind the scene living on the weaknesses of modern technology [FPPS07].

In fact, social engineering attacks are easy to perform and have astonishingly high success rates. Sophisticated staged social engineering attacks against any target are almost irresistible as is proofed by the work of our secret service organizations.

As part of our work related to the Psychology of IT-Security program at the University of Munich we had our students develop staged social engineering attacks using the attack tree methodology described in [Schn04, 318 ff]. This was an activity ranking among a security mindset training. Those attacks in many instances were of ingenious simplicity in exploiting hardwired or habitual behavioral routines of humans as done by influence specialists everyday everywhere in world. Even more ingenious was the ease how the exploitation of the social prerequisites that our electronic society relies upon was built in those staged social engineering attacks: authority, reputation, trust, implicit psychological contracts, loose coupling of obligations and many more social and individual automatisms that are the glue of our analogous world.

N. Pohlmann, H. Reimer, W. Schneider (Editors): Securing Electronic Business Processes, Vieweg (2009), 169-176

1.1 Observation

When running this security mindset program we noticed that most participants ran up to their possibilities only after some hours of explanation on the technological, legal, economical and administrative foundations of the digital information economy they were using in their everyday lives without thinking much about it.

Awareness training turned out to be a prerequisite for letting creativity fly and give the participants – theoretically – the chance to switch to the dark side of cyberspace. Before getting aware of the functioning of electronic commerce participants simply transferred concepts and metaphors of the world of analogous trade to the digital universe. After acquiring some digital literacy they could imagine scenarios that lead to good savings in time and money by exploiting inherent weaknesses of electronic commerce (while still staying legal). Interestingly virtually all participants only imagined those scenarios. No one planned to use the acquired knowledge for egoistic purposes.

1.2 Explanation

It comes to mind, that this altruistic good guy behaviour must be endemic. Compared to what could happen in electronic commerce and cyberspace we obviously are living in peaceful times. How come?

The answer lies in something that economists discover over and over again to their very surprise: individuals rarely behave as rational egoistic actors as the model of the *homo oeconomicus* prescribes [FiHe08]. People believe in moral values like

- honesty
- trust
- fairness
- equity
- veracity
- responsibility
- kindness
- politeness

and so on and would not defect from those moral standards without reason.[1]

2 Dangers

There is one looming danger however: people will defect from moral standards if the social commerce environment gives them reason to do so.

First of all the violation of the perceived psychological contract with the seller in the electronic commerce exchange has disastrous effects. Psychological contract violation not only changes people's emotions and attitudes toward the party who they perceive did them wrong, but also toward other parties who are perceived as belonging to the same group. Also psychological contract violation changes the "mental model" about electronic exchange relationships in general [PaGe05; LaJo03]. This generaliza-

---

1 Most of us are pretty high up in Kohlberg's stages of moral development most of the time (see [KoLH83]).

tion tendencies are reflected by comments like this: "I sent payment and never got the item. Very bad seller. Won't buy from eBay again."

Secondly results show that moral obligation is not spread evenly across electronic commerce situations. An "individual – known individual situation" as described by vignette "Loose coupling of electronic commerce exploitation" below is definitely considered fraud by most evaluators.

The case of shill bidding in eBay is not so clear to many people (individual – anonymous mass of individuals situation). In our research a significant percentage of reviewers considers this a crafty means to get a better price.

A staged attack against Amazon as described by vignette "Do it yourself refund of tuition fees" is considered fun and only a small percentage of reviewers found ethical problems with it (individual – social commerce system). The fault – if any – was definitely seen to be the fault of the system.

Since this attack includes many usually doubtful details like

- getting into the internet preventing being tracked to a personal account
- using a fake e-mail account
- using an identity of a person on vacation
- using disguise when collecting the shipment

there seem to be forces that weaken moral behaviour when transferring behaviour from the analogous world to the digital world.

3 Implications and Outlook

Social commerce providers are in constant danger that buyers stop transferring social interaction concepts from the analoguous world to the world of electronic commerce (including electronic banking).

3.1 Amazon versus ZVAB as an example

To illustrate what we think of, we would like to introduce a more detailed example. Amazon for example is obliged to provide customers with the rights to send back every item they ordered if the product does not meet their expectations. If this is done, it is Amazon who has to pay the postal charges. Amazingly enough, until now, only some customers make use of this opportunity. But what if more and more of them would extend usage of this offer and would start to use Amazon as a new kind of lending library? Someone who handles a book carefully can easily read each item he or she orders and then predict that he or she had a look at it and disliked it.

You can also imagine an organized denial of service attack: 100.000 activists ordering 100 books each and then sending it back. Book selling financial margins are low, so Amazon would have to cope with a major financial loss. On the other hand, to revoke the right of sending an item back under certain circumstances would cause the business models of social commerce to turn less attractive for honest customers. So there is no way out – Amazon relies on hopes that potential customers will use their rights modestly not only today but also in the future. It would be interesting to find out if this expectation is justified.

We assume that today customers transfer real world experience into social commerce. Someone who buys a book at the local book store does not read it under the eyes of the shop owner or takes it home and then brings it back later without good reason. This is justified, because in the shop the item can be evaluated well enough. Therefore, the right to return a book in is limited to certain circumstances – for example, if you find out that after page 125 the book goes on with page 182. It looks like customers who are used to this traditional book selling business model and its vendor – customer relationship tend to transfer the practice and ethics of this environment to the virtual environment. They feel a certain constraint preventing them from returning items just because they do not like them.

But what will happen if the number of digital natives in the customer community of a vendor like Amazon grows? Many of these people will have grown up by ordering products on web platforms. Buying at a local bookstore will be the exceptional case from their point of view. We estimate that this could have effects on the whole business model.

Interestingly enough, another model of book selling benefits even more from customers showing the same habits online as offline. ZVAB.COM is a search portal bringing together the catalogues of thousands of shops selling second-hand books worldwide. In Germany, most of these shops do not require payment in advance or by credit card when sending out a book. They just put it into an envelope and add a bill. Certified mail is seldom used. They simply rely on the honesty of their customers.

In this case, there may be another reason why this model works. Second-hand book shops have a certain image – most people think that their owners are idealistic and passionate preservers of the wisdom of the past. You do not get rich when running such a business. Vendors and customers are building a community, they are elitist accomplices in a more and more illiterate environment. Second-hand book sellers often help to find items desperately searched for over months and years. If you enter a second-hand bookshop, usually the interior of the shop and the exterior of the owner support the image of an old-fashioned, low-income business. A certain smell of old paper and dust fills the air. There is no chance of mistaking such a shop for a modern book store.

If you have a close look at ZVAB, you will discover that it is capable of transporting a little bit of these offline characteristics into the online world. In comparison to the bright online store world of Amazon the ZVAB portal looks simple and old-fashioned, too, while the search function and other services work perfectly and show that there is well-designed technology behind it. For every book, the individual book seller is represented. When the book arrives, the bill and other documents sometimes are written using a typewriter or a very old-fashioned printer. Often, a logo with calligraphic quality decorates the papers, telling the story of someone designing it at home with great artistry. So, as soon as you open the envelope and smell the book, the real second-hand book selling environments simply is there. Your imagination shows you the shop and the lady or the man who preserved the book for you. You won't betray him or her.

Our research uses vignettes depicting these situations.

3.2 Generalization

Borrowing from Clay Shirky [Shir03] one could say that social commerce is its own worst enemy. It relies heavily on the fact that customers transfer concepts from the analogous world to the digital world and that they do not recognize that there are subtle differences. Ordering merchandise from Amazon technically is sale on approval. But if people would do this on a high volume basis as they usually do in brick-and-mortar book stores as it is neatly shown above Amazon could hardly remain profitable.

It is highly improbable that digital natives will handle social commerce the same way as we digital toddlers do. If being digital means that you know how social commerce works you will use the mechanics to your own avail. This puts social commerce on par with brick-and-mortar commerce will consequently change revenues and force new added value models if it is to stay competitive with the old analogous methods of being serviced.

There is another mechanism to be taken into account. If transferring concepts from the analogous world to the digital world with Nass and Moon can be called a "mindless reaction to computers" and their environment [NaMo00], a possible "enlightenment" leading to a different view of social commerce not only may result from insights into its pure technical mechanisms. If computers are understood and treated as social actors [NaMo00], also ethics and fairness of these actors may be important to the users. A naive book shopper for example may understand the Amazon frontend as a friendly equivalent to a real helpful book seller in a shop as there is useful advice on the Amazon pages. Also help to discover products can be found and a chance to look into the books. But digital natives [PaGa08] who are used to produce their own content and online business models will certainly realize what Amazon also does: The vendor maximizes revenue from book sales by selling items with a lower headcount of employees than traditional shops by using technology and by transferring services like rating of products and product consulting to the customers themselves.

The finding that a system is inherently unethical or, in this case, simply based on pure commercial principles often leads to a less ethical behavior of those who inhabit or use the system – a lesson recently learned again from manifestations of the commercial crisis. This could endanger social commerce, too, at least those protagonists who do not build on acceptable business ethics.

4 Methodology

To corroborate the story of the fragility of current social commerce systems to changes in users conceptions and mindsets of what defines "good" behaviour in cyberspace authors set up a research design consisting of

- scenarios describing staged attacks against internet transaction systems exploiting the socio-technical nature of these systems
- implementing some of those attacks in a controlled experimental environment
- writing vignettes depicting those stages attacks using variations on damage to individuals vs mass of individuals vs social commerce systems, personal liability and outcome
- a study on the perceived ethical problems of the procedures depicted in the vignettes using focus groups and an online questionnaire study

Focus groups and questionnaire respondents are administered scales that measure cyber literacy, experience in the social commerce domain depicted in the vignette, moral judgement, prosocial orientation, justice/fairness, trust/trustworthiness and so on.

5 Conclusion

The research presented by the authors exemplifies the power of social engineering techniques in using the mechanics / the behavior of socio-technical systems to one's own avail as well as the current ineffectiveness of regulatory means and the noticeable lack of effective societal mechanism to prevent online fraud. People will be online wherever they are, all the time and in many different types of contexts, and these will all be known and processed by online services. We just do not know how such a world of physical/digital confluence will work out to the better or to the worse. But it seems worthwhile to point to role of human nature in this process.

In addition to the factors which make social, ethical and legal issues on the internet more complex the internet itself seems to present ethical issues that are distinct from those presented by traditional business activities.

6 Addendum – Sample Vignettes

6.1 Loose coupling of electronic commerce exploitation

In an eBay exchange a buyer reported the item (a computer) sold by Chad as "destroyed" and demanded and got a refund from Paypal. When the buyer shipped it back to Chad and he opened it, he found there was nothing wrong with it – except that the scammer had removed the memory, processor and hard drive. Now Chad is out $500 and left with a shell of a computer, and since the item was "received" Paypal won't do anything.

Chad accepted the return from UPS after a visual inspection, so UPS considered the matter closed. Pay-Pal and eBay both considered the matter closed. If the amount was large enough, the Chad could sue the buyer, but how could he prove that the computer was functional when he sold it?

6.2 Do it yourself refund of tuition fees

A group of students is upset because of the introduction of tuition fees in German universities and decides to perform a do-it-yourself refund of the tuition fees. They split up in teams of two and perform this plan:

Team 1 creates a fake mail account using personal data of a faculty member published in the university calendar.

Team 2 collects credit card information of some person using the receipts of the University card recharging terminals which are usually thrown into the waste basket next to the terminal.

Team 3 collects a university laptop allegedly for use in a course presentation.

Team 4 gets at vacation information of some university members, preferably high-ranking.

Team 5 connects the laptop to the University network via TP (no authentication), generates an Amazon account using the information above and orders some equipment to be delivered to the addresses of university members on vacation (express delivery)

Team 6 hangs around at the vacation address and collects merchandise if asked by the delivery driver.

Nobody is harmed, because every person is secured against loss by refund regulations or insurance.

References

[AnMo06] Anderson, Ross; Moore, Tyler, "The Economics of Information Security", Science, Vol. 314, 27.10.2006, pp. 610-613

[AvMy95] Avison, David E.; Myers, Michael D., "Information systems and anthropology: an anthropological perspective of IT and organizational culture", Information Technology & People, Vol. 8, No. 3, 1995, pp. 43-56

[Baka04] Bakan, Joel, "The Corporation. The Pathological Pursuit of Profit and Power", Free Press 2004

[FiHe08] Fischbacher, Urs; Heusi, Franziska, (2008) "Lies in Disguise. An experimental study on cheating", Thurgau Institute of Economics, Research Paper No. 40, November 2008

[FlRS05] Flechais, Ivan; Riegelsberger, Jens; Sasse, Angela M., „Divide and Conquer: The Role of Trust and Assurance in the Design of Secure Socio-Technical Systems",ACM Proceedings of the 2005 workshop on New security paradigms, pp. 33 – 41

[FPPS07] Franklin, Jason; Paxson, Vern; Perrig, Adrian; Savage, Stefan (2007), "An Inquiry into the Nature and Causes of the Wealth of Internet Miscreants", ACM CCS'07, October 29 – November 2, 2007

[Haid01] Haidt, Jonathan, "The Emotional Dog and Its Rational Tail: A Social Intuitionist Approach to Moral Judgment", Psychological Review, 2001, Vol. 108, No. 4, pp. 814-834

[Harf07] Harford, Tim, "The Undercover Economist", Abacus 2007

[KiBe06] Kiely, Laree; Benzel, Terry V., "Systemic Security Management", IEEE Security &Privacy, November/ December 2006, pp. 74-77

[KoLH83] Kohlberg, Lawrence; Charles Levine, Alexandra Hewer (1983). "Moral stages : a current formulation and a response to critics". Basel, NY: Karger, 1983

[KoPa04] Koskosas, Ioannis V.; Paul, Ray J., "The Interrelationship and Effect of Culture and Risk Communication in Setting Internet Banking Security Goals", ACM ICEC'04, Sixth International Conference on Electronic Commerce, pp. 341-349

[LaJo03] Lakoff, George; Johnson, Mark, (2003) "Metaphors We Live By", University of Chicago Press, 2003

[Lang00] Langford, Duncan, Internet Ethics, Palgrave 2000

[LeDu06] Levitt, Steven D.; Dubner, Stephen J., "Freakonomics", HarperCollins 2006

[Mans00] Manske, Kurt, "An Introduction to Social Engineering", Information Systems Security, November/ December 2000, pp. 53-59

[NaMo00] Nass, Clifford; Moon, Youngme, "Machines and Mindlessness: Social Responses to Computers", Journal of Social Issues, Vol. 56, No. 1, 2000, pp. 81-103

[NiBa08] Nikitkov, Alex; Bay, Darlene, "Online Action Fraud: Ethical Perspective", Journal of Business Ethics, Vol. 79, 2008, pp. 235-244

[ONei08] O'Neill, John, "Bank payment systems victim of elaborate social engineering scam", http://www.back-upanytime.com/blog/2008/08/bank-payment-systems-victim-of-elaborate-social-engineering-scam/

[Odly03] Odlyzko, Andrew, "Economics, Psychology, and Sociology of Security", Financial Cryptography: 7th International Conference, FC 2003, R. N. Wright, ed., Lecture Notes in Computer Science #2742, Springer, 2003, pp. 182-189

[PaGa08] Palfrey, John; Gasser, Urs, "Born Digital. Understanding the First Generation of Digital Natives", Basic Books 2008

[PaGe05] Pavlou, Paul A.; Gefen, David, (2005) "Psychological Contract Violation in Online Marketplaces: Antecedents, Consequences, and Moderating Role", Information Systems Research, Vol. 16, No. 4, December 2005, pp. 372-399

[Ruiu06] Ruius, Dragos, "Learning from Information Security History", IEEE Security & Privacy, January/February 2006, pp. 77-79

[Rush99] Rush, Jonathan J., "The "Social Engineering" of Internet Fraud", http://www.isoc.org/inet99/proceedings/3g/3g_2.htm

[Schn04]   Schneier, Bruce (2004), "Secrets & Lies. Digital Security in a Networked World", Wiley 2004

[Schn07]   Schneier, Bruce (2007), "Security in ten years", http://www.schneier.com/blog/archives/2007/12/security_in_ten.html, 3.12.2007

[Shir03]   Shirky, Clay, "A Group Is Its Own Worst Enemy", Speech a ETech, April, 2003, http://www.shirky.com/writings/group_enemy.html

[SpTa04]   Spinello, Richard A.; Tavani, Herman, T., "Cybertechnology, Ethical Concepts, and Methodological Frameworks: An Introduction to Cyberethics", Richard A. Spinello and Herman T. Tavani, (eds.), "Readings in Cyberethics", 2nd ed, Jones and Bartlett Publishers, 2004, pp. 1-12

[VaPL02]   Vaes, Jeroen; Paladino, Maria-Paola; Leyens, Jacques-Philippe, "The lost e-mail: Prosocial reactions induced by uniquely human emotions", Britisch Journal of Social Psychology, Vol. 41, 2002, pp. 521-534

[Vand09]   Vanderbeeken, Mark, "Taking a Broader View of the Human Experience", Interactions, March/April 2009, pp. 54-57

[Wals96]   Walsham, Geoff, "Ethical theory, codes of ethics and IS practice", Information Systems Journal, Vol. 6, 1996, pp. 69-81

[Whit09]   Whitson, Jennifer, "Identity Theft and the Challenges of Caring for your Virtual Self", Interactions, March/April 2009, pp. 41-45

How to Establish Security Awareness in Schools

Anja Beyer[1] · Christiane Westendorf[2]

[1] Generation:Secure
IT & Sicherheitsberatung
mail@generation-secure.de

[2] Dipl.-Medienwissenschaftlerin
(Degree in media science)
christiane.westendorf@gmx.de

Abstract

The internet is a fast changing medium and comprises several websites fraught with risk. In this context especially young age groups are endangered. They have less experience using the media and little knowledge on existing internet risks. There are a number of initiatives, which are engaged in the topic of internet safety. They provide information about measures on how to prevent and to deal with internet risks. However it is not certain if these initiatives do reach their target group (children and adolescents). In this regard schools bear a special relevance, since they have the knowledge about didactic methods and the chance to address measures directly to children and adolescents. The authors of this paper provide an overview of current security education in German schools, problems and open questions. Finally the authors make recommendations on how to establish internet safety in schools.

1 Introduction

It is not necessary to mention that education in the field of IT security is important as the ISSE conference has this topic on its agenda for years now. Responsible security officers in companies argue that educating employees in security issues is of great importance, but as well difficult. Awareness trainings often start with simple things like "do not stick your password to the monitor" or "do not give confidential data to untrustworthy people". More complex trainings cover topics like encrypting data on external hard disks or e-mail. These awareness teaching programmes can be cost-intensive, so that companies often do not make use of it.

By considering the fact that children already have contact with computers and the internet in their first years of school or even in kindergarten, the reader may agree that security education often begins too late. The problem here is that the young users are almost left alone with risks. IT security is a very complex field. Neither teachers nor parents are currently able to teach security topics. However, this is of great importance since there are risks that could even damage the children's development for example when it comes to pornographic or violent contents[1]. This is why the authors are convinced that IT/internet security education (awareness programmes) must start at school as soon as the kids start using computers and the internet. In this regard schools bear a special relevance, since they have the knowl-

---

1 The authors use the terms "IT/Internet security" and "IT/Internet safety" equivalently and define the terms as the protection against internet risks as well as raising the awareness for these risks.

N. Pohlmann, H. Reimer, W. Schneider (Editors): Securing Electronic Business Processes, Vieweg (2009), 177-186

edge about didactic methods and the chance to address measures directly to children and adolescents. Every young child living in a developed country visits a school – so school is the only institution where the majority of young computer users[2] can be reached.

"The European Parliament and the Council of the European Union recognize that it is necessary to [...] promote safe use of modern communication media and to protect consumers from undesirable content" and established the "Safer Internet Programme" in the EU [Klick09a]. The campaign, also known as the "Klicksafe"-initiative, provides an information portal with lots of material for children, parents and teachers. This programme also initiates annual events such as the Safer Internet Day. There are several information portals similar to that of the EU [Init09, BSI09, Medi09, Poli09]. But it is uncertain if these information portals do reach their target group because the people who visit these web pages must already have a certain level of awareness. But the main target group – the unaware people – can hardly be reached in such a way.

The initiative "Klicksafe" broadcasted several awareness spots on TV, for example "Wo ist Klaus?" ("Where is Klaus?") [Klick09b] with one majorly important statement for parents: if you want to protect your children in real life you shall do that in the digital world as well. But one important question remains unanswered: how can parents achieve that? Furthermore, it takes a big effort to stay informed. Teachers as well as parents are left alone with this task, for which reason it seems necessary that experts support teachers and parents.

The authors are convinced that the only way to establish security awareness in society is to start the topic in schools as soon as young people start using computers and the internet. In consequence school graduates already have this knowledge and bring it into the companies if they start working later.

Establishing security education in schools is a big step to take. In this article the authors give an overview of the state-of-the-art of security awareness programmes (in the educational domain the term "media literacy" is used) in German schools and show that the situation of schools can be improved immensely. The authors identify problems and give suggestions for future working programmes.

2 Current Situation in Schools (in Germany)

2.1 General Overview

First, the authors must mention that the situation is very different in various German federal states. Each federal state has its own educational system and in consequence its own school curricula. This is why we can only mention some general findings here.

Some federal states in Germany implemented internet safety into the curricula and some did not. Media related topics in general are either integrated in one subject as it is the case in Thuringia [Thür04, Thür02] or in different subjects e.g. in Mecklenburg-Western Pomerania [Mini04]. Though a holistic illustration of risks is missing, only a few isolated aspects are covered, for example data security or special risks of new media in Saxony [Säch07, Säch04]. Moreover the state Rhineland-Palatine created a training program, whereby teachers in schools are trained by state moderators so that teachers have a contact person who can inform and advise them of this topic [Czer08]. In addition in 2006 a project called "webclicker" started in Hesse. Students in small groups create e.g. a song or a photo story about a certain risk [LPRh06]. On the one side students learn about the importance of using the net safely.

---

2   University courses are even too late for effective accessibility because firstly, only a part of school leavers take up studies and secondly, in university age the people already use computer and internet for years.

On the other site the learning process is integrated in a creative context. Moreover there is the initiative "Schulen ans Netz" ("schools connected to the net") that provides schools with computers and internet access [Schu09].

Through an internet connection students might have access to websites with inappropriate content. In this respect schools must decide whether they want to use internet filters or not. Some states and cities developed specific internet filters for schools. For example there is the project "Jugendschutzfilter für Schulen" ("internet filters for schools") in Thuringia. More than 600 schools are attached to the internet filter already. The filter is based on a negative list so that all requests for websites from schools are checked before access is approved [Thür08]. Filter projects also started in other federal states [Schu05]. Still these filters do not offer enough protection. Till now no filter product was recommended since filter rates are relatively low, so that filters cannot prevent the access to inappropriate content effectively.

Nevertheless all these programmes and projects leave no conclusion on the situation of schools. Communication as well as exchanging knowledge and experience between the single schools and states could support projects and the revision of the curricula in all states.

2.2 Qualitative Study „Internet Safety in Schools"

In order to get a deeper understanding of what the current situation in schools is, the qualitative study "Internet Safety in Schools" was carried out [West09]. The aim of this study was to assess the situation of internet safety in schools of general education. Therefore guideline-based interviews with experts of seven different schools from Thuringia were conducted. Experts from primary schools, regular schools as well as grammar schools were interviewed. The questions in the interview related to measures of schools in class, extracurricular measures, IT measures and measures of supervision. Moreover the experts were asked to evaluate the meaning of teachers and parents in this context and the problems schools have regarding internet safety. Subsequently these interviews were transcribed and evaluated on the basis of a qualitative content analysis. The following chapters will provide an overview of the main findings.

2.2.1 Measures in Class

The study could identify several internet risks that teachers warn about in schools. These risks included websites with problematic content, technical risks like viruses, dubious offers in the internet, copyrighted material, publishing of personal data, being addicted to computers, Phishing and Cybermobbing. In this context teachers gave their students advices how to deal with these risks in a certain situation, such as the protection of the personal computer through a firewall, browser related advices, for example using Firefox as a safe browser, or specific principles on how to behave in chat rooms. In addition the experts referred to a systematic use of search engines, the consideration of copyright aspects like publishing an imprint on a private website, aspects regarding encryption and the cautious handling of personal data. In case students had problems, teachers named contact persons and tried to point out the importance of a critical, attentive, aware use of the internet.

The analysed schools showed large differences in the contents of teaching as well as in the didactic methods they used for teaching. Normally they used one lesson for internet safety. Internet safety was primary part of the subject "Medienkunde" ("media studies") and computer science, but also other subjects like ethics and social studies dealt with safety aspects. Within primary schools internet safety was part of the third und fourth grade whereas secondary schools integrated it mostly between the fifth and seventh grade.

2.2.2 Measures outside Class

Generally the schools conducted more measures in class than in extracurricular courses. Only a few courses for students could be found in this context like a specific project or an afternoon class of a working group. In this context schools rather tend to offer contact persons for students like teachers of computer science or media studies. Another measure outside class related to the communication process between teachers and students. Students talked with teachers during breaks or teachers exchanged information within meetings. Measures involved also trainings for teachers in and outside schools or the communication with parents. Schools organised thematic parent-teacher conferences or talked with parents in other meetings about a safe use of the internet.

2.2.3 Technical Measures

The experts were also asked to explain the IT measures, which were relevant in the context of internet safety. First of all methods to block specific websites were identified, such as internet filters or internal lists that contain links of websites schools block individually. The second group of IT measures contained systems whereby teachers had access to the student's computers. Schools used monitoring systems, so that teachers could control the websites students surfed on. The third part of measures concerned internal settings such as a personal login for students or the prohibition of specific actions like downloading files from the internet.

2.2.4 Measures of Supervision

The results of the study showed how the schools handled supervision, e.g. that always a person is present when students are using the internet. The experts mentioned several measures to support supervision. One measure was to beam the computer displays on the wall for instance so teachers can observe activities of the students from different positions in the class room. Moreover schools laid down different rules students had to obey. These rules prohibited to surf on pornographic websites for example. Also situations could be determined when students were intervened from using the internet. One situation concerned students visiting a website which is not useful for fulfilling the task that was given by the teacher.

2.2.5 Relevance of Schools

The experts were also questioned about the meaning of schools in respect of teaching a safe use of the internet. As one main result they named that schools have a big significance in this context. Hereby schools should explain risks, but also show practical ways on how to deal with these risks. Moreover schools should follow general measures and projects and communicate with parents on this topic.

In comparison experts were asked to name the functions of the parents. Parents should control their children's use of the internet and set up rules such as the duration of internet use or the activities children can use the internet for. If they do not obey, parents should also introduce sanctions. Furthermore parents need to strengthen a competent use of the internet of their children by showing up risks or talking to their kids about their experiences. In addition parents should inform themselves about internet safety and communicate with schools.

2.2.6 Problems

In the last part of the interview problems were discussed. The experts mentioned aspects of knowledge and personal positions. Often teachers lack of knowledge in this field or students are not interested in events about internet safety. Also the general organisation of the subject "Medienkunde" can be improved. For example schools do not have professional groups in the field of media, which are attended by the same teachers over years. Furthermore, general problems concerning internet filters exist. Filters do not offer a 100 percent safety against inappropriate content or even if schools use internet filters, students find a way to evade these filters. Issues also related to the supervision of students using the internet. Either computer labs were supervised seldom or there were computers which were never supervised. In addition, schools face difficult conditions. Often there is not enough room to provide a computer lab, financial resources are missing or teachers have little time to teach internet safety. Schools also need external support like special trainings or information material, that includes e.g. an overview on relevant risks especially intended for teachers who are not engaged much in internet safety. Finally experts referred to parents, who should control their children more often and intensively when they use the internet.

2.2.7 Differences, Similarities and other Criteria

Major differences could be found between primary schools and secondary schools. Primary schools conducted fewer measures than other schools. All schools offered students a contact person and set up rules for the use of the internet. Also all schools followed the rule that always a supervisor was present, when students were using the internet. Moreover schools mainly agreed that neither teachers nor parents have enough knowledge on this topic or that there are only a few teachers in the schools who have the knowledge of internet safety. Regarding regulary schools and grammar schools didactic methods can vary since measures attract students from both schools differently.

Finally further criteria could be identified, which have an influence on the situation of schools. These criteria included the school catchment area, the age of students, the dedication of teachers as well as the support through external persons like parents and institutions.

3 Situation in Europe

In combination with the Safer Internet Day 2005 the countries of the EU realised several projects. This chapter gives an exemplary review on projects relating to schools.

Iceland: In 2005 the SAFT (SAmfélag, Fjölskylda og Tækni or community, family and technology) educational package was released containing exercises about safer internet strategies. The aim of the exercises was to strengthen the awareness for a safer internet and was addressed to children (grade four to six) and parents. The package was distributed to all elementary schools, so that teachers could integrate internet safety into their lessons [Atlas05].

Ireland: In 2005 the Irish National Center for Technology in Education developed and offered an interactive online course for teachers. Teachers learned about safe internet strategies so that they could integrate these contents into their lessons [Wals05].

Poland: The Nobody's Children Foundation and NASK (Research and Academic Computer Network) organised in 2005 a safer internet conference. This conference was addressed to educators, psychologists, police and representatives from ministries etc. Similar conferences were held in 16 other cities throughout the country. Workshops and seminars dealt with an educational campaign and illegal internet content. An event for children was arranged to communicate a safe use also to the young group [Wrze05].

UK: The Semley CE VA Primary School was awarded for their work in the field of internet safety. The school taught internet safety for four years. The school cooperated with several agencies to raise the awareness of other schools and to demonstrate the importance of teaching internet safety. Moreover pupils cooperated with another school in London and tried to find ways how to encourage others to use the net safely [Hopwe05].

4 How to establish Security Education in Schools

Based on the current situation and the identified problems, suggestions are given of how security education can be established in schools. In this chapter we start with some general theses which can be seen as 'guidelines' for future projects. The second part of the chapter gives concrete examples of how security education could look like in detail. Finally, the third part of the chapter gives some recommendations for future working programmes.

4.1 General Theses

The following general theses are the basis for ongoing work:

1. The main target should be: each pupil in Europe must have the chance to get educated in security topics at school.
2. Security education should start at a very young age as soon as one has the first contact to PC or internet.
3. But also adolescents from age 17 to 19 should be a target group since they use the internet more intensively.
4. Curricula for primary schools and secondary schools should be elaborated and integrate a holistic presentation of relevant risks.
5. Working programmes should be based on measures for teachers imparting knowledge on internet safety. Platforms are needed which support the exchange of knowledge in this field between teachers and experts, e. g. media pedagogues, universities, institutes.
6. Those working programmes should concentrate especially on primary school teachers since children start using the internet at a very young age, so that internet safety becomes more and more relevant for primary schools.
7. Students can contribute enormously to security education and offer one way to communicate risks and security awareness to school mates.
8. It seems more reasonable to finance educational projects and courses for schools as to finance the development of internet filters. Filters cannot teach children and adolescents, how to use the internet safely.
9. Also parents should be involved in working programs so that measures have an effect on the behaviour and security awareness of children and adolescents.
10. Security education networks should be installed consisting of students, teachers, parents and experts.

4.2 Hands on Security Education in Schools

In this chapter the authors introduce some concrete examples on how security education can be established in schools. These examples were conceptualized by students during a university course called "Privacy and social Media – Media literacy goes schools" at the University of Technology Ilmenau in Germany. Some concepts are based in parts on existing material from different initiatives.

4.2.1 Comic and Quiz "Safe chat"

As IT security topics are quite difficult to understand – especially for young users – a way must be found to explain security risks easily and interestingly to kids. A comic and a corresponding quiz can be one possibility how this can be done.

This concept is based on the comics of "the Internauten". The Internauten is a project within the initiative "Deutschland sicher im Netz" ("Internet security in Germany") and focuses the education of kids about internet risks. There are several comics concerning different topics such as internet chat, search engines and Cybermobbing. In these comics the kids accompany the three friends Rio, Nina and Ben (the so-called "Internauten", see Fig. 1) at their adventures while fighting for a safe internet [Inte09].

The topic to deal with is the safe use of internet chats. Teachers can use the comic "Die falsche Paula" ("The false Paula") to read, to discuss and to reflect on "secure chat" (safe use of chat rooms). The first task for the students (for example in the fourth grade) is to read the comic and to explain their own experience with online chats. Through the comic students learn that chat partners can have a different identity as they expected, like an ugly old man instead of another student. After the students read the comic and discussed their own experiences they can test their knowledge in the quiz. In addition to the comic and the quiz, a guideline for teachers was developed providing some general information about the topic can be used in the lessons. This concept tried to deal with the topic "safe chat" in an easy and appropriate way for children.

Fig. 1: The Internauten [Inte09]

4.2.2 Project day "Safe usage of social networks"

This concept is oriented toward a full day where students can choose a project dealing with social networks.

The concept consists of several modules. Each module focuses on a concrete learning target. The first module is called "basic knowledge" and wants to provide general information about the topic. The students learn from videos and examples what social networks are and what kind of risks they must be aware of (for example privacy risks). The second module is a profile check where students can test their profiles (like in SchülerVZ) for aspects of privacy and security. In a third step the teacher organises a group discussion where students talk with their teacher about the advantages and disadvantages of social networks. In order to visualize the topic they create a wallpaper with all the discussion points. The installation of this wallpaper in the classroom remembers the students about the topic each day.

4.2.3 Media Trip with Blogging

This concept combines a "normal" school trip with a lesson on the media. Here the students have the task to comment on their experiences in a blog (weblog) during the Media Trip.

Based on an internal school server the students write comments or place pictures on an internet blog about their every day experiences. The aim is that students are able to make mistakes in this "internal community" where only teachers and school fellows have access to and can read the postings. Assuming that the students will write about the sightseeing-tour in the morning as well as the last nights party including loads of "not so nice" pictures. Students in this project will really "feel" what privacy means as they are directly affected and see the comments to their postings from the teachers and fellows.

The final important step is that the teachers start a discussion round with the student so that they can reflect their doings.

4.3 Recommendations

The findings in the former chapters lead to some recommendations. There a several ways how schools can improve their situation.

- Students should organise events and projects under the direction of teachers. Example projects are the writing of an article for the student's magazine or the website, the organisation of an open day or thematic parent-teacher conferences.
- Schools offer many places to attract the attention of students for internet safety. Information (material) can be put on the website, in rooms used for free time like the computer lab, the cafeteria, screensaver and posters can be put on walls.
- Teachers can be trained especially in the schools about risks and their consequences, but trainings should also include didactic methods and ways how to teach this topic. Often there are teachers who dealt with a safe use of the internet for a long time. An easy method to raise the awareness is to inform all colleges with a presentation held by experienced teachers in a staff meeting.
- To plan measures and projects schools must know how often and which websites their pupils use. Therefore teachers should talk with students about their experience in lessons or breaks or make an anonymous survey.
- As it is already practised by some schools, parents can be informed on the importance of a safe use of the internet in parent-teacher conferences, letters to the parents, open days. This can be the basis for a useful cooperation between schools and parents.

Schools need also external support. Following you find recommendations on how this support can be provided.

- Teachers must receive training in security and awareness topics. It is essential that teachers and schools get more support in this direction than they do at the moment.
- Schools need information material which gives an overview on the subject. Either useful existing material should be forwarded to schools such as research results of current studies and brochures (KIM study) or adequate material for schools' use must be prepared.
- The topic is of such great relevance that it is necessary to integrate it into the school curricula in every federal state. A good solution is the creation of a school subject like „Medienkunde" („me-

dia literacy") in Thuringia. Instead of creating too much „open" curricula it would be helpful to determine the exact topics that must be covered during one school year.

- Therefore teacher guidelines must refer to existing material which will help teachers to prepare for their lessons easier. The EU „Safer Internet Programme" must be seen as the first step towards „a safe use of modern communication media" [Kick09] and a society where people are aware of the internet risks. For the next steps it is necessary that the contact to the target group is deepened. The Safer Internet Day is a good possibility to initiate awareness programmes in schools directly at the place where the target group is. Also it would be possible to integrate some training courses.

- It is necessary that the schools receive support for the organisation and enforcement of the Safer Internet Day. Local networks consisting of scholars, teachers, parents and experts could provide such support (see Fig.2). Local experts are the first contact persons for schools for the task.

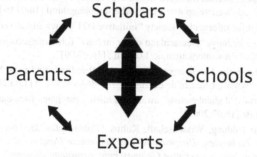

Fig. 2: Awareness Raising Network

- As it was shown in chapter 2.1, some German states started projects in this field or exchanged the contents of their curricula. A conference could help to exchange information about projects between schools, experts, parents, and other institutions. Firstly a conference could attract the attention of headmasters and teachers. Secondly it gives ideas about methods that show how schools can teach a safe use of the internet, especially those schools which conduct only a few measures.

- For a deeper security training the existing materials from Klicksafe, Internauten, Polizeiberatung should be used. It would be helpful if all initiatives would be accessible from one point of entry. At the moment each initiative has its own information portal which could lead to some confusion for the customers due to such a variety of information offers.

- Financial resources should be provided so that schools can start projects. Schools can also be supported through sponsoring special trainings. Also incentives should be given. If schools implement internet safety or improve their situation in an innovative way, they shall be awarded for their work.

- Also research in this field should be promoted. Contents of the internet are changing quickly, so that new risks occur easily. Only on the basis of current findings, schools can adapt their teaching programmes constantly.

References

[Atlas05] Atlason, G. *"Iceland launches new educational package on Safer Internet Day"* 2005. www.saferinternet.org/ww/en/pub/insafe/news/articles/iceland_launches.htm, [13.07.2009]

[BSI09] Website of the German Federal Office for Information Security, information about safe internet usage, http://www.bsi-fuer-buerger.de/, [16.07.2009]

[Czer08] Czernohorsky, S. *"Weiterbildung Jugendmedienschutzberaterin/-berater an Schulen in Rheinland-Pfalz. Medienkompetenz macht Schule"*, 2008. http://medienkompetenz.rlp.de/projekte.html, [11.05.2009]

[Hopwe05] Hopwood, K.: *"Semley School wins award for innovative work in internet safety"* 2005. www.saferinternet.org/ww/en/pub/insafe/news/articles/0707/uk3.htm, [13.07.2009]

[Klick09a] Safer Internet Programme "Klicksafe", www.klicksafe.de/ueber-klicksafe/die-initiative/project-information/what-is-klicksafe.html, [16.07.09]

[Klick09b] TV-Spot of the safer internet initiative "Klicksafe" named "Where is Klaus?", www.klicksafe.de/ueber-klicksafe/downloads/weitere-spots/eu-spot-cyber-mobbing.html [16.07.09]

[Init09] European Project for Information society "Initiative D21", www.initiatived21.de/, [16.07.09]

[Inte09] Project within the initiative "Deutschland sicher im Netz" („Internetsecurity for Germany") called „The Internauten",http://www.internauten.de/1.0.html , [16.07.09]

[LPRh06] LPR hessen (Hessische Landesanstalt für privaten Rundfunk und neue Medien) *"Webclicker – Wir clicken clever!"*. www.lpr-hessen.de/default.asp?m=86&s=1371 , [11.05.2009]

[Medi09] Information portal "Medienbewusst" awareness raising campaign focussing kids and the media www.medienbewusst.de,[16.07.2009]

[Mini04] Ministerium für Bildung, Wissenschaft, Kultus *"Rahmenplan Medienerziehung. Grundschule, Regionale Schule, Verbundene Hauptschule- und Realschule Hauptschule, Realschule, Gymnasium, Integrierte Gesamtschule, kooperative Gesamtschule. Erprobungsfassung"*, 2004. www.bildung-mv.de/export/sites/lisa/de/medien/medienerziehung/rpmedienerziehung.pdf , [08.01.2009]

[Poli09] Information Portal of the german police focussing security awareness raising, www.polizei-beratung.de/vorbeugung/medienkompetenz/internet/, [16.07.2009]

[Säch07] Sächsisches Staatsministerium für Kultus *"Informatik. Lehrplan Gymnasium"*, 2007. www.sachsen-macht-schule.de/apps/lehrplandb/downloads/lehrplaene/lp_gy_informatik_2007.p df , [05.05.2008]

[Säch04] Sächsisches Staatsministerium für Kultus *"Biologie. Lehrplan Gymnasium"*, 2004. www.sachsen-macht-schule.de/apps/lehrplandb/downloads/lehrplaene/lp_gy_biologie.pdf

[Schu05] Schulen ans Netz *"Jugendmedienschutz. Filterlösungen im schulischen Umfeld."* IT works Themenreihe, 2005. http://itworks.schulen-ans-netz.de/publikationen/dokus/Jugendmediensch utz 2006.pdf , [06.01.2008]

[Schu09] Schulen ans Netz „Entwicklung des Vereins," http://www.schulen-ans-netz.de/ueberuns /derverein/entwicklungdesvereins.php, [16.07.2009]

[Thür08] Thüringer Arbeitskreis Schulsoftware *"Jugendschutzfilter für Internetseiten"*, 2008. http://filter.th.schule.de [05.01.2009].

[Thür04] Thüringer Kulturministerium "Medienkompetenz in der Grundschule", 2004. www.schulportal-thueringen.de/c/document_library/get_file?folderId=20024&name=DLFE-69.pdf, [16.06.2008]

[Thür02] Thüringer Kulturministerium *"Handreichung für die Klassenstufen 5 bis 7 an Regelschulen, an Gesamtschulen, an Förderschulen mit dem Bildungsgang der Regelschule und an Gymnasien. Kurs Medienkunde"*, 2002. www.schulportalthueringen.de/c/document_library/ get_file? folderId =20024&name=DLFE-70.pdf, [16.06.2008]

[Wals05] Walsh, G. *"Online course for webwise teachers"*, 2005. www.saferinternet.org/ww/en/pub/ins afe/news/articles/0307/ie.htm, [13.07.2009]

[West09] Westendorf, C. „*Internetsicherheit an Schulen – Eine qualitative Untersuchung zum Stellenwert sicherer Internetnutzung an Thüringer Schulen"*, Diploma Thesis at University of Technology Ilmenau, 2009.

[Wrze05] Wrzesien, A. *"Warsaw kicks off series of conferences"*, 2005. www.saferinternet.org/ww/en/pub/insafe/news/articles/0705/pl.htm, [13.07.2009]

Privacy and Security – a Way to Manage the Dilemma

Walter Peissl

Institute of Technology Assessment
Austrian Academy of Sciences
wpeissl@oeaw.ac.at

Abstract

Privacy and security are often seen as opposites in a zero-sum game. The more you want from one, the less you get from the other. To overcome this dilemma the PRISE project (EU-funded by PASR/DG Enterprise) developed a methodology to establish sets of criteria for privacy enhancing security technologies. These sets of criteria are applicable on different levels (research, development, implementation) and by different actors (research coordinators, industry, policy-makers, public and private users). The use of these criteria is intended to contribute directly to a tangible and demonstrable improvement in security as accepted and acceptable security technologies will be more easily implemented, more widely used and confronted with less rejection by the general public and users of these technologies. A similar set of criteria is used for certification for the European Privacy Seal. Both the privacy by design approach and the certification scheme should increase the competitiveness of European security industries by providing guidance on the provision of widely acceptable security technologies.

1 Introduction

The broad use of ICTs in almost every part of daily life produces a huge amount of data. A great part of the stored and processed data is personal data of the user or people involved. It reveals a lot about users' behaviour and helps create a picture of people's personal lifestyles. Data stems from economic enterprises as well as from state surveillance systems and together they manifest a threat to privacy.

These new threats can no longer be dealt with by legal means alone. Interdisciplinarity is the key word. This paper will present new approaches that incorporate privacy-oriented thinking and PETs[1] principles early into the design-process. The starting point is the idea that even in data protection it is cheaper to make fundamental design-decisions earlier in the design-process rather than applying end-of-pipe solutions in order to ensure that a product or service complies with legal requirements or to gain acceptance on the market. These approaches will be discussed along with the presentation of results from two recent research projects in which ITA was involved: PRISE[2] und EuroPriSe[3].

In dealing with security and privacy you often hear that they are at odds with each other, e.g. you only get more of one by reducing the other. In order to overcome this kind of trade-off there will first be a short discussion of the term security and the political discourse on it. After that we will show that privacy and security are not a zero-sum-game. Rather, by applying some of the above mentioned approaches you can get more of both!

1	Privacy Enhancing Technologies (PETs)
2	http://prise.oeaw.ac.at
3	https://www.european-privacy-seal.eu/

N. Pohlmann, H. Reimer, W. Schneider (Editors): Securing Electronic Business Processes, Vieweg (2009), 187-196

2 Security – a dazzling concept

Security is a multi-facetted phenomenon and means different things to different people. It varies considerably from one scientific discipline to another and in the broader context of public and political debate. Basically, security derives from the Latin "securus", which itself is based on "sine" (without) and "cura" (concern/worry/problem). This means security may be defined as the status of no necessity to care see [1]. It is the absence of danger to individuals as well as to institutions. Because there is no situation without any danger or threat from outside, security is the condition of being protected against danger or loss. [2]

In the course of time the concept of security has developed and taken on different dimensions.[4] Since the 18th century security has included the protection of individuals, their rights and property. In 1948 the Universal Declaration of Human Rights[5] stated in Article 3 "Everyone has the right to life, liberty and security of person." And in Article 22 "Everyone, as a member of society, has the right to social security and is entitled to realisation, through national effort and international co-operation and in accordance with the organisation and resources of each State, of the economic, social and cultural rights indispensable for his dignity and the free development of his personality."

In the context of the PRISE project we defined security as the absence of danger – that is a state where the desired status quo is not threatened or disrupted in any way. Furthermore, in PRISE, security is understood as the security of society – or more precisely – of the citizens that constitute society [4]. Security has a twofold character: it is the security of society – organised in national states – and it is the security of the individuals forming a society.

There is a long tradition of security policy based on Hobbes' contribution to state philosophy, which saw the protection of the individual's security as a responsibility of the state. In that sense security prevailed over freedom [5] and [6]. Traditional state-centred security was the dominating concept and reached a peak during the Cold War. After World War II, diplomacy and international organisations began to play a more important role; organisations like the United Nations were widely acknowledged for dispute resolution. [3]. The Helsinki Final Act of the Conference for Security and Cooperation in Europe [7] established 10 basic principles (see [8] cit. in [3]). "Respect for Human Rights and Fundamental Freedom" was among them. Although security policy was state-centred for a long time, at least there remained a marginal aspect of security for individuals.

In recent years a new approach has become more important in the political sphere and centres more on the individual than on the national state. In 1994 the UNDP published the new concept of human security in its Human Development Report. This document is generally seen as the first significant attempt at articulating the broad approach to human security as a part of international policy. The report describes human security as having two principal aspects: the freedom from chronic threats such as hunger, disease and repression, coupled with the protection from sudden calamities [6].

Security policy on the level of the European Union has only recently been established[6]. In September 2006 ESRAB published its final report „Meeting the Challenge"[7], setting the European security research agenda thereby structuring the forthcoming research on security within Framework Programme 7 (FP7).

---

4   For details see: [3] ÖAW, Sicherheitsforschung, Begriffsfassung und Vorgangsweise für Österreich. 2005: Vienna., 20ff
5   http://www.un.org/Overview/rights.html
6   For a overview see: [9] Hayes, B., Arming Big Brother – The EU's Security Research Programme. 2006, Transnational Institute. TNI Briefing series 2006/1
7   http://ec.europa.eu/enterprise/security/articles/article_06_09_25_tc_en.htm

Besides these formal documents from EU bodies there has been an attempt to incorporate the human security concept into European policy. The so-called Barcelona Report [10] was written by members of the private Study Group on Europe's Capabilities and presented to the EU High Representative for Common Foreign Affairs and Security Policy Javier Solana in September 2004. It was an attempt to launch a discussion on Human Security as a part of the EU's Foreign Affairs and Security Policy. The report proposes a "Human Security Doctrine for Europe". The authors refer to human security as the "freedom for individuals from basic insecurities caused by gross human rights violations." [10]

The report aims at giving the Foreign and Security Policy of the EU a new direction through the incorporation of the Human Security Concept. However, critics say that "the authors of the Barcelona Report are not primarily interested in reflections about the concept of human security. They regard this term more or less as a valuable tool, which helps them to elaborate an alternative, partly avantgardistic foreign and security policy for the European Union."[11]

As shown above, security is a multifaceted phenomenon. It is individual security on the one hand and it is also security of enterprises and societal (national) security on the other. Neither is possible without the other. We argue that the underlying problem is a trade-off between these two dimensions of security rather than a trade-off between security and the fundamental right to privacy. It is the task of policy-makers as well as of the citizens to find a balance between the security of the individual and national security. Without security policies and law enforcement we may face anarchy in both foreign policy and internal affairs. Without individual freedom and autonomy, democracy itself is threatened.

The proportionality of measures is the key to acceptance[8]. It may be seen from two sides. Firstly it is the least necessary infringement, the least invasive measure to be taken in order to minimise the infringement of fundamental rights. In PRISE we give advice on how to do so and how to build this into security technology[9]. Secondly, proportionality may also be found in security gain. The more security you can gain from a measure the more it will be acceptable to infringe fundamental rights. The problem we are facing is that the security gain is not easy to calculate and, furthermore, people vary in the value they place on it. Although there are statistics on "objective security", like the number of attacks or of victims of attacks etc., there is a considerable problem in the legitimisation of measures and technologies. The difference can only be measured as compared with an equivalent period of time in the past – it is an ex-post statement. Even though a causality may be found between that difference and the measure or technology used, it can never be proven that an incident could not also have happened in an alternative scenario.

"Subjective security perception" is an important dimension of the issue. Because security is not something objective, many different influences may be involved in creating the feeling of security. One of these influences could be short-term focussed and non-proportionate measures. In that sense the implementation and use of security technologies may – despite their lack of an objective and measurable potential to contribute to a security gain – be an instrument which raises the level of perceived societal security. For the time being the main problem for the protection of fundamental rights is not a threat from a clear enemy, it is the lack of awareness of how privacy is affected by society's reaction to perceived risks. It is necessary to stimulate awareness of societal security as well as of the challenges that result from meeting the threats to this security with different means and technologies. Or as Louis

---

8 Again stressed by the European Parliament see: [12] European Parliament Resolution of 12 December 2007 on the fight against terrorism. 2007. http://www.europarl.europa.eu/sides/getDoc.do?pubRef=-//EP//TEXT+TA+P6-TA-2007-0612+0+DOC+XML+V0//EN Site visited 22nd July 2009

9 See [13] Raguse, M., O. Langfeldt, and M. Hansen, PRISE D3.3 Design Proposals, European Commission PASR, Editor. 2008, Unabhängiges Landeszentrum für Datenschutz Schleswig-Holstein,: Kiel. and [14] Raguse, M., et al., PRISE D6.2 – Criteria for privacy enhancing security technologies, European Commission PASR, Editor. 2008, Institute of Technology Assessment Austrian Academy of Sciences,: Vienna. Both can be downloaded from: http://prise.oeaw.ac.at/publications.htm

Brandeis put it: "Experience should teach us to be most on our guard to protect liberty when the Government's purposes are beneficent. Men born to freedom are naturally alert to repel invasion of their liberty by evil-minded rulers. The greatest dangers to liberty lurk in insidious encroachment by men of zeal, well meaning but without understanding."[10]

3 Theses and solutions

In order to structure the discussion of possible ways to overcome the privacy and security dilemma we present three theses as starting points:

Thesis 1: Privacy is a fundamental right. Nowadays it is endangered by a variety of means and can no longer be enforced by legal means alone. Reasons for this may be found in the very low level of awareness of users of ICT and in the lack of resources of data protection authorities [15-18].

Thesis 2: Privacy is increasingly on the political agenda. Indicators for this may be found on the one hand in the media coverage of data-loss scandals around Europe, the low level of acceptance of the data-retention directive and the protests against it in several European countries. On the other hand the EU publishes calls for data protection research and finances pilot projects like the EuroPriSe project. On a global level there are developments to establish a kind of data-protection standard [19].

Thesis 3: Privacy is often seen as a cost factor only. The main line of argument is that data protection systems cost money and cannot be afforded in a globally competitive market. It may be true that the adaptations needed to make an IT system comply with data protection regulation or to gain acceptance on the market are rather costly. However, in contrast to this end-of-pipe approach we argue that the privacy by design approach is cost-efficient. The early implementation of privacy-oriented thinking in the design process does not cost too much and furthermore "built-in-privacy" is an added quality feature of the respective IT product. As success in global markets is no longer solely dependent on competitive pricing, the new quality feature "privacy" is a comparative advantage for those who build it in at an early stage. How successful this kind of thinking already is may be judged by the success of the data protection seals in Schleswig-Holstein[11] and the European Privacy Seal[12].

Summing up: privacy should be seen as a quality feature of IT products and services; privacy can no longer be guaranteed solely by legal means. Therefore pro-active and constructive approaches seem to be necessary. Two of these will be presented in the following chapters: the first is the "engineer-oriented" approach, which takes up standards and guidelines from IT security and enhances them with the privacy dimension. The aim is to incorporate privacy know-how as early as possible into the design process. The second is the "market-oriented" approach which stands for self-regulation, audit schemes and quality seals.

3.1 The PRISE Approach

The PRISE project aimed at defining criteria for the privacy-friendly security technology research funded in Framework Programme 7. The PRISE Approach shows how privacy can be designed into security technologies and how privacy considerations can be operationalised in the research and development process and the deployment phase of a security product.

---

10 http://en.wikiquote.org/wiki/Liberty
11 https://www.datenschutzzentrum.de
12 https://www.european-privacy-seal.eu

By applying this evaluation procedure produced for Framework Programme 7 certain generalizations can be made. The method selected was a combination of classic expert Technology Assessments with analysis of literature and documents, and participative approaches.

The participative approaches had two components: on the one hand two stakeholder workshops were held with representatives of industry, science, and users of security technologies to discuss the research design and provisional results. The other component comprised so-called "Interview meetings"[13] which were carried out in six European countries[14]. The main purpose was to have an "informed debate" on the subject with approximately 160 participants and through it to discover their basic views, in particular lines of argument, and how these might be changed. By way of preparation the participants were given a variety of scenarios on the subject. The meetings began with an introductory talk, following which the participants were asked to fill in a comprehensive questionnaire. Using a list of questions the subject was then discussed in small groups.

The results show a high level of consensus in the non-specialist groups in all the countries. Among the key statements made, for example, was that a threat from terrorism does not justify an infringement of privacy, technologies that invade the very private (intimate) sphere are unacceptable, and the abuse of security technologies ought to be prevented. Of special relevance – and this was a distinguishing feature between countries – was the degree of trust that people had in different institutions. The independent judiciary in particular enjoys a high degree of public confidence which was also reflected in the list of values which participants said could improve acceptance of security technologies. Top of the list was the principle of proportionality which in turn would only appear to be assured if certain supervisory measures regulated by law were permitted together with strict checks. The fear of possible abuse was also expressed in the demand for strict controls and the emphasis people placed on security technologies which infringe privacy only being implemented as a last resort. More generally there were calls for informative and open debate on the subject involving as many as possible of all the groups concerned, and an obligatory analysis of the effects of implementation of such technologies [see 20].

Table 1: The PRISE matrix

	Criteria	Tools			Warning Interim Status	Recommendations for...		Conclusions
	Questions	Legal	Organisational	Technical	Red/Green Light	R&D	Users	
Baseline								
Data protection compliance								
Context sensitive trade-off								

The key result of PRISE is the so-called PRISE matrix. It is an evaluation instrument which allows the expected effects of a new security technology to be measured in three stages. The three areas evaluated are the so-called *Baseline of personal life*, which comprises very personal – intimate – data and which as a matter of principle should be free from any surveillance. The second area is concerned with *Data protection compliance*, which is asked about using existing principles, and the third is the *Context-sen-*

---

13 A short description of interview meetings can be found on the website of the Danish Board of Technology: http://www.tekno.dk/subpage.php3?article=1234&toppic=kategori12&language=uk
14 Denmark, Norway, Germany, Spain, Hungary and Austria

sitive trade-off. This final area examines whether a security technology promises a security gain which appears to make an infringement of privacy justified.

There are several evaluation stages in the course of designing a system or evaluating a project. If the initial evaluation of the project idea concludes that one of the first two areas is not fulfilled satisfactorily, there is a package of measures which could be used to contribute to alleviating a recognised problem of privacy. These have been summarised in the so-called PRISE Handbook. Altogether there are three types of instrument available – legal, technical and organisational – and these are also described in the report [21].

Using the matrix together with two check lists which enabled a quick evaluation to be made, an attempt was made to develop guidelines and support for enterprises proposing products, evaluators, and for research and development teams in general. The PRISE matrix and the PRISE Handbook can however also provide users of security technologies with valuable information on ICT use which complies with basic law and which enhances privacy.

In all it was possible to show that security and privacy are not necessarily opposites and that it is possible to have both at the same time if there is appropriate compliance with design principles.

Finally, the PRISE results were presented at an international conference where they were discussed by representatives of the security technology industry, users, NGOs and representatives from the scientific community. The conference concluded with the presentation of a Statement Paper[15], in which the project team and its international advisory committee had summarised the main results in terms of recommendations for action and policy options.

The Statement Paper contains the following conclusions and recommendations: an inviolable *baseline of privacy* needs to be established. There is no linear, interchangeable relationship between privacy and security, and the relationship between them is *not a zero-sum game.* Minimising the processing of personal data is an important principle of data protection. *The consolidation of databases* in order to analyse the behaviour of the entire population breaches the principle of the presumption of innocence and the principle of proportionality. The protection of privacy is the shared responsibility of all involved, and observance of *privacy should be a key non-functional requirement* of security technologies. In addition, the *criteria* for evaluating security technologies must be *continuously developed* and regulations should be introduced for a limited time and continuously reassessed [see 22].

3.2 The European Privacy Seal

Following on from this description of the "engineer-oriented" approach we now present a brief description of the "market-oriented" approach based on the example of the EuroPriSe project[16] which focuses on conditions for introducing a European Privacy Seal. Such a privacy quality seal is intended to certify "that an IT product or IT based service facilitates the use of that product or service in a way compliant with European regulations on privacy and data protection, taking into account the legislation in the pilot countries." [23]

The project had several aims. Firstly it was concerned with market analysis which was intended to assess the extent to which a European privacy seal might be viable on its own without subsidies from certification fees and could succeed in the market. The second aim was to promote awareness of data protection issues among manufacturers. The most challenging theoretical task was ultimately to develop

---

15 http://prise.oeaw.ac.at/docs/PRISE_Statement_Paper.pdf
16 https://www.european-privacy-seal.eu

criteria for evaluating data protection friendliness at a European level. EU Directive 95/46 already provides a standard framework for data protection legislation but there are wide variations in how it is interpreted by different member states. The project succeeded in establishing a common set of criteria based on the European framework [24]. The project also undertook to collect existing experience of the European certification of products and services and European admission criteria for the relevant experts.

The specific aims of the seal itself are to promote data protection per se, to improve consumer trust in IT products and services, to contribute to greater transparency in data processing and to demonstrate theoretically and empirically a possible competitive advantage for products which comply with data protection, which was carried out using the ROSI model – Return on Security Investment [25]. On top of this EuroPriSe aimed to simplify the certification procedure for businesses interested in data protection since certification that was recognised throughout Europe would mean that multiple certifications were no longer necessary, with immediate effect.

The certification procedure is largely based on the privacy seal of the Independent Centre for Privacy Protection Schleswig-Holstein (ICPP/ULD) established in 2002. The procedure comprises two stages which are basically voluntary but which are regulated by law. In each case the manufacturers or vendors of products and/or services to be certified select a legal and a technical expert from a register of accredited experts. Together they agree the "Target of Evaluation" (ToE). At this stage initial contact can be made with the certification body to clarify the ToE. After this the two experts can begin their independent evaluation of the product or service. Once the evaluation has been concluded the manufacturer submits the report to the certifying body which carries out its own examination of the report. If the result of the examination is positive, the seal is awarded and a short report is published on the Seal Homepage. An important factor is that the entire procedure remains confidential, that no business secrets are contained in the published short report, and that any negative examination results are not made public.

The only costs incurred by the business enterprise are the fees for the two experts and the fee charged by the certifying body.

A key factor in this process is the criteria used in certification. The fundamental question is: can the product or service be designed in such a way that its use will comply with data protection? This applies in particular to settings, configurations and also to pertaining documentation. The European Privacy Seal lays particular emphasis on the combination of law and technology. The certification criteria have been worked out in great detail and are also published in a comprehensive catalogue [24]. They basically follow the standard principles of data protection such as the legitimacy of data processing, purpose limitation, data subjects' rights, transparency and auditability, data minimisation and avoidance, as well as data security.

In the first 18 months from the time it was launched the project proved surprisingly popular with experts as well as manufacturers. No fewer than 67 experts from ten countries attended the first two training seminars in order to be trained, examined and accredited. Austria currently has seven experts (three legal and four technical experts). A total of 19 pilot certifications have started which in the meantime have resulted in the award of six seals. Twelve projects are still in the process of being evaluated by experts and one re-certification has been carried out due to further technological developments.

4 Conclusion

The starting point for the considerations of this article was the question of how to manage the apparent dilemma posed by privacy and security. It has been shown that, on the one hand, security is not simply synonymous with "national security", but rather that it is a complex phenomenon which has a very strong emphasis on the individual as well as on state elements. New concepts such as, for example, the Human Security Concept increasingly apply. EU policy-making too, within the framework of security research, is more and more concerned with fundamental rights and the right to privacy in particular. At the same time, security can also be seen as part of business security, infrastructure security – in short, the IT security debate. Given that the term security now covers such a variety of meanings, and in the light of the approaches to find solutions, it is no longer possible to speak of security and privacy as opposites.

Based on the evidence that privacy protection can no longer be assured by legal means, attempts have been made to find alternative solutions. These have shown that (new) instruments for ensuring privacy protection do already exist. On the one hand there is design-oriented assistance which supports early compliance with data protection aspects at the design phase involving only minimal additional costs. Fitting an IT system with PETs can qualify as a quality feature thereby giving the product a competitive advantage which in turn is reflected in a positive Return-on-Investment (ROI). On the other hand, market-oriented mechanisms of self-regulation, such as the Privacy Seal, can contribute to greater transparency on the market.

Particular responsibility in this respect falls to the policy-makers and those areas of public procurement which purchase large IT systems or are responsible for IT applications which are used widely. There is particular potential here in so-called "sensitive" areas such as, for example, security applications in the fight against crime, in e-government and above all in on line health.

Finally, the arguments and results discussed above are summarised in four theses:

1. Security and privacy are not necessarily opposites; security technologies can often be designed in such a way that they fulfil their function and enhance security without at the same time infringing the fundamental right of privacy.

2. The debate about data protection and privacy thus far has been concerned almost exclusively with legalities and now needs to be widened to include technical and social science aspects. This broader perspective has become necessary because of technological developments and changes in society. It would therefore appear helpful if in future we were to speak about privacy protection rather than "just" data protection.

3. The well trained and powerful statutory regulators which we have in Europe are needed as "support", but in themselves they are not enough. We need to remember that statutory regulation only makes sense if it can be enforced. This means that data protection authorities need to be equipped with the technology and legal resources required to be able to adequately meet new challenges.

4. Additional instruments and incentives need to be used. These include the promotion of the privacy by design approach, use of the PRISE matrix tools, Privacy Impact Assessments (PIA) etc. This represents a key task for public procurement and funding agencies. Also, from today's perspective it is clear that there is great potential for the implementation of self-regulation instruments such as, for example, data protection audits and quality seals. An additional and still too poorly funded public task is that of raising relevant awareness – including a debate of privacy issues and the inalienable right to privacy at an early stage in schools – which will play an important part in future privacy protection activities.

With a package of measures, an interdisciplinary approach and the appropriate political will at European as well as nation state level, it should still be possible in the future to preserve the fundamental right of privacy which is so important for our democracies.

References

[1]   Weinandy, K., *Sicherheitsforschung das Geschäft mit der Angst. Die Rolle der Ökonomie im (Un) Sicherheitsdiskurs – Eine kritische Betrachtung.* 2007, Unpublished manuscript: Vienna.

[2]   Wikipedia, *Security.* 2009.

[3]   ÖAW, *Sicherheitsforschung, Begriffsfassung und Vorgangsweise für Österreich.* 2005: Vienna.

[4]   NBT, *PRISE D2.2 Overview of security technologies v1.1,*, EC, Editor. 2007, Norwegian Board of Technology: Oslo.

[5]   Ullman, R., *Redefining Security.* International Security, 1983. 8(1): p. 129-153.

[6]   Owen, T., *Challenges and opportunities for defining and measuring human security.* HUMAN RIGHTS, HUMAN SECURITY AND DISARMAMENT, Disarmament Forum 2004, , 2004. 3.

[7]   Conference on Security and Co-operation in Europe (CSCE), *Helsinki Final Act,*. 1975.

[8]   Tretter, H., ed. *KSZE. Die Abschlussdokumente der Konferenz für Sicherheit und Zusammenarbeit in Europa. 1975 und der Nachfolgekonferenzen Belgrad 1978 und Madrid 1983,*. 1984: Wien.

[9]   Hayes, B., *Arming Big Brother – The EU's Security Research Programme.* 2006, Transnational Institute.

[10]   Study Group on Europe's Security Capabilities, *A Human Security Doctrine for Europe The Barcelona Report of the Study Group on Europe's Security Capabilities Presented to EU High Representative for Common Foreign and Security Policy Javier Solana.* 2004, Study Group on Europe's Security Capabilities: Barcelona. p. 35.

[11]   Wilfried von Bredow. *The Barcelona Report on a Human Security Doctrine for Europe, Overview and Some critical Remarks.* in *Berlin Symposium on Human Security and EU-Canada Relations Canadian Universities' Centre Berlin.* 2005. Berlin.

[12]   European Parliament *Resolution of 12 December 2007 on the fight against terrorism.* 2007.

[13]   Raguse, M., O. Langfeldt, and M. Hansen, *PRISE D3.3 Design Proposals*, European Commission PASR, Editor. 2008, Unabhängiges Landeszentrum für Datenschutz Schleswig-Holstein: Kiel.

[14]   Raguse, M., et al., *PRISE D6.2 – Criteria for privacy enhancing security technologies*, European Commission PASR, Editor. 2008, Institute of Technology Assessment Austrian Academy of Sciences: Vienna.

[15]   Cas, J. and W. Peissl, *Beeinträchtigung der Privatsphäre in Österreich – Datensammlungen über ÖsterreicherInnen*, Bundeskammer für Arbeiter und Angestellte, Editor. 2000, Institut für Technikfolgen-Abschätzung,: Wien.

[16]   Cas, J., W. Peissl, and T. Strohmaier, *Datenvermeidung in der Praxis – Individuelle und gesellschaftliche Verantwortung*, Bundeskammer für Arbeiter und Angestellte, Editor. 2002, Institut für Technikfolgen-Abschätzung der Österreichischen Akademie der Wissenschaften: Wien.

[17]   Klüver, L., Peissl, W., Tennøe, T., Bütschi, D., Cas, J., Deboelpaep, R., Hafskjold, Ch., Leisner, I., Nath, Ch., J., Steyaert, St., Vouilloz, N., *ICT and Privacy in Europe – A report on different aspects of privacy based on studies made by EPTA members in 7 European countries.* 2006, EPTA. p. 117.

[18]   Sterbik-Lamina, J., W. Peissl, and J. Cas, *Privatsphäre 2.0 (Beeinträchtigung der Privatsphäre in Österreich; Neue Herausforderungen für den Datenschutz)*, Bundesarbeitskammer, Editor. 2009, Institut für Technikfolgen-Abschätzung der Österreichischen Akademie der Wissenschaften: Wien.

[19]   Bennett, C.J. and C.D. Raab, *The Governance of Privacy.* 2003, Aldershot, Hampshire GB: Ashgate. 257.

[20]   Jacobi, A. and M. Holst, *PRISE D5.8 Synthesis Report – Interview Meetings on Security Technology and Privacy*, European Commission PASR, Editor. 2008, Institute of Technology Assessment Austrian Academy of Sciences: Vienna.

[21]   Raguse, M., *et al.*, *D6.2 – Criteria for privacy enhancing security technologies, Privacy enhancing shaping of security research and technology – A participatory approach to develop acceptable and accepted principles for European Security Industries and Policies* European Commission PASR, Editor. 2008, Institute of Technology Assessment Austrian Academy of Sciences: Vienna.

[22]   Čas, J., *Privatsphäre und Sicherheit Ergebnisse aus dem europäischen TA-Projekt PRISE*. TECHNIK-FOLGENABSCHÄTZUNG – Theorie und Praxis, 2008. 17(3): p. 79-82.

[23]   Bock, K., *European privacy Seal – Final report*, European Commission – eTEN, Editor. 2009, Unabhaengiges Landeszentrum fuer Datenschutz Schleswig-Holstein (ULD, Independent Centre of Privacy Protection): Kiel. p. 24.

[24]   Bock, K., S. Meissner, and K. Storf, *Description of EuroPriSe Criteria and Procedures (updated Version 1.1)*, European Commission – eTEN, Editor. 2009, Unabhaengiges Landeszentrum fuer Datenschutz Schleswig-Holstein (ULD, Independent Centre of Privacy Protection): Kiel. p. 41.

[25]   Borking, J.J., *The Business Case for PET and the EuroPrise Seal*. 2009.

Relative Anonymity: Measuring Degrees of Anonymity in Diverse Computing Environment

Claire Vishik[1] · Giusella Finocchiaro[2]

[1]Intel Corporation UK
claire.vishik@intel.com

[2]University of Bologna
giusella.finocchiaro@unibo.it

Abstract

In electronic communications today, multiple diverse connected devices are used, and messages and data are sent over heterogeneous networks. Devices and networks in these dynamic environments offer varying levels of security and privacy protections. The new models of usage require new more complex models to study and measure anonymity. Although anonymity of data has been subject to numerous studies, there is little research yet in establishing degrees of anonymity in complex electornic processes. This paper focuses on the relative nature of anonymity in electronic communications. We analyze the evolving concept of anonymity, discuss legal views on anonymity, connections of anonymity and data protection, and, finally, outline strategies for measuring anonymity from the user's point of view, in environments with multiple and diverse interconnected nodes.

1 Personal and Anonymous Data

The concept of anonymity is ancient and has not been formulated for the context of modern complex and dynamic computing ecosystems. The cultural influences support the treatment of anonymity as an absolute term. An anonymous individual is one without a name known for him/her. Consequently, what is anonymous cannot be connected to an individual, directly or indirectly. A formal definition of anonymity inlcudes two options: not having a name or impossibility to connect to an individual.

In this definition of anonymity there is room for the evaluation of the associability of a designation to an individual. The evaluation becomes crucial and more complex in the electronic environment that most people in the developed countries use today. If we use electronic communications, it is almost impossible to affirm that we can stay anonymous, although technologies are available today to obfuscate the association between an individual and a transaction. When handling data or messages, connectivity is often required or is, at least, possible. Connectivity implies data communication from one data processing point to another. In order to achieve this, some parameters in the data or message transmission have to be passed from the sender to the recipient, leaving a potentially reconstructible trail and making complete anonymity impossible.

It is important to define the distinction between anonymous and personal data. If data can –at least, from a theoretical point of view- be connected to a person, they may have to be considered personal, and,

N. Pohlmann, H. Reimer, W. Schneider (Editors): Securing Electronic Business Processes, Vieweg (2009), 197-205

theoretically, be subject to regulations with regard to personal data protection. Transmission of anonymous data via electronic networks is a different case; anonymous data are not considered personal data. Therefore, it is important to establish a good definition of anonymous data and anonymity.

How can personal data be distinguished from anonymous data? The European regulation on personal data protection is constituted by the Directive 95/46/EC on the processing of personal data and by the Directive 2002/58/EC on privacy and electronic communications. Personal data are defined in Article 2 of the EU Directive 95/46 as "any information relating to an identified or identifiable natural person ('data subject'); an identifiable person is one who can be identified, directly or indirectly, in particular by reference to an identification number or to one or more factors specific to his physical, physiological, mental, economic, cultural or social identity."

Although the definition of "anonymous data" is not included in the two EU directives mentioned above, there is a reference to anonymity providing that "(...) to determine whether a person is identifiable, account should be taken of all the means likely reasonably to be used either by the controller or by any other person to identify the said person; whereas the principles of protection shall not apply to data rendered anonymous in such a way that the data subject is no longer identifiable; (...)".

Similarly to personal data, anonymous data are defined based on the ability to connect data to the data subject. It has been clarified by the Opinion 4/2007 adopted by Art. 29 Working Party[1] and states that "'anonymous data' can be defined as any information relating to a natural person where the person cannot be identified, whether by the data controller or by any other person, taking account of all the means likely reasonably to be used either by the controller or by any other person to identify that individual"(p.21). The Opinion explicitly refers to a "case-by-case" analysis (p.21), which should be carried out with reference to the means of possible identification and cost of conducting identification for the intended purpose, the way the processing is structured, the advantage expected by the data controller, the interests at stake for the individuals, as well as the risk of organisational dysfunctions (e.g. breaches of confidentiality duties) and technical failures (p.15). Therefore, the definition of anonymous data is context-based and depends on multiple environmental parameters.

2 Modern Computing Ecosystems

Modern computing environment is characterized by ubiquitous connectivity among interoperable heterogeneous networks (from ad-hoc to G3 and TCP/IP) and diverse endpoints (from medical sensors to server farms). Although activities resulting in identical outcomes, e.g. sending electronic mail, can be performed in a variety of environments, their execution and security risks are not identical and depend on the path of a message. While the recipient may not distinguish between a message sent from an office PC or a smart phone, security and privacy risks associated with the two methods of sending a communication can be different. Similarly, the degree of anonymity if anonymity is desired is not identical in the two cases, either.

The transactions leave an electronic trail that can be captured if necessary, with some information stored for longer periods of time. Both user facing data and back-end data and messages flowing between the communications nodes can contain heterogeneous identifiers, making absolute anonymity difficult or impossible to achieve.

Simple systems and straightforward connectivity between two endpoints are no longer the foundation of computing. Today, heterogeneous environments are common, complicating security analysis and

---

1 http://ec.europa.eu/justice_home/fsj/privacy/docs/wpdocs/2007/wp136_en.pdf

measurement of anonymity. The levels of security protection, security and privacy rules, and support for security features, including encryption, are different in different components of the environment [SAPO07]. Therefore, the optimal degree of anonymity possible in a message varies depending on the stucture of a communication. Data from the simplest least protected device can be transferred to the end of the transaction, and ensuring a consistent level of security (and anonymity) in such an environment is very difficult because because the levels of security protection are diverse and the trail of a message is potentially reconstructable. For example, the choice of anonymization techniques is very limited for low power simple devices that don't have the computing power to execute complex protocols.

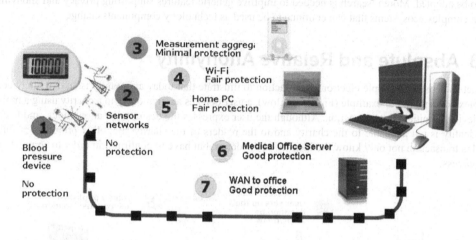

Fig. 1: Varying levels of protection/"anonymity readiness" in today's computing environments

Are data in the environment such as illustrated above personal or anonymous data? When examining issues associated with complex ecosystems consisting of multiple devices and networks, we discover that the analysis is almost always context-dependent. It is easier to distinguish between personal or anonymous data when describing individuals and their actions that when analyzing back-end transactions. The dynamic nature of the networks and their components (e.g. the use of different endpoints for sending the same messages or engaging in the same activities) also makes generalizations more difficult. Although we can assert that anonymized and minimized data can frequently be traced to the source by using information from various associated devices and networks, such tracing is very complex, considering diverse data formats, the fact that some data are not stored after the transaction has been completed, that data are overseen by different data controllers, and that legal constraints make analysis without authorization impossible. We can, therefore, conclude that, for most purposes, efforts required for re-identification will not fall within the definition of "reasonable."

In most devices and protocols, eliminating potentially attributable identifiers can result in the inability to use the tool, system, or protocol, for its primary purpose. A simple medical device (e.g.. blood pressure meter) needs to have an identifier to pass the data collected to an aggregation point. A wireless pedometer needs an ID in order to enable the device to connect to a "smarter" endpoint, such as an iPod or a PDA. A mobile phone requires a device number to connect to the mobile network as defined by applicable standards. A MAC address is necessary to locate the device in several protocols defined by open standards. When device identification is used to perform a primary technological function that benefits a user, with no aggregation and analysis of data involved, with data belonging to multiple controllers, it is likely that the device data, though potentially identifiable, could be defined as anonymous data. Additionally, numerous technologies exist that can obfuscate this information and make re-idenitification less likely.

Opinion 4/2007 points out that the tests applied to data must be dynamic and consider the state of the art in technology at the time of the processing and the possibilities for development during the period for which the data will be processed. Therefore, if the evolution of technology could lead to future re-identification, this eventuality has to be considered, and additional measures to protect anonymity need to be adopted. More research is needed to improve generic features supporting privacy and anonymity in complex ecosystems that can continue to be used as technology components change.

3 Absolute and Relative Anonymity

Let us consider a simple electronic transaction to illustrate that today anonymity is an extremely complex concept. In our example (Figure 2 below), a user donates anonymously to a charity using a mobile device to initiate the transaction. Although the user expresses the desire to be anonymous, and his/her identity is not available to the charity and to the readers of the charity site, other providers enabling this transaction not only know the identity of the donor, but have to confirm it in order to complete the process.

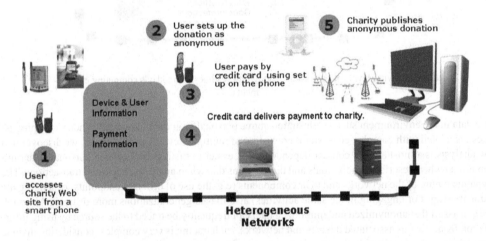

Fig. 2: Donating anonymously to a charity from a smart phone

Although the donor may believe that the transaction is completely anonymous, in reality, the degrees of anonymity vary, from complete anonymity to no anonymity at all, along the path of the transaction. The table below illustrates, in a simplified way, the degrees of anonymity that the user has at every stage of the transaction. The illustration demonstrates several possible research directions in this area that can improve anonymity, such as a „privacy device" that can help ensure anonymity with the provider at the origination point of a transaction.

Table 1: Degrees of anonymity in scenario on Figure 2.

Mobile Service Provider	Telephony and Network Operators	Payment Service	Charity Web Site	Readers of the Donors' list
Device and subscriber IDs are known to the service provider as well as the location when the connection is made.	Re-identification is possible if other data are made available	Identity and other user PII are known to typical payment providers	Identification may be possible, in rare cases, and with other data	The user possesses complete anonymity
User's level of anonymity: 0%	User's level of anonymity: intermediate	User's level of anonymity: 0%	User's level of anonymity: almost complete	Close to 100% anonymity

The example above demonstrates that, in many cases, absolute anonymity, i.e. impossibility to connect data to the data subject cannot be achieved for electronic transactions. But a different concept of anonymous data can be formulated. Instead of absolute, anonymity can be seen as "relative": data can be anonymous for some data users and service providers, but not for others, and anonymity has to be evaluated based on the context where a transaction takes place.

Some criteria for establishing anonymity have been already mentioned by the Opinion 4/2007. They can be summarized by the concepts of reasonableness and referability. **Reasonableness** is the criterion we propose to use in order to judge on the **referability** of the information to a person. If there is no possible connection, anonymity is **absolute**. If there is a possible connection, in the present or the future, then anonymity is **relative**, and relativity can be assessed through the **reasonableness** of the effort necessary to associate the data to a subject.

4 Strategies for Measuring Anonymity

Can we measure anonymity? Various quantifications of anonymity have been proposed by computer scientists, for example with the studies on k-anonymity [SAMA98]; [SWEE02]; [VAID06]; [GIAN07]. Additional research has been conducted on re-identification of data [SWEE98].The recent study at the University of Washington examined the levels of anonymity afforded by new connected devices [SAPO07]. However, most studies focus on data anonymity and data leakage and not anonymity available during a message transmission process in complex ecosystems. New strategies are needed to quantify anonymity available to users in electronic processes as opposed to data anonymity.

4.1 Data Anonymity

Technologies to support anonymity have existed for more than 25 years. David Chaum's mix networks were invented in the early 80s [CHAU81] However, the scenario described above and its simplified analysis indicate that, in a more complex environment that is typical today, new approaches (and new user expectations) are required. Anonymity with the data recipient only is no longer sufficient. Not only enabling technologies to support anonymity, but measurement techniques reflecting the user's and the data controller's views of the message are helpful. Reflecting the relative nature of anonymity when discussing anonymous delivery or anonymous data services has become a necessity.

[KELL08] acknowledge that

> *"an ability to confidently measure this information leakage and any changes in anonymity levels plays a crucial role in facilitating the free-flow of cross-organizational network data sharing and promoting wider adoption of anonyimzation techniques (p.31)"*

Numerous methods of analyzing anonymity exist, such as Anonymity Set Size (ASS), k-anonymity, Individual Anonymity Degree (IAD), or Entropy Anonymity Degree. Techniques have been developed also in order to address network anonymity metrics, including Combinatorial Anonymity Degree (CAD) or Evidence Theory Anonymity (ETA).

However, it is not easy to apply these methodologies to complex and dynamic environments rather than data sets. Not only data leakage, but the degree of anonymity at various stages of a message transfer is at stake, with new technologies affecting levels of anonymity, such as location-based services, further complicating the picture.

The emerging study of anonymity in social networks is an indication that the measurement of anonymity is moving from assessing anonymity in single node systems to more complex configurations [SING08]. It has been noted that identification of an individual or a device in a complex environment is easier than in some homogeneous environments where privacy policies and methods of privacy protection can be implemented and enforced consistently [BACK07]. As heterogeneous complex ecosystems proliferate, both technologically and in new Internet usage models, such as social networks, many researchers begin to ask if the study of network topology, in a social or physical network, can be utilized to measure anonymity in a way that is more dynamic. Numerous factors complicate such measurements, e.g., location services [XU07], [BAMB08]. But as traditional (low latency) anonymization services become less efficient [HOPP07], studies aimed at measuring various aspects of anonymity using new techniques become crucial.

In a dynamic heterogeneous environment, anonymity may depend on many factors, including the perception of the data subject. It has been noted that when using digital services, users consider themselves more or less anonymous, even if they are aware that message trails are identifiable. [CLAU06] contend that there are multiple and diverse anonymity metrics depending on the purpose of the measurements, and research in the area of anonymity supports this view:

> *"[]anonymity depends on how others act. In an environment where many individuals act in the same way one feels more anonymous than in an environment where only a few individuals are acting (p.55)."*

4.2 Strategies for Measuring Anonymity in a Process or Transaction

As Figure 2 and Table 1 show, the degree of anonymity is different along the path of a simple message/ execution path of a transaction. It is important to ensure that the users who wish to perform a transaction anonymously are aware that only relative anonymity can be reliably provided. In an example illustration (Figure 3 below) that can be understood by users, simplified indicators can be assigned to the nodes along the path of a transaction or a message and used to compute the "anonymity score" for adding all the indicators. If we use the approach based on the interpretation of anonymous data provided in 4/2007 Opinion analyzed in Sections 2 and 3, we can use simple indicators such as 0 (no anonymity), .5 (re-identification not possible without additional data) and 1 (complete anonymity is possible) to assess anonymity in the main nodes of the transaction. For the example scenario used in Section 3, the score can be computed as illustrated in Figure 3.

Anonymity Score: 2.5

Fig. 3: Simplified Anonymity Scoring

We recognize that Figure 3 is a simplification that lacks quantifiable definitions and objective measurements of anonymity for all nodes in order to provide useful inputs to the users and to avoid arbitrary and subjective evaluations. It is also clear that, in many cases, anonymity with some audiences (e.g., recipients) is much more important to the users than anonymity with, e.g., service providers. Different weights need to be assigned to nodes in order to reflect the true value of anonymity to the users. Nonetheless, a similar approach can be used to capture varying degrees of anonymity in complex ecosystems, to educate the users and facilitate technology development.

If anonymity is measured for each node in a process, then remedies can be devised to improve the available degree of anonymity where possible. Table 2 below illustrates remedies that can improve anonymity for some components of the scenario introduced in Section 3.

Table 2: Varying degress of anonymity and possible remedies

Mobile Service Provider	Telephony and Network Operators	Payment Service	Charity Web Site	Readers of the Donors' list
Identities of the device and subscriber, and the location of the transaction are known	Identity and origination are reconstructible, with other data (from other controllers)	Identity of the user has to be known, using normal financial ,mechanisms	Identity not available, but can be obtained in rare cases, as allowed by law	Complete anonymity possible
Anonymity: 0%	Anonymity: intermediate	Anonymity: 0%	Almost complete anonymity	Close to 100% anonymity
Remedy: "Privacy" device	E.g. proxies for redirection	Use anonymous wallet for payment	High degree of anonymity	High degree of anonymity

The degree of anonymity avalable in each node of the process can be improved with currently available technologies that can potentially become state-of-the-art and incorporated in common protocols as the use of electronic services for transactions where anonymity is desirable continues to increase. Similarly, refining electronic processes to permit, where allowed by law and where appropriate, greater degrees of anonymity, can change the „anonymity score" of a transaction.

5 Conclusions and Future Work

Relative anonymity is the reality of today's anonymous transactions, even though the users may believe their anonymity is nearly absolute. Techniques associated with enforcing data anonymity in relatively static datasets have been successfully devised, and various approaches to measuring anonymity currently exist. However, measuring anonymity along the path of a transaction or a message and establishing levels of anonymity available in complex systems, such as social networks, is an area that is beginning to be studied. New models and technologies are needed to support and measure anonymity in complex modern ecosystems.

Because anonymity is both a legal and technology concept, close cooperation between jurists and computer scientists is necessary. The role of the law is to establish fundamental principles and rules, while technology works to implement them. The complexities associated with relative anonymity can be solved when these two constituencies work together.

References

[CAME08] Camenisch, J. and Groß, T. Efficient attributes for anonymous credentials. In Proceedings of the 15th ACM Conference on Computer and Communications Security (Alexandria, Virginia, USA, October 27 – 31, 2008). CCS '08. ACM, New York, NY, 345-356.

[CAME08/1] Camenisch, J., Groß, T., and Heydt-Benjamin, T. S. 2008. Rethinking accountable privacy supporting services: extended abstract. In Proceedings of the 4th ACM Workshop on Digital Identity Management (Alexandria, Virginia, USA, October 31 – 31, 2008).

[CHAU81] Chaum, David L. Untraceable electronic mail, return addresses, and digital pseudonyms. Communications of the ACM, 24(2):84-90, 1981.

[BACK07] L. Backstrom, C. Dwork, and J. Kleinberg. Wherefore art thou r3579x?: anonymized social networks, hidden patterns,and structural steganography. In WWW '07: Proceedings of the 16th international conference on World Wide Web, p. 181–190, New York, NY, USA, 2007. ACM Press.

[FINO08] Finocchiaro, Giusella (ed.), Diritto all'anonimato, Padova, Cedam, 2008

[EIJK07] Eijck, J v and Orzan, S. Epistemic Verification of Anonymity. Electronic Notes in Theoretical Computer Science, vol. 168, pp. 159-174, 2007.

[GAJE07] Gajek, S., Sadeghi, A.R., Stüble, C., Winandy, M.: Compartmented security for browsers or how to thwart a phisher with trusted computing. In: 2nd Intl. Conference on Availability, Reliability and Security (ARES 2007), pp 120-127

[GAND04] Gandon, F. L. and Sadeh, N. M. 2004. Context-awareness, privacy and mobile access: a web semantic and multiagent approach. In Proceedings of the 1st French-Speaking Conference on Mobility and Ubiquity Computing (Nice, France, June 01 – 03, 2004). UbiMob '04, vol. 64. ACM, New York, NY, 123-130.

[GARC05] Garcia, F. D., Hasuo, I., Pieters, W., and van Rossum, P. 2005. Provable anonymity. In Proceedings of the 2005 ACM Workshop on Formal Methods in Security Engineering (Fairfax, VA, USA, November 11 – 11, 2005).

[GIAN06] Giannotti,F and Pedreschi, D. (eds.) Mobility, Data Mining and Privacy, Springer, 2007; Vaidya, Jaideep, Clifton, Chris, Zhu, Michael, Privacy Preserving Data Mining, Springer, 2006

[HONG04] Hong, J. and Landay, J. An Architecture for Privacy-Sensitive Ubiquitous Computing. In Mobisys, p. 177–189, 2004.

[HU05] Hu, Y and Wang, H. A framework for location privacy in wireless networks. In ACM SIGCOMM, Asiba Workshop, 2005.

[JACK07] Jackson, C., Boneh, D., Mitchell, J.: Transaction generators: Root kits for web. In: 2nd USENIX Workshop on Hot Topics in Security (HotSec '07)

[KELL08] Kelly, D. J., Raines, R. A., Grimaila, M. R., Baldwin, R. O., and Mullins, B. E. 2008. A survey of state-of-the-art in anonymity metrics. In Proceedings of the 1st ACM Workshop on Network Data Anonymization (Alexandria, Virginia, USA, October 31 – 31, 2008). NDA '08. ACM, New York, NY, 31-40.

[NICO03] Nicoll, Chris-Prins, Corien-Van Dellen,. M. J. M. (eds.), Digital Anonymity and the Law, Cambridge University Press, TMC Asser Press,The Hague, 2003

[PEIS08] Peissl, W., Raguse, M., Meints, M., Langfeldt, O., 2008, Criteria for privacy enhancing security technologies, Deliverable 6.2 of the PRISE project, Vienna May 2008

[SAPO07] Saponas, S., Lester, J., Hartung, C, Sameer, A., Tadayoshi, K. Devices that tell on you: privacy in consumer ubiquitous computing. Proceedings of the 16th USENIX Security Symposium, 2007.

[SINGH 07] Singh, L. Exploring graph mining approaches for dynamic heterogeneous networks. National Science Foundation Symposium on Next Generation of Data Mining and Cyber-Enabled Discovery for Innovation, October 2007.

[SWEE01] Sweeney, L Information Explosion. In Confidentiality, Disclosure, and Data Access: Theory and Practical Applications for Statistical Agencies, L. Zayatz, P. Doyle, J. Theeuwes and J. Lane (eds), Urban Institute, Washington, DC, 2001.

[SWEE02] Sweeney, L. k-anonymity: a model for protecting privacy. International Journal on Uncertainty, Fuzziness and Knowledge-based Systems, 10 (5), 2002; 557-570.

[TILL05] Tillwick, H. and Olivier, M. 2005. Towards a framework for connection anonymity. In Proceedings of the 2005 Annual Research Conference of the South African institute of Computer Scientists and information Technologists on IT Research in Developing Countries (White River, South Africa, September 20 – 22, 2005). ACM International Conference Proceeding Series, vol. 150. South African Institute for Computer Scientists and Information Technologists, 113-122.

[VAD06] Vaidya, J., Clifton, C., Zhu, M., Privacy Preserving Data Mining, Springer, 2006

[VISH07] Vishik, C., Johnson, S, Hoffman, D. Infrastructure for Trusted Environment: In Search of a Solution. In ISSE/SECURE 2007 Securing Electronic Business Processes, Vieweg, 2007, 219-227.

[CIAN07] Xian, H., Feng, D.: Protecting mobile agents' data using trusted computing technology. Journal of Communication and Computer 4(3) (2007), pp. 44-51

[XU07] Xu, T. and Cai, Y. 2007. Location anonymity in continuous location-based services. In Proceedings of the 15th Annual ACM international Symposium on Advances in Geographic information Systems (Seattle, Washington, November 07 – 09, 2007). GIS '07. ACM, New York, NY, 1-8.

User Privacy in RFID Networks

Dave Singelée[1] · Stefaan Seys[2]

[1]ESAT – SCD – COSIC, Katholieke Universiteit Leuven – IBBT
Kasteelpark Arenberg 10, 3001 Heverlee-Leuven, Belgium
Dave.Singelee@esat.kuleuven.be

[2]PricewaterhouseCoopers Enterprise Advisory
Woluwedal 18, 1932 Sint-Stevens-Woluwe, Belgium
Stefaan.Seys@pwc.be

Abstract

Wireless RFID networks are getting deployed at a rapid pace and have already entered the public space on a massive scale: public transport cards, the biometric passport, office ID tokens, customer loyalty cards, etc. Although RFID technology offers interesting services to customers and retailers, it could also endanger the privacy of the end-users. The lack of protection mechanisms being deployed could potentially result in a privacy leakage of personal data. Furthermore, there is the emerging threat of location privacy. In this paper, we will show some practical attack scenarios and illustrates some of them with cases that have received press coverage. We will present the main challenges of enhancing privacy in RFID networks and evaluate some solutions proposed in literature. The main advantages and shortcomings will be briefly discussed. Finally, we will give an overview of some academic and industrial research initiatives on RFID privacy.

1 Introduction

RFID (Radio Frequency Identification) is used to denominate a digital identifier that can be read using RF signals. There are three main types: passive RFID tags that require an external power source to operate, active tags that have an on-board battery and battery assisted passive (BAP) that require an external source to wake-up, but have a larger forward link capacity.

Today, RFID technology is used in a multitude of applications, for example:

- IT Asset Tracking
- RFID passports
- Mobile Credit Card payment systems
- Transportation payment systems
- Barcode replacements: product tracking, transportation and logistics
- Timing and tracing at sporting events (lap timing)
- Animal identification

As most RFID applications require massive deployment of tags, the cost of tags should be minimized. Because of this, security features have initially been close to non-existent and none of the basic security features one expects from a wireless communication system (such as authentication and encryption) were part of the first designs. As this opens the door for a large number of attacks and privacy issues,

N. Pohlmann, H. Reimer, W. Schneider (Editors): Securing Electronic Business Processes, Vieweg (2009), 206-215

researchers have started to investigate possible solutions. The main challenges these researchers have to tackle are explained in Section 2.

After a short selection of real-world security issues, we will present possible privacy enhancing techniques for RFID systems.

1.1 Selection of Real-World Security Issues of RFID systems

Privacy concerns related to the large scale deployment of RFID tags in consumer products

Replacing the ubiquitous bar code with RFID tags has many advantages, both for suppliers, retailers and consumers. Stock management and shipping can be further automated and your washing machine will detect whether you have combined coloured clothes and whites or not. Nevertheless, privacy concerns have been raised since day one. In general, bar codes cannot be read remotely, while this is exactly the main advantage of RFID tags. This means that the consumer will be carrying around a "cloud" of RFID tags at anytime that will leak information:

- The "cloud" itself will act as a unique identifier and can be used to track this individual;
- Certain RFID tags might reveal that you carry expensive items in your purse;
- Other RFID tags might reveal personal data such as medication you are taking, etc.

These concerns are not ignored by the legislation. For example, the European Commission recently issued "RFID Privacy Recommendations". One of the recommendations of the EC is that consumers should be actively involved when the RFID tag information is used. How this translates in technology still remains to be seen.

Cloning of the RFID chip in the UK's biometric passport

In 2006, Lukas Grunwald demonstrated at the Black Hat conference how to clone a UK biometric passport. After studying the publicly available standard used for the UK ePassports, he was able to read the data stored in the RFID of a genuine UK passport and copy it into a blank RFID chip. In this case, the complete RFID chip was cloned and the clone can no longer be distinguished from the original. Note that this attack could potentially be used to clone passports without having physical access to the passport.

2 Technological Challenges

RFID security is particularly difficult to design because of the specific properties of RFID chips and systems.

Virtually all applications of RFID systems require that the RFID chips are cheap to manufacture. Because of this, the resources available on typical RFIC chips are ultra limited. This is true on all levels: ultra low-power (in the best case a tiny battery), tiny CPU with limited processing power, very limited memory, very small bandwidth, no internal clock, etc. This has a large influence on the use of cryptographic primitives that can be deployed. In general, public key cryptography cannot be used in RFID networks, as these techniques are too computationally demanding.

Another consequence of the cheap production process is that RFID chips will not achieve the same level of physical security properties as their more expensive smartcard cousins. Because of this, they are not tamper resistant and thus more susceptible to physical attacks.

Another property of RFID systems is that are carried around by consumers in public places. This means that attackers will have ample opportunity to execute their attack. Furthermore, by employing tailored tag readers, attackers are able to eavesdrop on an RFID response from a much larger distance than the typical user expects. More advanced attacker models include active attackers (that can modify or replay communications) or even man-in-the-middle attackers that spoof a response to a tag reader over a large-distance relay using other communication means (e.g., forwarding the reader request over a cell phone connection to a tag at a completely different location and relaying the answer the same way back).

For the time being, there is no actual RIFD communication infrastructure that allows the use of central servers to assist with security (e.g., key servers to assist in key management).

All these limitations complicate the design of privacy preserving solutions for RFID systems.

3 Privacy Enhancing Solutions for RFID Networks

Various solutions to enhance the privacy of RFID applications have been proposed in the literature, taking into account the constraints on cost, energy efficiency and computational power. We will now give an overview of some of the proposed solutions, and evaluate their main advantages and drawbacks.

3.1 RFID Kill Command

One of the most straightforward solutions to provide privacy to the end-users of RFID tags, is just to permanently disable the tag's ability to transmit information (i.e. kill the tag) when it should not be used anymore (e.g., when the product with the RFID tag attached to it, leaves the store). This kill function is typically performed on a software basis (by sending a kill command to the tag). To protect against accidental or malicious killing of RFID tags, the kill function is password protected. To destroy the tag permanently, the kill command has to be accompanied by a tag-specific password, hard coded in the RFID tag. In the EPCglobal standard [EPC08], the kill password is 32 bits in length. Once this command is sent, there are three scenarios:

1. The password is correct and the tag is killed successfully ,
2. The password is incorrect, and the tag ignores the kill command, or
3. The password is correct, but the tag did not gain enough power to complete the kill function. The tag then sends an error message back to the reader.

The main technical challenge associated with kill commands is that they imply a vulnerability if kill-passwords are not properly secured. This could result in an attacker deactivating the RFID tag functionality and hence threaten the supply chain transactions [SpEv09].

The main advantage of using the RFID kill command is that it is a very straightforward solution and offers the best privacy guarantees for the end-user. From the moment it has been disabled, it cannot be tracked anymore. There are however also some drawbacks. The kill command solution is useless for situations such as access control, where legitimate readers need to verify the authenticity of the tag. This solution disallows transactions beyond the point of sale and hence conflicts with all use cases propagated by industry for after-sales services.

3.2 Physical Privacy

An alternative to sending a kill command to the RFID tag, is physically destroying the tag (i.e. a hardware kill function) when it should not be used anymore. IBM has proposed to use scratch-off material (similar to that found on lottery tickets) for the antenna of the RFID tag, so that customers can visually check that the tag's ability to transmit information has been disabled [IBM06, KaMo05].

The solution proposed by IBM is an example of physical privacy. The main idea of this solution is to use the physical RFID tag structures to permit a consumer to disable a tag by mechanically altering the tag in such a way that the ability of a reader to interrogate the RFID tag by wireless mean is inhibited [KaMo05]. These disabled tags are also called "clipped tags". An additional and desirable feature is to be able to reactivate the tag by using a physical contact channel. Such a reactivation requires deliberate actions of the RFID owner. Reactivation of the RFID tag should not be possible without the owner's knowledge and permission, unless the tag is stolen.

A similar approach to the "clipped tags" is shielding the wireless transmission of a RFID tag. By attaching a piece of metal to the RFID tag, one can construct a Faraday cage that blocks all wireless communication, and hence makes the tag invisible to readers. By removing the metal, the tag can be detected again. This is a simple solution to provide configurable privacy. However the main drawback is that such a Faraday cage is impractical if the RFID tags are attached to large objects (e.g., a pair of trousers).

The main advantage of the physical privacy solution is that it offers a visual confirmation to the customers that the tag is privacy protected. Mechanisms that enable the reactivation of a tag have the additional benefit that they support the industrial use cases for after-sales services. Physical privacy hence seems to be an interesting solution to enhance RFID privacy. There are however some drawbacks, including the extra production cost (to make tags that can be clipped) and the need of complex (technical) user interactions to reactive the tag. There is also the risk of sabotage, where a user disables the tag before the point of sale. In some scenarios, this could be beneficial to the customer (e.g., in a supermarket, where RFID tags could be used to scan all purchased products).

3.3 Cryptographic Authentication Protocol

Instead of physically altering the RFID tag or sending software commands to kill it, one can also deploy cryptographic techniques to solve the problem. There are two goals one typically wants to achieve by deploying a cryptographic authentication protocol in RFID networks: security (to guarantee the authenticity of tags being accepted by the authentication protocol) and privacy.

The goal of a privacy-preserving cryptographic authentication protocol is to enable a RFID tag to prove its identity to a legitimate reader without revealing its unique identity to any third party. Such a third party can be passive (eavesdropping the communication), but can also perform more active attacks (such as modifying or replaying the communication), or even perform man-in-the-middle attack. Designing an authentication protocol that tackles all these attacks is a challenging task.

There are essentially two approaches that have been proposed to solve this problem [SaVW09]. A first approach is to perform a challenge-response protocol between the RFID reader and the tag. This solution is schematically depicted in Fig.1. The protocol starts with the reader sending a challenge to the authenticating tag. The latter then computes a response, dependent on the challenge, by using a shared secret key (shared between the tag and the reader). In the last phase of the protocol, the reader performs an exhaustive search on all the keys its shares with RFID tags. If a match is found, it knows which particular RFID tag performed the authentication protocol. If none of the keys match, the authentication protocol fails. Instead of conducting a single round of a challenge-response protocol with both the challenge and the response having a bit length of n bits, one can also conduct n rounds using single bit challenges and responses. Examples of RFID challenge-response protocols are [EnHJ04, MoWa04, Tsud06, WSRE03].

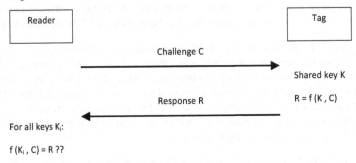

Fig. 1: RFID challenge-response authentication protocol

A second approach that has been proposed in the literature, is to have the tag use a temporary identifier (also called a "pseudonym") to identify itself. In each separate run of the authentication protocol, the pseudonym is updated (typically by using a secret key shared between tag and reader). This update is done in such a way that the different pseudonyms used by the tag, are unlinkable from the point of view of a third party. Only the legitimate readers can link the pseudonyms of a tag to each other, and hence identify the tags. This approach requires synchronization between a tag and all the readers in the system (otherwise, the reader will expect another identifier than the current pseudonym used by the tag). Various pseudonym schemes for RFID have been proposed in literature (e.g., see [Dimi05, HeMu04, JuWe05, MoSW05, SoMi08]).

The main advantage of using a cryptographic authentication protocol in RFID networks is that privacy is preserved automatically. Neither the end-user nor the retailer does have to perform any additional tasks. An additional benefit is that the RFID tag does not have to be disabled or altered. The tag continues to transmit (anonymous) data, even after the store exit, and privacy is always on. This solution hence supports the industrial use cases for after-sales services. There are however also some disadvantages of using cryptographic authentication protocols in RFID networks. The efficiency of using a challenge-response protocol with a shared symmetric key depends on the total number of tags in the system. A large number of tags will be inefficient and not scalable. The protocols that use temporary pseudonyms that are updated in each run of the protocol, are vulnerable to denial-of-service attacks that desynchronize the tag and the reader [JuWe06]. Another drawback is that several authentication protocols have been demonstrated to be broken and are hence not privacy preserving (e.g., see [Avoi05, FrSh09, JuWe07, Vaud07] for a security analysis of various RFID authentication protocols).

3.4 Distance Bounding Protocols

One of the attacks that need to be prevented when conducting a RFID authentication protocol, is a man-in-the-middle attack. By performing such an attack, the adversary can impersonate a legitimate tag to a RFID reader, even when both devices are not in each other's proximity. To prevent man-in-the-middle attacks, several researchers have proposed to incorporate the distance between RFID tag and reader in the authentication protocol. This leads to the concept of distance bounding protocols. These protocols enable a verifying party to determine an upper bound on the distance between itself and a prover, who claims to be within a certain range. By combining cryptographic and physical properties, one can design a secure authentication protocol that is resistant to man-in-the-middle attacks.

Secure distance bounding protocols typically measure the time of flight to determine an upper bound on the distance between prover and verifier. This measurement is performed during a challenge-response protocol, the main building block of the distance bounding protocol. This challenge-response protocol is executed n times. During each of the n rounds, the time between sending a challenge and receiving the response is measured. Multiplying the time of flight with the propagation speed of the communication medium gives the distance between prover and verifier. Several secure distance bounding protocols have been proposed in the literature (e.g., see [BrCh93, HaKu05, SiPr07]).

Since distance bounding protocols are a specific type of authentication protocols, they have the same properties as the latter (see Section 3.3 for more details). An additional advantage are their interesting security properties, as a consequence of implicitly incorporating the location between both devices. The major drawback is the large implementation cost. Distance bounding protocols impose very strict requirements on the hardware. It is unclear if these requirements can be achieved with the current state-of-the-art RFID technology.

3.5 Privacy Agents

Several researchers have introduced the concept of privacy agents. The idea is that consumers carry their own privacy-enforcing devices for RFID instead of relying on public RFID readers to enforce privacy protection. Users delegate the privacy management to a privacy agent that mediates tag-reader communication based on a privacy policy [SpEv09]. Three approaches have been proposed to conduct privacy agent schemes: using a RFID proxy, using a blocker tag, and using anonymizers.

3.5.1 RFID Proxy

The basic idea is that users carry a RFID proxy (also called "watchdog" or "RFID guardian") that acts as a personal RFID firewall [JuSB05, RiCT05]. Users delegate the privacy management to the RFID proxy, which implements their privacy policy. These policies are typically defined as follows: "Only reader x and y may scan tag t at location z".

All requests from the RFID reader to the tag are intercepted by the RFID proxy, which then analyzes the request and performs the necessary actions based on the user's privacy policy. If access is granted, the request can be forwarded to the tag, or the RFID proxy can reply itself. In other words, the RFID proxy then simulates the tags that are under its control. If a reader is not authorized to access a person's tags, then the RFID proxy selectively jams the wireless communication between the reader and the tag.

The main challenges of this approach are:

- techniques to securely have the RFID proxy acquire or release control over the tag,
- guarantee the correctness of authentication claims performed by the proxy,
- effectively cut off the tag-reader communication when access to a tag is denied, and
- having users specify their privacy policy and import this policy correctly into the RFID proxy.

Further research is necessary to tackle these challenges efficiently.

3.5.2 Blocker Tag

A simple but effective privacy policy could be to have two privacy states: on or off. When privacy is turned on, the tag is undetectable by the reader. When privacy is turned off, the reader can query the tag. This privacy policy can be implemented by a blocker tag. The concept was proposed by Juels, Rivest, and Szydlo to preserve privacy in RFID networks [JuRS03]. The basic principle of their solution is that a tag can act in two modes: the normal mode where it emits its unique identifier (e.g., in the shop), and a privacy mode (e.g., beyond the point of sale). To enable a tag to be in privacy mode, a blocker tag is used. When activated, it prevents undesirable scanning of RFID readers.

This is done by exploiting the anti-collision protocol used in RFID communication. To ensure that tag signals do not interfere with one another during the scanning process, the reader first ascertains what tags are present, and then addresses tags individually. A blocker tag impedes RFID scanning by simulating collisions. So in other words, the blocker tag just simulates that all possible RFID tags are present. It can also block a subset of all possible tags (e.g., only the tags which have a unique identifier starting with a '1').The blocker tag does not engage in an active form of jamming. Rather, by participating in the tag-reading process in a non-compliant way, it performs what may be thought of as a kind of passive jamming. Additional technical details on this technique can be found in [JuRS03].

A blocker tag creates a physical region of privacy protection in which a reader is incapable of reading RFID tags. It can however also be used as a malicious tool, to perform denial-of-service attacks. By employing blocker tags, the attacker can shield all tags (or a particular subset) from being read by a reader. This limits the use in a commercial environment.

3.5.3 Anonymizers

Another approach of delegating privacy management to a privacy-enforcing device, is the concept of anonymizers. The basic idea is to use temporary pseudonyms instead of the unique identifier of the tag in the tag-reader communication. The difference with employing cryptographic authentication protocols (as has been discussed in Section 3.3), is that the tags do not update their temporary identifier (i.e. the pseudonym) themselves because of efficiency reasons. Instead, they delegate this task to the anonymizer, a special device owned by the end-user. This device can be a dedicated device, but can also be implemented on a mobile phone or a PDA running anonymizer software [SaVW09]. Both the tag, reader and the anonymizer can then conduct an anonymizer-enabled RFID authentication protocol. Each time a tag is queried, it replies with its temporary pseudonym that it has stored in its memory. To avoid tracking, the pseudonym has to be updated regularly. This is done by the anonymizer and the tag conducting a protocol, where the anonymizer authenticates itself and sends an updated pseudonym to the tag. The tag always uses the current pseudonym to authenticate itself to the reader. By using an anonymizer, the user can implement its own privacy policy, and choose how regular the pseudonym of the tag should be updated.

Anonymizers are and interesting solution to preserve privacy in RFID networks. Since a mobile phone (or another personal mobile device) can be used as an anonymizer, the cost is reasonable low. One of the major drawbacks are the security properties of these schemes: most anonymizer-enabled RFID authentication protocols proposed in the literature are subject to impersonation attacks [SaVW09].

4 Academic and Industrial Research Projects

Security and privacy in RFID networks is an important research area that is intensively studied in the academic and industrial world. This is illustrated by the large number of academic and industrial research projects on this topic. Without having the intention to be complete, we give a brief overview of some of these initiatives:

- **RFID Guardian:** The RFID Guardian Project is a collaborative project focused upon providing security and privacy in Radio Frequency Identification (RFID) systems. The goals of this project are to investigate the security and privacy threats faced by RFID systems, design and implement real solutions against these threats, and investigate the associated technological and legal issues. The website of the project is: http://www.rfidguardian.org/

- **RFID Ecosystem:** The RFID Ecosystem is a large-scale project with participants from various research groups at the University of Washington's Department of Computer Science and Engineering. The project investigates user-centered RFID systems in connection with technology, business, and society. Past research on user applications of RFID has been limited to short-term technology and user studies in restricted scenarios. In contrast, the RFID Ecosystem provides a living laboratory for long-term, in-depth research in applications, databases, privacy, security, and systems. The project website is: http://rfid.cs.washington.edu/

- **PEARL:** The PEARL project performs research on a privacy enhanced security architecture for RFID labels. The goal of this project is to develop tools and methodologies as well as their theoretical foundations for using RFID systems while preserving the user's privacy. In this project, researchers will formally model the relevant privacy and security properties, develop new privacy enhancing protocols for the extremely resource constrained RFID environment, shape a context in which the user can check the privacy policies enforced by the RFID-based application, and develop methods to secure the integration of RFID tags and the back office applications that will support them. The project website is: http://www.cs.ru.nl/pearl/

- **BCRYPT:** This project intends to perform fundamental research into a number of selected disciplines that intend to address the information security challenges. WP7 of this project focuses on the application area RFID. This work package brings together research from the following fundamental areas: cryptographic algorithms and protocols, secure software and secure hardware. In this project, researchers investigate how privacy can be provided by the cooperation of new algorithms together with an extremely efficient hardware and software implementation. The website of the project is: https://www.cosic.esat.kuleuven.be/bcrypt/

- **STOA project RFID & Identity Management:** The STOA project "RFID & Identity Management" aims to provide insight into how Radio Frequency Identification is experienced by European citizens, draw a future scenario, and formulate challenges for this rapidly emerging technology. The final deliverable of the project can be found on: http://www.europarl.europa.eu/stoa/publications/studies/stoa182_en.pdf

- **RFID-AP:** The RFID-AP project performs research on the range of security threats to applications based on the deployment of RFID-tags and concentrates on two particular issues: those of authentication and privacy. The goal of RFID-AP is to design and prototype cryptographic algorithms and secure protocols for RFID deployment. Such algorithms and protocols could be used individually, or in combination. The project website is: http://www.rfid-ap.fr/

5 Conclusion

In this article, we have given an overview of privacy enhancing solutions for RFID systems. From this overview, it is clear that providing privacy within the limitations dictated by RFID technology is not straightforward and further research will be required to solve the issue. We have completed this report with an overview of ongoing research projects that try to advance the field of privacy and security for RFID systems.

Acknowledgements

Dave Singelée's work was supported by the Interdisciplinary institute for Broadband Technology (IBBT) and in part by the Concerted Research Action (GOA) Ambiorics 2005/11 of the Flemish Government and by the IAP Programme P6/26 BCRYPT of the Belgian State (Belgian Science Policy).

References

[Avoi05]   Avoine Gildas: Adversary Model for Radio Frequency Identification. In: LASEC Technical Report, 2005-001, Swiss Federal Institute of Technology (EPFL). 2005, 14 pages.

[BrCh93]   Brands Stefan, Chaum David: Distance-Bounding Protocols. In: Advances in Cryptology – EURO-CRYPT 1993, Lecture Notes in Computer Science, LNCS 765, Springer-Verlag. 1994, p. 344-359.

[Dimi05]   Dimitriou Tassos: A lightweight RFID protocol to protect against traceability and cloning attacks. In: Proceedings of the 1st International Conference on Security and Privacy for Emerging Areas in Communications Networks, IEEE Computer Society. 2005, p. 59-66.

[EnHJ04]   Engberg Stephan, Harning Morten Borup, Jensen Christian Damsgaard: Zero-knowledge Device Authentication: Privacy and Security Enhanced RFID Preserving Business Value and Consumer Convenience. In: Proceedings of the Second Annual Conference on Privacy, Security and Trust. 2004, p. 89-101.

[EPC08]   EPC global: Class 1 Generation 2 UHF Air Interface Protocol Standard version 1.2.0. In: http://www.epcglobalinc.org/home. 2008, 108 pages.

[FrSh09]   Frumkin Dmitry, Shamir Adi: Un-trusted-HB: Security Vulnerabilities of Trusted-HB. In: Proceedings of the 5th Workshop on RFID Security. 2009, p. 62-71.

[HaKu05]   Hancke G.P., Kuhn M.G.: An RFID Distance Bounding Protocol. In: Proceedings of the 1st International Conference on Security and Privacy for Emerging Areas in Communications Networks, IEEE Computer Society. 2005, p. 67-73.

[HeMu04]   Henrici Dirk, Müller Paul: Hash-based enhancement of location privacy for radio-frequency identification devices using varying identifiers. In: Proceedings of the 2nd IEEE International Conference on Pervasive Computing and Communications Workshops, IEEE Computer Society. 2004, p. 149-153.

[IBM06]   IBM: IBM Licenses Clipped Tag RFID Technology to Marnlen RFiD. In: http://www-03.ibm.com/press/us/en/pressrelease/20592.wss. 2006.

[JuRS03]   Juels Ari, Rivest Ronald, Szydlo Michael: The blocker tag: selective blocking of RFID tags for consumer privacy. In: Proceedings of the 10th ACM Conference on Computer and Communications Security, ACM. 2003, p. 103-111.

[JuSB05]   Juels Ari, Syverson Paul, Bailey Daniel: High-Power Proxies for Enhancing RFID Privacy and Utility. In: Proceedings of the 5th International Workshop on Privacy Enhancing Technologies, Lecture Notes in Computer Science, LNCS 3856, Springer-Verlag. 2005, p. 210-226.

[JuWe05]   Juels Ari, Weis Stephen: Authenticating pervasive devices with human protocols. In: Advances in Cryptology – CRYPTO 2005, Lecture Notes in Computer Science, LNCS 3621, Springer-Verlag. 2005, p. 293-308.

[JuWe07] Juels Ari, Weis Stephen: Defining Strong Privacy for RFID. In: Proceedings of the 5th IEEE International Conference on Pervasive Computing and Communications Workshops, IEEE Computer Society 2007, p. 342-347.

[KaMo05] Karjoth Günther, Moskowitz Paul: Disabling RFID tags with visible confirmation: clipped tags are silenced. In: Proceedings of the 2005 ACM workshop on Privacy in the electronic society, ACM. 2005, p. 27-30.

[MoSW05] Molnar David, Soppera Andrea, Wagner David: A Scalable, Delegatable Pseudonym Protocol Enabling Ownership Transfer of RFID Tags. In: Proceedings of the 12th International Workshop on Selected Areas in Cryptography, Lecture Notes in Computer Science, LNCS 3897, Springer-Verlag. 2005, p. 276-290.

[MoWa04] Molnar David, Wagner David: Privacy and security in library RFID: Issues, practices, and architectures. In: Proceedings of the 11th ACM Conference on Computer and Communications Security, ACM. 2004, p. 210-219.

[RiCT05] Rieback M., Crispo B., Tanenbaum A.: RFID Guardian: A batterypowered mobile device for RFID privacy management. In: Proceedings of the 10th Australasian Conference on Information Security and Privacy, Lecture Notes in Computer Science, LNCS 3574, Springer-Verlag. 2005, p. 184-194.

[SaVW09] Sadeghi A.-R., Visconti I., Wachtsmann C.: Efficient RFID Security and Privacy with Anonymizers. In: Proceedings of the 5th Workshop on RFID Security. 2009, p. 153-172.

[SiPr07] Singelée Dave, Preneel Bart: Distance Bounding in Noisy Environments. In: Proceedings of the 4th European Workshop on Security and Privacy in Ad Hoc and Sensor Networks, Lecture Notes in Computer Science, LNCS 4572, Springer-Verlag. 2007, p. 101-115.

[SoMi08] Song Boyeon, Mitchell Chris J.: RFID authentication protocol for low-cost tags. In: Proceedings of the 1st ACM Conference on Wireless Network Security, ACM. 2008, p. 140-147.

[SpEv09] Spiekermann Sarah, Evdokimov Sergei: Critical RFID Privacy-Enhancing Technologies. In: IEEE Security and Privacy, Vol. 7, no. 2, IEEE Computer Society. 2009, p. 56-62.

[Tsud06] Tsudik Gene: YA-TRAP: Yet Another Trivial RFID Authentication Protocol. In: Proceedings of the 4th IEEE International Conference on Pervasive Computing and Communications Workshops, IEEE Computer Society. 2006, p. 640-643.

[Vaud07] Vaudenay Serge: On Privacy Models for RFID. In: Advances in Cryptology – ASIACRYPT 2007, Lecture Notes in Computer Science, LNCS 4833, Springer-Verlag. 2007, p. 68-87.

[WSRE03] Weis S., Sarma S., Rivest S., Engels D.: Security and privacy aspects of low-cost radio frequency identification systems. In: Proceedings of the 1st International Conference on Security in Pervasive Computing, Lecture Notes in Computer Science, LNCS 2802, Springer-Verlag. 2003, p. 454-469.

Web Sessions Anomaly Detection in Dynamic Environments

Manuel Garcia-Cervigón Gutiérrez · Juan Vázquez Pongilupi
Manel Medina LLinàs

Politecnical University of Barcelona
{mgarciac | medina}@ac.upc.edu
juanillovp@gmail.com

Abstract

This paper presents a proposal for discovering anomalies in e-banking Web sessions by implementing different datamining techniques in a a graph-based environment.

Online banking is a good example of how millions of costumers rely on virtual channels for business transactions . Nevertheless, due to multiple scandals regarding security flaws, it becomes complicated moving a business from a physical scenario to the digital world. Therefore, security applications become highly necessary. Monitoring systems like HIDS intend to create a more reliable scenario for companies but because of the number of sessions linked to e-banking Web servers it is barely impossible to detect fraud in real time. We propose a novel method for detecting anomalies in e-banking services by integrating efficient clustering systems based in sequence alignment and graph mining.

1 Introduction

Online-banking has become increasingly popular in the recent years. Although the first online services appeared in the early 80's, people's fear to fraud delayed the growth of these kind of services. Nowadays, millions of users make their transactions through the Internet trusting to the alleged security provided by antispyware and antivirus and the confidence on the bank detections systems.

The truth is that unfortunately antivirus regular updating is still a pending job for most of users and few solutions have emerged in order to detect and react against many attacks that can easily be obfuscated to both client and server security applications. UK payments association APACS estimates that online fraud increased from £22.6m in 2007 to £52.5m in 2008.

Although authentication systems have been improved from the old user/password to two factor authentication, they may become useless in many fraud scenarios.

Many methods to steal Web banking credentials have arisen in the last years. Phishing and technical subterfuge have shown good results in order to steal costumer's identity. Keylogger systems can easily collect credentials on the end-user. Other types of trojans are in charge of redirecting users to sites the did not intend to go. Millions of e-mails are sent every day designed to trick costumers into exposing usernames and passwords.Only in December 2008, more than 31.000 new crimeware-spreading sites appeared[12].

N. Pohlmann, H. Reimer, W. Schneider (Editors): Securing Electronic Business Processes, Vieweg (2009), 216-220

On the bank side, incident detection systems (IDS) have been historically installed, but again, the poor effectiveness show that new focuses are needed. Signature detection systems are based on the comparison of certain information, normally URLs, with a data base of signatures representing known attacks. On the other hand anomaly detection systems (ADS) are able to detect known and unknown attacks by analyzing deviations from normal usage. In an e-banking environment, such deviations may be found in the clickstream and the operations made by users. As focused by many experiences, three main problems can be found in anomaly detection: high percentage of false positives, high computational costs due to the data mining algorithms, and the dependence on the training data.

The rest of this paper is organized as follows: Section 2 summarizes some of the research work as well as the preprocessing process to actually obtain a session data set. Section 3 gives detail of the proposed clustering methodologies. Section 4 proposes Section 5 concludes the paper with a summary and plans for future work.

2 Web usage mining and preprocessing

Web Usage Mining is the application of data mining techniques to discover interesting usage patters and behaviors from Web data, in order to understand and better serve the needs of Web-based applications [13].

It may be of importance to know how a user session differs from a normal behavior in order to detect a Web session impersonation. A session can be defined as the list pages a user visited during an interaction with a Web server. In an authenticated environment such can limited by the pages visited between logon and logoff or the logon and a timeout in case the user does not logoff in a certain time period.

Although it could be possible to find a navigation profile per user, it seems more efficient to compare new sessions with general profiles and therefore clustering seems to fit in that environment.

Application servers such WebLogic or WebSphere or Jboss have become a main part of financial and e-commerce portals architecture. Such new technologies imply a change in the clickstream clustering paradigm based in analysis of a sequence of static html pages found as part of the URL in the Web server logs.

Given the new scenario, where new languages such JSP or .NET work combined with multiple levels applications, queries found in logs are normally based in a domain, a SessionID (id URL Rewriting is used) and sequence of variable/value.

Preprocessing process includes the parsing of dynamic URLs to a categorical data in order to better study different navigation profiles and creation of sessions based on the sesionID, the logon and logoff variables and a timeout. Eclat algorithm was used to find the most frequent combinations of variables in URLs. Each frequent combination is then given an ID. Each URL is then parsed with the ID of the most frequent combination found. Finally a session data set is created.

3 Clustering

It was expected that a correct classification of sessions would help to find normal profiles of navigation and thus the be the base to find anomalous sessions. Clustering algorithms have been developed for continuous data [1][2][3][4] but in this case sequences of categorical variables must be compared and a similarity ratio must be found. Fortunately sequence alignment has been widely used in genomics in order to find similarities among DNA and protein sequences. In fact some investigations [2][6][7][8] have already taken use of sequence alignment for session clustering. JAligner was used to perform the operation but it was needed to reconfigure the application to accept URLs sequences instead of DNA or protein sequences.

Firstly, it was expected to design a cluster configuration in such way that most of the anomalous sessions would fall within the same group. That was achieved thanks to a distance matrix based in sequence alignment of sessions and a F Matrix that rewards the similarity of two sessions if frequency of the URLs (o combination of variables) is close. On the other hand many crimeware robots execute queries very fast so very short period between clicks punished.

Our first experiments with a synthetic data set of 2000 sessions showed detection rate of 75,2 % anomalous sessions. Although the results proved to be interesting some time is needed to create the distance matrix.

In order to perform a live detection of anomalies, it is necessary to compare each new session with the user regular navigation profile. Having a dendogram of sessions it is possible to get groups of similar types of navigations.

It must be taken into account that clickstream behaviors may vary. Although each user is assigned a general profile based in his first analyzed sessions, navigation behaviors can change so it will be mandatory to periodically study user profile changes. General profiles will be compared to each session and an anomaly scoring will be applied depending on the distance between the user's normal profile and the one fitting the studied session.

K-order Markov models are be extracted out of each cluster, that is each general profile of navigation, to better extract normality models for each general profile. K-order Markov techniques are useful to predict the next page to be visited from the information regarding the last k pages visited before.

Three different types of outcomes are possible. If the user regular profile model proves to fit the session, then it is a normal session. If some other model fits the session we can state that the user is changing its behavior. Finally, if the session if completely different to all profiles, we are in front a an anomalous session.

Again, the experiments were quiet successful with synthetic data due to a detection of 81% of anomalies.

4 Graph mining and anti-fraud heuristics

The increasing use of semi-structured data such as, XML, texts or trees benefited the use of data mining, but the amount of information grows exponentially and new ways of structuring data such as topological structures have emerged in order to better understand some environments [9]. Nowadays, the results expected from a query tend to be some relationships more than a list of entities.

As stated before, the amount of information to study and the need to have it analyzed within milliseconds is an important issue in online-banking. Information regarding money transactions made within a session is also a valuable source of information that must be correlated with the results extracted from the clickstream anomaly detection system.

In order to rapidly analyze each transaction the information is copied to Graphs Based Systems, where different types of nodes, new efficient relationships and levels of abstraction can be made in order to reduce the time to perform a query and manage different heuristics.

DEX [10] has been chosen as the graph storing system due to the high performance and the possibility of integrating different types of information sources. The query system facilitates the insertion of heuristics.

Moving data to nodes and edges involve some issues when e-banking transactions are handled. Information must be simplified into nodes, edges and attributes. For instance, different types of account identifiers must be merged into one type of node. Moreover, new information can be extracted: we can establish relation from account nodes to the countries nodes they pertain.

The graph system should be capable of creating new rules based on the analysis of click stream anomalies, that is, every time a anomalous clickstream is detected, the operations made during that session are compared to ones from other anomalous clickstreams with certain similitude.

Operations made during regular sessions are also important to update the different edges (transactions) among nodes (account) and the thresholds.

After analyzing different fraud techniques some basic heuristics have been included in order to study transaction validity in real time:

- Direct relationship. If the source and destination have been involved in previous transactions, no input will be added to the anomaly score.
- Family nodes relationship. Having a graph based forest it becomes in easy routine to find the number of account edges between source and destination. Depending on the distance between accounts, an anomaly scoring will be added.
- Transaction amount. Each account should have a transaction mount associated. The amount involved in a transaction should be within a threshold automatically updated and based in last non-anomalous transactions from the source account. The amount of transactions are studied by searching all the edges of a node.
- Money Mule's presence. The money mule's technique consists in convincing someone (the mule) to sign up for a new bank account and withdraw an amount of money after some transactions are made from hacked accounts to the mule's new account. Normally there is little time between the transactions and the moment the mule gets a phone call in order to withdraw the money. The automatic analysis of the number of account nodes that just generated edges to the mules account node as well as the period of time between the transaction and the withdraw can give a rapid idea of the presence of mules, that is, accounts from the same country as the source used to transfer money that will afterwards be again transferred from the mule account to a foreign country in a few amount of transactions.
- Level of suspiciousness. A Page Rank like algorithm has been developed in order to manage a level of suspiciousness per account node. If a node has been involved in an anomalous click stream session, a suspiciousness score is assigned. The level of suspiciousness can increase if the account is targeted by other suspicious accounts, that is, a virus like spreading is made.

Each heuristic has its own anomaly weight. A final score will show the level of normality of the operations of a session. We can define the final score as the sum of all weighted partial scores. Finally, the operation normality scoring must be merged with the clickstream normality scoring in order to define decisions.

5 Conclusions and Future Work

A new methodology has been developed to classify web queries in dynamic environments in order to obtain comparable clickstreams from a Web Server Log.

Partial experimentation has been done with synthetic data showing some promising results. The design of the system is completely finished, but test data is needed in order to establish the thresholds more accurately.

Neural Networks should be used in order to evaluate new costumer variables regarding the configuration of heuristics but data protection and privacy must be taken into account in order formulate investigations in an environment where mostly all variables belong to personal information sets.

References

[1] Er Strehl, Joydeep Ghosh, Raymond Mooney, Impact of Similarity Measures on Web-page Clustering, Workshop on Artificial Intelligence for Web Search, 2000

[2] Yue Xu, Li-Tung Weng, Improvement of web data clustering using web page contents, Intelligent information processing, 2004

[3] Xuanhui Wang, Dou Shen, Hua-Jun Zeng, Zheng Chen, Wei-Ying Ma , Web Page Clustering Enhanced by Summarization, Conference on Information and Knowledge Management , Proceedings of the thirteenth ACM international conference on Information and knowledge management , 2004

[4] Morteza Haghir Chehreghani, Hassan Abolhassani, Mostafa Haghir Chehreghani, Improving density-based methods for hierarchical clustering of web pages, Data & Knowledge Engineering, 2008

[5] Alberto P. García-Plaza, Víctor Fresno, Raquel Martínez, Web Page Clustering Using a Fuzzy Logic Based Representation and Self-Organizing Maps, Proceedings of the 2008 IEEE/WIC/ACM International Conference on Web Intelligence and Intelligent Agent Technology – Volume 01 , 2008

[6] Weien Wang, Osmar R. Zaïane, Clustering Web sessions by Sequence Alignment, Proceedings of the 13th international workshop on DEXA, 2002.

[7] Arindam Banerjee, Joydeep Ghosh, Clickstream Clustering Using Weighted Longest Common Subsequence, Proceedings of the Web Mining Workshop at the 1st SIAM Conference on Data Mining, 2001

[8] Chaofeng Li , Yansheng Lu, Similarity Measurement of Web Sessions by Sequence Alignment, 2007 IFIP International Conference on Network and Parallel Computing Workshops, 2007

[9] R. Angles and C. Gutiérrez, Survey of graph database models. Technical Report TR/DCC-2005-10, Computer Science Department, Universidad de Chile, 2008

[10] N. Martínez-Bazán, V. Muntés-Mulero, S. Gómez-Villamor, J. Nin, M. Sánchez-Martínez and J. Larriba-Pey, DEX: High-Performance Exploration on Large Graphs for Information Retrieval, Proceedings of 16th ACM Conference on Information and Knowledge Management, 2007

[11] Fu Y, Sandhu K, Shih M. A generalization based approach to clustering of Web usage session. International Workshop on Web Usage Analysis and User profiling, San Diego, 2000

[12] Antiphishing working group. Phishing Activity Trends Report. 2008

[13] J.Srivastava, R. Cooley, M. Deshpande, and P.N. Tan. Web Usage Mining: Discovery and Applications of Usage Patterns from Web Data. SIGKDD Explorations,1(2):12–23, 2000.

Standards and
Technical Solutions

KryptoNAS: Open source based NAS encryption

Martin Oczko

Utimaco Safeware AG, Aachen
Martin.Oczko@utimaco.de

Abstract

Even though more and more software based solutions exist that protect data of notebooks and workstations, NAS systems with integrated encryption mechanisms are very rare available on the market. At the same time it is possible to realize a cost optimized secure NAS device with good performance using freely available hardware and open source software. This article describes the research results of the KryptoNAS project which goal was to develop a NAS device with transparent Hard disk encryption based on open source software and standard hardware. The outcome of the project is a pre-product secure NAS device which meets the requirements of SOHO and SME users.

1 Introduction

Although primary Network Attached Storage was designed for the usage in datacenters and as storage for mainframe systems there appear more and more NAS devices on the market which are intended for the usage in SOHO and SME Networks. NAS devices become popular because of easy configuration and administration in contrast to the common server systems. These are indeed more flexible and can provide a bigger range of functions but the ease of use of NAS systems which offer specialized functionality convinced the users. In particular users of small offices and small enterprises without a dedicated IT department or IT administrator appreciate the simplicity of NAS devices. There are a couple of NAS devices available which aim on user groups like surgeries, law and tax consultant offices or home users. These users often have to satisfy security requirements and have to assure that their data is stored securely. Unfortunately, NAS devices which provide disk encryption functionality are very rare and unproportional expensive. This fact and the lack of adequate devices with the required functionality available on the market were the motivation for the KryptoNAS project. The idea behind the KryptoNAS project was to investigate the question whether it is possible to develop a secure and cost optimized high performance NAS device which is completely based on open source software and on minimalistic hardware. The goal was to develop a rudimental prototype of a NAS device which meets the defined requirements with the main focus on security and the performance and which acts as proof of concept for the idea of an open source based NAS device running on minimalistic hardware.

In the following this document defines different classes of NAS devices and describes the requirements for the NAS device which has to be designed. After this the paper describes the security concept of the NAS device and presents results of some performance measurements and finally ends with a conclusion.

N. Pohlmann, H. Reimer, W. Schneider (Editors): Securing Electronic Business Processes, Vieweg (2009), 223-229

2 NAS Categories

By analyzing the NAS market itself, in principle the available NAS devices can be divided in the three following categories:

SOHO Class: Cheap and low-performance devices without RAID functionality. The data transfer performance of these devices ranges between 3-8 Mb/sec.

SME Class: These devices usually come with RAID functionality and provide the option for several hard disk drives. The data transfer rate ranges between 8-20 Mb/sec assuming a Gigabit Ethernet interface.

Enterprise Class: These devices are designed for the usage in data centers. Devices in this class provide several TBytes of storage space with access over high performance fibre-channel interfaces. The data transfer rate often lies above 100Mb/sec.

Due to the fact that the demands on the devices in the enterprise class are completely different than the demands on devices of the SOHO and SME classes, the enterprise class devices are not considered in the following. Looking at SOHO or SME class NAS devices, there are only a few devices available with integrated encryption functionality. In addition some of the available devices with encryption functionality provide only weak encryption mechanisms and only one-factor authentication. Furthermore these devices come with very low performance (in some cases under 4Mb/sec) if the encryption function is activated.

3 Requirements

Based on this market research a concept for a secure and cost optimized NAS device with a performance according the needs of SOHO and SME users was being composed. The first step was to define the requirements for the new device. These requirements can be divided in general requirements and hardware requirements which are defined as follows.

3.1 General Requirements

- Transparent encryption on device level
- Performance on 100MBit Level (at least 8 Mb/sec)
- Two-factor authentication (token + password)
- Strong encryption (AES-256)
- Open Source software components

3.2 Hardware Requirements

- Minimalistic hardware (low energy consumption, passive cooling)
- Standard components
- Minimal costs

3.3 Hardware Platform

The fist step in this project was the selection of the hardware-platform, on which the KryptoNAS device should be operating on. A market research shows, that only two promising hardware platforms are available today which support the specified requirements for the KryptoNAS. One Platform is the AMD Geode [AMDGeode] processor family, which is used e.g. in Thin Clients and other low-performance systems. These processors offer an integrated crypto engine which accelerates cryptographic operations like symmetric encryption. The other potential Hardware Platform is the Eden processors family, offered by VIA [VIAEden], which also comes with an integrated crypto engine. Compared to the Geode processors, Eden processors support the AES encryption up 256 key length (whereas Geode only supports key lengths up to 128 bit). To meet the requirement for "strong encryption" the VIA Eden processors were chosen as the hardware platform for the project. Enclosed the datasheet for the KryptoNAS main board and a photo from the used hardware:

- 1 GHz VIA V4 Eden CPU with PadLock Security Engine
- Energy consumption : 9W
- Passive cooling
- Hardware acceleration for AES-128/256 and SHA-1
- 1 GB RAM
- 2 x SATA
- 2 GB Compact Flash Card boot device
- 2 x 100MBit LAN
- 4 x USB

Fig. 1: KryptoNAS mainboard ADE-2100

3.4 Software Architecture

The architecture of the KryptoNAS itself looks similar to usual NAS systems. Based on its own operating system, the KryptoNAS comes with a web based administration console and a fileserver interface.

Below you can find a list of the used software packages and figure 2 which denotes the high-level software architecture:

- **Operating System:** current version of Debian Linux [Debian]
- **WebServer:** Lighttps with Perl-CGI Module [Lighttpd]
- **Fileserver:** Samba [Samba]

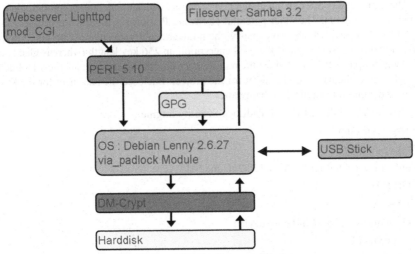

Fig. 2: KryptoNAS software architecture

4 Security concept

To integrate comprehensive encryption functionality, the security concept of the KryptoNAS consists of four components. First of all the basic encryption is done by the DM-Crypt kernel module [DMCrypt] which enables data encryption on blockdevice level. The additional key management layer LUKS (Linux Unified Key Setup) [LUKS] provides the missing Key-Management capabilities of DM Crypt. The authentication concept enables the use of security tokens in addition to password authentication. The last component is the tamper-evident hardware which avoids the manipulation of the installed operating system and prevents from attacks on hardware level.

4.1 DM-Crypt

DM-Crypt is a Linux kernel module which allows encryption and decryption of data stored on a blockdevice. The encryption is done on the blockdevice level so the DM-Crypt concept is very flexible and can be combined with other blockdevice oriented solutions like Linux software RAID or LVM. DM-Crypt creates a virtual blockdevice which provides a decrypted view of the encrypted data on the physical blockdevice. The read and write operations on the virtual blockdevice are decrypted and encrypted and redirected to the physical blockdevice. The encryption is done using AES-128/256 in CBC or CBC-ESSIV mode. The following figure describes the layer architecture with the DM-Crypt blockdevice. DM-Crypt sets up a logical blockdevice /dev/mapper/crypto and maps it to the physical harddisk blockdevice /dev/sda1. This logical blockdevice can be formatted with an arbitrary filesystem and used as a usual disk device. Figure 3 denotes the layer model with DM-Crypt mapper module between the filesystem and the physical harddisk.

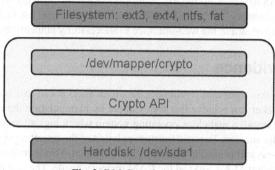

Fig. 3: DM-Crypt layer model

4.2 LUKS – Linux Unified Key Setup

DM-Crypt derives the symmetric key used for data encryption from the user password or takes the key directly as a parameter. If the user would like to change the password the whole data stored on the blockdevice must be decrypted with the old key and encrypted with the new one. LUKS avoids this complex operation by introducing an additional key management layer. By the creation of a new encrypted blockdevice, LUKS generates a random symmetric Master-Key and encrypts this key using the user input like a password or a binary key. Each instance of the encrypted Master-Key is stored in one of eight key slots in the partition header of the created blockdevice. Thus if the user is changing his password, only the encrypted Master-Key must be decrypted with the old password, encrypted with the new one and stored again in the key slot. At the same time the key slots allow to use up to eight different passwords or keys to authenticate different users. Figure 4 shows the design of the LUKs header.

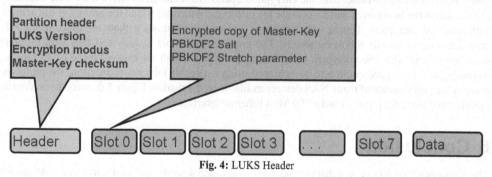

Fig. 4: LUKS Header

4.3 Two-factor authentication

The authentication concept is an essential component of the security concept. Common NAS devices are only using a user password to authenticate the user. One of the requirements in the KryptoNAS project was to develop a cost optimized but secure two-factor authentication concept. The idea is to use not only a password to authenticate the user but also a security token. This concept is implemented by using a simple USB Stick and the open source encryption tool GPG. If the user creates a new encrypted partition and selects a password using the web interface, a random key is generated by the NAS device. This random key is encrypted using GPG and the user password and is stored on a usual USB stick which has to be attached to the NAS device. Thus the following authentication chain is created: "userpassword" -> "key stored on the USB medium" -> "LUKS Master Key". Now the user has to attach the USB medium and needs to enter his password in the web-interface to successfully authenticate with the device.

4.4 Tamper-Evidence

The most secure encryption algorithm is without effect if an attacker can gain access to the key used for the encryption. An attacker can achieve this for example by manipulating the operating system of the NAS device. He could install a malicious operating system which logs all secure passwords and keys and forwards them to the attacker. To avoid the manipulation of the operating system which is stored on the CF-Card, a tamper-evident is used to secure the boot medium. This is realized by casting the part of the system board in which the CF-Card and the RAM memory reside. The casting material encloses the CF-card and the memory module whereby it is impossible to detach these components. This measurement prevents the attacker from manipulating the operating system or performing a cold-boot attack on the memory module.

5 Performance

The performance of the prototype was tested with the NAS Performance Tool [NASPt] developed by Intel. This test application creates test files in different sizes and copies these files to and from the device and measures the time each operation takes. The results of these benchmark tests meet the expectations and the requirements specified in the beginning. With activated AES-256 encryption the prototype was able to copy the test files from the client pc with an average speed of 9 Mb/sec. Considering the fact that the system was featured only with a 100 Mbit Ethernet device the results correspond to the maximum transfer rate which can be reached using the CIFS protocol. So it seems that the slow ethernet connection was the bottle-neck rather than the encryption operations themselves. More tests were necessary to circumvent the bottle-neck and to measure the maximum data rates which the prototype can achieve with activated encryption. Testing with local copy and move operations without the usage of the Ethernet interface yields the following results. The prototype was able to copy test files with different sizes between an AES-256 encrypted partition and the ramdisk with the average speed of 30 Mb/sec. Assuming that this speed could also be achieved using a Gigabit Ethernet connection, the prototype exceeds the performance of many NAS devices available on the market. Figure 5 denotes the read/write performance via CIFS protocol and a 100 Mbit Ethernet interface.

6 Conclusion

The KryptoNAS project proves that it is possible to develop a secure and cost optimized NAS device based on open source software and low priced hardware. Considering the fact that the chosen system board was developed for the usage in thin clients and set-top boxes and comes with functionality which is obsolete in a NAS device (VGA, sound system, etc.) it should be easily possible to reduce the hardware costs by choosing a system board without these components. Because the most manufacturers of NAS devices neglect the matter of data security, the developed security concept and prototype NAS device has a special standalone feature and provides unique data security combined with high-performance.

Literature

[AMDGeode] Inc. (AMD) Advanced Micro Devices. Amd geode lx processor family. http://www.amd.com/usen/ConnectivitySolutions/ProductInformation/0502330986313022,00.html

[VIAEden] Inc. VIA Technologies. Via padlock security engine. The worlds fastest x86 military-grade security engine, http://www.via.com.tw/en/downloads/whitepapers/initiatives/padlock/VIAPadLockSecurity-Engine.pdf

[Lighttpd] Lighttpd Community, lighttpd dokumentation, http://redmine.lighttpd.net/wiki/lighttpd

[Debian] Internationales Debian Projekt, Debian – das universelle betriebssystem, www.debian.org

[Samba] Opening Windows to a Wider World, www.samba.org

[DMCrypt] dm-crypt project. dm-crypt: a device-mapper crypto target, http://www.saout.de/misc/dm-crypt/

[LUKS] http://www.saout.de/tikiwiki/tiki-index.php?page=LUKS

[NASPt] Intel R Software Network. Intel R nas performance toolkit, http://software.intel.com/en-us/articles/intel-nas-performance-toolkit

Secure Network Zones

Peter Kai Wimmer

atsec information security GmbH
Steinstraße 70, 81667 Munich, Germany
peter.wimmer@atsec.com

Abstract

Large networks, which are often distributed over physically separate locations, require a coherent security approach. This paper introduces the concept of secure network zones, arranged in "onion-like" layers, providing increasing security levels towards the inner, more secure zones.

Increased security is provided by both protective layers around sensitive networks and additional (cumulative) security measures, ranging from basic measures such as hardening and firewalls to more sophisticated techniques such as intrusion detection and encryption of transmitted and stored data.

The implementation of secure network zones is described, including classification of data, assignment of applications to zones, and data flow. A path for the migration of existing environments is discussed and recommendations for special use cases are provided.

1 Introduction

Internal networks used to be flat entities, separated only from the Internet by a single firewall. With the increasing use of electronic services such as e-mail and web, internal networks grew rapidly, and were – at least logically – separated along department boundaries. A growing awareness of the value of confidential information (e.g., design specifications, financial data) and of increased dependency on the electronic infrastructure led to implementation of further security measures, such as access control and strong authentication mechanisms.

Malware with the ability to spread without user interaction by replicating itself to other systems on a network (a.k.a. worms) imposes a tremendous threat to flat network structures. Humans, either acting as insiders (e.g., employees) or outsiders ("hackers", spies, script kiddies, etc.), pose a similar threat. Thus, additional protection for networks against each other, as well as for systems within these networks, is required.

In addition, legacy applications that cannot be patched with security fixes due to restrictions from the vendor (e.g., support only for a specific configuration) or simply due to the sheer number of missing updates are considered a major risk for the whole environment. By separating such applications into a protected subnet, both the risk of being compromised and the impact of compromise on the surrounding systems are efficiently reduced.

The secure network zones model provides a sophisticated and granular approach to protecting assets, focusing on *information* as the most valuable (electronic) asset. Sensitive data is surrounded by additional layers of protection, providing both network and logical security measures such as access control, confidentiality protection, and intrusion prevention. The segmentation of networks efficiently restricts

N. Pohlmann, H. Reimer, W. Schneider (Editors): Securing Electronic Business Processes, Vieweg (2009), 230-241

vulnerabilities and the associated threats and risks to a limited environment. The secure network zones model implements *defense in depth* through its layered model and *diversity in defense* through an adequate protection profile for each zone.

The author originally developed a secure network zones model in 2003, and some similar approaches exist. However, few related papers focus on data security and restrictions for the traversal of zones. Indeed, most papers proposing an extended zone model for secure networks discuss "classic" network separation, e.g., isolating the server LAN from client LANs. This separation model also references "zones"; however, such zones usually represent a flat separation of subnets with differing security requirements.

The work of Bell and La Padula, as well as the "hierarchical protection domains" model (see chapter 5, Related work) for protecting data and resources, serve as foundation for the secure zones model introduced in this paper.

2 Architecture

A "secure network zone" is a dedicated network segment, with a well-defined communication flow to other zones and implementing specific security measures.

Three internal zones are defined, and these zones are nested, i.e., the innermost zone is protected by the surrounding zones (see **Fig. 1**). An internal zone may consist of various subnets and even span several locations.

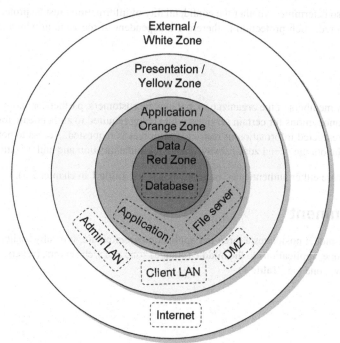

Fig. 1: Secure network zones

An external zone represents all networks that are not controlled by the organization; this includes not only the Internet but also "attached" networks of outsourcing partners, suppliers, and service providers.

Zones may be divided into segments (labeled "zone instances", implemented as subnets), since further separation is often desired, e.g., for a DMZ and client LANs. This structure also supports the protection of critical applications by isolating them from other parts of the network.

Availability and accountability are individually defined for each segment, independent from the data security level. For example, a web server providing information classified as "public" may require high availability, while an internal system with confidential data may only need to be available during business hours.

2.1 Classification

The focus of this approach is data security, i.e., the confidentiality and integrity requirements of information. Therefore, it is necessary to classify data according to the information classification guidelines of the organization. The three essential levels are *public*, *internal* and *confidential*. Further granularity usually may be reduced to one of these three levels. For information not (yet) classified, a reasonable approach is to consider such data as internal.

Although confidential data must be stored in the inner, most secure zone, a subset of this data is typically processed in an application in the zone "below", which in turn forwards part of this (processed) data to the presentation layer in the adjacent lower zone.

Classification also determines whether the confidentiality of information must be protected while being transferred or stored; such protection is therefore independent of the zone in which data is currently processed.

2.2 Users

Users are usually members of the organization, but may be customers, partners or anonymous users. Users may remain anonymous for certain services, while being required to authenticate for others, usually when access to restricted information or restricted resources is requested. Access to non-public data or resources (i.e., the orange or red zone) always mandates authentication and authorization.

Therefore, users are either authenticated or anonymous (see **Table 1** in chapter 2.3).

2.3 Assignment

The secure zone model postulates a three-tier application architecture, typically assigning databases to the inner (red) zone, applications to the middle (orange) zone and web servers, (reverse) proxies, etc. to the outer (yellow) zone (see **Table 1**).

Table 1: Zone and user level assignm

Zone / Layer	Typical contents	User level
Internet (white)	Public Customers Partners	Anonymous
Presentation (yellow)	Client LANs (Reverse) proxy Web server VPN endpoint DMZ	Authenticated
Application (orange)	Applications Admin jump station	Authenticated
Data (red)	Databases	Authenticated

The location where information is actually *stored* determines the assignment to zones (see also 2.1).

Examples of common assignments:

- Web server providing public information only – yellow zone
- File server providing internal documents, such as guidelines – orange zone
- Database with confidential customer data, such as a CRM – red zone, and the application server – orange zone

Clients may be in either the yellow or white zones; for access to internal and confidential information, clients must be authenticated and authorized (see also chapter 2.4).

2.4 Data flow and zone traversal

Data flow is restricted to and from *adjacent* zones only, thus restricting direct access to sensitive data from networks considered insecure (see **Fig. 2**). This restriction applies both from outer to inner layers, as well as vice versa. Although the inner zones are considered "more secure" (actually, better protected), direct connection from an inner (e.g., database) zone to the Internet would allow a Trojan to transfer sensitive data without any further obstacles.

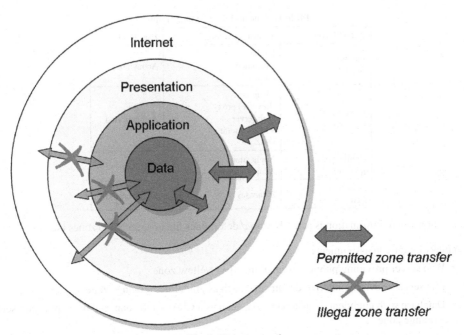

Fig. 2: Zone traversal

Any user accessing resources or data in the orange or red zone must be authenticated and authorized.

Applications in the orange zone may need to be accessed from the Internet, e.g., by members of the organization working in remote locations. A number of such applications do not provide a separate presentation layer due to the limitations of a two-tier architecture. As no direct access from the Internet to the orange zone is allowed, a gateway is required in the yellow zone (internal users are already located in the yellow zone). Depending on the frontend provided, such gateways include reverse proxies (for web services) or terminal servers for Windows applications.

For additional security, these gateways may implement content filtering and virus scanning, to prevent malicious code from entering higher zones.

2.5 Security measures

In addition to the firewalls between secure zones, the security of the systems and applications themselves must be maintained. Security measures to be applied are authentication, logging (for accountability), and virus scanning. A reverse proxy may provide authentication for external users; a web application gateway – a.k.a. web application firewall, usually acting as a (transparent) reverse proxy – restricts traffic that is considered malicious, e.g., containing SQL injection attacks. Organizational security measures include user account management and user authorization, as well as physical protection of the data center, such as fenced-in premises, a guarded entrance, and no unaccompanied physical access to systems.

Table 2 provides an overview of which zones must implement which technical security measures, and references the subchapter where the respective measure is described. The measures are cumulative, i.e., each zone implements all measures of the zone "below" and possibly additional measures.

Table 2: Security measur

Zone	Security Measure	Ref.	Remarks
Presentation (yellow)	Firewalls	2.5.1	
	Hardening	2.5.2	
	Data transfer encryption	2.5.3	
	Virus scanners	2.5.4	
	Audit trail	2.5.5	
Application (orange)	Access control	2.5.6	
	IDS	2.5.7	
Data (red)	Data storage encryption	2.5.8	optional

2.5.1 Firewalls

Each zone implements its own filtering, typically using firewalls with several network interfaces to accommodate a number of zone instances (subnets) within that zone. The firewalls protect zones by filtering incoming and outgoing connections as well as traffic between zone instances according to the documented communication flow for the applications within the zone.

As an example, the firewall for the orange zone controls access both from the yellow and red zones, and also between zone instances (subnets) within the orange zone. It denies all other access, e.g., from the white zone.

2.5.2 Hardening

System and application hardening are *the* most important step towards protecting data and assets.

Security updates for the operating system and all software packages must be installed as soon as they become available. Furthermore, services not required on a system must be uninstalled or at least disabled.

The configuration of the applications and the operating system must follow best practices for security. Tools to determine insecure configurations are often provided by the manufacturer, as well as information on secure configuration.

Therefore, hardening is not a one-time measure at the time of deployment of a system, but must be implemented as an ongoing process.

2.5.3 Data transfer encryption

Confidential data that is transferred over a network must always be encrypted, regardless of the zone(s) it traverses.

The amount of (sensitive) information typically becomes less from the database layer (red) towards the Internet, since the application layer (orange) usually queries more data than it actually needs from the database and then passes on a subset of this data to the presentation layer (yellow); see also 2.6. Nevertheless, such sensitive information is also less protected towards the outer zones, and therefore must be encrypted all the way.

Table 3 lists some replacements for unencrypted or unauthenticated protocols.

Table 3: Data transfer encryp

Insecure protocol	Secure replacement	Remarks
HTTP	HTTPS	via SSL / TLS
FTP	SFTP	Secure FTP
	scp	secure copy
telnet	ssh	secure shell
SQLNET	SSL	e.g., Oracle and DB/2 provide several authentication and encryption mechanisms

The use of insecure protocols such as ODBC for the transfer of sensitive information must be prohibited. In case there is no authentication and encryption mechanism intrinsic to a specific type of transfer, end-to-end communication may also be embedded, e.g., in an SSH or SSL tunnel between the source and target components.

2.5.4 Virus scanners

Virus scanners are mandatory on internal clients and must also be implemented on gateway or proxy servers, such as web and ftp proxies, as well as mail servers.

Depending on the applications used, it may also be feasible to install a virus scanner on specific servers. For example, a system used to convert files (pictures, MS Word docs, etc.) for anonymous users may want to verify that no buffer overflow occurs due to a deliberately manipulated file.

2.5.5 Audit trail

For accountability and non-repudiation purposes, logging of critical events is mandatory:

- Important application events like start / stop, critical errors, etc.
- Security relevant events, i.e., login / logout of users, including failed logins, as well as configuration changes

Write access to log data must be restricted to the application that is the source of the audit trail. A remote log host is highly recommended to protect the audit trail from manipulation and to provide centralized log analysis.

Log data must not include confidential information, like passwords. Log entries must always include date and time, as well as the source of the event. If available, user name and IP address should also be part of a log entry.

2.5.6 Access control

Access control is the ability to permit or deny the use of a resource by an entity. Access control includes *identification* and *authentication, authorization* and an *audit trail* (see 2.5.5).

Access can be granted or denied based on a wide variety of arbitrary criteria, such as the network address of the communication partner, the time of day, type of request, etc. These criteria may bear no reference to the attributes of a particular request.

2.5.6.1 Identification and authentication

Applications that process internal or confidential data must only be accessed by an authenticated entity for which specific access rights have been defined. Humans and also applications may communicate with a service; therefore, the following two types of authentication apply:

- **User authentication**
  Individual accounts (instead of shared logins) must be set up for each end user to ensure accountability. Depending on the sensitivity of information, strong authentication mechanisms are recommended.

- **Service authentication**
  Services usually authenticate using a "technical user", which must only be used in this context, for example, access to a database or to a bus in an SOA environment. Especially for web services, certificate-based authentication is recommended.

It is assumed that *applications* implement access control mechanisms controlling end users' access to resources. Therefore, other services like databases have to rely on access control mechanisms implemented in the application from which a query originates. This ensures that end user access control only has to be implemented once, in the application the end user is communicating with.

For large environments with a substantial number of users, a single sign-on service is recommended, which greatly reduces the various passwords to be remembered while ensuring that no stale accounts remain after a user leaves the organization or is transferred to another department.

2.5.6.2 Authorization

Authorization is the process of providing and restricting access to resources. As such, it is very much credential-focused and dependent on specific rules and access control lists preset by the application administrator(s) or data owners. Typical authorization checks involve querying for membership in a particular (user) group, possession of a particular clearance, or an entry in the approved access control list of a resource.

Any access control mechanism is clearly dependent on effective and forge-resistant authentication controls used for authorization.

2.5.7 IDS

An intrusion detection system (IDS) alerts administrators if an intrusion attempt or a successful compromise occurs within a network or on a host. Since an IDS requires considerable resources to implement and maintain, an IDS is only required for the red zone, which typically consists of only a few systems. A host-based IDS provides more reliable information about whether an intrusion attempt was successful, while a network-based IDS also sees undirected traffic (e.g., reconnaissance), which is expected to be rather limited within a red zone.

2.5.8 Data storage encryption

Data storage encryption is strongly recommended at the application level (see 2.5.8.1).

2.5.8.1 Application data encryption

In order to protect the confidentiality of sensitive data against intruders or malevolent administrators on the database server, application-level encryption is recommended, where available.

2.5.8.2 File system encryption

If application-level encryption is not an option, file system encryption at least protects confidential data against physical theft or loss, e.g., when old or non-functional hard drives are improperly disposed of.

2.6 Example – online banking

In **Fig. 3**, an online banking application is illustrated as an example of a typical implementation in a secure zones environment.

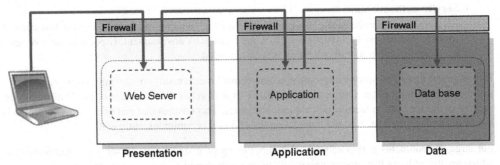

Fig. 3: Online banking example

The client is somewhere in the Internet, the white zone, and accesses the online banking frontend, which executes on a web server in the yellow zone of the bank. The web frontend authenticates the customer, and only after the user's credentials are verified successfully, forwards the requests to the actual online banking application in the orange zone. If the online banking application needs further data to fulfill the request, it queries the database in the red zone, processes the data, and returns a dynamic web page via the web server in the yellow zone to the customer's client.

Since all banking data is considered confidential, each communication link is encrypted.

3 Special cases

This paper also discusses the compliance of several use cases, such as system administration, MAN / WAN interconnectivity, backup, and small enterprises with this security model.

3.1 System administration

For system administration, a „jump station" is placed in the orange zone, from where it is allowed to access this zone, as well as the red and yellow zones (see **Fig. 4**). Administrative access to other systems is only permitted from the jump host, requiring administrators to log on to this jump host first.

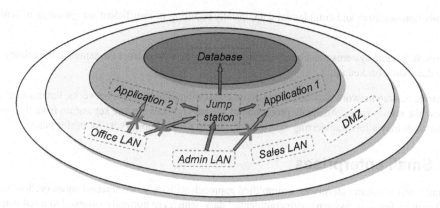

Fig. 4: System administration with a jump station

The jump station holds ssh keys and certificates required to authenticate to other systems, providing central control over credentials, as well as accountability via logging of user activity.

According to best practice, unencrypted or insecure protocols, such as telnet, rsh, or http, must not be used for system administration. Also, trust relationships such as `.rhost` never were a valid security concept and must not be employed.

3.2 Interconnectivity

The interconnectivity between remote locations is not logically different from local networks organized in network zones. Routers and transfer networks are not considered part of zone instances, but part of the network infrastructure (see **Fig. 5**).

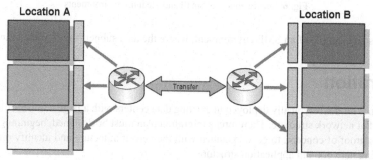

Fig. 5: Location interconnectivity

The zone traversal paradigm (see 2.4) applies to interconnected zones. Zones are considered adjacent (as defined in **Fig. 2**) across transfer networks. Zones of the same level may connect directly, e.g., red zone in location A with red zone in location B.

3.3 Backup

Existing (additional) backup networks often interconnect all hosts to be backed up, thus circumventing intermediate firewalls. Furthermore, backup media often is not clearly classified, and backup procedures intermix non-sensitive and confidential data, usually resulting in insufficient safeguarding of sensitive data.

As a result, backup systems must be placed in a secure zone with at least the same confidentiality level as the data being backed up.

A separate backup network may be used to avoid congestion of production networks, but must not compromise the secure zones. Adequate protection of the backup network and separation from the productive network may allow transferring data unencrypted to the backup servers for performance.

3.4 Small enterprises

For small and medium enterprises, a simplified approach with only two internal zones (yellow and orange) may be feasible. Systems with confidential data, which are normally assigned to a red zone, are placed into the orange zone.

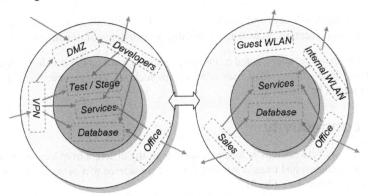

Fig. 6: Secure zones for small and medium environments

Fig. 6 shows an example of an SME environment, where the data subnet is part of the orange zone.

4 Migration

A secure zones model is typically deployed in existing data centers with a large number of legacy applications in a flat network structure. Therefore, a migration plan must be designed, beginning with a pilot migration as proof of concept, to get acquainted with the new architecture and identify pitfalls caused by the existing network and application structure.

Applications need to be separated into their three tiers (presentation, logic and data); the logic tier usually is an application server. The communication flow for the application must be documented, i.e., source, target, protocol, and content must be identified. This information is required to define access controls (see 2.5.1), as well as for classification of data (see 2.1).

For the data tier, it is feasible to implement a centralized database service which provides table space to the applications. A centralized approach also reduces maintenance costs, while concentrating on a secure and redundant implementation of that service.

The presentation layer either is a client in a local LAN or a (reverse) proxy providing access for external clients. Such a proxy authenticates external clients, forwards client requests and delivers server responses, and optionally filters incoming data for malicious content. In addition, data transfer mechanisms may have to be adapted to provide encryption.

Some protocols are quite easily switched to their encrypted equivalent, e.g., HTTP to HTTPS (see 2.5.3). However, some (proprietary) protocols may not provide any option for encryption at all, or the application can not be changed (e.g., no source code available). Therefore, there are always some legacy applications that cannot be migrated and that will remain in the insecure, flat network until they are obsolete.

5 Related work

Bell and La Padula ([BeLP73], [BeLP76]) developed a security policy for access control for military and government applications. This model is based on security labels on information objects and clearances on subjects. The security labels are classifications, such as "secret", whereas the clearances represent roles and the corresponding (access) rights. The Bell and La Padula focus on data confidentiality and data flow was adapted for the secure zones model.

A mechanism to protect data and resources called "hierarchical protection domains" or "protection rings" has been developed to provide layers of privilege. Typically this is implemented in hardware, e.g., CPU architectures that use "supervisor" mode (a.k.a. "kernel" mode) and "user" mode for different levels of access. This hierarchical approach was adopted for the secure zones.

6 Conclusion

Secure network zones provide in-depth protection for sensitive data and vital systems by implementing several layers of increased security. The impact of malicious code or attacks is effectively contained, and the standardized approach for securely deploying applications also improves data center operation efficiency.

References

[BeLP73] Bell, David Elliott and La Padula, Leonard J.: Secure Computer Systems: Mathematical Foundations. MITRE Corporation, 1973.

[BeLP76] Bell, David Elliott and La Padula, Leonard J.: Secure Computer System: Unified Exposition and Multics Interpretation. MITRE Corporation, 1976.

[LaHM84] Landwehr, C.E., C.L. Heitmeyer, and J. McLean, "A Security Model for Military Message Systems," ACM Trans. on Computer Systems Vol. 9, No. 3 (Aug. 1984), pp. 198-222.

[Zelt00] Zeltser, Lenny: Firewalls, Perimeter Protection, and VPNs. GCFW Practical Assignment, SANS, December 2000, p. 13-35.

[Zelt02] Zeltser, Lenny: Firewall Deployment for Multitier Applications. http://www.informit.com/articles/article.aspx?p=26254, informIT, April 5, 2002.

[BCF+07] Buecker, Axel; Carreno, Ana Veronica; Field, Norman; Hockings, Christopher; Kawer, Daniel; Mohanty, Sujit; Monteiro, Guilherme: Enterprise Security Architecture. IBM Redbook, IBM International Technical Support Organization, August 2007, p. 29-39.

ETSI Specifications for Registered E-Mail REM

Franco Ruggieri

UNINFO Liaison to ETSI
On behalf of ETSI[1] TC ESI, STF318
franco.ruggieri@fastwebnet.it

Abstract

ETSI TS 102 640 – basis for actual REM interoperability

Trustable e-mail, suitable to provide users with at least reliability similar to that of the *physical* registered mail, is an actual need within Europe as well as outside. This is confirmed by the number of existing or under development systems aiming to meet this need. All these systems address only their own country, so, even if some of them can technically exchange messages outside their own domains, being they based on standard protocols, there is no mechanism in place providing senders and recipients of different countries with evidence on the transmission of one e-mail, not to mention content, trustable enough to stand even in court.

Technical Specification ETSI TS 102 640 for interoperable Registered E-Mail systems that has been issued by the European Telecommunications Standards Institute – ETSI in August 2008, based on a previous broad survey outcomes, is suitable to provide not only technical interoperability, but even, where applicable, the basis for legal validity. By 2009 end a further refinement, fine tuned with the support of a number of organizations running or implementing systems of this kind, will also be available. This ETSI TS 102 640 has been drafted by the STF 318[2] to whose members is addressed the Acknowledgement in Clause 5.

The next achievement will be, in the 2010 – 2011 timeframe, the development of an interoperability test bed and of a mechanism to enable systems based on different protocols, such as SMTP and SOAP, to interact.

1 Forewords

Relationships between companies, between Public Administrations, across these two entity types, and between them and what they respectively call "consumer" and "citizen", increasingly require the availability of a trustable e-mail system, suitable to exchange e-messages with a reliability comparable to the registered paper mail's.

The above sentence may appear as the usual, worn out way to draw the reader's attention on the writing.

---

1 *ETSI produces globally-applicable standards for Information and Communications Technologies (ICT), including fixed, mobile, radio, converged, broadcast and internet technologies and is officially recognized by the European Commission as a European Standards Organization. ETSI is a not-for-profit organization whose 700 ETSI member organizations benefit from direct participation and are drawn from 60 countries worldwide. For more information, please visit: www.etsi.org*

2 *"STFs are teams of highly-skilled experts working together over a pre-defined period to draft an ETSI standard under the technical guidance of an ETSI Technical Body and with the support of the ETSI Secretariat. The task of the STFs is to accelerate the standardization process in areas of strategic importance and in response to urgent market needs. For more information, please visit: http://portal.etsi.org/stfs/process/home.asp"*

N. Pohlmann, H. Reimer, W. Schneider (Editors): Securing Electronic Business Processes, Vieweg (2009), 242-254

This time it is not, since it is a matter of fact that e-documents are now ubiquitous, especially the ones structured in a way compatible with the sender's, and even more with the recipient's, ERP. Yes, they might, indeed, be sent on a CD or on a similar media sealed in an envelope, but the advantage of e-mail in terms of time and workload for the recipient is obvious, not to mention the hassle for the sender to physically go to the Post Office, possibly to send to different recipients a number of registered envelopes each carrying the same, identical text, apart of the recipient's name. Yet, as of now, physical mail has still one undisputable advantage when registered mail is used (even more when a delivery receipt is requested): trust.

Indeed, it is a fact that the Postal Authorities throughout the world provide for a trustable paper documents exchange, therefore a paper delivery receipt has it its own intrinsic validity and can be even used in court as an evidence. However, on the other hand, the content (i.e. the text) of this paper registered mail does not enjoy the same trust: in order to have an undisputable proof of this, one user must, in addition to using registered mail with delivery receipt, also create what can be called an "envelope-less parcel". In other words: the letter must be folded to make an envelope with it in a way that the address is externally readable, moreover, when it is wanted to make the letter content confidential its edges must be pasted or taped. Only if the sender enacts all these cares it would be impossible to the recipient to pretend having received something different from what the sender claims having sent.

One simple e-mail, instead, needs a strong enough technical proof, and preferably also an underlying legal substrate, to provide evidence that it was actually sent by a specific user, and/or delivered to a precise recipient. To say nothing of the text integrity.

The above mentioned increasing need for trusted e-mail systems lead several countries, even outside the European Union, to set up a number of projects suitable to achieve this goal. Nowadays many of them are already operational, are being developed or at least are planned. Just to mention a few cases, it is worth saying that in Italy this system[3] is operational with legal validity since 2005, in Belgium a law was issued in May 2007 and a reliable mailing system basing its legal validity on such law is way ahead in its development, in Germany the Bürgerportale is part of a Federal Government programme, etc. Also in Switzerland, not (yet?) a EU Member State that is moving towards building ever tighter links with the Union, such a system, IncaMail, is provided by the Swiss Post since a few years and, although there is still no legislation formally endorsing it yet, it is a de facto recognised mechanism.

In other words, such a trusted e-mail service is no more wishful thinking.

Unfortunately, all these systems have been or are being designed to address and to serve each one its own national environment. Consequently there is no structure suitable to allow achieving also international *legal* interoperability, even if for some of them there is no technical hindrance to exchange messages with foreign users. Therefore, even when they are technically interoperable, these, indeed technically secured, messages have no feature that allow foreign users to ascertain the actual reliability of the sent or received message.

In order to help fill this gap, ETSI launched in 2006 a multi-phased project with the purpose to produce one technical specification, broad enough to encompass likely all of the above needs, suitable to be applied at least in the EU, and possibly elsewhere, with a user friendly interface and mechanism. The e-mail system developed by this project is named "Registered E-Mail" – REM and is specified in TS 102 640[4].

---

3 Named "Posta Elettronica Certificata" – PEC
4 "Registered Electronic Mail (REM): Architecture, Formats, and Policies" Downloadable from URL http://pda.etsi.org/pda/queryform.asp by specifying TS 102 640.

ETSI believes that the goal was achieved in such a way that it can enjoy a cross-border recognition when complemented with another ETSI Technical Specification, TS 102 231 – TSL. The TSL can be used to make known what service providers, among which e-mail providers, are positively assessed by the relevant governing authority. It is worth mentioning that the TSL has been chosen by the EU Commission as the mechanism to ensure EU-wide cross-border recognition for electronic signature certificate issuers, to become operational in 2009.

2 ETSI Specialist Task Force – STF 318 past, present and future

The ETSI became aware of the rapid growth of the market need for trustable and interoperable e-mailing systems in 2006, as well as of the risk that, had no suitable timely answer been given to this need, an unmanageable archipelago of monadic (i.e. non interoperable) solutions would have soon been developed. ETSI therefore in 2006 launched one project, under the responsibility of its Technical Committee (TC) Electronic Signatures and Infrastructures (ESI), with the purpose of producing a Technical Specification (TS) specifically addressing the implementation of REM systems issuing reliable evidences. Where applicable, these evidences can even be endorsed by the relevant legislation to enjoy a higher standing.

Projects in ETSI are carried out by specifically focused STFs: this project was entrusted to STF 318 the activity of which was initially structured in the following three phases:

1. analysis of the market needs and expectations
2. specification development
3. investigation in, and confrontation with, the "real world".

At the end of Phase 3, as it will be later further addressed, it became clear within the TC ESI that another Phase was necessary with additional activities, not to repeat some previous, far from exciting, experiences a few countries already had in the past. A fourth project phase has, therefore, just been proposed and is undergoing the approval phase.

In the following sections each Phase, past, present and future, will be synthetically described, along with its outcomes.

2.1 Phase 1 – Analysis

This phase began in September 2006 and ended in July 2007. Its purpose was to collect from the largest possible number of entities of different kinds (Governmental agencies, experts, implementers of REM-like systems) the actual market views on what should the REM systems possible structure be.

A broad questionnaire was sent out to 61 organisations of 20 different countries, from within and from outside the EU, that initially accepted to cooperate and also to 4 international organisations. It interesting to remark that among these organisations only few were, directly or indirectly, linked to Postal Authorities and that this trend is still progressing. Just to mention a notable example: in Italy, where REM-like systems are legally in force since 2005, only two out of the currently registered 22 REM services providers are linked to Poste Italiane.

The questionnaire was very much detailed: 74 multi-replies questions were posed, structured in 9 main sections, with an overall number of 563 possible replies. Such depth likely discouraged some of these organisation, nevertheless the STF got 39 replies, to which it was able to add 3 more questionnaires that the STF members were able to fill in, due to their personal and direct knowledge of the related situations

It is however to be remarked that a few of these replies were received even from organisations outside the EU.

The STF summarised the outcomes of this phase in ETSI TR 102 605, available for free download (as any ETSI deliverable) from the address: http://pda.etsi.org/pda/queryform.asp.

It became apparent, however, from the vast majority of replies, that the preferred basics for the REM trust were the electronic signature and a consistent and exhaustive structure of evidence types covering at least all the main steps of an e-mail transmission. An additional and remarkable outcome was the ISO/IEC 27001 standing as a means to ensure security and therefore reliability.

Another item that arouse from this survey was that there were already services of different kinds addressing the REM needs in at least 10 European countries, serving an overall community of over 500.000 users with a potential catchment area of even 100 million.

2.2 Phase 2 – Specification development

Starting from the findings of Phase 1, the STF in this second Phase, launched in September 2007, designed the all-encompassing structure for an exchange between different REM services providers. For these providers an X.400 term was exhumed: "Managed Domain"; so these providers have been given the name of "REM Managed Domain" – REM-MD.

The logical model is as in Figure 1, that presents the entities involved in an exchange of REM, including also non-REM providers, and the related interfaces[5].

Evidence types and structure and information security policy requirements were also developed in detail.

All above aspects are addressed in the ETSI Technical Specification TS 102 640 three parts:
1. Architecture.
2. Data Requirements and Formats for Signed Evidences for REM.
3. Information Security Policy Requirements for REM Management Domains.

Parts 1, 2, 3 were produced during Phase 2 of the STF 318, were published in August 2008 and will be improved by 2009 end, due to Phase 3 findings.

---

5 All figures in this document are taken from the ETSI Technical Specification TS 102 640.

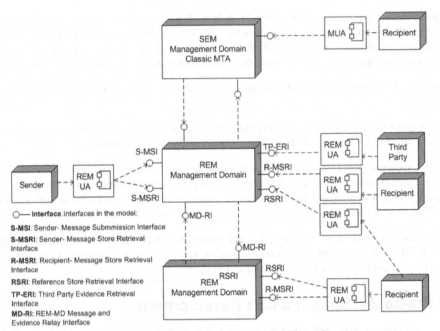

Fig. 1: REM Logical Model – Functional Viewpoint

2.3 Phase 3 – investigation

The purpose of this phase was stated in its Terms of Reference – ToR:

- *"Investigating among the REM market actors and the Universal Postal Union to identify what requirements, specified in the TS" ... "are more suitable to enable interoperability; depending on the outcomes of this investigation the STF will assess if updating the Technical Specification";*
- *Drafting one or more REM profiles, one of which will harmonise with Universal Postal Union requirements."*

This Phase activity was articulated in the subsequent stages:

- Investigating with a number of market actors, among which: Swiss IncaMail, German Bürger-portale, Italian CNIPA (Authority supervising the Italian PEC), Italian Postecom, Belgian CER-TIPOST, European Notary eWitness, Spanish Correos, etc.
- Issuing a new Part 4 of the ETSI TS 102 640 profiling two sets of requirements, one basic and one advanced, ensuring one e-mail services provider is actually a REM-MD.
- Issuing a new Part 5 of the ETSI TS 102 640 profiling a common set of requirements suitable to ensure interoperability among REM-MDs that implement them.

Parts 4 and 5 will be published by 2009 end.

2.4 Phase 4 – "going beyond"

As hinted to above, during Phase 3 it was acknowledged, while STF 318 was progressing mainly based on SMTP, that other projects have been launched based on SOAP.

It was also found that there is an actual strong interest by most of actors and developers of REM-like systems to become mutually interoperable. These entities had seen the ETSI REM as one readily available solution.

It was then proposed to launch one new Phase aiming to:

1. cooperate with developers of SOAP based systems in order to agree on an interchange mechanism;

2. facilitate the take up of the REM specifications by the interested entities by means of consultancy provision and by the definition of a common test bed, supported by a central testing facility to be installed in ETSI.

   It is to be noted that ETSI is already accustomed to implement this kind of testing facility for a number of application domains, among which electronic signature.

This option is still in the evaluation stage.

3 Description of the REM ETSI Technical Specification (TS 102 640) five Parts

3.1 Part 1 – Architecture

The basics of the REM design is to provide trust through issuance by REM-MDs of:

1. evidence of when the original message was sent and, if the user authentication policy implemented by the REM-MD allows for this, also of who was the sender; this is achieved by creating a new message structure, REM Dispatch, signed by the REM-MD, that carries both the original message and the evidence created by the REM-MD;

2. evidence of when the REM Dispatch has been delivered to the recipient's mailbox or when the original message was downloaded from the relevant REM-MD repository;

3. evidence of the occurrence of all other possible positive or negative events;

4. evidence of integrity and authenticity of what is conveyed within the REM Dispatch.

The possible Architectures are depicted in the figures of this section. They differentiate on the style of operation of the interacting REM-MDs:

- Store & Forward (S&F) – Figure 2: REM Store & Forward Logical Model – REM Sender and REM Recipient subscribers of different REM-MDs[6]

- Store & Notify (S&N) – Figure 3: REM Store & Notify Logical Model – REM Sender's REM-MD creating the REM-MD Message / Figure 4: REM Store & Notify Logical Model – Recipient's REM-MD creating the REM-MD Message.

Briefly and with much simplification:

---

6 All figures in this paper are extracted from the ETSI TS 102 640.

- in the S&F style, the original message is included as is along with the suitably built evidence in the above mentioned REM Dispatch that is conveyed to the recipient;
- in the S&N style, one REM-MD stores the original message in a repository under its own control and builds a new REM Dispatch carrying, instead of the original message, a notification to the recipient that the original message can be downloaded from a URL that is specified in the same REM Dispatch; this latter is then delivered to the recipient who can download the original message from the URL; there are two subcases, depicted in the following figures, depending on what REM-MD performs the above action:

1. the sender's REM-MD – Figure 3: REM Store & Notify Logical Model – REM Sender's REM-MD creating the REM-MD Message
2. the recipient's REM-MD – Figure 4: REM Store & Notify Logical Model – Recipient's REM-MD creating the REM-MD Message.

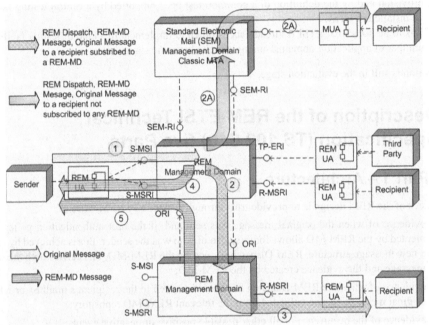

Fig. 2: REM Store & Forward Logical Model – REM Sender and REM Recipient subscribers of different REM-MDs

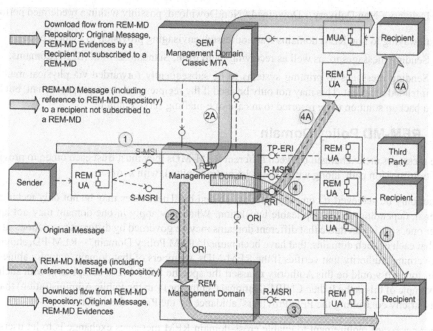

Fig. 3: REM Store & Notify Logical Model – REM Sender's REM-MD creating the
REM-MD Message

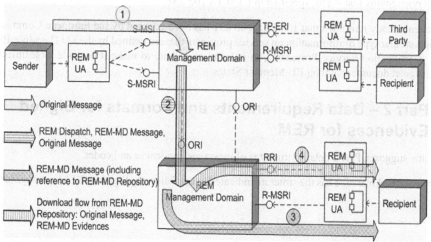

Fig. 4: REM Store & Notify Logical Model – Recipient's REM-MD creating the REM-
MD Message

Part 1 also indicates what evidences are generated to assert the occurrence of specific events. The main
evidences are :

- Sender's Message submission acceptance or rejection by the sender's REM-MD
- Acceptance / Rejection by the REM Recipient's REM-MD

• Delivery / Non Delivery – Download / Non Download, possibly within a predefined period.

Also gatewaying to non REM domains was addressed, envisaging provision of evidence for:

• Sending messages to, as well as receiving them from, Standard E-Mail (SEM) domains;
• Sending messages to printing systems to be subsequently forwarded via physical mail to the intended recipient. This may not only be used if the recipient only accepts paper mail, but also as a backup solution to be resorted to in case of e-mailing service failure.

3.1.1 REM-MD Policy Domain

Where messages are exchanged between different REM-MDs they must trust each other, to provide the whole transmission path, along with what is being transmitted, with *trust*.

This can only be achieved if common rules are abided by. These rules may be not only technical, but also legal, depending on the applicable legislation. What may apply in one domain may not apply in another one, so it is inevitable that different domains may be governed by different regulations. It is also clear that each of such domains, that have been named "REM Policy Domain" – REM-PD, should have one governing Authority that verifies if the REM-MDs, members of that domain, actually abide by the rules in force. It would be this Authority to assert the specific REM-MD's compliance with such rules. One example of this is the Italian CNIPA (National Centre for IT in the Public Administration) that since 2005 is strictly controlling the PEC Providers' abidance by the PEC rules in force.

Another necessary requirement to enable cross-domain REM messages exchange is to let users know whether one specific REM-MD complies with the relevant REM-PD rules. It is recommended to this purpose that the above Authorities make such information public. One recommended mechanism is the Trust-service Status List – TSL specified in ETSI TS 102 231.

It has been already reminded that ETSI TS 102 231 has been adopted by the European Commission to provide a similar type of information on service providers that are defined by the EU Directive 1999/93/EC as "Certification Service Providers", in order to contribute to make it possible to seamlessly exchange signed document among EU Member States.

3.2 Part 2 – Data Requirements and Formats for Signed Evidences for REM

As its title suggests, Part 2 details structures of messages, evidences and codes.

The typical REM message has the structure indicated in the following Figure 5: REM message structure.

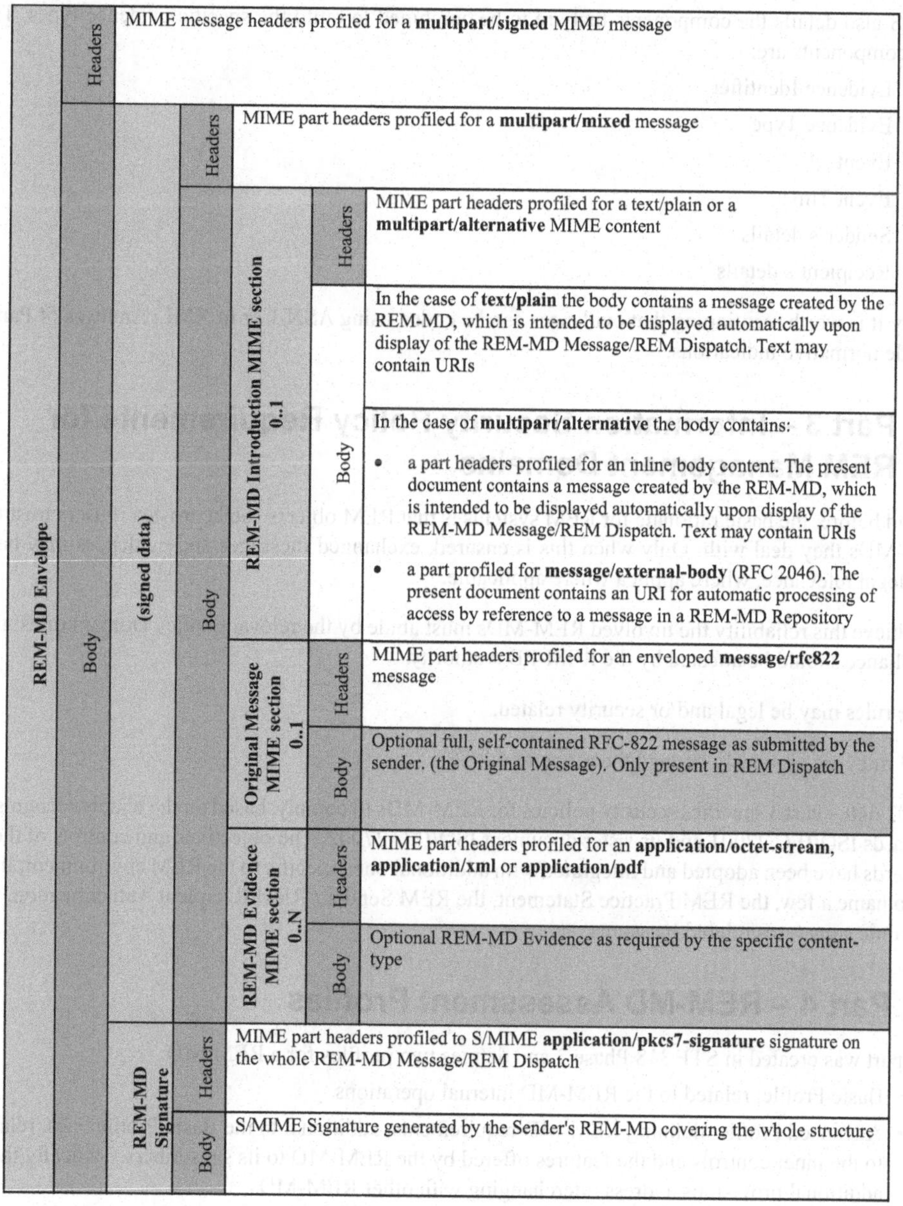

REM-MD Envelope						Description
	Headers					MIME message headers profiled for a **multipart/signed** MIME message
	Body (signed data)	Headers				MIME part headers profiled for a **multipart/mixed** message
		Body	REM-MD Introduction MIME section 0..1	Headers		MIME part headers profiled for a text/plain or a **multipart/alternative** MIME content
				Body		In the case of **text/plain** the body contains a message created by the REM-MD, which is intended to be displayed automatically upon display of the REM-MD Message/REM Dispatch. Text may contain URIs
						In the case of **multipart/alternative** the body contains: • a part headers profiled for an inline body content. The present document contains a message created by the REM-MD, which is intended to be displayed automatically upon display of the REM-MD Message/REM Dispatch. Text may contain URIs • a part profiled for **message/external-body** (RFC 2046). The present document contains an URI for automatic processing of access by reference to a message in a REM-MD Repository
			Original Message MIME section 0..1	Headers		MIME part headers profiled for an enveloped **message/rfc822** message
				Body		Optional full, self-contained RFC-822 message as submitted by the sender. (the Original Message). Only present in REM Dispatch
			REM-MD Evidence MIME section 0..N	Headers		MIME part headers profiled for an **application/octet-stream, application/xml** or **application/pdf**
				Body		Optional REM-MD Evidence as required by the specific content-type
		REM-MD Signature	Headers			MIME part headers profiled to S/MIME **application/pkcs7-signature** signature on the whole REM-MD Message/REM Dispatch
			Body			S/MIME Signature generated by the Sender's REM-MD covering the whole structure

Fig. 5: REM message structure

The basic issue is that whatever is exchanged through REM systems is signed by the relevant REM-MD, thus ensuring its authenticity and integrity. The signed object, generally speaking, includes the original message and/or the evidence.

The TS also details the components that are to be combined to build the specific evidence types. The main components are:

- Evidence Identifier
- Evidence Type
- Event
- Event Time
- Sender's details
- Recipient's details

Finally it is worth mentioning that evidences can be coded using ASN.1 or in XML. Annexes of Part 2 provide normative indications.

3.3 Part 3 – Information Security Policy Requirements for REM Management Domains

As said before, the basic rationale for REM systems is that REM objects can be trusted if users trust the REM-MDs they deal with. Only when this is ensured, exchanged messages and evidences may have even legal relevance, where applica where applicable.

To achieve this reliability the involved REM-MDs must abide by the relevant Policy Domain rules; this compliance should be attested by the REM-PD Authority.

These rules may be legal and/or security related.

Legal rules are obviously beyond the scope of the TS.

TS 102 640 – Part 3 specifies security policies for REM-MDs to comply, based on the widely recognised standards ISO/IEC 27001 and its sister document ISO/IEC 27002. The objectives and controls of these standards have been adopted and integrated with additional ones specific to the REM environment, like, just to name a few, the REM Practice Statement, the REM Sender / REM Recipient Authentication, the electronic signatures related measures.

3.4 Part 4 – REM-MD Assessment Profiles

This part was created in STF 318 Phase 3 and defines two profiles for a REM-MD:

- Basic Profile: related to the REM-MD internal operations
- Advanced Profile: defining REM-MD requirements, additional to the Basic Profile ones, related to the inner controls and the features offered by the REM-MD to its subscribers. Typically these additional provisions address interchanging with other REM-MDs.

The Basic Profile details provisions related to:

- REM-MD Management: procedures and documentation to be implemented;
- Roles: one REM-MD shall implement at least specific roles;
- Authentication: authentications measures to be adopted;
- Interfaces and protocols to be used;
- Evidence: minimum set of Evidences to implement/dealt with;

- Information Security: minimum set of Security controls, with the meaning as in ISO/IEC 27001, to be implemented by the REM-MD.

The Advanced Profile details provisions, additional to those specified in the Basic Profile that are to be also implemented, related to:

- Evidence;
- Information Security controls.

3.5 Part 5 – REM-MD Interoperability Profile

This Part, also developed in STF 318 Phase 3, defines one profile of the REM specifications suitable to ensure interoperability between REM-MDs that implement their systems based on these common provisions.

The core Parts of the TS, i.e. Parts 2 and 3, indicate which requirements are mandatory, which ones are recommended and which ones are optional.

This Part 5 specifies what other requirements, among those indicated in parts 2 and 3 as "recommended" or "optional", must also be implemented to ensure interoperability.

It is worth mentioning that among these mandatory requirements a "core" subset of the Evidence types specified in Part 2 has been identified, that covers:

- SubmissionAcceptanceRejection – provides information on the outcomes of the sender's original message submission to the related REM-MD;
- DeliveryNonDeliveryToRecipient – provides information on whether the REM Dispatch was/ was not successfully delivered to the recipient's mailbox;
- DownloadNonDownloadByRecipient – provides information on whether the recipient has successfully downloaded within a predefined time the message intended for him/her;
- RelayToREMMDAcceptanceRejection – provides information on whether the recipient has accepted to download the message intended for him/her;
- RelayToREMMDFailure – provides information on possible failures during the transmission of the REM Dispatch to the recipient's REM-MD.

4 Acknowledgment

The STF 318 that drafted the above mentioned five parts of TS 102 640 was led by Juan Carlos CRUEL-LAS IBARZ, Professor at Universitat Politècnica de Catalunya (Spain).

The other members were:

- Paloma LLANEZA of LLaneza A+A (Spain) – Editor of Parts 1 and 4,
- Luca BOLDRIN of Infocert (Italy) – Editor of Part 2,
- Nick POPE of Thales (UK) – Editor of Part 3 v1,
- Franco RUGGIERI of FIR DIG Consultants, representing UNINFO (Italy) – Editor of Part3 v2,
- Santino FOTI of Critical Path (Italy) – Editor of Part 5,
- Gregory SUN of Macau Post (Macau – China),
- Benjamin VOITURIER of Certipost (Belgium).

5 Conclusion

Since a number of years, reliance on e-mail has been addressed (it can be mentioned to this regard that IETF in 2004 issued RFC 3798 "Message Disposition Notification", but it addressed solely reporting *"the disposition of a message after it has been successfully delivered to a recipient"*). Unfortunately, lacking a common specifications basis to be used as a reference, a number of non fully interoperable systems were developed. Some of them have technical structures suited to convey nearly all kind of evidence types, some other ones aim to a broader and "lighter" service type, but, although some of them can actually enforce the delivery of a processable message, they leave to the user non belonging to their "circuit" to understand the meaning of the evidence content. Similarly, the recognition of the counterpart provider standing is left to the user's acceptance.

ETSI TS 102 640, with its five parts, addresses the whole spectrum of e-messages exchange, spanning from the style of operation (Store & Forward – Store & Notify), through the provision of a complete evidence structure and of security policy requirements, to finish with profiles suitable to allow assessing if one e-mail provider is actually a REM-MD and one profile that allows to achieve interoperability not only related to the technical aspects, but also to the messaging providers' "formal recognition".

This TS is already available, with the exception of assessment and interoperability profiles that will be published by 2009 end.

It is also reasonable to expect a further step to be implemented, that will help achieve interoperability by means of skilled consultancy and factual support in performing functional interoperability tests. This will require some more time: up to early year 2011.

Acceptance of Trust Domains in IT-Infrastructures

Arno Fiedler · Selma Gralher

Gesellschaft für Telematikanwendungen der Gesundheitskarte mbH
www.gematik.de
{Arno.Fiedler | Selma.Gralher}@gematik.de

Abstract

Creating non-hierarchical trust domains for healthcare applications with ETSI Trust-Service Status Lists

Healthcare applications demand a complex telematics infrastructure, with strict participant authorisation rules and high-security technical components. In principal, all identities in such a network can be managed using X.509 certificates. The following article shows how to combine the involved certificate authorities into a single trust domain using bridge configurations from the ETSI-TSL concept.

1 Introduction

Despite tremendous cost pressures, the German Health Service keeps growing due to the progressive developments in medicine. As in many other areas, the effective gathering, processing, and storage of information are vital for the success of the project. In healthcare, the requirements regarding user-control and data privacy protection are most severe.

With the introduction of an electronic medical card Germany is setting up a comprehensive health network which allows hospitals, health insurers, doctors, pharmacists, and patients to exchange information in a reliable and trustworthy manner.

The underlying infrastructure must fulfil severe security requirements regarding

- confidentiality,
- integrity,
- access authorisation,
- availability, and
- nonrepudiation.

All sensitive data are repeatedly encrypted to ensure confidentiality. The decryption codes are stored in safety-evaluated "High-Security-Modules", e.g. "Crypto" chip cards, which have an additional PKI chip packed aboard.

To gain acceptance it is essential that access to data within the telematics infrastructure is restricted to authorised participants only, and that they can only access those data that are relevant to them.

A higher, "trustworthy" authority issues X.509 identity certificates which identify persons and their professional accreditation. Certificates are also allotted to all technical components in the network to

N. Pohlmann, H. Reimer, W. Schneider (Editors): Securing Electronic Business Processes, Vieweg (2009), 255-261

secure it, and to limit access to it logically. Some components, like the connectors, which connect the local healthcare appliances to the Telematic Infrastructure, even use several certificates.

The trustworthiness of these higher authorities (certificate Authorities, Trust-Service-Providers/TSPs) which issue these certificates is crucial for the security, availability and the acceptance of the whole infrastructure. For the verification of certificates it is essential that the signing TSP is absolutely trustworthy. To inspire confidence in the system as a whole all involved TSPs have to meet uniform security requirements. Compliance has to be confirmed regularly by an independent third party.

In the eighties and nineties the common, "classic" approach was to use a PKI-hierarchy to authenticate the identity of a trustworthy TSP. In this model the TSP is subordinate to the operator of a central root. An example is a system the German Federal Network Agency operates for accredited providers of certification services, based on the Signatures Law (SigG). This approach does not always meet the user requirements for flexibility and individual configurations, though. And, quite often, psychological barriers exist which lower acceptance, especially in a federalistic system.

After careful evaluation the decision was reached to dismiss the common, hierarchical approach in the trust domain for the telematics infrastructure in health care in favour of centralised (online-) certificate verifications for the X.509 certificates of the issuer authorities (or their TSP).

The practical implementation of this new approach was based on the experiences gained at the European Bridge CA of TeleTrusT e.V. [EBCA]. Accreditation is granted on the condition that compliance with a uniform and concerted certification policy is proven, e.g. through an independently audited security concept.

Following this new approach all TSP certificate verification information is collected centrally in an XML file named "Trust-service Status List" (TSL) [ETSI]. This file, in turn, is either signed by gematik GmbH or an assigned service provider.

gematik uses two of these lists for the telematics infrastructure, one for people and organisations, the other one for technical components. Thus, the respective TSLs represent the shared trust domain in the sense of a "White List".

Using Trust-service Status Lists holds a number of advantages over the hierarchical approach, namely:

- integration of the existing heterogenous and complex structures in health care with little effort,
- mapping of different security levels of personal or organisational certificates in one infrastructure,
- quick implementation of necessary adjustments for new or changed general conditions,
- transparency of the trust status of all TSPs for the technical community.

2 Using ETSI as a Foundation

Usage and verification of certificates through third, relying parties, who are not directly involved in the infrastructure and its technical specifications, are paramount for the success and the acceptance of PKI.

This interoperability requisition was identified at an early stage by the international standardisation committees. At the European level, CEN and ETSI share the responsibilities:

CEN focuses on "Crypto" chip cards, the secure "Signature Issuer Units" as well as specialised applications.

ETSI focuses on issuing specifications on the basis of international "best practises", e.g. for signature formats, certification policies and their implementation, as in the areas of "registered e-mail" and "eInvoice".

Particularly remarkable is the standardisation process of the "Trust-service Status List" in the years 2002 to 2004, where an integrative approach for building trust domains was developed that respects the legal framework of all of the different European countries.

The national Italian supervisory authority CNIPA has been using a mechanism based on a similar logic since 2000 to document the trust status of all accredited Certification Authorities that issue Qualified Certificates. This mechanism is to be shortly replaced by the TSL.

Also, the SEPA Core Direct Debit ("SDD") Scheme owned by the European Payments Council [EPC] will follow the general approach of multiple CAs with the establishment of a Trust-Service Status List (TSL) for e-Mandate Services based on ETSI 102 231. It contains the relevant public key certificates of all EPC approved CAs for e-Mandate Services.

3 The TSL Concept

The goal of ETSI TS 102 231 – Electronic Signatures and Infrastructures (ESI); "Provision of harmonized Trust Service Provider status information" – TSL – is to provide, in a standardised, signed, and machine-readable form, information on the Trust Service Providers – TSP – listed in the TSL by its issuing Authority. The TSL can be used for any kind of TSP, for which it can also bear information on past dates.

Users can fully exploit the features of TSL Version 1 within a trust domain managed by a trustworthy CA, but not outside of it.

TSL Version 2, published in May 2005, also allows verification of the status of TSPs belonging to other domains, provided that the authorities that govern them adopt ETSI TS 102 231. To achieve this, one TSL must point to the TSLs issued by the authorities governing the external domains.

The cryptographic components used by Signature Creation Devices as well as their certificates are subject to strict requirements concerning the quality of the algorithm, key length, private key protection, and system availability.

The concept of a flat, two-tiered hierarchy, which is legally mandatory for qualified electronic signatures from a certified provider, is not enforceable on a cross-sector level for encryption (ENC/ENCV), authorisation (AUT/AUTN) and organisational (OSig) certificates, because of the expected growth in the number of certificate issuers as well as the necessity to integrate existing structures.

Figure 1 shows the PKI participants and emphasises the complexity of the system: Different types of certificates on various cards have to cooperate in a multi-domain system:

- SMC-B: Institutional Cards for organisational signatures;
- HBA: Health Professional Cards with advanced and qualified certificates,
- eGK: for protecting the patients data and
- CVC: Card Verifiable Certificates for Card-to-Card-Authentication.

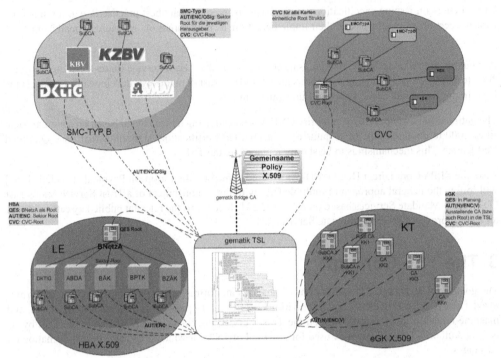

Fig. 1: PKI participants and emphasises the complexity of the system

So fundamental differences exist regarding:

- data protection,
- liability issues,
- identification and registration by the sponsors,
- decryption mechanisms for data in case of an ENC key loss,
- launch duration and costs,

compared to the regulations regarding qualified certificates. Thus, a bridge structure in which the independent trust information for the TSPs is stored in a signed XML file (ETSI Trust-service Status List) was chosen as a trust model. [gemX.509_TSL] contains more detailed information on TSLs.

A comprehensive certificate policy was developed for the ENC, AUT and OSig certificates of both eGK (electronic health card) and SMC-Typ-B (Institution Identities surgery/hospital/pharmacy) of on the basis of the regulations for the use of PKI components defined in the security concept. All participating TSPs must guarantee compliance with these guidelines in their "Certification-Practise-Statement". Accredited testing institutes survey whether the security measures are precisely implemented in the TSP's day-to-day operations.

Every certificate authority (CA) in this trust model has to be authorised by a central body. This happens through the inclusion in a Trusted-service Status List. The TSL contains the public keys of all trustworthy CAs, information on the accredited certificate type for these CAs, and the address for the certificate status services (OCSP responder and CRL provider). The TSL is signed by the gematik TSL service provider.

Similar conditions concerning issuer and structural diversity exist for the component certificates assigned to devices and services, so these certificates are processed along the same lines. The trust information of the certificate issuers are stored and published in a separate TSL. It is called "Trusted-Component-List" for easier distinction. [gemX.509_TCL] contains more detailed information on TCLs with certificate domains for Server and Services, Card-Terminals and VPN-Devices "Konnektor".

4 Verification of trust domains

Normative arrangements concerning the verification of the trust domain (does the certificate originate from a trustworthy source?) as well as the certificate status (is the certificate valid or revoked?) are essential for certificate evaluation. Certificate verification checks:

- whether the certificate can be trusted,
- the role acknowledged by the certificate, and
- the identity acknowledged by the certificate.

For verification purposes, the component in question must have a locally stored and valid TSL. Also, the validation chain has to be traversed in its entirety to effectively evaluate the certificate's validity.

In general, certificate verification includes OCSP-checking the End Entity certificate and checking issuer certificate validity on the basis of the TSL. In this context, the TSL provides a shared trust domain in the sense of a White List of all approved issuers. An issuer certificate can only be verified when a current and valid TSL exists in the validating system.

These are the steps for checking a trust domain:

- download the TSL,
- check the validity of the TSL
- check the TSL signature certificate using a securely stored gematik TSL root key,
- check the TSL's integrity by testing the TSL's signature

New TSL service provider certificates (e.g. when a generational change occurs) are integrated into the TSL in due time. This applies to the following certificates:

- TSL signature certificate
- TSL root certificate

Thus the valid, old keys safeguard the integrity of the new keys.

5 Mechanisms for Validation

Every CA in the telematics infrastructure has to supply information on the certificates it has signed or revoked. This ensures that individual certificates, or all certificates signed by a certain CA, can be revoked when necessary.

Inside the telematics infrastructure, all status queries for certificates have to be performed using the Online Certificate Status Protocol (OCSP). Each CA has to provide an OCSP responder for the certificates which it has signed.

The advantage of this approach is that the status of a certificate can be queried without the unnecessary distribution of information on revoked certificates. To improve scalability and reduce complexity Certificate Revocation Lists can be used on demand – and only as an exception – to verify non-qualified signatures. The OCSP responder address for each CA (and that of the CRL provider, where necessary) is included in the TSL entry of the respective CA certificate.

The following section describes in more detail the validation of X.509 certificates in combination with the trust domain TSL. The process is geared towards the requirements of the telematics infrastructure.

For certificate validation the following prerequisites have to be met:

- an up-to-date TSL exists,
- the trust domain was successfully initialised, and
- the TSL is evaluated and loaded, e.g. into a trust store.

The following use case diagram exemplifies the corresponding system activities.

The steps to go through for the validation of an advanced certificate are listed here briefly:

- verify validity,
- verify the trust chain back to the respective issuer until identification through the TSL is effected,
- verify the mathematical correctness of the certificate (signature test),
- verify the revocation status of the certificate in comparison to the OCSP responder referenced in the field "ServiceSupplyPoint" in the TSL, and then verify:
  - the authority of the OCSP certificate (is the OCSP responder registered in the TSL ?),
  - the contents of the OCSP answer (revocation status).
- verify the role.

In each of these tests, the mathematical-cryptographical correctness of the mechanisms has to be verified, and also whether these mechanisms are approved. A certificate signed with a hashing algorithm without approval, for example, may be classified as valid. Though it may entail judicial insecurities regarding its evidentiary value.

The certificate is considered not valid if, for technical or other reasons, any one of the above tests fails. Information from certificates may be used only when the respective certificate was validated successfully.

6 TSL and QES

The fundamental aspects of the verification of qualified electronic signatures are:

- validation certificates are regarding the signature creation or the authentification date as well as the underlying validation model,
- validation of the certificate status, for which the CA provides the appropriate queries,
- validation of the certificate's application range and restrictions,
- use of key pairs and certificates only within their respective application range to accomplish nonrepudiation and content commitment,

- validation is performed only by approved signature application components from the official register of the German Federal Network Agency,
- checking whether the extension QCStatement exists.

Validating a qualified certificate means identifying checking the whole path back to the root. This results in special requirements concerning the detection and storage of the "secure keystore". The TSL could be used for certificate path configuration. Hence, it constitutes a safe certificate store.

7 Acceptance and Conclusion

The CROBIES study aims at improving eSignature interoperability. It recommends the creation of a trusted list at Member States' level of supervised or accredited qualified certification service providers (QCSPs), i.e., certification service providers issuing qualified certificates to the public. In a first step, a list is compiled of all QCSPs established in the Member States.

ETSI is finalizing the review of ETSI TS 102 231 for incorporating the requirements identified now.

Fortunately, a implementation of this concept has commenced its Europe-wide realisation. Many national supervisoring authorities plan to implement "Trust-service Status Lists" of all nationally recognised TSPs.

Given the heterogeneous structures in German health care, the TSL is a pragmatic and flexible approach to build a shared trust domain. The advantages outweigh those of a strictly hierarchical approach.

If all involved, including all medically insured, trust this infrastructure for impartial (e.g. certification and accreditation) as well as for subjective reasons ("sensed" security), the necessary process changes can be implemented quickly. The concept of the Trust-service Status List as the foundation of a transparent trust domain is a good basis on which to build.

References

[EBCA]   European Bridge CA https://www.bridge-ca.org/

[EPC]   TSL Trust Body for EPC Approved Certification Authorities (CAs) in support of SEPA e-Mandate Services http://www.europeanpaymentscouncil.eu/documents/EPC249-09%20TSL%20RFP.pdf

[ETSI] ETSI Technical Specification TS 102 231 ('Provision of harmonized Trust Service Provider (TSP) status information') http://pda.etsi.org/pda/AQuery.asp

[COMMON-PKI] Common COMMON-PKI- Specification For PKI-Applications, T7 & TeleTrusT Version 2.0 (former known as ISIS-MTT)

[CROBIES] ec.europa.eu/idabc/servlets/Doc?id=32145

[gemX.509_TSL] PKI für die X.509-Zertifikate: Registrierung eines Trust Service Provider, gematik, Version 1.2.0

[gemX.509_TCL] PKI für X.509-Zertifikate: Konzeption und Registrierungsanforderungen der Trusted Component List (TCL), gematik, Version 1.3.0.

Proposal for an IT Security Standard for Preventing Tax Fraud in Cash Registers

Mathias Neuhaus[1] · Jörg Wolff[2] · Norbert Zisky[2]

[1]cv cryptovision GmbH
Munscheidstr. 14, Gelsenkirchen, Germany
mathias.neuhaus@cryptovision.com

[2]Physikalisch-Technische Bundesanstalt (PTB)
Abbestr. 2-12, 10587 Berlin, Germany
{joerg.wolff | norbert.zisky}@ptb.de

Abstract

This paper describes a technology solution for preventing tax fraud in electronic cash registers (ECR) and point of sale (POS) systems. The solution is based on electronic signatures, and as a result, any alterations to protected data will be detected. The signed transaction data can be stored on various electronic memory devices. Technical provisions enable the estimation of transaction volumes, even after tampering or loss of data. In this way the solution presented here differs significantly from other fiscal solutions where a pattern of approvals for ECRs and permanent technical supervision of the market is necessary. This paper is focused on the architecture, the protocols and the usability of the proposed system.

1 Introduction

Tax fraud has become a serious problem in our society. This is especially true in countries with high value-added tax (VAT) rates. As a result, it has become necessary to fight against manipulations of cash takings. This problem exists in all member states of the European Union. Anyone dealing with this area of tax fraud will find that the key words include skimming, phantom-ware and zappers:

"Skimming cash receipts is an old fashioned tax fraud; a fraud traditionally associated with small or medium sized enterprises. .... Businesses that skim frequently keep two sets of books (one for the tax man, the other for the owner). In its simplest (nontechnological) form there are two tills, and the cashier simply diverts some cash from selected sales into a secret drawer.... Technology is changing how businesses skim. The agents of change are software applications – phantom-ware and zappers. Phantom-ware is a "hidden," pre-installed programming option(s) embedded within the operating system of a modern electronic cash register (ECR). ...

Zappers are more advanced technology than phantom-ware. Zappers are special programming options added to ECRs or point of sale (POS) networks. They are carried on memory sticks, removable CDs or can be accessed through an internet link. Because zappers are not integrated into operating systems their use is more difficult to detect. Zappers allow owners to place employees at the cash register, check their performance (monitor employee theft), but then remotely skim sales to cheat the taxman." [AINS09]

Deficits in tax revenues caused by manipulations of electronic cash registers (ECR) are a major problem of all industrial countries.

"The German financial authorities are not able to detect forged statements of cash earnings when using state of the art electronic cash registers. In modern PC-based ECRs it is possible to tamper internal records without leaving any traces. ... It is not unlikely that the tax fraud in cash transactions runs into many billions of Euros." [translated from BUND03]

Thus, an immediate remedy is needed. In 2003 a number of different activities to detect and prevent this fraud were started in Germany. The Ministry of Finance engaged the German federal states in discussions about a number of solutions. The outcome was the development of a new approach for the protection of ECR against manipulations. The proposal was advanced by the German National Metrology Institute (Physikalisch-Technische Bundesanstalt – PTB), and a working group on cash registers was founded. From 2003 to 2008 this group published two reports and developed an operational concept for the use of a smart card solution. In 2008 a project named "INSIKA" (INtegrierte SIcherheitslösung für messwertverarbeitende KAssensysteme – integrated security concept for ECRs) was launched with the goal of making the technical solution for this problem a reality.

Other countries have developed different solutions. One of the oldest answers is to regulate ECRs. Bulgaria, Italy, Turkey, Lithuania, Latvia, Poland, Russia, Hungary, Brazil, Argentina, and Venezuela are some of the countries that rely on classical fiscal law regulations with strong requirements for ECRs. Detailed requirements for ECRs mandate a complex governmental approval process and involve reasonably sophisticated technical field observations. As the threats to such a system are very high, the security and enforcement demands need to be equally high. The conditions are similar to regulation of the banking sector.

"Globally, two policy orientations guide enforcement actions in this area – one approach is rules-based; the other is principles-based. They are not mutually exclusive – degrees of blending are common. Rules-based jurisdictions adopt comprehensive and mandatory legislation regulating, and/or certifying cash registers. Jurisdictions taking this approach include Greece and Germany. These jurisdictions are classified generally as "fiscal till" or "fiscal memory" jurisdictions.

Principles-based jurisdictions rely on compliant taxpayers following the rules. Compliance is enforced with an enhanced audit regime. Comprehensive, multi-tax audits (the simultaneous examination of income, consumption and employment returns) are performed by teams that include computer audit specialists. Audits are frequently unannounced and preceded by undercover investigations that collect data to be verified. Jurisdictions taking this approach include the UK and the Netherlands. " [AINS09]

Classical fiscal system are best characterised as "security by obscurity". In most cases they consist of a fiscal memory in a separate device and/or a fiscal printer. Often the fiscal memory and the fiscal printer form a single unit. The key element of the fiscal solution is the printed receipt indicating that the fiscal data set has been stored inside the fiscal memory. Often the receipts have to contain special characters. The technical requirements differ substantially from country to country.

The on-line data transfer to central tax servers in real time is another solution of a fiscal system which was introduced in Serbia: "Additionally Serbian Tax Administration introduced GPRS terminals for remote readouts of fiscal cash registers in 2005. Since 2006, fiscal certification is also necessary for

POS applications. By Serbian law, all printers are obliged to have a journal, unfortunately an electronic journal is still not accepted." [SERV09]

2 Goals, requirements and measures

2.1 Goals

The ultimate goal is the development and implementation of a mechanism for the protection of ECR and POS against tax fraud. The solution should provide protection against manipulations of cash registers and offer a wide range of testing opportunities for tax auditors. The system itself should be revision-safe. The general costs of all system components have to be minimised.

2.2 Requirements

2.2.1 General requirements

As a general requirement transactions have to be recorded completely, correctly, orderly and timely. Cash receipts and expenditures should be kept daily. In cases where changes are made, the original content must always be able to be retrieved.

Data, which contains fiscal-relevant information, must be protected in such a way that subsequent changes are prevented or recognised with a high probability to provide manipulation protection.

The highest level of protection is achieved if all registration procedures and access to the cash register are durably stored. A long-term archive of cumulated values of exactly defined periods could offer data reduction.

In the case of registration and processing of turnovers a high threat potential is to be expected.

Techniques must be used which ensure substantial manipulation protection in cases where high potential threats are expected.

The sum of all costs for subsystems guaranteeing protection from manipulation, including expenditures for examinations, test maintenance as well as operation, training etc. for all participants are to be compared with the expected benefit of unstinted tax revenues. In the end, all costs are ultimately born by the community.

2.2.2 Technical requirements

As a technical requirement all data referred as fiscal-relevant information must be stored in electronic systems in such a way that any change or falsification is not possible or must be readily detectable.

- It must take into account fixed system architecture, data formats and access methods
- Each ECR or POS must be clearly identifiable.
- It must keep non-erasable logs with exactly specified registrations.

2.3 Essential measures

Some of the most critical measures for implementing a fiscal system are listed below:
- Definition of the data that must be protected
- Definition of protection requirements, technical requirements for the approval of technical systems for the recognition of manipulations by cash registers,
- Specification of testing instructions (test criteria)
- Specification of inspection intervals
- Deposit of critical software
- Development of evaluation software for revenue offices
- Control of version numbers and digital signatures of software modules
- Keeping safety logs
- Specification of sanctions/penalties in case of non-compliance

3 Solution

3.1 Establishment of the INSIKA project

The German working group on cash registers, headed by the German Ministry of Finance, has been examining automated sales suppression within the country. Two reports have been released in 2004 and 2006. The problem is deemed to be serious. Finally, in 2008 this group proposed an operational solution for the protection of ECR against manipulations which was based on a general concept of the PTB from 2004. A parallel development was the publication of a draft law which clearly defined the main topics of the solution. The working group supported the set-up of a technical project for developing and testing of the system. This was a lesson learned from other countries. In February 2008 the INSIKA project was started. INSIKA is funded by the German Ministry of Economics and Technology within the MNPQ program for small and medium-sized enterprises. Four ECR manufacturers and the PTB are the project partners. This project group is supported by security specialists from cv cryptovision. In addition to the technical specifications of the smart card it was critical that there was a determination of the data structures and formats, communication protocols and the security analysis. Currently the technical solution is entering the final stages of testing.

3.2 System concept, architecture and protocols

3.2.1 System concept

The essential concept involves the signing of critical data from the ECR by the use of a smart card. This technique is used in many other areas. The PTBs experience includes the securing of metering data by the use of electronic signatures. Within the SELMA project a technically-based secure architecture had been developed and rigorously tested for secure communication of measuring instruments (see SELMA project – www.selma.eu).

The basic idea of the INSIKA concept is very simple. It is compulsory that all transactions are recorded. Each transaction is signed with an electronic signature, generated by a smart card. The cryptographic functions involve the Elliptic Curve Digital Signature Algorithm (ECDSA, 192 bit) [ECDSA00] and the Secure Hash Algorithm (SHA-1, 160 bit) [SHA08]. As the system makes use of asymmetric cryptography, the smart card contains a public and private key. The total length of data to be signed is less than 168 bytes. The tax payer is responsible for the use of the smart card. A Public Key Infrastructure (PKI) is used, and the public key is personalised to the tax payer of each ECR. The German working group on cash registers planned that the Federal Central Office for Taxes will operate as the central authority. Tax auditors must have access to the electronic data in a direct or indirect way. After the recording each manipulation of transaction data is detectable now. Audits by the revenue authority can validate the records of the cash register by the use of the public key and can determine if the data has been tampered.

Based on these basic principles some additional features are defined. It is absolutely necessary, that for each transaction a printed receipt must be presented to the customer. In doing so, the usage of the signature device is shown. The data of the receipt must contain the same data as in the electronically recorded one, including the signature. As a result, the printed receipt can be verified by its digital signature too. In the case of lost data, monthly turnovers can be estimated by the use of totalisers, located in the secure memory of the smart card. These totalisers have to be read out by the ECR daily and stored within the electronic journal as signed reports.

The fiscally relevant data records can be examined both locally and after their transmission over various communication channels. Processes will be fully automatic with respect to data's integrity and authenticity.

3.2.2 System architecture

The solution uses a centralised system architecture, as seen in Fig.1. The smart cards will be distributed by the central authority. For the generation of electronic signatures and the recording of totalisers special smart cards have to be used. The tax payer may request as many smart cards as he needs from the central authority. For each smart card a certificate will be generated, which will be stored on a central server and the smart card itself. The distinguished name of the certificate contains the tax payer identification and a consecutive card number. For generating valid transactions the smart card must be integrated into the ECR or POS system. The data sets are well defined within the interface specification. By reading the totalisers the case of cards not being used can be checked easily.

The first step of a taxpayers' audit is the delivery of stored tax data to the auditor. This can be done via various mediums, e.g. memory sticks, CDs or web services. The data format is specified as an XML-export description. Therefore there is no need for the auditor to have direct access to the taxpayer's system. For the verification of the transactions the auditor will need a standard PC or laptop and the verification software only. Aside from the tax data, the public key of the particular smart card is necessary. This key can be obtained either by a request for the certificate from the central server, from the XML-audit-file or from the smart card itself. Both latter versions additionally require access to the certificate revocation list, which is distributed by the central authority.

Of course one can think of other system architectures. Some of them are currently under discussion – keeping in mind that each system architecture needs a discrete threat analysis. Systems with decentralised architectures can operate quite well, especially when there are no stringent fiscal regulations and the system is used for in-house control purposes.

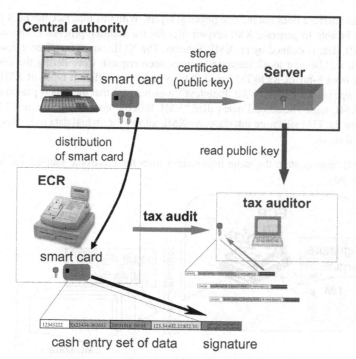

Fig. 1: System architecture

3.2.3 Protocols and interfaces

As described above, INSIKA defines two interfaces only. As seen in Fig. 2 one of them is the interface between the ECR and smart card, called TIM signature interface. As the smart card has some special features, it is named TIM (Tax Identification Module). The data transfer is based on the T=1-protocol according to the ISO/IEC 7816 standard. The data itself follows the Simple-TLV approach, which means that the data is coded according to the pattern Tag-Length-Value. Approximately 50 tags were defined to cover the data model. Mainly three commands (transaction, report, read certificate) are needed in the communication between ECR and TIM. Because of this the handling with the TIM is very easy from the ECR's point of view.

A consecutive sequence number – which is a very important security feature – is generated inside the TIM and will be added by it to the signed data set automatically. This sequence number is sent to the ECR together with the signature as the response of the TIM. It must be stored and printed by the ECR together with other relevant data. If this is not done, the verification will fail. The detailed specification of the TIM signature interface is available for all interested parties. It will be sent for free upon request and registration.

The INSIKA concept does not define any specification for the internal journal of the ECR. The ECR manufacturer is free to decide these specifications. This is one of the main advantages of this solution. Even embedded ECRs with an 8-bit-architecture should be able to implement this system. That means that a high number of older ECRs can be easily upgraded to work with this system.

The second system interface does not include physical layers. With this interface the ECR itself or any other system will be able to generate XML-export files for the auditing processes. The structure and content of the XML data is defined by an XML-Schema. The XML export interface is also defined in a document which will be sent to all interested parties upon request. Considering the wide range of computing power from 8-bit ECRs to PC-based POS systems two different types of XML-data were defined. The first type is specified as "XML Plaintext", which means that the data is placed the classical way in-between XML-tags. The second type called "XML Base64" contains the original TLV-requests and responses from the TIM signature interface. As XML allows for textual data only, this binary data must be coded as Base64.

Both types of XML-data contain the same information from the electronic journal, i.e. transactions, reports and certificates.

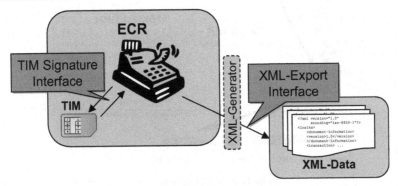

Fig. 2: System interfaces

3.2.4 Usability of the system.

The INSIKA solution is based upon open and established cryptographic algorithms and widely used microchips. Digital signatures have advantages over any other mechanisms for protecting data. The data is protected between the two end points of signed data sets/printed receipts to tax auditor's software. Therefore it is "end-to-end" security. The security is not based on keeping technical secrets but on generally accepted mathematics. As there is no proprietary technology used, the security of the system can be verified independently. Finally, the solution is based on state-of-the-art cryptographic algorithms. The applied ECDSA-192-algorithm has not been broken and is expected remain secure for many years. And as the signatures of this algorithm are comparatively short, they qualify for being easily printed on receipts.

The digital signature is not only visible in the export file, but also on the printed paper receipt that is generated by the ECR for each transaction. On the receipt the signature can be coded as an ASCII string or a two-dimensional code, depending on the ECR's and the printer's capabilities.

All data verification is based on stored and signed transaction data. Any imaginable manipulation of cash register's reports or master data is ineffective because the entire data set cannot be modified without being discovered. Even intentionally installed manipulation functions within the cash register cannot compromise the system, making any device certification procedure obsolete.

Stored data can be verified automatically to a large extent, which is more efficient than previous audits. As the verification of printed receipts is based on the printout information only, there is no need to use saved transaction data. Hence, every printed receipt can be checked to see whether it was generated by an ECR with a valid smart card. All printed receipts without or with faulty signatures clearly signal tampering. Vice versa, taxpayers are able to prove the validity of their cash registers data very easily.

4 Conclusion

A protection system is proposed and implemented for ECRs and similar systems. The solution offers a new approach for fiscal systems in the fight against tax fraud. No system approvals and technical observations are needed for checking the running system. Without doubt, market observations by auditors will be necessary as they are today. But the auditors will have a powerful auditing tool at their disposal. Within a short time they will be able to examine the accuracy of any system.

The concept and specifications developed by INSIKA have raised interest in many countries. The specification details were published in the beginning of 2009. The system could be a template for an European solution. The solution offers flexibility for ECR manufacturers combined with a high level of security. It can break down the trade barriers that are raised when extensive national approval procedures for ECR and POS are instituted. Plans are underway to adapt this technique for use in the taxi business and other related fields.

The INSIKA project is supported by the German Ministry of Economics and Technology under the grant MNPQ 11/07.

References

[AINS09] Ainsworth, Richard: CALIFORNIA ZAPPERS: A PROPOSAL FOR CALIFORNIA'S COMMISSION ON THE 21ST CENTURY ECONOMY, Boston University School of Law Working Paper No. 09-01 (January 8, 2009)

[BUND03] Deutscher Bundestag – 15. Wahlperiode Drucksache 15/2020 Teil II 54: DROHENDE STEUERAUSFÄLLE AUFGRUND MODERNER KASSENSYSTEME, 24.11.2003, http://drucksachen.bundestag.de/

[ECDSA00] U.S. Department of Commerce and National Institute of Standards and Technology, FIPS PUBLICATION 186-2: DIGITAL SIGNATURE STANDARD (DSS), Januar 2000 und Change Notice 1, Oktober 2001 http://csrc.nist.gov/publications/PubsFIPS.html

[SHA08] U.S. Department of Commerce and National Institute of Standards and Technology, FIPS PUBLICATION 180-3: SECURE HASH STANDARD (SHS), October 2008 http://csrc.nist.gov/publications/PubsFIPS.html

[SERV09] Service Plus D.O.O. : INFORMATION TECHNOLOGIES FOR RETAIL, accessed on July 6th, 2009, http://www.serviceplus.rs/eng_txt__serbian_fiscal_printers_comparison.php

The Operational Manager – Enemy or Hero of Secure Business Practice?

Wendy Goucher

Security Empowerment Consultant
Idrach Limited
wendy@idrach.com

Abstract

This paper will investigate the role of the non-IT manager in information security. He can, for example, be the reason why sensitive work is carried out on the move and security focused spending is given a low priority in the budget. Alternatively, he can also be the driving force behind empowering the team to have a dynamic attitude to protecting data both at work and at home. Now is the time for managers to stop pushing information security issues away from their desk and into the in-tray of the IT department.

Goals

- To highlight the growing profile of information security incidents
- To discuss how the attitudes and directives of non-IT managers can lead to insecure business practice.
- To discuss the role of security empowerment in the development of a more effective business culture.
- To examine how managers can make a positive contribution to the success of information security policies and procedures.

My Perspective

My background is that of a social science graduate with a first career in lecturing in management and economics. While I spend much of my time working with clients to improve their security awareness and devising policy and procedure my default perspective is always to ask why the human interface in information security continues to be the weak point. If I ever find a good answer to that then, I suppose I will have to move to another one, but somehow I think the question is big enough to keep me busy for a while yet.

1 Introduction

In the last year the media has carried many examples of lapses in operational business security which have lead to a loss, or suspected loss, of sensitive information. These have included the loss of a USB key by Lothian and Borders Police in Scotland in January 2009. The key contained registration details of 750 cars and their owners. Also an incident at New York City Payroll Administration where 3,470 items of payroll data were lost when an employee used conventional postage. The data went missing and there is no trace as to where. It is important to realize that data loss is not just about computers. In The US a school in Nashville left student paperwork in a public street. The documents contained names, social security numbers and details of student disabilities. In these incidents, and many more like them, the media need to focus a story on an individual for maximum impact, means that the blame, in the public perception at least, is entirely with the careless employee. In many cases that is a shallow and unhelpful view.

2 The Fuzzy Boundary

When we talk about information security in many cases we are focusing on technical issues and other aspects that are under the direct control of the responsible person or team. This discussion is a little removed from direct control. It might best be sited within a 'Fuzzy Boundary' of the organisational system. The fuzzy boundary is important because it is an area through which much sensitive business information flows. However, it is difficult to reliably monitor and requires different perspectives and techniques to influence adherence to security controls and standards. There are 7 categories of egress by which information moves through the fuzzy boundary [1]

- Management or Organisational Pressure.
- Risk by Association
- Mergers and Acquisitions
- Out in the Open
- Indiscretion
- Calling in the Dark
- Virtual Booth

While all these categories are interesting, for the purposes of this discussion I am going to focus on the first. Management and organisational pressure.

Where security awareness is concentrated on the end-user within an organisation focus is often put into delivering a series of rules and guidelines of prohibited or risky behaviour. The motivation for adherence will vary but will often primarily take the route of avoiding punishment of those who fail to meet the standards.

There are many examples of organizational pressure which leads to a weakening of the fuzzy boundary.

- **The pressure to work long hours, especially at home.** The European working time directive is a good thing. However, one way it is often circumvented is to encourage staff to work at home. This means that data must travel home on a laptop hard drive, USB key or other medium. Every time this happens it is a risk. It would be best if these risks were taken when strictly necessary, rather than routinely.
- **The pressure towards mobile working.** As well as the technical risk of using WiFi connections while on the move there are also the risks of being 'shoulder-surfed or overheard on the phone. Staff may be aware of this, but if they are encouraged to be in touch with colleagues while they are traveling, then it is likely that this communication need trumps the security concern.
- **The organizational pressure.** Having a strong security policy may appear to be a good thing, but if it does not consider the operational demands then the shortcuts or subversions that staff would need to take in order to do their job then these may well render the policy ineffective. Take an example, that a colleague of mine came across when conducting a pre-audit evaluation of a London hospital 5 years ago. The secure data access policy required all staff to attend a security awareness briefing before they were given a logon password onto the database. The budget constraints meant that these briefings were not available to short term agency and temporary night

staff. Staff circumvented this problem by sharing their passwords with those colleagues who did not have them. There was no real concern that sensitive patient information would get into the hands of people who would not, in a more effectively implemented system, have had access. It did, however, mean that it was not possible to identify actions and changes in the system and attribute them to the staff member concerned, and therefore any audit trail was undermined.

3 Why is the manager role unrecognised?

In our news-hungry age of 24-hour transmission, it seems that has the general attention span decreased. In the opinion of Dr.Ted Selker [2], until recently of MIT, attention span while on the internet can be a little as 9 seconds. At the same time the power of the 'Blame Vacuum' has increased. When the aircraft was blown up over Lockerbie in December 1988, while there was shock and a keenness to find out the cause there was also an acceptance that time would be needed to assemble the evidence. By the time of the Twin Towers attack in 2001 that acceptance was all but gone. While direct parallels between the crash of one flight on a Scottish town and the hijacking of 4 flights targeting the towers, the Pentagon and possibly even the White House cannot reasonably be drawn, the anxiety to identify the exact circumstances of the incidents, and bring any remaining perpetrators who played a supporting role to justice was noticeably stronger, and could be seen as indicative of the increase in this blame vacuum phenomenon in the intervening years. And where there is a demand, as economists will tell you, there will be a supply and the stronger that demand then the more likely that the supply will focus on speed of delivery rather than quality. So then, when there has been a security incident the demand is for the perpetrator, the easy target of blame. Public interest is not going to stay in town long enough to examine the background to the story, and the norms of operational practice set by the organisation and the management which will take longer to emerge. In other words the role of management is likely to take longer to uncover than outside attention will last. The identity of the 'looser' and, if it seems appropriate, the notionally responsible Member of Parliament- in the case of HMRC the Home Secretary, will be of more immediate interest as it will be quicker to identify. In this case the 'junior member of staff' was never publically identified and the person thrown in to plug the 'Blame Vacuum' was HMRC chairman Paul Gray. While he was undoubtedly ultimately responsible, he almost certainly did not have any first hand influence on what went wrong. The managers who might be said to have had that sort of influence were, and are, still unknown to the outside world.

4 The Negative Effect of the Manager.

One of the most common security risks that staff take is often the result of pressure of office norms or culture. That is the sharing of passwords. In the summer time it is common to find people giving on their password to their colleague so they can 'keep and eye' on their in-tray in their absence. I came across a PA in a large organisation who had the passwords to the three board members she worked for on her desk. Technically of course she could have got her own 'log – in' to their accounts. However that was probably perceived as not allowed, or was complicated to authorize, so having their passwords was the easiest solution. And a very risky one. A few years ago a friend of mine found themselves suspended from their job as someone, from within the business, had spoofed his e-mail account and sent inappropriate mail to senior managers under his guise. Fortunately, my friend was at a social event, with no computer access at the time of the incident (it was pre-Blackberry) and had a number of witnesses who could attest to his attendance. Even so it took several weeks to fully untangle the story and identify the perpetrator. If my friend had shared his password with a colleague, or colleagues, then it may well have proved harder, or even impossible, to demonstrate the innocence of all concerned and that would certainly have had a big impact on his career, which, I suspect, was the perpetrator's intent. So pressure to share passwords amongst staff can be a problem. And if you don't think there is pressure, try being the one person in the team who appears not to trust their colleagues enough to share

4.1 Attitude

Two of the most powerful and dangerous attitudes in business, as regards information security, are ignorance and arrogance. In the case of security the ignorance may not be willful it may be the result of overwork and a well developed 'SEP' filer which was defined, by Douglas Adams [3] as "something we can't see, or don't see, or our brain doesn't let us see, because we think that it's Somebody Else's Problem". However many organisations of any size now require their staff to agree to, and abide by, the acceptable use policy for computer and data handling. I had to do this each time I logged into collect my mail with a previous employer.

However, this should not be taken as a method of ensuring the removal of ignorance. Most people I spoke to while in that job could only guess at what they were supposed to know. Nobody had actually read the policy. No surprise actually. It was written and presented in a format only a lawyer could love. However, if you are the manager, and your staff have to agree to a such a policy surely you should at least understand what is in it. The other side of this coin is where the manager is aware of secure procedures, but believes that they are wrong and that he needs to avoid them. It is ultimately unfortunate that they feel unwilling, or unable to make any real contribution to drawing up policies and procedures that do work. Although that may be the fault of those responsible for information security. Budgets are tight all over, and it is more cost efficient to treat all non- information security people as straightforward end-users. If another category is created that needs to be serviced and considered – and that is expensive

5 The Reluctance of the Non-IT Manager

All of the points in this section are, I believe, linked. They reference the perception of the manager.

As I have mentioned before the non-IT manager is often busy and so simply does not feel they have the time, or indeed that is the most cost efficient use of their time, to be involved in information security. What is the point? Really, it is a serious question. What is the motivation for investing time and effort? It is a key point and one I will return to later.

The protection of personal data has always been a combination of people based solutions and technical solutions. The Elizabethan spymasters such as Sir Thomas Walsingham in the 16th century, knew all about balancing these two aspects. Indeed they helped to devise a means whereby Mary, Queen of Scots, who had been subject to imprisonment by Elizabeth 1st for many years, could send and receive messages which could, unbeknown to Mary, then be intercepted and copied. The technical solution alone was not enough to entrap Mary, however. It was necessary for a 'double agent', Gilbert Gifford to persuade Mary of the safety of the method and encourage her to contact those who would conspire to free her. She wrote encrypted messages which were put in a watertight container and then placed into the stopper in beer barrels taken to, and from, her prison at Chartley. As a result of this she was successfully tried for treason and executed. It can seem that, in this modern age, we have lost the appreciation of the human interface and are concerned principally with the technical solutions. This has many impacts on the effectiveness of information security and awareness programs, one of the most serious of which is the belief that if the solutions are technical, and the manager who is not employed for his technical skill can believe that it is not his problem.

A significant difficulty with the operation of information security is that it not what politicians would call 'A vote winner'. A study by Dietmar Pokoyski [4] found that staff perceived information security as a tool of control over staff. This means that if staff want to be able to do something out of the ordinary, such as take their laptop on a sales and marketing trip to China, the assumption is that the answer will be "no". As the participants do not want to go without their machine then they will not raise the issue in the hope that they are able to take their laptop before anyone notices. The three basic thoughts that enable that rejection of co-operation are

- "I don't believe it is a problem.
- If I ask for advice or help the info sec people will just stop me taking a machine; which will reduce my ability to do my job.
- Any help would not be tailored to my need. The staff won't work with me they will just refer to the rule book.

Pokoyski refers to the perception of the implementation of information security as being "Inhuman and objectifying". While it may well be true that the information security team, especially in the larger organisations needs an element of detachment because they must be accepted as fair arbiters by both staff and management. They also need to be accepted as the first point of call for the pre-emptive queries and assisting secure, and safer data handling.

A final issue, often raised as a justification for reluctance to get involved in information security programs , is budget and funding. Some managers, although sympathetic to the information security message do not see it as something that should they should spend their limited budget on. Price, Waterhouse and Cooper, carried out an investigation on behalf of ENISA in 2007 [5] with the aim of offering

> "A perspective on what governments and private companies are currently doing for assessing the impact and success of awareness raising activities. "

In so doing they found that security awareness was most commonly perceived as a compliance issue, rather than an investment. As a result managers were reluctant to spend above the minimum level that would allow them to achieve the compliance they require.

Security awareness, especially, suffers from being difficult to measure in its effectiveness in any objective way as one might, for example use absenteeism to measure staff morale. If the only available measure is whether it is good enough to achieve compliance then that will be the attractive solution. It is, in fact, possible to measure effectiveness, provided measurable targets is based on security objectives set beforehand. For example while having staff wearing ID badges within a building can make strangers apparent and easy to watch, if they wear them to go to the local café for lunch on a regular basis that will then make them, and their conversation, most interesting. It could even make the wearer a possible target for attack if their job title implies that they handle special or high value accounts at a bank, for example. If they are walking to the station in the dark of a winters evening, carrying their laptop then the temptation to try and part the employee from their laptop which could carry interesting, even valuable information is clear. So if there was a campaign to reduce the number of people wearing badges outside the building then, justification is clear and success can be readily recorded by means of a simple observed count.

So, while the demands of budget are significant, they should demonstrate the need to be clear on the aim of any security awareness activity.

5.1 Security Empowerment in the Workplace

Attempts to entice managers to improve the security awareness and behaviour in their team could be equated to addressing the petulant teenager in every manager [6] – so believes Urs Gattiker. He asserts that initiatives with teenagers often aim to make them wiser, less impulsive, less short sighted.- i.e. change them! At for that reason are doomed to failure as it is that pressure that teenagers are primed to resist.

Urs Gattiker was very forthright in his assertion that traditional security awareness programmes do not work. It should be considered that his statement is made in the context that he has a business product to sell and so will make the point more strident that he might otherwise have done. However, it is still helpful to examine his point. He says that the standard training approaches treat staff as an interested and motivated audience who are just waiting to be guided in safe practice by the words of the experts. In practice, however, the audience is more likely to be like a bunch of petulant teenagers who have better things to do and probably feel that they know more about balancing security and operational issues than those presenting to them. Looking at the situation from that perspective then it is a tall order for training sessions to be effective if they dictating future practice. Gattiker promotes the concept of Security empowerment, as do I, as you can see from my job title 'Security Empowerment Consultant'. Security empowerment seeks to build security awareness from within. Building on knowledge and experience of staff to devise operations that are consistent with the requirements of audits and data protection legislation while still enabling operations to continue. On the face of it, it may seem to be a 'cuddly' approach, from the same stable as 'group hugs' and other modern manifestations of the human relations approach. However, it is not. At the core is the need to engage with staff, both end-user and managers and give them the means to make security work for them. One effective technique which has been used in many places, including Royal London assurance is to beginning with helping staff to take more care with their own sensitive data away from work. Nick Harwood, Head of Security and Governance at Royal London Assurance believes that this is a key tool in their security armoury.

> *"My view was (and is) that if people are aware of the issue, because they are protecting themselves or own stuff, they are firstly more likely to take notice and then are more likely to demonstrate the same behavior at work thereby protecting the corporate environment."* '*Harwood's Law'*

Another financial institution in Edinburgh, towards the end of November last year set up a series of 10 minute workshops next to the canteen covering such subjects as shopping on line, telephone banking and advanced fee fraud. These were very popular. Indeed I was fortunate to speak with some of the staff in another context and they said that not only had they felt that the sessions were useful, but it also helped them to feel more valued as staff members. Of course, while they are valued, what that statement showed was that they had also been, to a certain extent, 'duped'. They were seeing the puppet and not the strings. They did not realise that this would make them safer in their business operations too and that was the main motivation behind the provision of the sessions.

However there is no escaping the fact that empowering staff is harder than just issuing policy and setting up a couple of training sessions. Surely though, what business needs to be concerned about more than ever at the moment, is value for money. Sometimes you have to invest a bit more and get a tailored product that will, ultimately be more effective if properly maintained.

6 The Manager as the Information Security Driver

The title of this piece implied that not only can the manager be the cause of insecure business practice, but they can also be a solution. As Hertzberg identified in his 'Hygiene Factors' [7] sometimes removing the negative factors is all that is required to get the motivation to swing towards a positive direction. Indeed removing the requirement for staff to call the office on their mobile once they come out of a meeting, or exercising discretion as to when to discuss business outside the office, can make a significant step towards improvement. It is best to be clear here, I think, that using a security empowerment approach does not mean that each and every manager needs to become an expert in information security. There will, hopefully, be at least one expert within the organisation, or contracted to assist when needed. Where the manager can be the turbo boost of effective implementation is to:

- Ensure that they, along with their team, understand why there needs to be care and security surrounding the handling of certain types of information.
- Be willing to work with those responsible for information security to identify and develop sound operational practices.
- Lead staff by encouragement and example.

The first point may seem a little obvious, but it includes also being aware of potential hazards such as those involved in working in public places and taking work home. If staff don't realise there is a problem then they are going to be much less interested in working on a solution.

The second point is key. At the very least there needs to be a dialogue between the implementers and users where proposed policy or procedure could make current business practice difficult. Take, for example the company referred to earlier who is going to market it's services to China. This has been a growing trend over the last years and security awareness and practices have not always kept track. Established information security experts in the field of international travel tell me that there is significant risk of data loss during these sorts of journeys. This can be due to physical removal of laptops or other storage media from hotel rooms or bags, or in can be due to data interception. One large consultancy of my acquaintance dealt with this issue with a combination of secure VPN connection and re-use of old equipment. When staff travelled to China they were given laptops which held only the data that was necessary for their trip and any required software. This meant that any loss or damage was inconvenient rather than embarrassing or, worst still, a real problem. The IT department also were more than happy to find a use for retired laptops.

It is worth saying here that even when the chairman of the board went out to China he took one of the old machines. This leads me neatly to my final, and probably most important point. T

6.1 The importance of Management Setting an Example.

If an organisation is going to have improved information security and awareness then for greatest effectiveness it needs to be part of the culture of the whole organisation. From the highest to the part time temporary staff covering for sick leave. The power of example to put that message across should not be under-estimated. Stephen P Robbins [8], in his book discussing organisational behaviour, cites a perfect example of this. The story concerns Thomas Watson Jr who was the president of IBM from 1952 to 1971. There was a young woman who was working as a plant security supervisor. One day Mr Watson, and his entourage, approached the women and moved to continue into one of the secure areas of the plant. They were all wearing their orange security badges which allowed them into almost all areas of the plant. However, as this was a sensitive area those wishing to enter had to wear a special green badge. The security supervisor stopped the party, even though she recognised Mr Watson. The group were, apparently, amazed and were keen to see what would happen next. Mr Watson was not noted for his benevolent approach. The story goes that some of the group even expected that she would be fired on the spot. When she admitted that she did recognise Mr Watson, but would still not go against the policy that only green badge wearers could enter he area it was a high tension confrontational moment. Thomas Watson raised his hand for silence and one of the group went back to the senior office suite and returned with the appropriate badge, which Thomas put on and then entered the area. The supervisor was not fired and the clear implication was that she had done the right thing. Stories like this travel at lightening speed around organisations and that story said that the security rules are to be respected by everyone, with no exceptions. That one action was probably worth several thousand pounds of training.

7 Summery

Whether non-IT managers advocate more effective information security measures and awareness amongst their staff or not, there is one thing for sure. Their role is central to the success of any initiative. The problem with being a manager is that their role in central to the success of a great deal within an organisation. From customer care to product development, through staff retention and motivation to staff development and succession planning and, off course efficiency and budgetary control. Everyone needs, and in many cases expects, the busy manager to focus on their perspective. Is it any wonder that executive stress is such a big issue? However, whilst one can be sympathetic it is important to see that whether they are aware or not, the actions of the ordinary operational manager have an effect on the security of the data within the organisation. Indeed a recent strategy devised by the Knowledge Council on behalf of Her Majesty's Government to look at the management of information [9] stressed the importance of capable 'Professional Leadership' in maintaining the high standards expected and required.

However we, as information security professionals cannot escape our responsibilities to the managers within an organisation. For example, if is believed that their opinion is required then it needs to be gathered in a reasonable and appropriate way that does not waste time and leaves the majority at least feeling that their opinions were respected. We need to look at how we get information to all staff, baring in mind that information security, in most organisations, is a support service, not the core function. While a high standard may be required, especially in the financial sector and aspired to in certain sections of government, they must fit with the core operational function. Padres or other religious figures within the armed forces understand this. They know that bringing spiritual support and guidance to the people under their care is what they have been appointed to do. But they must, at the same time, be mindful that theirs is a support service. It is only if they respect the core function of the organisation that they can truly give the ministry to those who serve with them.

Managers can be the inhibitors or the advocates of good security operation. The determining factor between the two will often be the information security team.

8 Conclusion

So the answer to the question as to whether managers are the heroes or the inhibitors of secure business practice lies, at least in part in the hands of those of us who work with them.

Literature

[1] First presented to the ISACA Europe conference, November 2008 and available as a white paper at www.idrach.com

[2] Ted Selker: http://news.bbc.co.uk/1/hi/sci/tech/1834682.stm

[3] Douglas Adams; Life the Universe and Everything

[4] Dietmar Pokoyski. Security in the Workplace

[5] Information Security Awareness initiatives; Current Practice and the Measurement of Success. July 2007.

[6] Urs E Gattiker, Why information security assurance initiatives fail and will continue to do so.

[7] F.Herzberg, B.Mausner, and B Snyderman, The Motivation to Work. (New York: John Wiley, 1959)

[8] Stephen P Robbins, Organizational Behaviour, 6th Edition 1979 Prentice-Hall International Editions

[9] Information matters: Building government's capability in managing knowledge and information. HMG November 2008.

Secure Software, Trust and Assurance

A Structured Approach to
Software Security

Ton van Opstal

Ericssonstraat 2, Rijen, The Netherlands, Ericsson Telecommunicatie BV
Research & Development
ton.van.opstal@ericsson.com

Abstract

Security is an important aspect of software that needs to be considered during the entire System Development Life Cycle (SDLC). A structured and practical approach to handle Software Security is proposed by defining the concept of Security Architecture and by using this Security Architecture as key concept to relate all security activities that need to be performed as defined by the SDLC. The Security Architecture itself is described using a structured definition format, called the Extensible Security Architecture Description Format (XSADF). XSADF can be used as input format for tools that can assess the security aspects of a system under development.

To support the work on a Security Architecture, a Security Architecture Framework is proposed. Software Architects can use this framework as a template to define the Security Architecture for the system they are developing.

The structured approach using XSADF, with a central place for Security Architecture, is a step to achieve „security by design".

1 Introduction

It is now widely accepted and advocated that security should be considered throughout the entire software development life cycle ([HoLi06], [McGr06], [KSS+08]). Considering security during development should lead to a more pro-active "security by design" approach, rather than the current practice of "security by patching".

As part of a "security by design" approach, we should also ensure that the software being developed complies with applicable standards, guidelines, best practices and laws. Software security shall be measurable, to make the result of the effort on software security visible.

However, striving for "security by design" is easier said than done. The current practice in industry typically involves a lot of paperwork. For starters, there is a lot of documentation in the form of standards, guidelines and best practices that serves as input to the development process. On top of this customers provide additional documents with more specific security requirements. In most cases the origin and rationale for these security requirements is not clear. Next to that, development processes require security activities to be performed and security documentation to be produced as a result of these activities. Examples of such activities are: Architectural Risk Assessment, security requirements definition/selection, hardening, and vulnerability analysis.

It is not clear if all the documentation that is produced is actually used in later stages. Doing a security review in the end, e.g. to check compliance to standards, is a tedious task, as it means reading through

N. Pohlmann, H. Reimer, W. Schneider (Editors): Securing Electronic Business Processes, Vieweg (2009), 281-290

piles of documentation filled with details and hidden cross references. Tracking security issues described in all these documents is hard.

We propose a more structured way to realize the "security by design" idea in practice ([Opst08]). Firstly, we introduce the concept of Security Architecture that can be used as the key concept to relate all security activities that need to be performed as part of the development life cycle and as the basis to organise all the associated documentation. Secondly, we propose an XML format for this, so that tool support can be used to find or select relevant information.

Together, this provides a way to get a grip on all existing documentation related to the security, taking the architecture as a base.

2 Software Security Approach

Our proposed approach is a natural extension of the practice at the National Institute of Standards and Technology (NIST) to describe security checklists in a standard format. For our purpose we considered the Extensible Configuration Checklist Description Format (XCCDF), described in [ZiQu08]. A small extension of this format allows us to use this format not just for security checklists, but to describe the whole Security Architecture. We call this the Extensible Security Architecture Description Format (XSADF).

2.1 Security Architecture

The definition of *Security Architecture* that we propose to use is as follows:

> *"The fundamental organization of a system, embodied in its components, their relationships to each other and the environment, and the principles governing its security design and evolution. The Security Architecture comprises Security Requirements, Security Controls, Business and Security Architecture Assets (including associated threats, vulnerabilities, and risks), security documentation, and security definitions and abbreviations. It contains those aspects of Software Architecture that are needed to assess the security of a system."*

This definition is in line with the more general definition of Software Architecture and defines what comprises a Security Architecture. A Software Architect is typically the responsible person for assessing the security of a system.

The Security Architecture comprises security requirements, Security Controls, assets (including associated threats, vulnerabilities, and risks). It effectively documents all the steps in the development life cycle, from security Architectural Risk Assessment to choosing and implementing Security Controls, in the same XML format.

A Security Architecture Framework is proposed that can be used as a template for the definition of a Security Architecture. This framework is defined in our proposed XML format as well. Software Architects define the Security Architecture of the system they are working on using the Security Architecture Framework as a base. This framework is more than a template, since it is constant being updated with new requirements, controls, threats, assets, etc.. It can be expected that a Security Architecture Framework is developed, or further improved, for specific areas or technologies.

The Security Architecture Framework proposed consists of:
- Security Requirements
- Security Controls
- Business Assets (including known Threats and Vulnerabilities per asset).
- Security Architecture Assets (including known Threats and Vulnerabilities per asset)
- Threats and Vulnerabilities
- Definitions and abbreviations: consistent use of this terminology within the Security Architecture Framework is considered important.
- Mapping between Security Controls and Security Requirements
- Mapping between Business Assets and Security Controls
- Mapping between Security Architecture Assets and Security Controls

The base for the Security Controls part of the Security Architecture Framework is taken from NIST Special Publication 800-53 ([RKJ+07]). The reason is to achieve alignment between Information Security and Software Security. NIST Special Publication 800-53 is targeted at Information Security. The mappings are needed to create compliance statements.

2.2 Extensible Security Architecture Description Format

We introduce an XML-based format, called XSADF. This format is based on XCCDF, as stated before. In the table below, we describe the usage of the XSADF XML elements and make a comparison to the XCCDF original intent of these elements.

Table 1: XCCDF and XSADF

XCCDF Element	XCCDF original intent	XCCDF used for Security Architecture (XSADF)
Benchmark	A Benchmark holds descriptive text, and acts as a container for the other elements. An XCCDF document holds exactly one Benchmark object.	Used as in XCCDF.
Profile	A Profile is a collection of attributed references to Rule, Group, and Value objects. A Profile is used to define a baseline of Security Controls; more than one Profile can be defined in an XCCDF document.	A Profile holds (1) baseline of Security Requirements, (2) Security Architecture Assets, (3) definitions and abbreviations and (4) security activities of a SDLC.
Group	A Group can hold other elements and can be selected.	Used as in XCCDF.
TestResult	A TestResult holds the results of performing a compliance test against a single target device or system.	A TestResult holds (5) statement of compliance against a baseline of Security Requirements, (6) statement of compliance against a baseline of Security Controls.
Value	A Value holds a named data value that can be substituted into another XCCDF element's properties.	Used as in XCCDF. In addition a Value holds definitions and abbreviations.
Rule	A Rule holds check references, a scoring weight, and may also hold remediation information.	A Rule holds Security Controls and Security Requirements.
Asset (new)	-	Asset is introduced to hold Business Assets and Security Architecture Assets. Assets marked abstract are part of the Security Architecture Framework, and contain references to applicable Security Controls, Threats and Vulnerabilities.
Risk (new)	-	Risk is introduced to hold business and Security Architecture risks.

CWE™ (http://cwe.mitre.org/) is used in our Security Architecture to refer to software weaknesses (which are the source of vulnerabilities) in an Architectural Risk Assessment. CAPEC™ (http://capec.mitre.org/) is used in our Security Architecture to refer to threats in an Architectural Risk Assessment. Threats are described in CAPEC™ using attack patterns; these attack patterns can be used during Vulnerability Analysis to verify whether the implemented Security Controls are effective to mitigate or reduce the observed risks. CPE™ (http://cpe.mitre.org/) is used in our Security Architecture to refer to hardware.

MITRE (http://www.mitre.org/) mentions Asset Management, but does not have concrete examples on how to do this. Our approach is to extend XCCDF with the necessary elements Asset and Risk. Furthermore some changes are proposed to the existing definitions. These changes are backwards compatible with the original XCCDF specification.

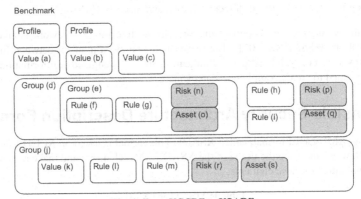

Fig. 1: From XCCDF to XSADF

In the following paragraph the most relevant XSADF elements are discussed in more detail.

Group
Groups are used to create structure in the Security Architecture Framework. During the work of defining a Security Architecture, groups that are not applicable are deselected. By default a group is selected.

Rule
Rules are used to define Security Controls and Security Requirements.

Begin (example: rule)

```
<cdf:Rule id="AU-8-Rule">
    <cdf:title>Time Stamps</cdf:title>
    <cdf:description>The information system provides time stamps for use in audit
                    record generation.</cdf:description>
    <cdf:rationale>Supplemental Guidance: Time stamps (including date and time) of
                    audit records are generated using internal system clocks.
                    </cdf:rationale>
</cdf:Rule>
```

End (example)

During the work of defining a Security Architecture, rules that are not applicable are deselected. By default a rule is selected.

Asset

Assets can be divided as follows:

- Business Assets: these assets have to be protected by the systems that provide them. An example of a business level asset is "a customer database holding details of mobile phone subscriptions". These assets are considered as part of the focus on Information Security by enterprises, but need already to be considered during an Architectural Risk Assessment performed for a development project (Software Security). When performing such an assessment, the risks related to these assets need to be considered from the viewpoint of the enterprise.
- Security Architecture Assets: these assets form the Security Architecture for a system and need to be considered during an Architectural Risk Assessment performed for a development project (Software Security).

During the work of defining a Security Architecture the assets defined in the framework that are not applicable are deselected. By default an asset is selected.

In the Security Architecture Framework it must be possible to represent a class of assets. This is achieved by using the notion of an abstract asset, which is indicated by assigning the value "true" to attribute abstract (abstract="true"). An example of an abstract asset can be 'Password', while a concrete instance (like 'root password') represents an occurrence of that asset in the system under consideration. Abstract assets can be used to include applicable Threats, Vulnerabilities and Security Controls.

Assets are defined in the following way. This example contains one abstract asset and one concrete asset.

Begin (example: Access Control Groups asset)

```
<cdf:Group id="AccessControlGroups">
   <cdf:title>Access Control Groups</cdf:title>
   <cdf:description>Overview of all Access Control Groups. Depending on the
                   operating system, each access group has different
                   attributes. Attribute names are between =..=</cdf:description>
   <cdf:Asset id="access_control_group_abstract" level="data"
              category="information" abstract="true">
      <cdf:title>Access Control Group</cdf:title>
      <cdf:description>A Group is a list of principals (Security Engineering, Ross
                      Anderson).</cdf:description>
   </cdf:Asset>

   <!--Concrete Assets -->
   <cdf:Asset id="acg-root" level="data" category="information"
              extends="access_control_group_abstract">
      <cdf:title>root</cdf:title>
      <cdf:description>=Name='root'</cdf:description>
      <cdf:description>=Members='root'</cdf:description>
      <cdf:description>=Description='Standard Linux group'</cdf:description>
      <cdf:platform idref="SLES 10 Service Pack 2" />
      <cdf:component>Operating System</cdf:component>
      <cdf:deployment>'/cluster/etc/groups'</cdf:deployment>
   </cdf:Asset>
</cdf:Group>
```

End (example)

Now we have defined Security Architecture and XSADF, we can look at the security activities that typically are performed. Our approach how to deal with these activities is described.

2.3 Security Activities

Now we are going to look at the security activities in the SDLC. The following security activities are the most relevant:

- Define Security Architecture
  - Select Security Requirements
  - Select Business Assets
  - Define concrete Business Assets
  - Select Security Architecture Assets
  - Define concrete Security Architecture Assets
  - Select Security Controls
- Perform Architectural Risk Assessment
  - Relate threats/vulnerabilities to assets
  - Determine risks
  - Propose treatments to mitigate/reduce/transfer/accept risks
- Determine compliance
- Create security documentation

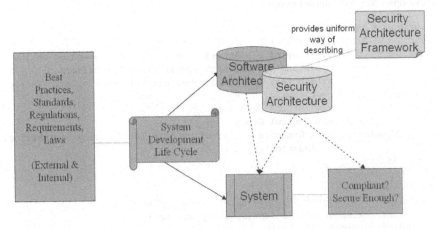

Fig. 2: The challenge for a Software Architect

The Software Architect works closely with the product owner to ensure proper alignment with the business needs, and to determine priorities for the security related activities.

In Figure 5 the challenge for a Software Architect regarding Software Security is graphically depicted. The Security Architecture provides structure to help him focus on security.

In the following sections some of these security activities are described in more detail to show the usage of XSADF.

Define Security Architecture

The Software Architect needs to define the Security Architecture for the system he is working on. It is the task of the product owner and Software Architect together to make sure that the relevant security requirements are selected and defined in XSADF using a Profile. This can be an existing Profile that is already defined in the Security Architecture Framework, but it might be that some requirements are not relevant for the system under consideration. In this case a new Profile needs to be defined in which those requirements are not selected.

Security Controls can be selected from the complete set of controls defined to form a specific baseline for the system under consideration.

Assets forming the Security Architecture can be linked to a Security Control. A Security Control can be linked to a Security Requirement.

In the following example, part of a Security Architecture is depicted. The ← points to ids that are used to refer to other elements in the Security Architecture.

Begin (example Defining Security Architecture)

```
<!- NIST SP 800-53 Security Controls
<cdf:Rule id="SC-7-Rule">
   <cdf:title>Boundary Protection</cdf:title>
   <cdf:description>The information system monitors and controls communications
                   at the external boundary of the information system and at key
                   internal boundaries within the system.</cdf:description>
   <cdf:reference>specific.Base_filter_001_m</cdf:reference>
   <cdf:reference>specific.Base_filter_007_m</cdf:reference>
   <cdf:reference>specific.Base_filter_008_m</cdf:reference>
</cdf:Rule>

<!-Ericsson Security Requirements
<cdf:Rule id="Base_filter_001_m" severity="high">
   <cdf:title>Ability to Filter Traffic</cdf:title>
   <cdf:description>The node shall provide a means to filter IP packets on any
                   interface implementing IP. The node shall provide a mechanism
                   to allow the specification of the action to be taken when a
                   filter rule matches.</cdf:description>
   <cdf:reference>IETF RFC 3871 Operational Security Requirements for Large
                  Internet Service Provider (ISP) IP Network
                  Infrastructure</cdf:reference>
   <cdf:reference>WCDMA MRS03-R2370</cdf:reference>
   <cdf:rationale>Packet filtering is important because it provides a basic means
                  of implementing policies that specify which traffic is allowed
                  and which is not. It also provides a basic tool for responding
                  to malicious traffic situations. Examples: Access control lists
                  that allow filtering based on protocol and/or source/destination
                  address and or source/destination port would be one example.
                  Actions like "permit" (allow the traffic), "reject" (drop with
                  appropriate notification to sender), and "drop" (drop with no
                  notification to sender) etc must be possible to be defined.
                  </cdf:rationale>
</cdf:Rule>
```

```
<!—Security Architecture Assets
<cdf:Group id="BoundaryProtectionDevices">
    <cdf:title>Boundary Protection Devices</cdf:title>
    <cdf:description>Devices protecting the system boundary.</cdf:description>
    <cdf:Asset id="firewall_abstract" level="technology"
               category="hardware/software" abstract="true">
      <cdf:title>Firewall</cdf:title>
      <cdf:reference>SC-7-Rule</cdf:reference>
    </cdf:Asset>
</cdf:Group>
```

End (example)

Asset Firewall has a reference to Security Control SC-7-Rule, which in turn has references to related Security Requirements Base_filter_001_m, Base_filter_007_m and Base_filter_008_m. These references are used for compliance checking.

Perform Architectural Risk Assessment
During the System Development Life Cycle an Architectural Risk Assessment needs to be performed. As you can see the Security Architecture is also used to document the results of the Architectural Risk Assessment by introducing assets, and relate the associated risks to security requirements and implemented Security Controls.

The Security Architecture Framework includes per asset known Threats, Vulnerabilities and Security Controls (see Figure 6). These can be used during the risk assessment as input to discover security related risks. During the risk assessment, risks are identified for the key assets. Each risk indicates (if applicable) a possible threat and vulnerability, and available or planned Security Controls to mitigate or reduce that risk.

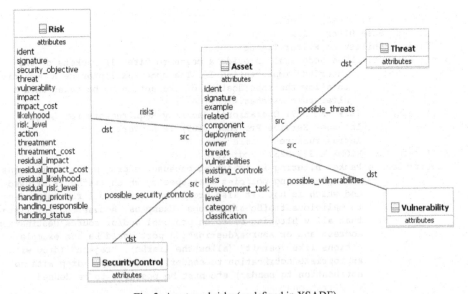

Fig. 3: Assets and risks (as defined in XSADF)

Note: Since XCCDF is set up as kind of hardening language, it is also possible to define hardening actions to be performed on a system in XSADF, since it is based on XCCDF. These hardening actions are then directly related to a Security Control for which a risk has been identified. Being able to capture hardening activities in the same format as used for the Security Architecture indicates that our approach is flexible and able to support additional security activities.

In the following example, part of the results of an Architectural Risk Assessment is depicted.

Begin (example Architectural Risk Assessment)

```
<cdf:Group id="Files">
  <cdf:title>File</cdf:title>
  <cdf:description>The primary reason for listing file information is to identify
               the application critical files and their required file
               permissions. Especially important is to identify configuration
               files, log files and files with requirements for special access
               permissions (set-uid, world writable etc).</cdf:description>
  <cdf:Group id="ConfigurationFiles">
    <cdf:title>Configuration Files</cdf:title>
    <cdf:Asset id="password_file_abstract" level="application"
               category="information" abstract="true">
      <cdf:title>Password File</cdf:title>
      <cdf:description>A password file contains passwords.</cdf:description>
      <cdf:owner>System Administrator</cdf:owner>
      <cdf:threats idref="password_file_abstract_threats">capec-2 capec-7
               </cdf:threats>
      <cdf:vulnerabilities idref="password_file_abstract_vulnerabilities">
                           cwe-320 cwe-178 </cdf:vulnerabilities>
      <cdf:existing_controls idref="password_file_abstract_controls">AC-6-Rule
                           </cdf:existing_controls>
    </cdf:Asset>
  </cdf:Group>
</cdf:Group>
```

End (example)

Looking at the example above:
- Known threats are referring to CAPEC™ (capec-2 (Inducing Account Lockout), and capec-7 (Blind SQL Injection)).
- Known vulnerabilities are referring to CWE™ (cwe-320 (Key Management Errors), and cwe-178 (Failure to Resolve Case Sensitivity)).
- An existing control to mitigate the risk is AC-6-Rule (Least Privilege).

2.4 Experiences Using this Approach

The approach described has been developed during the security work for a project within Ericsson. Although tool support is still limited we already experienced a positive impact. The fact that all security related information is stored in one central place is beneficial. Having the results of the Architectural Risk Assessment at hand makes it more easy to use a risk-based approach when developing the system, since the information is constantly visible while defining the architecture.

3 Conclusion

Using a formal XML-based description format to document the Security Architecture leads to a less ambiguous description of the system. Just using text often leads to more prosaic text which can be interpreted in different ways. If done properly we also achieve common terminology which enables easier communication and discussion over a Security Architecture.

A Security Architecture described in our proposed XML format makes it possible to use tools to assess the Security Architecture. An example of such use is generating a statement of compliance towards a selected set of security requirements.

Using a Security Architecture also enables a structure to measure software security, for instance by measuring the level of compliance to requirements defined by a certain security standard.

Using the Security Architecture Framework leads to a uniform way of documenting a Security Architecture which enables unambiguous communication around "security by design".

The following benefits are most notable:

- Having all relevant information in one place, in one format, and using consistent terminology.
- Keeping track of the interdependencies and relations in all this information through cross-references.
- Being able to use tools to browse or search through this information or produce selections from it, e.g. all information pertaining to the compliance with a certain set of guidelines, or relevant for a certain security requirement.

To conclude, we believe that our idea for a more structured approach is a major step forward to make „security by design" workable in industrial practice. We realize that more work is still needed to develop tools that support and extend the approach, but this will evolve when the approach is used in more projects. Also more work needs to be spent on the Security Architecture Framework in order to get an agreed framework that can be used by several projects/organizations. In the end standardization of the proposed XML format should be investigated if we want this practice to become a standard for communicating the security aspects of a system using a Security Architecture.

References

[HoLi06]   Howard, Michael – Lipner, Steve: The Security Development Lifecycle. Microsoft, 2006, ISBN: 978-0-735-62214-2.

[McGr06]   McGraw, Gary: Software Security Building Security In, Addison-Wesley, 2006, ISBN: 0-321-35670-5

[KSS+08]   Kissel, Richard – Stine, Kevin – Scholl, Matthew – Rossman, Hart – Fahlsing, Jim – Gulick, Jessica: NIST Special Publication 800-64, Revision 2, Security Considerations in the Information System Development Life Cycle, NIST, November 2008, http://csrc.nist.gov/publications/nistpubs/800-64-Rev2/SP800-64-Revision2.pdf

[Opst08]   van Opstal, Ton: A Structured Approach to Software Security, Introducing the Extensible Security Architecture Description Format. Master Thesis TiasNimbas Business School, November 2008

[RKJ+07]   Ross, Ron – Katzke, Stu – Johnson, Arnold – Swanson, Marianne – Stoneburner, Gary – Rogers, George: NIST Special Publication 800-53, Revision 2, Recommended Security Controls for Federal Information Systems, NIST, December 2007 http://csrc.nist.gov/publications/nistpubs/800-53-Rev2/sp800-53-rev2-final.pdf

[ZiQu08]   Ziring, Neal – Quinn, Stephen D.: Specification for the Extensible Configuration Checklist Description Format (XCCDF) Version 1.1.4, NIST, January 2008 http://csrc.nist.gov/publications/nistir/ir7275r3/NISTIR-7275r3.pdf

Using Compilers to Enhance Cryptographic Product Development

E. Bangerter[1] · M. Barbosa[2] · D. Bernstein[3] · I. Damgård[4]
D. Page[5] · J. I. Pagter[6] · A.-R. Sadeghi[7] · S. Sovio[8]

[1]Bern University of Applied Sciences
endre.bangerter@jdiv.org

[2]Departamento de Informática, Universidade do Minho
mbb@di.uminho.pt

[3]Department of Computer Science, University of Illinois at Chicago
djb@cr.yp.to

[4]Department of Computer Science, Aarhus University
ivan@cs.au.dk

[5]Department of Computer Science, University of Bristol
page@cs.bris.ac.uk

[6]Centre for IT Security, Alexandra Instituttet A/S
jakob.i.pagter@alexandra.dk

[7]System Security Group, Ruhr-University Bochum
ahmad.sadeghi@trust.rub.de

[8]Nokia Research Center, Helsinki
sampo.sovio@nokia.com

Abstract

Developing high-quality software is hard in the general case, and it is significantly more challenging in the case of cryptographic software. A high degree of new skill and understanding must be learnt and applied without error to avoid vulnerability and inefficiency. This is often beyond the financial, manpower or intellectual resources available. In this paper we present the motivation for the European funded CACE (Computer Aided Cryptography Engineering) project. The main objective of CACE is to provide engineers (with limited or no expertise in cryptography) with a toolbox that allows them to generate robust and efficient implementations of cryptographic primitives. We also present some preliminary results already obtained in the early stages of this project, and discuss the relevance of the project as perceived by stakeholders in the mobile device arena.

N. Pohlmann, H. Reimer, W. Schneider (Editors): Securing Electronic Business Processes, Vieweg (2009), 291-301

1 Introduction

Bjarne Stroustrup, inventor of the C++ programming language, has been quoted as stating that "our civilisation runs on software'" and therefore, by implication, the engineers who create it. From the perspective of other industries this might seem like a wild claim. However, the increasing ubiquity of computing in our lives somewhat justifies the statement. Beyond software running on desktop and laptop computers, we are increasingly dependent on huge numbers of devices that have permeated society in less obvious ways. Examples include software running on embedded computers within consumer products such as automobiles and televisions, and software running in a mobile context such as on smart-cards within mobile phones and chip-and-pin credit cards. All of these examples form systems on which we routinely depend; from domestic tasks to communication, from banking to travel, computers and software are ingrained into almost everything we do.

However, as put by Computer Scientist Donald Knuth in one of the standard textbooks on the subject, "software is hard". Given our dependency on said software, the implication of this hardness is a significant problem. For example, a 1994 report [Stan94] published by consultants at The Standish Group paints a bleak picture of software quality. They found that 31% of software engineering projects were cancelled before they were completed; only 16% were deployed on time, on budget and with the full set of originally specified features. A 2002 study [Nist02] by the National Institute for Standards and Technology (NIST) estimated that software errors cost $59 billion annually. High profile examples litter the trade press, including the UK government's attempt to modernise the National Health Service (NHS) computer system in a scheme that is now predicted to cost more than double the initial estimate of £6 billion; complexity and under specification are cited as key sticking points.

Moreover, computing devices are increasingly used to store, communicate and process security sensitive information. This fact puts the field of cryptography, a key enabling science for such applications, at the heart of IT-related product development. The design and implementation of cryptographic hardware and software components often draws on skills from mathematics, computer science and electrical engineering. This fact presents a major hurdle to software engineering, and further exacerbates the so-called software crisis. In a nutshell, while developing high-quality software is hard in the general case, this is *significantly* more challenging in the case of cryptographic software.

In particular, when implementing cryptographic software, a high degree of new skill and understanding must be learnt and applied without error to avoid vulnerability and inefficiency. This is often beyond the financial, manpower or intellectual resources available; even if engineers can learn all the required skills, human nature dictates that errors and oversights will inevitably occur. In an ideal world, the engineer would be assisted somehow. For example, the development of non-cryptographic hardware and software components is facilitated by a design flow or tool-chain (e.g., compilers and debuggers) which automates tasks normally performed by experienced, highly skilled humans. However, in both cases the tools are generic in that they seldom provide specific support for a particular domain. Indeed, current language and compiler technology does not do an adequate job of supporting an engineer who writes mathematically rich, security and performance sensitive cryptographic software. Moreover, the fact that a variety of cryptographic solutions can be understood by few experts only has a further consequence: some business models with sophisticated security and privacy requirements are not implemented *at all* in practice, even though said solutions provide the appropriate basis.

In this paper we present the motivation for the European funded CACE (Computer Aided Cryptography Engineering) project, which aims to fill the technological gap outlined above, as well as some preliminary results already obtained in the early stages of this project. The main objective of CACE is to provide engineers (with limited or no expertise in cryptography) with a tool-box that allows them to generate robust and efficient implementations of cryptographic primitives. The tool-box provides new cryptography-aware high-level programming languages and compilers aimed at (i) automatic translation from natural specifications, (ii) automatic security awareness (e.g., to avoid some side-channel attacks), analysis and correction, and (iii) automatic optimisation for diverse platforms. In Section 2 we further expand on motivation and present real-world examples of how and why the implementation of cryptographic software can, and often does, go wrong. We also show that important achievements by the cryptographic community, which are often perceived as being of theoretical interest only, are actually realisable with the appropriate tools and can have a high impact in practical applications. In Section 3 we describe the CACE project and how it tackles the stated challenges. We describe the rationale behind the development of the CACE tool-box, the challenges that the project faces, and the current status of ongoing work. We conclude our paper in Section 4 with a discussion of the potential added value of the CACE toolbox to industry, as perceived by stakeholders in the mobile device arena.

2 Motivation

Cryptography often goes wrong. An engineer who implements cryptographic software is faced with hurdles which do not exist in other areas. Firstly, the engineer is expected to be expert in an extremely broad and fast moving field, which touches areas of mathematics, computer science and even electrical engineering. The assumption that such a rich body of research can be absorbed and applied without error is tenuous for even an expert engineer. Secondly, the programming tools presented to the developer to assist the construction of software within this specific context are relatively rudimentary. This implies that cryptographic software implementations are potentially more error-prone than other software components, a dangerous state of affairs for security-critical applications which we will illustrate with some real-world examples.

OpenSSL is an open-source implementation of the Secure Sockets Layer (SSL) and Transport Layer Security (TLS) protocols. The core library (written in the C programming language) implements basic cryptographic functionality, and provides various utility functions; wrappers allowing the use of the OpenSSL library in a variety of computer languages are available. Versions of OpenSSL are also available for many platforms, which justifies its widespread use and importance within modern e-commerce work-flows, particularly in realisation of secure HTTP connections. OpenSSL is an interesting case-study which affords some pertinent examples:

- An OpenSSL security advisory[1] states that due to "a coding error", the random number generator was not implemented correctly. More specifically, the memory checking tool Valgrind reported that part of OpenSSL was incorrectly accessing uninitialised data. A call to a hash function was incorrectly commented out in an effort to solve the problem and, as a result, OpenSSL became insecure.

- Another vulnerability was uncovered when OpenSSL signature verification was found to be quite lax in the sense that mis-formulated control-flow logic allowed malformed signatures to be reported as valid[2].

- A further security advisory[3] states that a time-based side-channel attack is possible on the RSA implementation in particular versions of OpenSSL. Although correct configuration of the library would avoid the problem, the "opt-in" nature of countermeasures means that they are often not used (potentially since they represent a performance overhead). We refer the interested reader to [JoKo07] for more information on OpenSSL side-channel vulnerabilities.

---

1 http://www.openssl.org/news/secadv_20071129.txt
2 http://www.openssl.org/news/secadv_20090107.txt
3 http://www.openssl.org/news/secadv_20030317.txt

Cryptographic failures are not limited to open-source software. A prominent example is the widely used MiFare Classic system, a member of the product family from NXP Semiconductors (formerly Philips Semiconductors). According to NXP more than 1 billion MiFare cards have been sold, and there are around 200 million MiFare Classic tags in use around the world covering 85% of the contact-less smart card market. In [GGM+08] the security mechanisms (e.g., the authentication protocol and the symmetric cipher) of the MiFare Classic were reverse engineered and shown to be breakable in under one second of computation.

Performance compromising security. Pressure on developers to improve the performance of their cryptographic implementations is often the underlying cause for the occurrence of vulnerabilities. Two examples of this are:

- In 2004, Nguyen [Nguy04] described a now famous attack on GPG (version 1.2.3), an open-source implementation of the OpenPGP standard. Partly as a result of demands for efficiency, certain sections of the source code were mis-optimised: the size of security-critical parameters was reduced, which meant computation using them was faster. However, this reduced size also allowed attackers to compute GPG private keys in a few seconds of computation.

- Cryptographic researchers have shown that 1024-bit RSA is breakable by botnets, large companies, etc. For example, at Crypto 2003, Shamir (the "S" in RSA) and Tromer [ShTr03] described an attack machine on the scale of $ 10 M that could factor a 1024-bit RSA key in one year. RSA Laboratories and NIST recommended moving to 2048-bit RSA by the end of the decade. However, for the sake of performance, most web-security software continues to use 1024-bit keys by default.

In both cases, lack of understanding on the part of the engineer is a critical failing. However, it is also clear that the same engineer was badly supported by development tools: they were unable to automate the optimisation processes safely, or check for security vulnerabilities for example.

The additional hurdle of physical security. Side-channel attacks are an additional threat which makes life even harder for engineers. These attacks are, in some sense, *unfair* to the engineer: a functionally correct implementation may still be vulnerable to attacks launched at the physical level. The basic idea is for the attacker to passively observe execution, and infer details about the internal device state from the features that occur; information is said to "leak" through the resulting side-channel. An attack typically consists of an observation phase, which provides the attacker with profiles of execution, and an analysis phase which recovers otherwise secret values from the profiles. Any embedded or mobile device (e.g., smart-card) that is carried into and used within an adversarial environment is an attractive target; in this case, a local attacker might gain physical access to the device. However, it is important to note that remote attack (e.g., of an e-commerce server over a network) is often viable. Although the general concept is older, cryptographic side-channels came to the fore after seminal work by Kocher et al. who describe attacks based on timing variation [Koch96] and power consumption [KoJJ99]; this was later extended to consider electromagnetic emission [AARR02]. More recently, a range of micro-architectural side-channels have emerged that focus on standard processor components; examples include cache [Bern05] and branch prediction [AcSK07] systems. Again, one can easily point to concrete examples of this challenge being too much for an engineer unsupported by suitable development tools:

- In 2008, Eisenbarth et al [EKM+08] mounted a side-channel attack against KeeLoq, a type of RFID device used for car access control by companies such as Chrysler, GM and Volvo. By observing only a few uses of a key fob, an attacker can duplicate the key.

- In 2008, Halderman et al. [HSH+08] describe a "cold boot" attack based on the physical characteristics of memory: contrary to intuition, memory retains state for sometime after being powered-off. The attack capitalises on this feature to attack popular full disk encryption mechanisms such as the BitLocker (found in Windows Vista), recovering key material and negating the security such mechanisms afford.

Lack of implementation of high-level primitives. Cryptographic research has generated many useful results that, in theory, allow the implementation of applications and business models with very sophisticated security requirements. Prominent examples are secure multi-party computation (MPC) and zero-knowledge proof of knowledge (ZKPoK) protocols. MPC allows different parties, who have conflicting interests and each hold secret values, to perform computation involving said values without revealing them. MPC is useful for many security-critical applications such as electronic voting and various types of auctions. ZKPoK allows a party to prove to another party that it knows a secret value, without revealing anything about the value itself. ZKPoK is a crucial building block for various privacy preserving systems, such as privacy friendly authentication; also, ZKPoK is used as a sub-protocol within MPC.

Despite the range and importance of the applications they enable, MPC and ZKPoK are unfortunately complex cryptographic primitives; this means they are currently accessible only to specialists with substantial expertise in the respective field. As a result, we have not yet experienced a widespread usage of these primitives and the novel paradigms they support remain underutilised.

3 Computer Aided Cryptographic Engineering

3.1 Implementing Low-Level Cryptography

Implementation of cryptography at a low-level typically focuses on "building blocks", or primitives, that support higher-level schemes; examples include hash functions such as SHA-1, block ciphers such as DES and AES, and arithmetic operations such as modular multiplication. Within this context, the quality of an implementation is dictated by a careful trade-off between efficiency (e.g., execution speed and memory footprint) and security.

Performance. For (at least) two reasons, the efficiency of cryptographic primitives is an important issue within many applications. Firstly, many primitives represent an inherently expensive workload comprised of computationally-bound, highly numeric kernels. Secondly, said primitives are often required in high-volume or high-throughput applications; examples include encryption of VPN traffic and full-disk encryption, both of which represent vital components in e-business.

For an engineer, the first challenge is to understand the high-level specification of the primitive they intend to implement; often this alone demands specialist training. The next challenge is understanding and effectively utilising the diverse range of potential platforms. On one hand, standard desktop or server platforms may be the target. Although such platforms appear well understood, in this setting efficient implementation can still be difficult: the programming model is often complex (e.g., cache memories, out-of-order execution) and include exotic features (e.g., multiple cores, vector instruction sets). On the other hand, embedded or mobile platforms (e.g., smart-cards, mobile phones and PDAs) may be the target. In this case, the platform is vastly less able: it will be much more constrained in terms of computation and storage. The engineer must find an efficient way to map a complex, high-level specification of some primitive onto the characteristics of a demanding target platform, potentially using a low-level programming languages and tools. Both the semantic gap between specification and implementation, and the skills gap between cryptography and engineering are vastly problematic.

Security. The specification of cryptographic primitives and schemes are often "proved" secure; there are a variety of proof methodologies which typically reason about the attacker within a mathematical model. However, once such a primitive or scheme has been deployed, there is potential for physical attack: the attacker is free to utilise any aspect of the implementation itself to their advantage. Approaches to defend against physical attacks are increasingly well understood on a case-per-case basis. However, it is obvious that a trade-off exists between performance and security; reasoning about and implementing suitable countermeasures while limiting their computational overhead is an ongoing research challenge.

Towards a solution. The CACE tool-box includes three components which address the issues of cryptographic implementation at this level. CAO and *qhasm* are two domain-specific languages and associated compilation tools; CAO operates in a roughly similar way to a traditional compiler, and *qhasm* as a traditional assembler. Both languages support a rich set of mathematical types and operations on them: their goal is to permit the description of cryptographic primitives in a natural form, and to automate analysis and transformation phases which translate them into an efficient and secure implementation. Although CAO and *qhasm* can be used as stand-alone tools, the aim is to expose them to other components in the CACE tool-box via a fixed interface. This interface is a library called NaCl, which includes stubs for cryptographic primitives and communication.

3.2 Implementing High-Level Cryptography

Secure multi-party computations (MPC) and zero-knowledge proof of knowledge (ZKPoK) protocols are high-level cryptographic primitives that are about to make their way from the more theoretically oriented research community into real world applications. These novel primitives are exciting since they enable novel business models and applications which are not otherwise feasible. ZKPoK, for instance, are a key-enabler for privacy preserving systems such as anonymous authentication systems. MPC are the foundation for many novel variants of trading and bidding platforms.

MPC and ZKPoK were believed to be too inefficient and, loosely speaking, too obscure for practical use. However, work in recent years has shown that these concerns and objections are not justifieFor example, ZKPoK are the main primitive underlying the Direct Anonymous Attestation (DAA) protocol [BrCC04] specified by the Trusted Computing group (TCG) for the Trusted Platform Module (TPM) [TPM1.2]. Current realizations of TPMs are cryptographic chips embedded into millions of computer platforms (i.e., desktops, laptops and servers) and shipped by almost all major vendors. Another example is the identity mixer anonymous credential system [CaHe02], which was released by IBM into the Eclipse Higgins project, an open source effort dedicated to developing software for "user-centric" identity management.

Today, due to rapid development of the available computational power and fast communication networks, MPC protocols can be deployed in practice. Especially in the two-party setting highly efficient implementations are available [LiPS08]. The two-party setting is very common in client-server applications over the internet and allows for many privacy-enhancing services such as medical diagnostics, secure data classification, secure face-recognition, or privacy-preserving credit checking.

On January 14, 2008, the first large-scale and practical application of MPC with more than two parties was launched in Denmark to auction production licenses for sugar beets. The auction involved 1229 bidders and the computation among three standard laptops lasted about 30 minutes [BCD+09]. Since then, further steps have been taken towards extended practical use. A commercial company has been formed (http://www.partisia.com) and in 2009 the sugar beet auction will run for the third successive time, while efforts are being made towards using MPC in other similar auctions. Also, in another application of the same MPC platform, a so-called "lowest unique bid" auction has been implemented. This has been used several times to showcase the MPC technology by auctioning of iPods to the visitors of the Danish "Technology Caravan" (http://www.teknologikaravanen.dk).

New challenges. These novel primitives are subject to the same concerns (with regard to the efficiency and security of their implementations) as the already established primitives discussed in the previous section. Furthermore, there are also challenges that are specific to these primitives. In fact, MPC and ZKPoK each refer to a class of protocols and not to concrete instances of protocols. That is, when using these primitives, an engineer needs to go through the following steps:

1. Formulate the goal of a protocol, i.e., specify what expression shall be proved in a ZKPoK or the function to be evaluated in a MPC.

2. Find an appropriate protocol instance that realizes the specified protocol goal set out in step 1, and implement that protocol.

3. Assert, by proving formally, that the protocol found in step 2 meets the required formal security properties of a MPC or a ZKPoK, respectively.

The first of the above steps is reasonably easy and intuitive since protocol goals typically arise naturally from the application context. However, it is important to note that finding an adequate protocol in the second step, as well as performing the formal security proofs in the last step, are far more difficult tasks. This difficulty means, in many cases, it is impossible for people who do not have extensive expertise and intricate knowledge of the respective protocols to carry out steps 2 and 3. As a result, neither ZK-PoK nor MPC are used widely, and the unique potential of these primitives remains under-utilized.

Towards a solution. On a high-level, our approach is to assist engineers in the completion of the three steps outlined above by providing appropriate components in the CACE tool-box (see Figure 1 for an overview). More precisely, to carry out step 1, we provide domain specific-languages that allow non-experts to precisely yet intuitively specify the goal of ZKPoK or MPC protocols, respectively. Given such specifications as inputs, corresponding compilers automatically find appropriate protocols and generate their implementations. As such, the compilers take away the burden of step 2 from protocol designers. Similarly, we are researching tools that semi-automatically perform the formal verification in step 3.

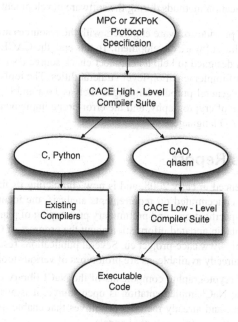

Fig. 1: The CACE tool-box

The protocol implementations produced are either described in existing programming languages (e.g., C or Python), or in the CACE domain specific languages CAO and *qhasm* described in the previous section. The clear advantage of the latter case is that the implementations inherit the code security and efficiency features provided by CAO and *qhasm*.

The challenge is clearly to conceive and implement the compilers, which need to absorb a great deal of protocol design expertise. To this end, we intend to analyze and pick the most appropriate existing protocol design and composition techniques and, when necessary, to advance the current state of the art of MPC and ZKPoK.

3.3 High Assurance Through Formal Methods

An essential part of any software development process is verification that an implementation meets a pre-specified set of requirements. Requirements can be functional (i.e., define what a program is meant to do) or non-functional (i.e., constrain the way in which a program calculates its results); security policies are typically non-functional properties that ensure that an implementation does *only* what it is meant to do. For example, the implementation of a digital signature algorithm should not only compute the digital signature correctly, but also be trusted not to leak (explicitly or implicitly through some covert channel) the value of the secret key used.

The level of assurance that is placed on a software implementation can be increased using a wide variety of techniques, including quality control procedures and extensive testing during development. However, formal methods are generally recognized as being the ideal tools for achieving the highest degrees of assurance since they enable the construction of mathematically sound proofs that attest the validity of developers' claims. An important example of the relevance of formal methods is the requirements imposed by the Common Criteria standards [CCRA06] for implementations seeking certification at the highest levels of assurance. Indeed, for assurance levels 6 and 7, the Common Criteria *mandates* the use of formal models and verification methods during the software development process.

The CACE project aims to provide software engineers with the resources necessary to incorporate formal methods in cryptographic software development. To this end, the CACE tool-box will include a set of formal verification tools designed to help an engineer check source code for implementation errors, and rule-out the existence of implementation-level vulnerabilities. The tools follow the same approach used in other scenarios for general-purpose languages such as Java and C. However, they are geared towards the specific domain of cryptography, and the error-prone implementation of low-level cryptographic primitives in the CAO language.

3.4 CACE Status Report

The CACE project commenced in early 2008, and is now completing its first year of activities. Work carried out on the project concentrated on requirements analysis, the identification of research challenges, language and tool specifications, and preliminary prototyping of planned tool-box components. The interested reader can obtain updated information about the progress of CACE project activities via the project web-site at http://www.cace-project.eu. Several publications resulting from research activities within the project are already available, as are prototypes of various tool-box components:

- The first release of cryptographic components of the NaCl library can be found at http://nacl. cace-project.eu. The NaCl implementation is open-source, it is available for use without any licensing restrictions, and already includes primitives that enable the implementation of high-performance and high-assurance secure channels.

- An initial version of the ZKPoK compiler has been developed and will be published as an open source project soon. The current version can already be used to automatically implement a large number of protocols found in the literature, such as various group-signature or ring-signature schemes. We currently are adding support for protocols in hidden order groups, which will allow to automatically generate the protocols used in the DAA protocol.

- A framework and compiler for the specification and automatic generation of two-party MPC protocols with semi-private functions is available as an open source project at http://www.trust.rub. de/FairplaySPF. This framework allows a service provider (server) to partially hide the evaluated functionality from the customer (client). This is necessary in many cases to protect the intellectual property of the service provider (evaluated function) while protecting the customer's privacy (data containing sensitive information) at the same time. The framework allows to specify and automatically generate secure protocols for many new privacy-friendly services such as those mentioned in Section 3.2.

- Viff (Virtual ideal Functonality Framework) is an open source framework, written in Python, for doing general Multiparty Computation, and is available at http://viff.dk. Using Viff one can perform secure function evaluation of arbitrary functions in different trust models using a range of different multiparty computation protocols. Using operator overloading, Viff allows the programmer to express a desired secure computation directly as standard arithmetic without worrying about which underlying protocol is used, or how communication is scheduled. Viff is designed so it can be easily extended with new protocols. The current version includes standard protocols based on Shamir secret-sharing plus some more recent work for efficient comparison. CACE plans to add a range of new protocol implementations, including some that are developed within the project

On top of Viff, a new programming language PySMCL will be developed, together with a tool for static analysis that will help the programmer spot security problems.

During the first quarter of 2009, the first deliverables of the CACE project were made available on-line. These include a comprehensive report on security properties which are applicable to cryptographic software and therefore relevant to the CACE tool-box, full specifications of CACE languages and tools, and early prototypes of tool-box components.

4 Benefits for Industry: The Mobile Example

Use of open innovation has been fruitful within research and development activities, especially in industries connected to mobile computing platforms. Opening the platform and/or parts of the innovation process means that a larger community can contribute to products and services, reduces manufacturer dependence on specific components (e.g., embedded processors and operating systems), and makes it easier to integrate tailored solutions for specific market demands. However, competition within this industry has traditionally been very tough. From an engineering perspective, any new product or feature must i) have a minimal time-to-market delay, ii) not consume unnecessary resource (e.g., battery life, computational effort or (secure) storage), iii) cope with the expense of updating deployed devices, and iv) contain as few flaws as possible.

Any development process that yields an implementation of high-quality can be a significant help in mitigating pre- and post-deployment cost and thus maximise success in the marketplace. This implies emphasising efficiency, modularity and reuse at all levels.

The security of hardware and software plays a significant role in this industry. Various stakeholders contribute to mobile platforms, many of whom have assets that they want to protect. For example, telecoms operators subsidise mobile phones and therefore require subsidy-locking mechanisms that make this business model sustainable. Companies that provide digital content to said mobile phones often want to set DRM policies for content access and consumption. Also, end-users rely on their devices in their daily lives and do not want to succumb to, for example, virus infection or allow thieves to easily extract data from a stolen phone. A crucial precondition for meeting all of these market requirements is to have adequate platform security, which in turn crucially and necessarily depends on cryptography.

Platform security can be seen as the basis of trust that makes it possible to build secure real-world solutions. Two well known standards for platform security are the Trusted Platform Module (TPM) [TPM1.2] and Mobile Trusted Module (MTM) [EkKy07]. The latter is designed to meet additional industry-specific requirements; for example, the MTM module can verify signatures from different parties without common trust, thereby allowing different stakeholders to specify policies on how a device should behave. The problem is, at least in their current specification, that the TPM and MTM do not provide the large selection of cryptographic functions and primitives that are needed for real-world solutions. Even if they did, it is necessary to allow a mechanism for algorithm agility whereby existing cryptographic algorithms are updated or new algorithms deployed. It is therefore necessary to have cryptographic implementations that are not part of secure hardware solutions; such implementations are mainly software-based even though some primitives may derive benefit from accelerators commonly included in processors that support mobile phones. If the cryptographic primitives include vulnerabilities, or if they are misused, this may invalidate *all* security mechanisms that are built on top. For example, successful utilisation of an MTM requires flawless, and properly used cryptographic primitives; even when cryptographic algorithms are implemented by experts this is hard to fully guarantee. An illustrative example of this is the vulnerability of the DSA verification in OpenSSL described in Section 2.

The CACE project is developing a tool-box that eases the effort of developing high-quality secure software. For example, the high abstraction level provided by CAO enables the fast development of high-quality secure software; when CAO and *qhasm* have been successfully integrated, even non-expert users can develop secure implementations with excellent performance. Since the CACE toolbox is targeted to the non-expert engineers, it is even more crucial to apply verification to the results; the examples in Section 2 show that the importance of testing cannot be over-emphasised. The CACE tool-box will offer tools for the formal verification and validation of the code that is written with other CACE tools. The expected results of the CACE project are therefore very interesting and useful to mobile device and platform vendors. These vendors continuously implement cryptographic algorithms and protocols for new device security features, communication protocols and services. Through the promise of minimal implementation and testing effort, their resources can be put to optimal use without sacrificing the quality of the end result; ultimately this affords any new product or feature a better chance of success in the marketplace.

References

[AARR02] D. Agrawal, B. Archambeault, J.R. Rao and P. Rohatgi. The EM Side-Channel(s). In Cryptographic Hardware and Embedded Systems (CHES), Springer-Verlag LNCS 2523, 29-45, 2002.

[AcSK07] O. Acriçmez, J-P. Seifert and Ç.K. Koç. Predicting Secret Keys via Branch Prediction. In Topics in Cryptology (CT-RSA), Springer-Verlag LNCS 4377, 225-242, 2007.

[BCD+09] P. Bogetoft, D. L. Christensen, I. Damgård, M. Geisler, T. Jakobsen, M. Krigaard, J. D. Nielsen, J. B. Nielsen, K. Nielsen, J. Pagter, M. Schwartzbach, T. Toft. Multiparty Computation Goes Live. To appear in Financial Cryptography and Data Security (FC), 2009. Available as ePrint Archive, Report 2008/069 at http://eprint.iacr.org.

[Bern05] D.J. Bernstein. Cache-timing attacks on AES. Available from: http://cr.yp.to/antiforgery/cachetiming-20050414.pdf

[BrCC04] E. Brickell, J. Camenisch, and L. Chen. Direct anonymous attestation. In Proc. ACM CCS 2004, pages 132-145. ACM, 2004.

[CaHe02] J. Camenisch and E. V. Herreweghen. Design and implementation of the idemix anonymous credential system. In Proc. ACM CCS 2002, pages 21{30. ACM, 2002. http://www.zurich.ibm.com/security/idemix/.

[CCRA06] The Common Criteria Recognition Agreement Members. Common criteria for information technology security evaluation. Available from: http://www.commoncriteriaportal.org/, September 2006.

[EkKy07] J.-E. Ekberg and M. Kylänpää. Mobile trusted module, 2007. NRC report NRC-TR-2007-015 http://research.nokia.com/files/NRCTR2007015.pdf.

[EKM+08] T. Eisenbarth, T. Kasper, A. Moradi, C. Paar, M. Salmasizadeh, M.T. Manzuri Shalmani. On the Power of Power Analysis in the Real World: A Complete Break of the KeeLoqCode Hopping Scheme. In Advances in Cryptology (CRYPTO), Springer-Verlag LNCS 5157, 203-220, 2008.

[GGM+08] F.D. Garcia, G. de Koning Gans, R. Muijrers, P. van Rossum, R. Verdult, R. Wichers Schreur and B. Jacobs. Dismantling MIFARE Classic. In European Symposium on Research in Computer Security (ESORICS), LNCS 5283, 97-117, 2008.

[HSH+08] J.A. Halderman, S.D. Schoen, N. Heninger, W. Clarkson, W. Paul, J.A. Calandrino, A.J. Feldman, J. Appelbaum and E.W. Felten. Lest We Remember: Cold Boot Attacks on Encryption Keys. In 17th USENIX Security Symposium, 45-60, 2008.

[JoKo07] M. Joye and Ç.K. Koç. Side-channel attacks against OpenSSL. In The Security Newsletter, 5:5-6, 2007.

[Koch96] P.C. Kocher. Timing Attacks on Implementations of Diffe-Hellman, RSA, DSS, and Other Systems. In Advances in Cryptology (CRYPTO), Springer-Verlag LNCS 1109, 104-113, 1996.

[KoJJ99] P.C. Kocher, J. Jaffe and B. Jun. Differential Power Analysis. In Advances in Cryptology (CRYPTO), Springer-Verlag LNCS 1666, 388-397, 1999.

[LiPS08] Y. Lindell, B. Pinkas, N. Smart. Implementing two-party computation effciently with security against malicious adversaries. In Security and Cryptography for Networks (SCN), Springer-Verlag LNCS 5229, 2-20, 2008.

[Nguy04] P.Q. Nguyen. Can We Trust Cryptographic Software? Cryptographic Flaws in GNU Privacy Guard v1.2.3. In Advances in Cryptology (EUROCRYPT), Springer-Verlag LNCS 3027, 555-570, 2004.

[Nist02] National Institute of Standards and Technology (NIST). Software Errors Cost U.S. Economy $59.5 Billion Annually. Available from: http://www.nist.gov/public_affairs/releases/n02-10.htm, 2002.

[ShTr03] A. Shamir, E. Tromer. Factoring Large Numbers with the TWIRL Device In Advances in Cryptology (Crypto), Springer-Verlag LNCS 2729, 1-26, 2003.

[Stan94] The Standish Group. The CHAOS Report. In http://www.standishgroup.com/, 1994.

[TPM1.2] Trusted Computing Group (TCG). TPM Specification Version 1.2 Revision 103. October 2006. http://www.trustedcomputinggroup.org/developers/trusted_platform_module/

Why Secure Coding is not Enough: Professionals' Perspective

John Colley

CISSP, (ISC)² EMEA
259-269 Old Marylebone Rd London, UK NW1 5RA
john.colley@isc2.org

Abstract

This paper outlines basic concepts the software community must consider if they are to develop applications and software that is secure. In particular it explains why the common practice of depending on secure coding mechanisms are not enough. Beginning with the drivers for more secure applications and software, and why it is now becoming such an issue, if not a new issue, it examines the problem in terms of why software and applications are delivered without security built in to them and goes on to discuss what we should be doing about it and how we need to go about it, sharing insights that have recently been accumulated by the new and growing community of Certified Secure Software Development Lifecycle professionals.

1 Why Secure Coding is Not Enough

My career of twenty years in software and systems development covers virtually every role you might think of as far as IT development is concerned. I started off in programming, moved into systems analysis, spent some time in business analysis, was a development project manager, an implementation project manager and held many other posts.

I also spent time in systems maintenance. It's in systems maintenance that you realise what bad programming much of the development community produces. You also realise that some of the problems you have to sort out have nothing to do with the programming but are due to missed requirements or bad systems design or architecture.

Today, there are a number of drivers that are causing a lot of big organisations to look at how they can deliver more secure software and applications. The two main drivers are both related to costs: The first is that it is estimated that 80% of all breaches are application-related. The estimated annual cost of this is thought to be about US $180 Billion a year[1]. The other aspect is that it is expensive to retrofit security after software or an application is delivered. IBM estimates that it is 30 to 100 times more expensive to retrofit security compared with building it in at the beginning.

So there are good financial reasons why we should be trying to make the software we develop, or that which we buy, or that which we use, more secure.

N. Pohlmann, H. Reimer, W. Schneider (Editors): Securing Electronic Business Processes, Vieweg (2009), 302-311

2 Why Now?

This situation has been around for some time, so why is it an imperative now? Part of the answer lies in the growing incidences of reputational damage. Companies that have not been featured in the media have started to ask themselves, or more accurately their IT and security managers, whether they are likely to. Since 2005, when the Privacy Rights Clearinghouse started collecting and publishing the Chronology of Data Breaches, not one year has gone by without noteworthy data breaches. By mid-2008, 226 million records had been reported to have been disclosed or breached. All of these instances have things in common: large numbers of records disclosed; consumer victims; and colossal punitive damages and fines levied on the organisations involved. Analysis of the cause of these and other data breaches invariably indicate one of, a combination of, or all of, the following:

- Insufficient protection of data during transit or at rest
- Insecure software designed, developed, and deployed (in built or third-party)
- Improper or inadequate configuration of software security controls
- Wireless and physical security breaches (thefts) leading to data compromise
- Lack of layered security defensive measures at the perimeter, hosts, and applications[1]

Software security issues featured in three of the five concerns listed above, yet it is not yet well understood across the development community.

Further, the infrastructure is generally secure, and the people who want to exploit the systems and software are moving up the ISO stack to the application layer. This aside, today's business environment dictates that in order to maintain a competitive advantage, organisations need open connected relationships. Sensitive customer and business data and the applications that house it are now available to privileged third parties, including contractors, outsourcers, business partners, supply chain nodes, and other business network users/stakeholders.

Finally, the use of software is ubiquitous; there is nothing that we do in our daily lives that doesn't usually use some software or other. End users and real customers are dependent on software and applications in their dealings with businesses. The need for better and more secure software and applications is a pressing problem that needs to be solved.

3 Why do we have this Problem?

In any development environment, be it software, building a house, making a motor car or anything else you might think of, there is always a trade-off between functionality, timescale and cost. You can't really change one of these without affecting one or more of the others. If you want more functionality, it will probably cost you more, and it will probably take longer. If you want to reduce the cost, then you can't usually do it without reducing the functionality. Given that IT projects have a track record of over-running and over-spending, then this problem is exacerbated.

At one of the organisations I worked at recently, they had a reputation for not overrunning on cost and for delivering on time. How did they do this? Simple, when they realised they were not meeting their targets, they simply re-scoped the project to see what functionality they could drop out. If they are specified when projects go through the rescoping process, security requirements and functionality are soft targets for dropping.

It's not just about requirements though. Usually, no testing is undertaken of the security requirements and functionality. Testing concentrates on whether the software or application delivers what it should deliver when it is operated correctly. Little time is spent testing situations where the system is not operated as it should be.

I've been in situations when I've pointed out a problem where an application would behave peculiarly under certain conditions – the response – "Why would anyone want to do that?"

Why then is secure coding not enough? The answer is pretty simple: not all of the breaches we see are caused by insecure code. Sure, buffer overflows and breaches caused by bad input may be caused by insecure coding, but quite often the breaches are caused by bad design or inadequate requirements definition or bad operation or bad maintenance processes.

Probably the best example of poor design causing problems is that of the way TCP makes a connection. A TCP connection is very much like a telephone call – we have to follow a protocol. You make a phone call, the person at the other end answers, and you make a response. TCP is exactly like that. In order to establish a connection, you have to send a SYN packet, the Server should then send you a SYN-ACK packet and the you send an ACK packet back and the connection is then open to receive traffic. In the well known denial of service attack that was first used around 1996, the attacker sent a number of SYN packets but never acknowledged the SYN-ACK that was returned. The result, rather like if when you make a phone call, the caller answers you don't say anything, and the person you have called hangs on the line for a while before hanging up. This was exactly what happens in the Denial of Service attack. The attacker floods the server with SYN packets leaving the server with so many half-opened connections that genuine users could not use the service. This is not a coding problem. It is a design problem.

Since software, like anything else that goes through a manufacturing process, is designed and developed to a blueprint, it is of paramount importance that security requirements are determined alongside the functional and business requirements. A preliminary risk assessment at this stage serves to determine the core security necessities of the software while a security plan should be generated as part of the design phase of the project to be revisited and adjusted as the development progresses. Other imperatives include:

- The business must be engaged during the requirements-gathering stage to address security aspects and aid in the understanding of the risk or protection requirements;
- Software developed must respect established policies and standards for the organisation and be compliant with audit requirements. Software requirements must also take into consideration the regulatory (legal), compliance, and privacy requirements at a local and international level;
- It is essential to develop the confidentiality, integrity, and availability (CIA) objectives of the software. Is the data or information open for viewing by all or should it be restricted (confidentiality requirement)? What are the factors that allow for authorised alterations, and who is allowed to make them (integrity requirement)? What is the accessibility of the software and what is the allowable downtime (availability requirement)?
- It is also necessary to consider the software Authentication aspect (proving of claims and identities), Authorization aspect (rights of the requestor), and Auditing aspect (accountability or building historical evidence).
- If software is to be bought, rather than built in-house, developing the a set of requirements for the procurement process is important.
- With the rise in access to inexpensive labor and outsourcing, software development projects have been exported to countries in the emerging/establishing marketplaces of Eastern Europe,

Russia, India, and China. Gone are the days when software development was contained within an organisation's perimeter, or even within the borders of a country.

- In the interest of business operations, demarcating network access devices such as the firewalls and demilitarised zones that separated the outside from the organisational assets start to slowly disappear, and the world has become one big, global development shop.

4 What Should we do About it?

At (ISC)^2, we have been looking at the whole area of secure software and application development, consulting the pioneers in this area over several years and have concluded that we have to consider security at every point in the systems development life cycle:

1. Requirements

   At the requirements stage, we should be considering what the security requirements are. Are there any specific business security requirements that need to be built in? Is the data being processed particularly sensitive? Are there any specific requirements that have to be met, for example, if the system is processing credit card information, in which case the Payment Cards Industry Digital Security Standards have to be incorporated into the requirements.

2. Design

   From an architectural design viewpoint, consideration must be given to how the security requirements can be designed into the system. Design should also consider how the system might be misused or what could go wrong, a perspective missed by developers that instinctively think about how to build rather than break things. We should also think about what are the main threats to the design of the system – SQL injection is a typical example of a threat to the design of the system.

3. Coding

   Coding is important, and we must make sure that the coding is robust and secure. There are many tools that can be used to check coding, and code inspection can also be used in the testing phase. The approach to coding should be to trust nothing and to be able to process anything:

   - Don't rely on the length of the input
   - Don't rely on the content of the input

   Input should be obtained a character at a time rather than a buffer at a time. The input should be validated as well as parsed.

4. Testing

   - Testing should test the security functionality along with the other functionality.
   - Testing should ensure that the system is resilient to attack.
   - And of course, testing should test incorrect operation of the system as well as correct operation.

5. Operations and maintenance

   It doesn't matter how well the system has been designed coded and tested. If it is operated insecurely, then all of that effort has been wasted. Maintenance presents two main problems. Firstly, any changes should be designed, coded and tested with the same rigour as the initial implementation. Secondly, it is important to have a good change management and source management system. Too many upgrades are released with errors that were corrected in previous versions resurfacing in the new version. This is because the corrections were not retrofitted back into the previous development environment or because flawed source code was deployed.

6. Disposal

Don't forget the disposal of the system. We have seen losses to reputation where data has been left on hard drives when systems have been replaced or updated. Make sure what has been left behind is considered both from a software and a hardware viewpoint.

An often cited example of the controls and issues that can be addressed at each phase are summarised in the following table taken from the US National Institute of Standards and Technology (NIST) system development lifecycle.[1]

Table 1: Security in the Systems Development Life Cycle

NIST Phase	SDLC Phase	Security Control
Initiation (Envisioning & Planning)	Requirements Gathering	Business Partner Engagement Identify Policies & Standards Identify Regulatory & Legal Requirements Identify Privacy Requirements Identify Compliance Requirements Develop C,I, A Goals & Objectives Develop Procurement Requirements Perform Risk Assessment
	Design	Use and Abuse Case Modeling Secure Design Review Secure Architecture Review Threat & Risk Modeling Generate Security Requirements Generate Security Test Cases
Acquisition/ Development	Development	Writing Secure Code Security Code Review Security Documentation
	Testing	Security Testing Redo Risk Assessment
Implementation/ Assessment	Deployment	Secure Installation Vulnerability Assessment Penetration Testing Security Certification & Accreditation Risk Adjustments
Operations/ Maintenance	Maintenance	Change Control Configuration Control Recertification & Reaccreditation Incident Handling Auditing Continuous Monitoring
Sunset (Disposition)	Disposal	Secure Archiving Data Sanitization Secure Disposal Learn and Educate

5 Guiding principles

There are a number of different development methodologies: The waterfall methodology is the most well known, but there are many others – Iterative development, Spiral development, Agile and many more. There are also a number of different languages that software and applications are written in – Java, Objective C, Python, .Net and many more. Should we develop a set of rules for one methodology and then adapt them for another? Or a set of coding standards for Java, another set for C++ and yet another set for .Net? This could be an approach at the code-specific level, but there is much broader need to recognise the principles of secure application and software development that apply across different development methodologies and different programming languages. This is no different than what we do with policies and standards. The top levels are usually control objectives or principles that are implemented on different platforms or situations. So we already use this approach in information security where we may have overall security controls that are implemented differently in a Windows environment than in a Unix environment.

Examples of design principles include things like "Economy of Mechanism", "Open Design" and "Least privilege". Many of these terms will be familiar to the reader. For example, "Economy of mechanism" means keeping the design simple and less complex – KISS or Keep it Simple Stupid. This can be implemented by modular code, shared objects and centralised services.

"Least privilege" means rights are kept to a minimum and users granted access explicitly. An example of this is having non-administrative accounts and access granted on a need to know basis.

Another example is "Fail safe defaults" where access is denied by default and only granted explicitly.

The good news is that we don't have to go out and develop theses principles. People already involved in secure development are sharing experiences and developing a common body of knowledge that provides the development community with guiding principles on how to develop software securely. It is imperative that we, in the security community, make an effort to enssure they become better known to all stakeholders involved in development. As a professional body dedicated to the support of professionals working in all specialism of information security, (ISC)² has put its resources behind documenting this common body of knowledge and providing a professional certification program against it, thereby promoting awareness through education.

6 Stakeholders

It is important that the people involved in the whole of the software development life cycle understand what needs to be done in order to produce secure applications and software.

There are a great number of players or stakeholders in the systems development life cycle, and all of these to a greater or lesser extent need to be involved in building security into the life cycle so that we have better and more secure software and applications.

The obvious stakeholders are the security specialists – us, our teams along with the developers and coders. Equally important are the architects and designers, the quality assurance managers and the business analysts, the business unit heads and the project managers also need to be involved so that when the famous rescoping exercises are undertaken, the relative importance of the security requirements are considered.

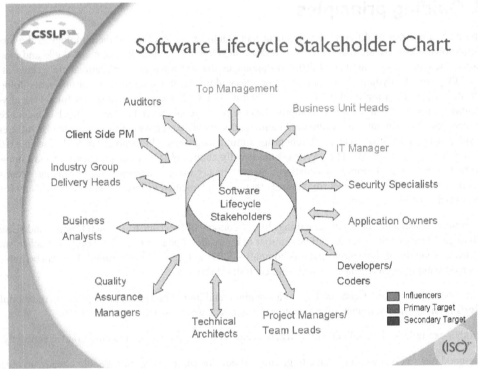

Fig. 1:

7 Best Practices[2]

Clearly, the infamous release-and-patch cycle of software security management can no longer be tolerated. There is a growing community of professionals who understand that escaping this vicious cycle requires a systemic approach to ensuring software can be designed, developed and deployed with a secure mindset, factoring in necessary security controls that minimise both the likelihood of exposure and the impact of exploitation. The ten best practices reflected by this community include:

1. **Protect the brand your customers trust**

   As cybercriminals evolve, so must the defenders. It's the defenders and their organisations that need to stay a step ahead of the cybercriminals, as they will be held responsible for security breaches. Breaches leading to disclosure of customer information, denial of service, and threats to the continuity of business operations can have dire financial consequences, yet the real cost to the organisation will be the loss of customer trust and confidence in the brand. Such a loss may be irreparable and impossible to quantify in mere monetary terms. Fundamentally, the recognition that the organisation is obligated to protect the customers should powerfully motivate the organisation in creating more secure software.

2. Know your business and support it with secure solutions

The answer to the question – "why were brakes invented?" could be answered in two ways, "to prevent the vehicle from an accident" or "to allow the vehicle to go faster". Similarly, security can prevent the business from a crash or allow the business to go faster. One must work with a thorough understanding of the business, to help in the identification of regulatory and compliance requirements, applicable risk, architectures to be used, technical controls to be incorporated, and the users to be trained or educated.

3. Understand the technology of the software

A thorough understanding of the existing infrastructural components such as network segregation, hardened hosts, public key infrastructure, to name a few, is necessary to ensure that the introduction of the software, when deployed, will at first be operationally functional and then not weaken the security of the existing computing environment. Understanding the interplay of technological components with the software is essential to determine the impact on overall security and support decisions that improve security of the software. Further, when procuring software, it is vital to recognise vendor claims on the 'security' features, and also verify implementation feasibility within your organisation.

4. Ensure compliance to governance, regulations and privacy

An industry that is not regulated is today an exception to the norm. Governance, Risk and Compliance (GRC) is a means to meeting the regulatory and privacy requirements. One must understand the internal and external policies that govern the business, its mapping to necessary security controls, the residual risk post implementation of security controls in the software, and the compliance aspects to regulations and privacy requirements.

5. Know the basic tenets of software security

When it comes to secure software, there are some tenets with which one must be familiar: protection from disclosure (confidentiality), protection from alteration (integrity), protection from destruction (availability), who is making the request (authentication), what rights and privileges does the requestor have (authorisation), the ability to build historical evidence (auditing) and management of configuration, sessions and exceptions. Knowledge of these basic tenets and how they can be implemented in software is a must-have, while they offer a contextual understanding of the mechanisms in place to support them. Some of these mechanisms include encryption, hashing, load balancing and monitoring, password, token or biometric features, logging, configuration and audit controls, and the like.

6. Ensure the protection of sensitive information

Any information upon which the organisation places a measurable value, which by implication is not in the public domain, and would result in loss, damage or even business collapse, should the information be compromised in any way could be considered sensitive. While it may be easy to identify the sensitivity of certain data elements like health records and credit card information, others may not be that evident. One must consider data classification and protection mechanisms against disclosure, alteration or destruction. Data classification is the conscious decision to assign a level of sensitivity to data as it is being created, amended, stored, transmitted, or enhanced, and will determine the extent to which the data needs to be secured, while software that either transports, processes or stores sensitive information must build in necessary security controls.

7. **Design software with secure features**

When one is exclusively focussed on finding security issues in code, we run the risk of missing out on entire classes of vulnerabilities. Security issues in design and other concerns, such as business logic flaws, need to be inspected by performing threat models and abuse cases modeling during the design stage of the software development lifecycle. Threat modeling, an iterative structured technique, is used to identify the threats by identifying the security objectives of the software and profiling it. Attack surface analysis, a subset of threat modeling, can be performed when generating the software context in which sections of the software exposed to un-trusted users is analysed for security issues. Once the software context is generated, pertinent threats and vulnerabilities can be identified. Threat Modeling should be performed during the design stage so that necessary security controls (safeguards) can be developed during the development phase of the software or application.

8. **Develop software with secure features**

It is imperative that secure features not be ignored when design artifacts are converted into syntax constructs that a compiler or interpreter can understand. Once developed, controls that essentially address the basic tenets of software security must be validated to be in place and effective by security code reviews and security testing. This should complement and be performed at the same time as functionality testing. Definition of the scope of what is being reviewed, the extent of the review, coding standards, secure coding requirements, code review process with roles and responsibilities and enforcement mechanisms must be pre-defined for a security code review to be effective, while tests should be conducted in testing environments that emulate the configuration of the production environment to mitigate configuration issues that weaken the security of the software.

9. **Deploy software with secure features**

Secure deployment ensures that the software is functionally operational and secure at the same time. It means that software is deployed with defense-in-depth, and the attack surface area is not increased by improper release, change, or configuration management. It also means that assessment from an attacker's point of view is conducted prior to or immediately upon deployment. Software that works without any issues in development and test environments, when deployed into a more hardened production environment, often experiences hiccups. Post mortem analyses in a majority of these cases reveal that the development and test environments do not simulate the production environment. Changes therefore made to the production environment should be retrofitted to the development and test environments through proper change management processes.

Release management should also include proper source code control and versioning to avoid a phenomenon one might refer to as *"regenerative bugs"*, whereby software defects reappear in subsequent releases. The coding defect (bug) is detected and fixed in the testing environment and the software is promoted to production without retrofitting it into the development environment. Further, vulnerability assessment and penetration testing should be conducted in a staging pre-production environment and if need be in the production environment with tight control.

10. **Educate yourself and others on how to build secure software**

As Charles Dickens once eloquently said: "Change begets change." When one who is educated in turn educates others, there will be a compound effect on creating the security culture that is much needed – to create a culture that factors in software security by default through education that changes attitudes. IT security is everyone's job.

8 Conclusion: Security Mindset

Contrary to popular opinion that software security is all about writing secure code, and although it is a very important and critical step in the software development life cycle (SDLC), secure code writing is only one of the various steps necessary to ensure security in software, it must be recognised that security is a process to be woven into the SDLC. Since software, like anything else that goes through a manufacturing process, is designed and developed to a blueprint, it is of paramount importance that security requirements are determined alongside the functional and business requirements.

The first step is philosophical. Designers and developers must develop a security mindset if we are going to address this issue. Traditionally they are so busy concentrating on making systems work that they don't stop to see how they might fail or be made to fail. As security professionals it is imperative we help the development community understand why and how this must change.

References

Paul, Mano CISSP, MCAD, MCSD, Network+, ECSA, Software Assurance Advisor, (ISC) 2 Whitepaper: *The Need for Secure Software*, (ISC) , 2008

Paul, Mano CISSP, MCAD, MCSD, Network+, ECSA, Software Assurance Advisor, (ISC) 2 Whitepaper: *Ten Best Practices for Secure Software Development*

Proactive Security Testing and Fuzzing

Ari Takanen

Codenomicon Ltd
ari.takanen@codenomicon.com

Abstract

Software is bound to have security critical flaws, and no testing or code auditing can ensure that software is flawless. But software security testing requirements have improved radically during the past years, largely due to criticism from security conscious consumers and Enterprise customers. Whereas in the past, security flaws were taken for granted (and patches were quietly and humbly installed), they now are probably one of the most common reasons why people switch vendors or software providers. The maintenance costs from security updates often add to become one of the biggest cost items to large Enterprise users. Fortunately test automation techniques have also improved. Techniques like model-based testing (MBT) enable efficient generation of security tests that reach good confidence levels in discovering zero-day mistakes in software. This technique is called fuzzing.

1 Reactive versus Proactive

Security has traditionally been reactive, focused on defending from attacks. A proactive approach should focus on fixing the actual flaws enabling these attacks. An attack does not work if there is no vulnerability. Majority of flaws reported publicly are found by third parties, and require expensive and time-sensitive process for disclosure of the vulnerability data, building of corrections (patches) and distribution/deployment of the corrective measures. A bug found as part of the software development process will not go through this extensive process but is handled just like any other critical flaw in the system.

1.1 Fuzzing as a Proactive Measure

Proactive security testing approaches include fuzzing, protocol mutation, robustness testing, and the like. Especially fuzzing is a very effective way of discovering software vulnerabilities, as it requires no intelligence of the internal operations of the device or system under test. Legacy fuzzing was based on randomly mutated inputs (white-noise testing), and was only used by professional security specialists and selected researchers. But today most fuzzers are based on intelligent model-based test automation techniques. Besides making the use of fuzzing tools much easier, this enables much higher vulnerability detection rates.

1.2 Automation equals Efficiency

Fuzzing is a rather new test automation technique for finding critical security problems in any type of communication software. It is a negative software testing method (negative testing) that feeds a program, device or system with malformed and unexpected input data in order to find critical crash-level defects. The tests are targeted at remote interfaces, but can also test local interfaces and API. Focus on most critical remote interfaces typically means that fuzzing is able to cover the most exposed and critical attack surfaces in a system relatively well, and identify many common errors and potential vulner-

N. Pohlmann, H. Reimer, W. Schneider (Editors): Securing Electronic Business Processes, Vieweg (2009), 312-319

abilities quickly and cost-effectively. Only recently, it was mostly an unknown hacking technique that very few quality assurance specialists knew about. Today, both quality assurance engineers and security auditors use fuzzing. It is a mainstream testing technique used by all major companies building software and devices for critical communication infrastructure.

1.3 Focus on Finding Vulnerabilities

Fuzzing is focused on detecting implementation issues in software. Vulnerability databases indicate that programming errors causes 80% of the publicly known vulnerabilities. Inclusion of the vulnerabilities caught in the software development would probably increase this even further. Today, no more than 25% of vulnerabilities are found with the traditional software quality assurance processes, with majority of the software companies catching less than 5% of the vulnerabilities in hiding. Static analysis tools cannot be used in post-release testing, or in third party security analysis. Improving the software testing practices can eliminate these worm-size holes before product launch, and without requiring access to the source code.

1.4 Evolution of Fuzzing

The term 'fuzzing' or 'fuzz testing' emerged around 1990, but in its original meaning fuzzing was just another name for random testing, with very little use in Quality Assurance (QA) beyond some limited ad-hoc testing. Still, the transition to integrating the approach into software development was evident even back then. During 1998-2001, in the PROTOS project (at University of Oulu) we conducted research that had a focus on new model-based test automation techniques, and other next generation fuzzing techniques [Kaks02]. The purpose was to enable the software industry themselves to find security critical problems in a wide range of communication products, and not to just depend on vulnerability disclosures from third parties. Codenomicon is a spin-off from the project, founded in 2001, that today continues to lead the state-of-the-art in fuzzing techniques. Later, around year 2007 also other companies became fascinated in the topic, and a new highly competed test and measurement market domain was created. Finally in 2008, among several other books on the topic, we also released a book (with the help of other fuzzing specialists) which gives a broader and but also more detailed look on how fuzzing can be used in different steps in the software lifecycle [TaDM08]. This started the move towards making fuzzing a best practise in software development.

1.5 Attack Surface

Communications function in layers of protocols. Data is transmitted in protocols running on top of each other, and much of the security analysis only looks at the highest layers, ignoring protocol level attacks. Fuzzing can be conducted on all layers of communications. Security research focusing on one layer fuzzing only (such as the publicly available PROTOS research results) indicate that more than 80% of all software will crash when tested with negative testing. Additional studies where more layers were included show that any interface on any communication device taken for analysis has less than 10-30% survival rate, with majority of devices failing in more than half of the interface tests. With a sample of products under tests, no device was found to be secure on all layers of communication (Figure 1).

	AP1	AP2	AP3	AP4	AP5	AP6	AP7	
WLAN (*	INC	FAIL	INC	FAIL	N/A	INC	INC	33 %
IPv4	FAIL	PASS	FAIL	PASS	N/A	FAIL	INC	50 %
ARP	PASS	PASS	PASS	N/A	FAIL	PASS	PASS	16 %
TCP	N/A	N/A	FAIL	N/A	FAIL	PASS	N/A	66 %
HTTP	N/A	PASS	FAIL	PASS	INC	FAIL	FAIL	50 %
DHCP	FAIL	FAIL	INC	N/A	FAIL	FAIL	N/A	80 %
	50 %	40 %	50 %	33 %	75 %	50 %	25 %	Failure %

Fig. 1: Test results from fuzzing seven WiFi access points against six different interfaces/
protocols

1.6 Test Efficiency

Comparing fuzzing tools is difficult, and there is no accepted methodology for that. The easiest method is based on the enumeration of interface requirements. One toolkit might support about 20 or so protocol interfaces where another one will cover more than 100 protocols. Testing a web application requires a different set of fuzzers than testing a voice over IP (VoIP) application. Some fuzzing frameworks are powerful at testing simple text-based protocols, but provide no help in testing complex structures such as ASN.1 or XML. Other fuzz-tests come in pre-packaged suites around common protocols such as SSL/TLS, HTTP, and UPnP, whereas in other cases you need to build the tests yourself. The test direction and physical interfaces can also impact the usability of some tools, as some of them only test server side implementations in a Client-Server infrastructure.

In one research for studying fuzzing test efficiency [TaDM08], fuzzers were compared by running their tests against a piece of software that had intentionally planted security vulnerabilities in it. Selected protocol interfaces and open source implementations were selected, and common vulnerabilities were created to the implementations. The fuzzer efficiency was noted to range from 0% up to 80%. The detection rates of fuzzers ranged from 10-30% for random fuzzers and up to 70-80% for model-based fuzzing tools. Majority of the security problems intentionally created for the open source implementations were caught and some previously unknown flaws were also detected, adding up to an estimate of 90% detection rate through fuzzing. The tool with most test cases very rarely was the most efficient one, so looking at the number of test cases will often lead into selecting a tool that has least intelligence in the test generation. The testing technique had no false positives, as each found issue was truly a remotely exploitable weakness in the tested software.

2 Product Security

Recent studies [McCM09] indicate that all major software security initiatives have included fuzzing in their activities. Market studies by leading analysts and reports by leading commercial fuzzing companies indicate that the adoption of fuzzing is still in rapid growth. Users of fuzzing tools come from all industries, and from all parts of the organizations. Some users look at fuzzing as a quality assurance technique. Others use fuzzing in penetration testing. And finally leading Enterprises have integrated fuzzing in acceptance testing and procurement processes. The range of use cases for fuzzing is growing fast, and integration capabilities of fuzzing tools are improving as the use cases become clearer.

2.1 Software Requirements

To understand the principles behind fuzzing, we need to look how it fits into the entire software lifecycle. As the software development process starts from requirements gathering, so let's first look at how the requirements for security and fuzzing can be mapped together. A software requirements specification often consists of two different types of requirements (Figure 2). Firstly, you have a set of positive requirements that define how software should function. Secondly, you have a set of negative requirements that define what software should not do. The actual resulting software is a cross-section of both of these. Acquired features, and conformance flaws, map against the positive requirements. Fatal features and unwanted features map into the negative requirements. The undefined grey area in-between the positive and negative requirement leaves room for the innovative features that never made it to the requirements specifications or to the design specifications, but were implemented as later spontaneous decisions (or by mistake) during the development. These are often difficult to test, as they might not make it to the test plans at all. The main focus of fuzzing is not to validate any correct behaviour of the software but to explore the challenging area of negative requirements. [ErLa05]

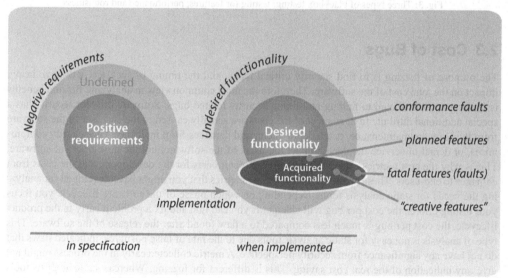

Fig. 2: Mapping requirements to flaws in delivered software

2.2 Types of Testing

Looking at different types of black-box testing, we can identify three main categories of testing techniques (Figure 3). These are feature testing, performance testing, and robustness testing. Feature testing is the traditional approach of validating and verifying functionality, whereas performance testing looks at the efficiency of the built system. Both feature testing and performance testing are exercising the system with valid inputs. Robustness testing on the other hand tests the system under invalid inputs, focusing on checking the system stability, security and reliability. Comparing these three testing categories, we can note that most feature tests map one-to-one against use-cases in the software specifications. Performance testing on the other hand uses just one use-case, but loops that either in a fast loop, or in multiple parallel executions. In robustness testing, you build thousands or sometimes even millions of misuse-cases for each use-case. Fuzzing is one form of robustness testing, focusing on the communication interfaces and discovery of security related problems such as overflows and boundary value conditions, in order to more intelligently test the infinite input space that is required to try out in robustness testing.

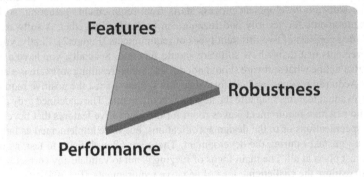

Fig. 3: Three types of blackbox testing: testing for features, performance and robustness

2.3 Cost of Bugs

The purpose of fuzzing is to find security critical flaws, and the timing of such test will have heavy impact on the total cost of the software. Therefore the most common view in analyzing fuzzing benefits is looking at costs related to finding and fixing security related bugs. Software product security has a special additional attribute to it, as most of the costs are actually caused to the end user of the software from the software maintenance, patch deployment, and damages from incidents. The security compromises, or denial of service incidents impact the users of the software, not the developers of software. This is why the cost metrics often include both the repair costs for the developers, and the costs from damages to end-users. These are often the very same metrics that you might have developed for analyzing the needs for static analysis tools. Depending on which phase of the software lifecycle you focus your testing efforts, the cost per bug will change. If you can find and fix a problem early in the product lifecycle, the cost per bug is much less compared to a flaw found after the release of the software. This type of analysis is not easy for static analysis tools due to the rate of false positives, indicated flaws that do not have any significance from security perspective. A metric collected early in the process might not give any indication of the real cost saving. This is different for fuzzing. Whereas static analysis tools create poor success rate based on analyzing the real security impact of the found flaws, there are no false positives in fuzzing. All found issues are very real, and will provide a solid metric for product security improvements.

2.4 Uses of Fuzzing

Although originally fuzzing was mainly a tool for penetration testers and security auditors, today the usage is much more diverse. Soon after the exposure caused by PROTOS, most network equipment manufacturers (NEMS) quickly adapted the tools into their quality assurance processes, and from that the fuzzing technologies evolved into quality metrics for monitoring the product lifecycle and product maturity. Perhaps because of the rapid quality improvements in network products, fuzzing soon also became a recommended purchase criterion for enterprises, pushed by vendors who were already conducting fuzzing and thought that it would give them a competitive edge. As a result, service providers and large enterprises started to require fuzzing and similar testing techniques from all their vendors, further increasing the usage of fuzzing. In short, today fuzzing is used in three phases at the software lifecycle:

1. QA Usage of Fuzzing in Software Development,
2. Regression testing and product comparisons using Fuzzing at test laboratories and
3. Penetration testing use in IT operations.

As the usage scenarios range from one end to another, so does the profile of the actual users of the tools. Different people look for different aspects in fuzzers. Some users prefer random fuzzers whereas others look for intelligent fuzzing. Other environments require appliance-based testing solutions, and other test environments dictate software-based generators. Fortunately all those are easily available today.

3 Test Automation

Let's then review how fuzzing maps to different test automation techniques. Different levels of test automation are used in all testing taking place today, and fuzzing is just one additional improvement in that domain (Figure 4) [Puol08].

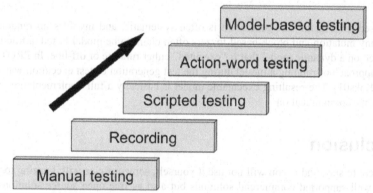

Fig. 4: Test automation maturity levels (based on presentation by Olli-Pekka Puolitaival, VTT, 2008)

In fact, test automation experts are often the first people that familiarize themselves with fuzzing and other related test generation techniques. Test automation often focuses only on the repeatability of tests, but another significant improvement from some test automation techniques is the improvements in test design and test efficiency. The more advanced tools you use, the less work is required for the entire testing cycle. The most basic transition into test automation is moving from manual testing into test recording and replaying methodologies. The most extreme developments in test automation are in model-based testing. In fact, the laborious test design phase is mostly skipped in model-based testing, as the tests are automatically generated from system models and communication interface specifications.

3.1 Test Automation in Fuzzing

Not all fuzzing tools are model-based, but all types of fuzzing techniques are always highly automated. When people conduct fuzzing, there is close to zero human involvement in the testing. In fuzzing, the tests are automatically generated, executed, and the test reporting is also automated so that most of the work can be focused on analyzing and fixing the found issues.

3.2 Capture-Replay versus Full Model

Two different test automation techniques are popular in fuzzing. The major difference is in where the "model" of the interface is acquired. The easiest method of building a fuzzer is based on re-using a test case from feature testing or performance testing, whether it is a test script or a captured message sequence, and then augmenting that piece of data with mutations, or anomalies. The simplest form of mutation fuzzing is based on just randomly doing data modifications such as bit flipping and data insertion, in order to try unexpected inputs. The other method of fuzzing is based on building the model from communication protocol specifications and state-diagrams.

Mutation-based fuzzers break down the structures used in the message exchanges, and tag those building blocks with meta-data that helps the mutation process. Similarly, in full model-based fuzzers each data element needs to be identified, but that process can be also automated as that information is often already given in the specifications that are used to generate the models. Besides information on the data structures, the added meta-data can also include details such as the boundary limits for the data elements.

In model-based fuzzing the test generation is often systematic, and involves no randomness at all. Although many mutation and block-based fuzzers often claim to be model-based, a true model-based fuzzer is based on a dynamic model that is "executed" either runtime or off-line. In PROTOS research papers, this approach of running a model during the test generation or test execution was called Mini-Simulation [Kaks01]. The resulting executable model is basically a full implementation of one of the end-points in the communication.

4 Conclusion

Fuzzing is here to stay, and if you will not use it yourself, someone else will. Fuzzing tools are easily available as well supported commercial solutions but also as free open source solutions. Not doing fuzzing at all could be considered negligence. Fuzzing is a very efficient method of finding remotely exploitable holes in critical systems, and the return of time and effort placed in negative testing is immediate. Just one flaw when found after the release can create enormous costs through internal crisis management, and compromises of deployed systems. No bug will stay hidden if correct tools are used. Still, there is room for development in fuzzing research, and we are happy to see that research teams are embracing fuzzing as a new security research topic.

In this paper (and related panel talk) we focused in use of fuzzing in software development. As part of that we looked at the brief history of fuzzing and the different technologies used by different fuzzers. The techniques behind different types of fuzzers were explained to give the reader an understanding on how different fuzzers work. By studying the use cases of fuzzing we aimed to assist the audience in integrating fuzzing in their own software development lifecycle. Attention was also paid on various metrics related to fuzzing, to enable comparison of efficiency of various tools. We also explained various aspects of test automation to help you map this proactive security testing technique to other quality assurance practises.

References

[ErLa05]   Eronen, Juhani; Laakso, Marko: A Case for Protocol Dependency. In proceedings of the First IEEE International Workshop on Critical Infrastructure Protection. Darmstadt, Germany. November 3-4, 2005.

[Kaks01]   Kaksonen, Rauli: A Functional Method for Assessing Protocol Implementation Security (Licentiate thesis). Espoo. 2001. Technical Research Centre of Finland, VTT Publications 447. 128 p. + app. 15 p. ISBN 951-38-5873-1 (soft back ed.) ISBN 951-38-5874-X (on-line ed.).

[McCM09] McGraw, Gary; Chess, Brian and Migues, Sammy: Building Security In Maturity Model. www.bsimm.com, 2009, 53 p.

[Puol08]   Puolitaival, Olli-Pekka: Model-based testing tools. Presentation at Software Testing Day at TUT. March 25-26, 2008.

[TaDM08] Takanen, Ari; DeMott, Jared and Miller, Charlie: Fuzzing for Software Security Testing and Quality Assurance. Artech House. 2008. 230p. ISBN 978-1-59693-214-2.

Protecting Long Term Validity of PDF documents with PAdES-LTV

Nick Pope

Thales Information Systems Security
Aylesbury, United Kingdom
nick.pope@thales-esecurity.com

Abstract

This paper describes an extension to Portable Document Format (PDF) signatures to facilitate the long term validity of electronic documents. It presents the work of ETSI (European Telecommunications Standards Institute) published summer 2009, in ETSI TS 102 778, aiming towards an extension to the ISO 32 000-1 PDF standard.

The paper describes the problems with assuring the authenticity of a signed document over long periods (from about 1 year onwards) and outlines how these issues can be resolved using the PDF extensions for Long Term Validation (LTV).

The LTV extension is specified as part of a series of profiles for PDF Advanced Electronic Signatures (PAdES) recently published by ETSI [ETSIPAdES].

1 Introduction

The Portable Document Form (PDF) is widely recognised as the format to be used for electronic document output from a wide range of document preparation systems. PDF provides an electronic analogue to paper with the information being presented consistently, independent of platform used. PDF documents can be displayed in human readable form as well as used as input to a computer system for automatic processing (e.g. invoice received input into accounting system). The features of PDF account for its popularity and widespread usage as organizations move to electronic forms of information distribution and commerce.

With the widespread adoption of PDF as a part of day-to-day business, ensuring the authenticity and integrity is becoming important for their use. For example, as recognised under VAT legislation (European directive on VAT harmonisation [EUVAT06]), when receiving an electronic invoice a business needs to ensure that the invoice comes from the true source and the invoiced values have not been modified. The mechanism most widely recognised for providing authenticity and integrity is the digital signature (termed advanced electronic signature in European directive on electronic signatures [EUSig99]).

PDF has for a number of years included support for digital signatures. This not only provides for the use of digital signatures which "certify" the authenticity and integrity of documents, but also signatures which can be represented in visual form as well as a digital providing further comparability with hand written signatures. This use of signatures is already recognised in the ISO standard for PDF (ISO 32000-1 [ISOPDF]) and is supported in the billion or so of PDF readers that have been loaded onto user machines.

N. Pohlmann, H. Reimer, W. Schneider (Editors): Securing Electronic Business Processes, Vieweg (2009), 320-327

ETSI, an official European standardisation organisation for information and communications standards, as part of its work in the technical committee on Electronic Signatures and Infrastructures (TC ESI) supporting use of electronic signatures in line with European legislation [EUSig99], has developed a set of "profiles" for the use of PDF Signatures. This describes the use PDF Signatures as "Advanced Electronic Signatures" as defined in [EUSig99] in a multi-part technical specification TS 102 778 [ETSIPAdES]. These specifications are based on the existing PDF signature format specified in ISO 32000-1 [ISOPDF] and define extensions that may be used to provide additional security features. The profiles also support signed XML structures carried with PDF documents using techniques such as XFA [Adob07]. The role of each of the parts is as follows:

Part 1: **PAdES Overview – a framework document for PAdES:** This part provides a general framework for the use of PDF signature, outlining the provisions already in ISO 32000-1 [ISOPDF] and the specific features of PDF signatures as profiled in the other parts of TS 102 778.

Part 2: **PAdES Basic – Profile based on ISO 32000-1:** This part specifies the use of PDF signatures as currently defined in ISO 32000-1 [ISOPDF]

Part 3: **PAdES Enhanced – PAdES-BES and PAdES-EPES Profiles:** This part specifies the enhancements to PDF signatures to create signatures with additional security features as defined in a separate ETSI specification for binary format Advanced Electronic Signatures extending the standard CMS structure [Hous04] as specified in ETSI TS 101 733 [ETSICAdES].

Part 4: **PAdES Long Term – PAdES-LTV Profile:** This part specifies enhancements to the PDF syntax to enable verifiers to extend the life-time of signatures created in accordance with other parts of PAdES.

Part 5 **PAdES for XML Content – Profiles for XAdES signatures of XML content in PDF files:** This part specifies the use of the XML Advanced Electronic Signature format, as specified in ETSI TS 101 903 [ETSIXAdES], to protect signed XML data within PDF files either embedded directly as an XML documents or using XFA [Adob07].

This paper describes the enhanced features of Part 4 of TS 102 778 [ETSIPAdES] to support the verification of PDF signatures, such as specified in part 2 or part 3, long (many years) after the signature has been created.

This paper is based on the work of ETSI (European Telecommunications Standards Institute) Technical Committee on Electronic Signatures and Infrastructures, Specialist Task Force 364. Members of this group are:

Alexander Funk	TeleTrusT Deutschland e. V.
Giuliana Marzola	InfoCert s.p.a.
Juan Carlos Cruellas	DAC-UPC
Julien Stern	Cryptolog International
Leonard Rosenthol	Adobe Systems
Marc Straat	Adobe Systems
Nick Pope	Thales

2 Example Scenarios Addressed by PAdES-LTV

Consider the situation for a major governmental procurement contract where an offer is made online taking the form of an electronic document – a PDF. The CEO from the supplier digitally signs the offer document PDF specifying the terms and conditions for supply, and this document is then accepted by the government. A few days later, the CEO is fired from his position for incompetence. However, the supplier continues with the contract until several years into the contract (say 6 years) it is found that the goods offered are not as durable as expected. The offer document is found by the new CEO to contain penalty clauses which would almost bankrupt the company. So the lawyers are brought in.

One potential avenue for trying to avoid the penalty is to dispute the validity of the contract and the digital signature 6 years after it was created. The signing certificate used by the CEO was revoked very soon after the signing date, but after this time the applicable revocation list is no longer available. Also, the certification authority records at that time are no longer available as the CA was subsequently taken over and the old records were not kept. Thus, there is no proof as to whether the signer's certificate was valid at the time of signing. The PDF signature was time-stamped, in line with recommended practice for PDF signatures, and so there was no dispute over the signing time (assuming that the time-stamp certificate is still valid). However, the certificate revocation status is unknown and hence the signature cannot be verified.

A further problem with validating the signature 6 years after it was created is that all the certificates which form the trust path from the signer's certification authority (CA) to a trusted root may no longer be available. Again without the full path the signature cannot be verified.

With the rapid development of cryptanalysis further problems exist with assuring that the algorithm can withhold attack over more than a number of years. Already over the 15 years or so that signature algorithms have been in widespread use the length of key acceptable has moved from 512 bits to 756 bit and now 1024 bit with 2048 for long periods. Also, old hashing algorithms such as MD5 are no longer considered strong enough for general use [WaYu05].

With retrospective verification of signatures it can be uncertain exactly what time should be used for verification. In some environment systems are required to await a grace period to ensure that security problems which result in revocation are given time to be reported and pass through the revocation management system. In other environments a signature time-stamp applied by the signer in creating the signature is used to indicate the verification time.

These issues apply to a range of situations. The current European legislation for VAT requires that authenticity and integrity of documents is "guaranteed", not only on transfer between trading partners, but also for the full period of time that invoice need to be stored for review by tax auditors (from 5 to over 10 years). Without special controls over the storage of invoices additional measures need to be taken to assure the authenticity and integrity of signed documents throughout their lifetime.

Applications such as governmental archives holding key government legislative and administrative documents which may needed to confirm historical facts may depend on signatures to assure the authenticity of the archives. Without the use of additional measures, such as those described in this paper, the validity of those signatures may be called into question.

From this and other similar scenarios the following issues have been identified with the validation of signatures stored over long periods:

1. Revocation information may not be readily available for certificates beyond the expiry period,

2. CA Certificates used in the certificate path may not be readily available,
3. The time to be used for retrospective verification can be uncertain.
4. Algorithms and key lengths used for signatures have to be regularly upgraded to keep apace with developments in cryptanalysis.

3 Description of PAdES LTV

The measures defined in [ETSIPAdES] part 4 makes use of two additional sets of fields added to the end of a PDF document which has already been signed, as illustrated in the following figure:

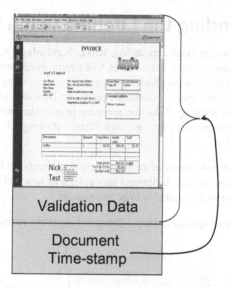

Fig. 1: Illustration of PAdES LTV extension fields

The first area contains data that was used to validate the signature (termed Validation Data). The second area contains a time-stamp applied to the rest of the document, including the original signed document and Validation Data.

The LTV information is added to the signed PDF document, when it is initially verified, by any party wanting to assure the long term validity of the document. For example, a buyer first receiving a signed invoice might apply LTV before storing the document in an archive so that it is verifiable by the tax auditor when a company accounts are reviewed several years later. In such a scenario the seller may also apply LTV to its own invoices, subsequent to signing and sending off the invoice, before storing invoices for its own audit purposes.

The Validation Data contains all the data that was used to initially verify the PDF signatures. This can include all the CA certificates up to a trusted root as well as information used to check the revocation status of the user and all the CA certificates. The revocation information can either be in the form of Certificate Revocation Lists (CRL as specified in RFC 5280 [SFBH08]), or an On Line Certificate Status protocol response (OCSP as specified in RFC 2560 [MAMG99]). By including this validation information in with the signed PDF anyone wishing to re-verify the signature may repeat the verification using the same validation used to initially verify the signature.

The Document Time-stamp is a time-stamp as specified in RFC 3161 issued by a trusted time-stamping authority. This provides proof of existence of the Validation Data as applied to the PDF document at the verification time as indicated by the time-stamp. This proof extends the lifetime of the Validation Data beyond the expiry date of the certificates employed using the proof of existence at verification time given by the time-stamp. Furthermore, the time-stamp, by using stronger algorithms and key lengths, can further protect the signature and validation data against later weaknesses identified in the original signature algorithms.

This approach is equivalent to that already applied in the existing ETSI specifications for advanced electronic signatures TS 101 733 [ETSICAdES] and TS 101 903 [ETSIXAdES].

4 Further extending the Lifetime using LTV

Where documents are held for extended periods (e.g. tens or hundreds of years) further issues come into play in assuring validity. Time-stamping certificates will expire, acceptable key lengths will increase, and new algorithms may come into use. Such issues can be countered by repeated application of the LTV extension. Certificate status and CA certificate paths can be added to assist in the verification of earlier time-stamps. Also, the integrity of the document can be refreshed with new time-stamps to maintain the integrity of the document using stronger algorithms with longer key lengths to lock the earlier validation information in place.

Consider, for example, a national library or archive where documents are to be held in digital form for perpetuity. The media used to hold the documents may change as new technology is introduced but the authenticity of the document as an original is to be maintained.

The LTV extensions may be re-applied to keep a document signature verifiable for as long as necessary as illustrated below:

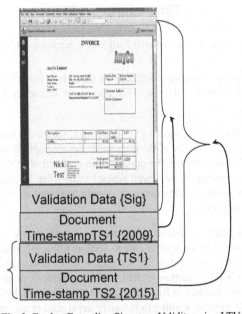

Fig. 2: Further Extending Signature Validity using LTV

A party concerned with maintaining validity of a PDF signature in an archive, can take the LTV extensions applied when initially verifying a document, for example, in 2009 (containing Validation Data {Sig} with Document Time-tamp TS1{2009}) and extend the protection using additional LTV structures Validation Data {TS1} and Document Time-stamp TS2 {2015} at a time before the previous TSA certificate expires, say 2015. The new Validation Data {TS1} add certificates and revocation information needed to validate the previous document time-stamp. The new document time-stamp TS2 proves the existence of the validation data for the previous time-stamp at the time when it was validated (2015). Also, the new time-stamp may use stronger algorithms or key lengths to protect against any potential weaknesses in the previous time-stamp.

By re-applying the LTV Validation Data for the previous time-stamp and with a new Document Time-stamp, say every 10 years, after checking the validity earlier time-stamps and signatures, its validity can be maintained for as long as required. Even if old algorithms are considered weak, by refreshing the document with newer time-stamps, using stronger algorithms, the authenticity is preserved, potentially forever.

5 Example use of PAdES in an e-Invoicing Workflow

Considering an example e-invoicing scenario where a company AnyCo is invoicing its customer for an extra cup of coffee had at a "free" training session. Both companies have to keep their own copies of the signed invoice for the tax auditor, AnyCo for 8 years, the Customer for 3 years. The signature steps required by each party are as illustrated in the following figure:

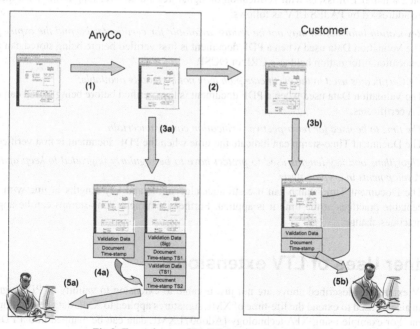

Fig 3: Example use of PAdES in e-Invoicing Workflow

1. The PDF invoice is signed by AnyCo using a signature as specified in either Part 2 or Part 3 of TS 102 778 [ETSIPAdES].

2. AnyCo sends the invoice to the Customer.

3a. AnyCo verifies its own signature and adds Validation Data for its signature with a Document time-stamp before storing the document in its archive.

3b. The customer verifies AnyCo's signature and adds the Validation Data it uses with a Document Time-stamp before storing the document in its archive.

4a. As the invoice is stored by AnyCo for a period longer than the time-stamp authority validity, the invoice in the archive is updated after 5 years with additional Validation Data and Document Time-stamp is added to protect the previous Document Time-stamp.
Note: The same step may be applied by the Customer, but as the storage period is only 3 years, less than the document time-stamp certificate lifetime, this is not necessary for this scenario.

5a. AnyCo's tax auditor can verify the validity of the invoice held in the archive by verifying the sequence of time-stamps and then the original signature using the Validation Data stored with the document linked to a trusted anchor certification authority.

5b. The Customer's tax auditor can verify the validity of the invoice held in the archive by verifying the sequence of time-stamps and then the original signature using the Validation Data stored within the document starting from a trusted anchor certification authority.

6 LTV countering Identified Issues

In section 2 a number of issues with verification of signatures stored over long terms were identified. These are addressed by PAdES LTV as follows:

1. *Revocation information may not be readily available for certificates beyond the expiry period,*
The Validation Data used when a PDF document is first verified before being stored can include revocation information held as a CRL or OCSP.

2. *CA Certificates used in the certificate path may not be readily available;*
The Validation Data used when a PDF document is first verified before being stored can include CA certificates.

3. *The time to be used for retrospective verification can be uncertain.*
The Document Time-stamp can indicate the time when the PDF document is first verified.

4. *Algorithms and key lengths used to protect have to be regularly upgraded to keep apace with developments in cryptanalysis.*
The Document Time-stamp can use stronger algorithms and key lengths in line with the acceptable practices at the time it is applied. Further Document Time-stamps can be applied as practices change.

7 Other Uses of LTV extensions

The LTV extensions described above are not just useable to extension to validity of PDF signatures. They can also be used to extend the life-time of XML signatures applied to XML data held within a PDF document. For example using XFA technology [Adob07] XML data can be mapped into a PDF form. This XML data can be signed. Using LTV technology the lifetime of XML signature can be extended in the same way as a PDF signature (described in Part 5 of PAdES).

Also, even if a PDF document is not signed, the LTV Document Time-stamp can be used to protect the integrity of the document and prove its existence at a point in time. This can be used, for example, to support patent claims proving that a given idea existed at a given time.

8 Conclusions

This paper presents the application of the latest advanced electronic signature techniques to the most widely used portable document format. It makes it feasible to use signed PDF with assurance of their authenticity over tens or even hundreds of years.

References

[EUVAT06] EU COUNCIL DIRECTIVE 2006/112/EC of 28 November 2006 on the common system of value added tax.

[EUSig99] EU DIRECTIVE 1999/93/EC of the European Parliament and of the Council of 13 December 1999 on a Community framework for electronic signatures

[ETSIPAdES] ETSI TS 102 778 (2009-07) Electronic Signatures and Infrastructures (ESI); PDF Advanced Electronic Signature Profiles; Part 1 to 5; July 2009

[ISOPDF] ISO 32000-1 (2008): "Document Management – Portable Document Format – PDF 1.7".

[Hous04] R. Housley, IETF RFC 3852 Cryptographic Message Syntax (CMS), July 2004

[ETSICAdES] ETSI TS 102 733 (2008-07) Electronic Signatures and Infrastructures (ESI);CMS Advanced Electronic Signatures (CAdES)

[ETSIXAdES] ETSI TS 101 903 (2009-06) XML Advanced Electronic Signatures (XAdES)

[SFBH08] S. Santesson, S. Farrell, S. Boeyen, R. Housley, W. Polk: IETF RFC 5280: Internet X.509 Public Key Infrastructure Certificate and Certificate Revocation List (CRL) Profile, May 2008

[MAMG99] R. Ankney, A. Malpani, S. Galperin, C. Adams IETF RFC 2560: X.509 Internet Public Key Infrastructure Online Certificate Status Protocol – OCSP, June 1999

[WaYu05] Xiaoyun Wang and Hongbo Yu, How to Break MD5 and Other Hash Functions, Eurocrypt 2005

[Adob07] Adobe XML Architecture, Forms Architecture (XFA) Specification, version 2.5, (June 2007), Adobe Systems Incorporated.

RE-TRUST: Trustworthy Execution of SW on Remote Untrusted Platforms

Brecht Wyseur

Katholieke Universiteit Leuven,
Department of Electrical Engineering ESAT / COSIC-IBBT
Kasteelpark Arenberg 10, 3001 Heverlee, Belgium
brecht.wyseur@esat.kuleuven.be

Abstract

A major challenge in software security is preserving software integrity. Traditionally, this problem is addressed through the development of software (self-) checking techniques that verify the integrity of its code and execution. Unfortunately, no satisfactory solutions for run-time verification of software integrity have been presented. In this paper, we approach the problem of run-time software integrity verification in a networked context. That is, we present techniques to enable remote verification of the execution of software, given the availability of a continuous network connection between the verification entity and the untrusted execution platform.

1 Introduction

One of the major challenges in software security is the issue of trustworthy execution of software components. Since software, computers and networks are converging and becoming part of our daily lives, various security and trust issues are emerging. We depend on secure execution of software when using online banking applications or relying on medical care, while many businesses rely on the fact that their software performs as expected. For example, the gaming industry heavily depends on the fact that their games do not get hacked, while the music industry suffers from theft and uncontrolled distribution of multimedia content.

In this paper, we discuss the issue of integrity of software that is executed on an untrusted machine. The term 'untrusted machine' refers to the fact that the adversary has complete access to this computing platform: the adversary has full access to the system resources (CPU, memory, etc.), has full access to the software implementation, and any tool that is available to the adversary (debuggers, emulators, disassemblers, etc.) share the same privileges. As a result, the adversary can always tamper the binary software implementation; its objective will be to modify the binary in such a way that he gains extra functionality or privileges. For example, an adversary wants to tamper a music player in such a way, that any rights enforcement techniques (e.g., "do not re-distribute") are circumvented.

The contributions presented in this paper are techniques that enable remote verification of run-time integrity of software. This mainly constitutes the results of the RE-TRUST project, a European Framework Programme 6 project that has been studying the problem of trustworthy execution of software.

N. Pohlmann, H. Reimer, W. Schneider (Editors): Securing Electronic Business Processes, Vieweg (2009), 328-338

Outline. In section 2, we discuss techniques for software tamper resistance and analysis techniques that have been presented in existing literature. The general conclusion will be that local tamper verification is hard to achieve. The direction we pursue is to address the problem in a networked context. In Section 3 we introduce an architecture for remote run-time verification of software that is the basis of the RE-TRUST project. The solutions that were proposed in the project can be classified into two categories: pure software solutions, which we discuss in Section 4, and hardware assisted solutions that leverage the software solutions with lightweight hardware such as Smart Cards and TPMs in Section 5. In Section 6, we discuss the challenges that were addressed, identify open issues, and discuss the security analysis of the proposed techniques.

2 Software Tamper Resistance

Software tamper resistance techniques aim at providing a significant level of robustness against targeted tampering. That is, making it intractable or costly for an adversary to modify sensitive components of an application. In practice, there is a focus on the protection of static software modules, e.g., by verifying a signature of compiled code with its originator. Such techniques work well to verify software at load-time, and are usually deployed in systems where a trusted code base (e.g., a trusted operating system) is present. These static protection techniques do not satisfy in the case where the adversary controls the execution environment, since the execution can be tampered with at run-time.

Dynamic software authentication in real-time during execution is more appropriate in this case. Commonly, dynamic software tamper resistance techniques involve verification techniques that supplement the original program with additional controls that verify at execution time the integrity of code, variables, and context (e.g., memory). These include control flow verification techniques that check the transitioning through expected valid traces, while invariants monitoring techniques monitor if variables maintain values between accepted constraints. Data duplication techniques rewrite a program to compute on several copies of data, and compare for consistency at run-time.

On computing platforms that are under complete control of the adversary, no satisfactory dynamic software tamper resistance techniques seem to exist. Given sufficient time and effort, an adversary is able to circumvent these techniques and tamper with the execution of the program. One of the main reasons for this, is that an adversary that has full access to the execution environment can tamper with the execution of the program even without modifying its code. Instead of executing the program on the actual processor, the attacker could run it also on a simulated processor, and pause the execution when a specific event occurs. After analysis and modification of the context (memory etc.), the execution can be resumed. Calls to libraries, the operating system, and I/O can be intercepted and parameters in the memory can be modified.

Cloning attack. The cloning attack [OoSW05] applies to verification techniques that compare signatures of code at execution time, and can be deployed on Von Neumann architectures (which constitutes almost all major computing architectures commonly used). In this attack, two copies of a program are used. One copy is the original, untampered version. Here, all code is genuine and its execution behaves as expected. The second copy is a tampered copy which is maliciously modified by the adversary. The idea is to execute the altered copy, and point every instruction that accounts for a verification to the original (unmodified) code. Other instructions account to the tampered version. Since it is not common for applications to read (rather than execute) code, it is most likely that such instructions come from verification code that has been supplemented to the original program. The effectiveness from this attack comes from the fact that on a Von Neumann architecture, one can easily distinguish between read instructions that point to code pages and those to data pages. What it takes, is to modify the behavior of the *Translation Lookaside Buffer*, which manages the buffering of memory pages, such that instructions point to the right copy of the code.

The cloning attack defeats software self-checking techniques, a popular protection method that is widely used as a software tamper resistance technique. Countermechanisms have been presented, such as the use of self-modifying code [GiCK05]. However, with sufficient time and effort, an adversary might eventually trap these modifications (e.g., by virtualizing the execution of the targeted software) and circumvent protection techniques.

Note that the original cloning attack does not apply to verification techniques that monitor run-time information such as local variables. In this attack, only the tampered copy is executed and takes into account static information of the untampered copy to circumvent verification techniques. To defeat verification techniques that incorporate dynamic information such as variables, one could augment this kind of attacks by executing the tampered copy and untampered copy next to each other and use run-time information from the untampered copy to fool verification techniques. Further development in protection techniques would need to make it as hard as possible for an adversary to distinguish functionality that accounts for verification techniques from the original functionality. It is clear that this will remain an arms race, and that dynamic verification techniques remain unsatisfactory as a solution. Specifically, how to ensure that a trusted code base is running on an untrusted machine at all times and that the original functionality has not been modified prior to or during run-time is an open research challenge.

To obtain tangible solutions that ensure the trustworthiness of a code base that is running on an untrusted machine, we see two main directions possible:

1. restrict the capabilities of the adversary, or
2. address this challenge in a networked context.

In the first case, access restrictions to the software implementation can be imposed by implementing (parts of) the code in tamper resistant hardware devices such as Smart Cards, while usage restrictions on the execution platform can be imposed, e.g., in the case of Trusted Computing.

Trusted Computing. The issue of executing software in a trusted computing (TC) environment has received significant attention in recent years. The main initiative for a new generation of computing platform is taken by the Trusted Computing Group (TCG), a consortium of most major IT companies. The TCG defines the addition of a small hardware security module called Trusted Platform Module (TPM), which together with the initial software component of the platform acts as *root of trust* [BCP+02]. Trusted computing initiatives offer technology to verify the integrity of software. The idea is that at load-time, the application is measured by computing a cryptographic hash of its code. These measurements can be signed by the TPM and be used to verify the system's integrity; this is called *load-time binary attestation*. The main issue however, is that TCG solutions require a bootstrap from the root of trust to the application that needs to be authenticated, which implies the deployment of a non-legacy operating system. An enabling technology to increase the trustworthiness of computing platforms is *virtualization*. These activities are somewhat complementary to the work we present in this paper, since they are hardware-based and consequently not available on all existing computing platforms.

3 Architecture

In this paper, we aim to address the problem of run-time software integrity for general computing platforms. The idea is to exploit the continuous availability of a network connection between a verification entity and the execution platform. Since we are converging to computing systems that are connected to networks (e.g., grid computers, servers and laptops that are connected to the internet; mobile phones that are connected via wireless networks), the continuous availability of a (broadband) network at run-time is reasonable to assume. The applications that are most conceivable to protect in this case, are those that rely on a remote service (e.g., in the case of online gaming or online banking). Applications of an offline nature (such as music players or office programs) can be forced to accept a network connection by deploying a system of delivery of software updates containing functionalities needed to continue the execution of the software.

Remote attestation. The basis of the architecture is a remote attestation scheme. Attestations are pieces of code that intend to provide some "proof" of authenticity. In this case, they are sent from the (remote) untrusted execution platform to some verification entity. Attestations are some signature of the binary code that is loaded. Since they are computed on an untrusted computing platform, it is a hard problem to guarantee that the correctness of attestations corresponds to the authenticity of the software. An adversary could for example compute signatures on binary code of an untampered copy, while executing a tampered version of the application. Trusted Computing initiatives approach this problem using special hardware that computes a (cryptographic) signature, but require non-legacy operation systems. Moreover, most attestations are computed at load-time and cannot guarantee the execution at run-time. Instead, we aim to provide a level of assurance of run-time execution of software on legacy operating systems and computing platforms.

The main paradigm shift in the solutions presented in this paper is that they are designed to emanate attestations continuously. We denote this paradigm of continuous run-time authentication of software on untrusted platforms as *remote entrusting*. Initial work [BaOY03] introduced this idea of generating such a stream of attestations with software only.

The basic architecture consists of two communicating parties:

1. The trusted entities, which include a verification server that monitors the execution of the software. Based on its verdict, the application host may decide to stop the service to the user, or stop providing software updates the application needs to continue its execution.

2. The untrusted host, which is the computing platform for the software.

The original program needs to be extended with extra functionality, which we capture with the concept of "monitor". This includes code to compute and send the attestations, code that manages the software updates, code that could force the application to stop when a trigger arrives from a trusted entity, and so forth. We also envision the usage of lightweight hardware to enforce the solutions that we develop. Examples of such lightweight hardware include Smart Cards and Trusted Platform Modules. Figure 1 depicts the basic architecture extended with trusted hardware.

In the following sections, we will provide an overview of the major scientific results of the project. Their objective is to provide a trusted code base on the untrusted host using the architecture described above.

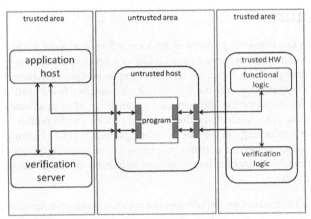

Fig. 1: The RE-TRUST architecture

4 Pure software solutions

A first dimension of solutions conceives the software-only techniques. The solution that applies to generic applications mainly constitutes of two stages to realize the concept of remote entrusting.

- Stage 1: Complement the original software with a functionality to construct the attestations. This is a part of the code we denoted as the "monitor".
- Stage 2: Deter analysis and improve tamper resistance.

It is important that the monitor is integrated into the original client application in such a way that it becomes difficult for an adversary to distinguish its code and functionality. If an adversary were to distinguish the monitor, he might isolate its functionality from the execution of the original application, and as a result remove the link between the correctness of the attestation and the authenticity of the execution of the program. Protection techniques consist of 'interlocking' techniques, which will interweave the execution of different functions of the program. An initial direction in this research was provided by Aucsmith [Aucs03] who introduced the concept of *Integrity Verification Kernels*, which are small pieces of code that are injected in a program. These kernels include verification code to verify the integrity of code, and re-order instructions to make it difficult for an adversary to distinguish independent functionalities.

The attestation generation functions that are used in the monitor, compute a signature from static and dynamic (run-time) information of the application. This includes binary code and memory pages. The objective would be that if an adversary modifies any crucial component of the application in an unacceptable way, this should be detectable by the verification entity. Note that some degree of modification can be allowed (e.g., from a security point of view, we do not mind if an adversary modifies the background color of banking application, as long as all transaction operations perform as expected). We refer to our recent work [BDH+09] on a theoretical framework of software tamper resistance for a discussion on verification predicates. A candidate attestation generation function would be a cryptographic hash function or MAC algorithm. However, it is more advisable to use functions that consist of only a few simple operations, for two reasons: 1) attestations need to be generated very often, and hence impose an overhead in the execution time of the protected applications; hence they should be efficient. 2) The attestation generation function should consist of instructions that appear to be quite common in generic applications; hence, using very specific cryptographic functions could be identifiable and give enough information for an adversary to find a point of attack. We refer to the work by Horne *et al.* [HMST02] on efficient check-summing techniques for software verification.

Below, we present a number of techniques that were developed or improved within the context of the RE-TRUST project. Note that this is only a selection of techniques that have been explored.

Crypto Guards. Crypto guards [CPA+08] represents an on-demand decryption scheme that applies small grained code encryption/decryption (e.g., on a function level). It tries to protect both against analysis and against tampering. Protection against analysis is achieved by encrypting all code and keeping only the executing code portion in clear. As such, an attacker can only observe a minimal portion of the program in time. On the other hand tamper resistance is improved as code encryption/decryption relies on the integrity of other code portions. Several predefined schemes specify that decryption of the next block should rely on a previously executed block, and vice versa, that encryption of a block should rely on the executing block. Hence, if code is tampered with no matter statically or dynamically (off line or during execution), the modification will trigger errors that propagate back and forth along the control flow graph resulting in undefined program behavior.

Code encryption only protects the program statically, i.e., executing code should be in clear, thus code is decrypted sooner or later. This implies that initially some portions should be in clear. A crypto guards consist of an hash function that verifies code integrity and derives a key from the hash. This key is then passed on to a decryption routine, part of the crypto guard as well. The strength of this scheme relies on a complex network of inlined guards and how they monitor each other. However, in a stand-alone (i.e., non-networked) solution, this techniques relies on some other techniques to avoid easy guard detection, namely: code diversity and code obfuscation.

Code Obfuscation. Code obfuscation is a technique that tries to hinder code analysis. By applying one or more code transformations it alters the code in such a way that analysis becomes hard(er), but program functionality is preserved.

However validation of code obfuscation is hard as it is hard to measure how much complexity is added to the analysis. Furthermore, analysis is often a combination of automated tools and human observation. While the former can be fooled by e.g., violating coding conventions or destroying common software patterns, the latter is more subjective due to the expertise of the attacker. During the year several metrics have been proposed to measure obfuscation and its cost. However, they never got fully adopted by both the industry and the scientific world such that code obfuscation remains an ad hoc technique, which usually comes down to a trade-off between security, performance, and cost.

Typically an attacker will first disassemble code and then decompile it to a higher level to get better understanding of the program. Obfuscation transformations try to make these steps harder.

White-Box Cryptography. The solutions that we develop might include cryptographic information in the software that is executed on the untrusted host. For example, a secure channel can be established between the client applications and the entrusting server based on a secret key. The purpose of such a channel would be to enable secure communication, e.g., to provide software updates or transfer application specific content (such as licence information in DRM applications). Extraction of the secret key from the application can compromise this covert channel. As a second example: in the basis architecture, attestations are sent to the trusted server. These can be signed by the software to assure that they originate from the executing software. Compromise of the signing key might compromise this correlation.

In general, we want to assure that cryptographic primitives (such as signing functions or encryption routines) remain secure when they are under attack by the adversary that we envision (a full access software adversary, often denoted as a white-box adversary). Since traditionally, cryptographic primitives are not designed against such type of adversaries, this is an important point to consider. The research topic that aims to address these issues is coined *"white-box cryptography"*. We refer to [Wyse09] for an overview of this research field, and to [SaWP09] for a theoretical framework that was presented within the scope of the RE-TRUST project.

Dynamic replacement. A key concept is the dynamic replacement strategy. The objective is to narrow down the window of exposure of the protection techniques to the adversary, and conceives the fact that at execution time, software updates are provided to the untrusted host at execution time. This approach has similarities to software aging, where updates of a program are frequently distributed. This limits the spread of software cracks and allows the renewal of software protection techniques embedded in the application. In order to make sure that the adversary accepts the software updates, two strategies can be pursued:

1. the original program is incomplete and needs to include updates at run-time in order to guarantee further execution, or

2. the service on which the execution depends might modify its protocol or authentication procedure, such that the application needs to accept the corresponding modifications in order to keep the connection to the service established.

The usage of code replacement techniques forces the adversary to deploy his attack within a well-defined period of time. Here the idea is that the amount of effort is only applicable during a limited period of time and that the effort of reverse engineering does not give knowledge on future release of software updates. We refer to the technique of *orthogonal replacement* [CPMT09] that has been developed in the RE-TRUST project for this purpose.

5 Hardware assisted remote attestation

In a second major part of this project, hardware-assisted approaches have been considered to enforce the pure software-based solutions. These hardware-assisted approaches rely on the usage of light-weight hardware such as Trusted Platform Modules or Smart Cards, which are relatively inexpensive and widely available in the marked of set-top boxes and personal computers. These hardware components facilitate the development of solutions that achieve a higher level of robustness against illegitimate software tampering, since we assume that they are able to provide secure storage or can employ (constraint) secure computations.

TPM–based Remote Attestation. In [SLS+05], a pure software-based technique to address the cloning attack, called *"Pioneer"*, was presented. The basic idea is to detect if an adversary is performing a cloning attack, by measuring the execution time of a verification mechanism. This exploits to fact that the TLB needs time (extra instructions) to swap between the tampered and untampered memory pages.

The Pioneer protocol works as follows: the verification server triggers a routine that is running on the untrusted platform. This routine computes a checksum of memory pages that are selected according a challenge that is randomly selected by the verification server. Based on the resulting value, the verification server is able to make a trustworthy verdict: if the value is correct and computed within a reasonable timeframe, the integrity of the memory pages is believed to be untampered. There are a number of issues with this protocol, including the fact that network delay has to be incorporated since the execution time needs to be measured by the verification server, and a reliable timeframe needs to be decided upon (based on CPU speed, cache load time, etc.). We have addressed most of the issues with Pioneer, by developing a system that uses the trusted clock of a TPM, and by deploying a benchmark service in the trusted boot loader. We refer to [ScWP08] for details on our new verification protocol.

FPGA-based Protection. This protection solution proposes the use of mobile hardware agents implementing monitoring techniques for securely producing and delivering attestations of code integrity of an application. It tries to join the benefits in terms of security of hardware-based verification, together with the flexibility of mobile software techniques.

Code mobility is nowadays widely used to build complex distributed systems. Systems supporting mobility are inherently dynamic and are particularly advantageous for networked infrastructures made of distributed and heterogeneous nodes [Picc00]. The idea of code mobility is however mainly limited to software. This is somewhat obvious when looking at the traditional partitioning of computers into physical, static hardware and logical, mobile software. However, such partitioning is being more and more blurred by the emerging field of reconfigurable computing [CoHa02]. The term reconfigurable computing refers to systems incorporating hardware programmability enabling a distinction between physical and logical hardware, as well as run-time hardware reconfigurability (e.g., Field Programmable Gate Arrays – FPGA). Reconfigurable computing, coupled with code mobility opens up a range of new opportunities for distributed digital systems, including the possibility of achieving adaptability, functionality extension, dependability, and security.

The proposed protection techniques exploits the possibility of sending mobile hardware agents able to implement different monitoring techniques (e.g., code checksumming), and to send back attestations of the integrity of the target software to the entrusting server (Fig. 2). We consider here an extended notion of mobility taking into consideration the possibility of migrating logical hardware components in a distributed infrastructure to protect remote software applications. Monitors implemented using reconfigurable hardware have the main advantage of having direct access to system resources (e.g., program code and data) without relying on software routines that might be under the control of the adversary.

Replacement of hardware modules guarantees to provide limited amount of time to the adversary to defeat the protection technique. Moreover, the increasing complexity of hardware reverse engineering allows in general to keep the replacement rate at a reasonable level. Finally, all hardware agents embed a secret (e.g., a key) that guarantees a secure communication between the monitor itself and the entrusting server.

The proposed solution perfectly targets embedded computational nodes that are nowadays commonly equipped with reconfigurable hardware components (e.g., FPGA) exploited for solving different problems.

Smart Dongle. A smart dongle [AuDa08] is a USB device that is made of a controller, a flash memory and a smart card. The flash memory is split in several partitions (CD-ROM, private, public). The original program is located in the CD-ROM partition and cannot be statically modified. In the RE-TRUST architecture, the smart dongle has the role as a trusted server and will monitor the behavior of the software at execution time. When the USB device is connecting to a computer, a session key will be injected into the application that will be loaded from the CD-ROM partition to the untrusted computing platform. Messages between the USB and the executing software can be secured with a communication protocol based on this session key.

The technique to verify the execution of the software that is loaded on the untrusted computing platform is based on checksums that are computed on code segments and compared to pre-computed values that are stored in the USB dongle. This method is referred to as the thumbprint mechanism. Session key renewability mechanisms guarantees freshness of the software.

The smart dongle may interact with a remote server in a secure way via a set of keys that are shared between the server and the smart dongle. This feature is used at connection time to check if a replacement of the CD-ROM partition is to be performed.

6 Security Analysis

The major challenge in evaluating the security of RE-TRUST solutions is to quantify the 'cost' and 'time-period' for a successful attack. To this purpose an extensive security analysis has been performed. In general, the objective of the security mechanisms is to construct efficient schemes for which it is infeasible to violate the security features. In modern cryptography both notions of efficiency and infeasibility have a common definition; such definitions are not trivial to construct for software protection mechanisms. In fact, the effort for breaking a protection technique is not easily evaluable in terms of computational resources. Starting from the consideration that an attack against solutions may require to perform complex comprehension tasks, we developed a model of the attacker behavior inspired on software evolution and maintenance. Although at a first glance software maintenance and malicious software tampering present major differences, mainly due to the underlying purpose and objectives, they share a very similar life-cycle and require a cognitive intensive effort to map the request for change (bug fix, new features or the attack goal) to the changes to software. For this reason, we used the *micro cycle of change* [RaBe00], a well-known software engineering paradigm that stresses the common aspects and focus on fast changes.

According to the effect that they have against the attack behavior techniques have been categorized in solutions that reduce the comprehensibility of the program's code (local e.g., obfuscation, and remote, by executing part of the program on the entrusting server), solutions that preserve the integrity of the code (both locally, as for crypto guards, and remotely, as for the TPM-based solution), and solutions that limit the available time by dynamically replacing the program's code. Since mounting an attack often involves the presence of men, the infeasibility need to be measured by means of the *empirical software engineering* to accumulate knowledge about the complexity of mounting an attack to different programs (e.g., through a set of experiments aimed at evaluating the effect of specific parameters, case studies, surveys, and statistical analyses) and to combine them using ad hoc metrics [WRH+00].

7 Conclusion

In this paper, we discuss the issue of trustworthy execution of software on untrusted computing platform. The challenge to guarantee that software is running and that it is running as expected is a major problem for which no satisfactory solutions exist. We present an overview of solutions for run-time software authentication, with the assumption of continuous availability of a network connection between the untrusted computing platform and trusted entities. These solutions constitute techniques that have been developed in the context of the RE-TRUST project, and can be classified in two major categories: pure software solutions which complement the original program with extra run-time monitoring functionalities; and hardware assisted protection techniques that rely on the presence of lightweight hardware such as Trusted Platform Modules, Smart Cards, or FPGAs.

To narrow down the window of exposure of our protection techniques, we present dynamic replacement techniques. This forces an adversary to deploy an attack within a well-defined period of time. Finally, we discuss the security analysis of the protection techniques and introduce a model based on the micro cycle of change.

Acknowledgements

This work has been partially funded by the IAP Programme P6/26 BCRYPT of the Belgian State (Belgian Science Policy) and the European Commission through the IST Programme under contract IST-021186 RE-TRUST.

The author would like to thank the colleagues and partners of the RE-TRUST project, in particular Cataldo Basile, Jan Cappaert, Stefano Di Carlo, and Yoram Ofek.

References

[Aucs03]   David Aucsmith "Tamper Resistant Software: An Implementation", In Information Hiding 1996.

[AuDa08]   Jean-Daniel Aussel, Jerome d'Annoville, "Smart Cards and remote entrusting", in proceedings of The Future of Trust in Computing, 2nd conference, Berlin, Germany, June 30-July 2, 2008.

[BaOY03]   M. Baldi, Y. Ofek, M. Young, "Idiosyncratic Signatures for Authenticated Execution of Management Code", 14th IFIP/IEEE International Workshop on Distributed Systems: Operations and Management (DSOM 2003), Heidelberg, Germany, Oct. 2003.

[BDH+09]   Cataldo Basile, Stefano Di Carlo, Thomas Herlea, Jasvir Nagra, and Brecht Wyseur. "Towards a Formal Model for Software Tamper Resistance". Work in progress, 16 pages, 2009.

[BCP+02]   Boris Balacheff, Liqun Chen, Siani Pearson, David Plaquin, Graeme Proudler, "Trusted Computing Platforms: TCPA Technology in Context", Prentice Hall, 2002.

[CPA+08]   Jan Cappaert, Bart Preneel, Bertrand Anckaert, Matias Madou, and Koen De Bosschere, "Towards Tamper Resistant Code Encryption: Practice and Experience", In Information Security Practice and Experience, 4th International Conference, ISPEC 2008, Lecture Notes in Computer Science 4991, L. Chen, Y. Mu, and W. Susilo (eds.), Springer-Verlag, pp. 86-100, 2008.

[CPMT09]   Mariano Ceccato, Mila Dalla Preda, Anirban Majumdar, Paolo Tonella. "Remote software protection by orthogonal client replacement". In Proceedings of the 24th ACM Symposium on Applied Computing. ACM, March 2009

[CoHa02]   K. Compton and S. Hauck, "Reconfigurable computing: A survey of systems and software," ACM Computing Surveys, vol. 34, no. 2, pp. 171–210, 2002.

[GiCK05]   Jonathon T. Giffin, Mihai Christodorescu, and Louis Kruger. "Strengthening Software Self-Checksumming via Self-Modifying Code," In Proceedings of the 21st Annual Computer Security Applications Conference (ACSAC 2005), pages 23–32, Washington, DC, USA, 2005. IEEE Computer Society.

[HMST02]   Bill Horne, Lesley R. Matheson, Casey Sheehan, and Robert Endre Tarjan. "Dynamic self-checking techniques for improved tamper resistance." In DRM '01: Revised Papers from the ACM CCS-8 Workshop on Security and Privacy in Digital Rights Management, pages 141–159, London, UK, 2002. Springer-Verlag.

[OoSW05]   Paul C. Van Oorschot, Anil Somayaji, and Glenn Wurster. "Hardware-Assisted Circumvention of Self-Hashing Software Tamper Resistance," In IEEE Transactions on Dependable and Secure Computing, 2(2), pp. 82-92, 2005.

[Picc00]   G. Picco, "Understanding code mobility," in Proceedings of the 2000 International Conference on Software Engineering, 2000., 2000, pp. 834–834.

[RaBe00]   Vaclav T. Rajlich and Keith H. Bennett. "A Staged Model for the Software Life Cycle". IEEE Software, 33(7):66–71, July 2000.

[SaWP09] Amitabh Saxena, Brecht Wyseur, and Bart Preneel, "Towards Security Notions for White-Box Cryptography," In Information Security – 12th International Conference, ISC 2009, Lecture Notes in Computer Science, Springer-Verlag, 18 pages, 2009.

[ScWP08] Dries Schellekens, Brecht Wyseur, and Bart Preneel, "Remote Attestation on Legacy Operating Systems with Trusted Platform Modules,". in Science of Computer Programming 74(1-2), pp. 13-22, 2008.

[SLS+05] Arvind Seshadri, Mark Luk, Elaine Shi, Adrian Perrig, Leendert van Doorn, and Pradeep K. Khosla. "Pioneer: Verifying Code Integrity and Enforcing Untampered Code Execution on Legacy Systems," in Proceedings of the 20th ACM Symposium on Operating Systems Principles 2005 (SOSP 2005), pages 1–16. ACM Press, 2005.

[WRH+00] Claes Wohlin, Per Runeson, Martin Höst, Magnus C. Ohlsson, Björn Regnell, Anders Wesslén. "Experimentation in Software Engineering: an Introduction". The Kluwer International Series In Software Engineering, 2000.

[Wyse09] Brecht Wyseur, "White-Box Cryptography," PhD thesis, Katholieke Universiteit Leuven, Bart Preneel (promotor), 169+32 pages, 2009.

Future of Assurance: Ensuring that a System is Trustworthy

Ahmad-Reza Sadeghi[1] · Ingrid Verbauwhede[2] · Claire Vishik[3]

[1]Ruhr University Bochum
ahmad.sadeghi@trust.rub.de

[2]KU Leuven
ingrid.verbauwhede@esat.kuleauven.de

[3]Intel Corporation UK
claire.vishik@intel.com

Abstract

Significant efforts are put in defining and implementing strong security measures for all components of the computing environment. It is equally important to be able to evaluate the strength and robustness of these measures and establish trust among the components of the computing environment based on parameters and attributes of these elements and best practices associated with their production and deployment. Today, the inventory of techniques used for security assurance and to establish trust -- audit, security-conscious development process, cryptographic components, external evaluation – is somewhat limited. These methods have their indisputable strengths and have contributed significantly to the advancement in the area of security assurance. However, shorter product and technology development cycles and the sheer complexity of modern digital systems and processes have begun to decrease the efficiency of these techniques. Moreover, these approaches and technologies address only some aspects of security assurance and, for the most part, evaluate assurance in a general design rather than an instance of a product. Additionally, various components of the computing environment participating in the same processes enjoy different levels of security assurance, making it difficult to ensure adequate levels of protection end-to-end. Finally, most evaluation methodologies rely on the knowledge and skill of the evaluators, making reliable assessments of trustworthiness of a system even harder to achieve. The paper outlines some issues in security assurance that apply across the board, with the focus on the trustworthiness and authenticity of hardware components and evaluates current approaches to assurance.

1 Trust, Trustworthiness, and Security Assurance

Ubiquitous nature of connectivity and computing in the 21st century led to the reassessment of security and security assurance. In the past, assurance relied on encryption and a few other methods, but today the area has grown to include everything that could disrupt creation, processing, transmission, and storage of information, sometimes summarized as confidentiality, availability, and integrity (see, e.g., PFLE07). The field of security assurance became so broad that it is now part of most subfields of computing [MYER08]. Faster product and technology development cycles and emergence of new development methodologies led to the revision, and sometimes to the relaxation, of assurance requirements [BEZN04]. The field continues to be very active, with a lot of technology development done in most areas that now are part of security assurance.

N. Pohlmann, H. Reimer, W. Schneider (Editors): Securing Electronic Business Processes, Vieweg (2009), 339-348

The broad approach to security assurance is not always helpful (as opposed to broad applicability of assurance technologies), and we attempt to provide clearer definitions for the issues associated with hardware assurance in this paper. The concept of security assurance is linked to the concepts of trust and trustworthiness [SMIT05], [BAZL05]. What needs to be done to develop the level of assurance that would permit users and operators to trust all types of modern computing systems? Before attempting to answer this question, it is important to define the meanings of trust, trusted and trustworthiness as these concepts are important for understanding security assurance.

In recent years, a lot of attention has been dedicated to the study of trust in hardware, defined as adherence to expected behaviors in components and systems. As the behaviour and composition of computing and electronic systems became more complex, manufacturing of the components of these systems was deployed globally, and connectivity of these systems became nearly universal, the definition of the expected behaviors grew more complicated as well.

Definitions of trust and security assurance consequently are more nuanced today than in earlier literature. E.g., [SMIT05] explains that, in an average transaction, the devices are, to some degree, worthy of trust, the relaying party has some ability to choose to trust a device, based on the capability of the device to communicate information confirming its trustworthiness (page 2). As a result of these linkages, some authors (e.g. [BAZL05]) use trust establishment and the relationship between trustworthiness and trust as the basis of the definition of trust:

> **trusted:** *the degree to which the user or a component depends on the trustworthiness of another component. For example, component A trusts component B, or component B is trusted by component A. Trust and trustworthiness are assumed to be measured on the same scale.*

However, the limited ability to establish and communicate trust that exists in generic devices and platforms is not sufficient to provide adequate levels of assurance across the computing environment. This is demonstrated by continued efforts to create high-assurance devices (from PCs to cellular phones) that can be trusted on a basis of better protections and more reliable proof of their trustworthiness and that are used in high security environments. In the past three decades, numerous projects aimed at building high assurance systems took place, many of them successful for the niche applications that they served. But the task of extending assurance to the entire computing environment remained elusive, since numerous components of the ecosystems (the term is "used here synonymously with "computing environment") need to work together to ensure that the ecosystem can be trusted.. Various approaches have been proposed (see, e.g. [GREV03] or [ALVE06]), with Trusted Computing achieving some level of success in both research and industry as evident from a significant body of research in TC and a list of Trusted Computing products developed internationally[1].

As electronic processes replace other methods in all activities, including those processes that require higher security assurance, from essential records management to supply chain execution and electronic commerce, building higher assurance systems for all tasks is increasingly challenging. General use ecosystems and higher security environments are now interconnected at many levels and share common elements. It is urgent, therefore, to assess assurance needs of these complex systems and environments [PHAM07] in order to develop a higher degree of automation as well as new tools and technologies and define design and evaluation approaches that could support a higher level of assurance in a broad spectrum of common electronic systems. The work in this area is starting, but it builds on long and successful tradition of developing trusted systems. Many foundational questions require additional re-

---

1 A list of such products is available from the Trusted Computing Group Web site at http://www.trustedcomputinggroup.org/

search, however, starting with the articulation of the general assurance requirements and achievement of a greater automation of the evaluation process [see, e.g., IRVI08].

2 Hardware Assurance – High Level View

When determining the level of assurance of a system (and consequently the level of trust that can be afforded to such a system), we can formulate some questions to help us define areas of assurance:

1. Is the system secure (does it have the expected security properties and configuration)?
2. Is it in good standing (did is sustain attacks or unauthorized modifications)?
3. Is it trustworthy (can it be trusted for the type of tasks it is expected to perform)? Even if 'broken' in the future, can past operations be trusted?
4. Is the system genuine (does it comprise only authentic components that are correctly implemented and are those parts assembled together in a genuine way for both hardware and software)?
5. What was its path from manufacturing to deployment?
6. Was the design of its elements compliant with the best industry and technology practices?

If technology were available to answer most of these questions in an automated fashion for all components of the ecosystem, the state of security assurance would be more adapted for the dynamic nature and complexity of today's computing environment. Considerable body of research is available in many areas outlined above, but the gaps remain. The problem of assurance is exacerbated by both the complexity of computing devices and heterogeneous nature of the computing environment. Establishing adequate levels of assurance in a transaction such as the example outlined in Figure 1 below (and, consequently, establishing trust among all the nodes of such a process) requires a broad and unified approach to technologies that enable security and provide assurance and trust in heterogeneous devices and communication protocols. As illustrated below, ensuring trust and developing technologies for security assurance in a complex environment is not a simple matter.

It is important to note also that various aspects of security assurance receive varying levels of attention. Frequently, resistance to vulnerabilities and threats is considered the main (or the only) basis to establish trustworthiness of a platform or a device (see, e.g., IRVI08). Consequently, sometimes process oriented assurance practices are believed to be the only (or the best) means to reliably assess the trustworthiness of a device [IRVI08], and an external evaluation of these processes is considered the best benchmark that can be trusted. Without wishing to diminish the value of security evaluations, such as Common Criteria, and their positive influence on increasing the security of ICT (Information and Computer Technology) products, it is important to understand the limitations of such approaches. They cannot address all the assurance needs reflected in the list of assurance questions above. We will discuss the issues of security evaluation in Section 2.2 below.

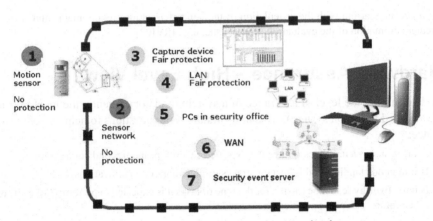

Fig. 1: Varying level of security in devices & networks supporting the same process

Of the assurance problems outlined earlier, the authentic nature of a component or a device is frequently overlooked by researchers, although counterfeiting of goods and intellectual property violations have reached a level that threatens industrial production, organizational functions, and even national security. Non-genuine systems are more likely to become a weak link in an otherwise robust computing environment, since their quality and integrity cannot be guaranteed in the same way as is the case for authentic components. While the problem of authenticity of the systems is different from other problems in security assurance (e.g. trustworthiness after deployment), the methods that can be used to prove authenticity of systems and their trustworthiness defined as resistance to threats and adherence to expected behaviors may be similar. Best practices currently available to reduce the occurrence of counterfeit goods, such as sound purchasing practices, use of certified providers and checking product authenticity where available, are important. However, considering the complexity of an average device or platform as well as supply chain practices, without solid support in technology and trust in technology providers, it will be increasingly hard to rely on best practices only. It is necessary, therefore, to develop assurance and evaluation methodologies that can cover all aspects of trustworthiness in hardware and ecosystem in general.

Insufficient levels of assurance can be expressed in economic terms. General losses from security failures are significant, for example, losses just from the theft of data are estimated to be one trillion dollars in 2008□. The total annual value of the trade in fake goods has risen from $200 Billion in 2002, to $450 Billion in 2006 [KON03],[ICC05],[OECD07]. It involves a wide range of items, from electronics to multimedia content and pharmaceuticals. Counterfeit electronics are estimated to account for 1-10% of global sales [TUY06]. But non-genuine components and products could also house undetected malicious elements capable of bringing significant damage to the foundation of today's digital economy and even critical information infrastructure.

Electronics contain specific ICs such as ASIC (Application-Specific Integrated Circuit), ASIP (Application Specific Integrated Processor) or FPGA (Field-Programmable Gate Array) that implement innovative features. A substantial proportion of electronic products (e.g., routers, PCs, electrical grid management devices) are used as part of the critical infrastructure. Commercial off-the-shelf (COTS) hardware (from mobile phones and removable storage to PCs) is increasingly deployed for government use and in higher security areas and is used by both consumers and organizations.

The same components are frequently used for lower grade and higher security devices, and techniques used to defeat protections in consumer systems can potentially be used to break more secure implementations. This is not unusual: as the technology environment develops, new attacks are performed, and new remedies against them are devised. The challenge is the diversity of the computing environment today and the need to provide a good level of assurance across the board. New approaches are necessary to protect a broad range of hardware devices, and new broadly applicable methodologies need to be defined for hardware assurance and evaluation. The same technologies can be used in packaging or other controlling features to increase assurance of other types of products. In general, approaches to assurance are needed that are applicable to all the elements of the computing environment.

The ability to ensure functional correctness of ICs is important to provide assurance in all types of hardware. Progress has been made in research in this area [WAGN07], [HARD08]. A combination of formal verification methods and reliance on trusted processors is beginning to be used for security assurance, e.g., [WAGN07], [AUST00]. While these methods and approaches have potential for improving some aspects of assurance, they cannot resolve the problem of authenticity.

Various types of security hardware, from secure co-processors to Trusted Platform Modules, are also viewed as part of the solution to build a safer, more trustworthy, ecosystem, supporting both secure storage and secure execution of programs. Indeed, they go a long way towards improving the safety of the computing environment. But security hardware is susceptible to the same counterfeiting issues as general purpose hardware.

As hardware becomes more complex, more security features are built into different hardware components. Functional blocks, such as USB or Ethernet, are produced by or licensed from multiple manufacturers. Undetected malicious or test functions in these blocks could potentially become an origination point for dangerous security attacks. The problem of assurance spans the whole device and the computing environment where it operates.

Any of the issues mentioned above can lead to serious consequences for security and many general purpose components and systems, spanning from loss of revenue to loss of privacy to negative impacts on critical infrastructure.

These concerns call for new approaches to design and evaluation of hardware components that are applicable across the board – enabling technologies that support unique features that can be measured or evaluated, but not cloned. However, technology advances necessary to produce higher security architectures covering the whole ecosystem as well as methodologies for evaluation to help detect forgeries and potentially malicious elements in a more automated fashion continue to require attention. The field of hardware assurance needs new technologies that are broadly applicable to enable a safer computing environment, in order to assert the trustworthiness of other elements of the computing ecosystem.

2.1 More on Authenticity of Hardware

Counterfeiting and forgery are serious global issues causing significant economic losses as well as other negative impacts. We can distinguish between two types of counterfeiting. The first is overproduction or overbuilding. Manufacturers who are not technology developers or owners, but have access to the blueprints of the original products can create perfect forgeries by manufacturing unauthorized exact copies after hours. Since the product is unchanged, overproduction is passive counterfeiting. However, the conditions of unauthorized manufacturing can be slighly different, and quality control can be relaxed, potentially leading to malfunctions and weaknesses.

There are two types of *active counterfeiting*. One is sometimes related to outsourcing in manufacturing. Overseas manufacturers may try to cut costs by omitting or reducing the features from the original design, with possible effects on security features. There is also a risk that the functionality has been deliberately modified or supplemented with a backdoor or a hardware Trojan. For instance, a circuit might be added to leak the key materials, the random number generator can be altered or the IC might have a kill switch. The other type of active counterfeiting is related to cloning and/or reverse engineering of products to obtain design information for future reproduction, with alternations or without changes.

To summarise, counterfeit or altered hardware systems or components can emerge as a result of multiple activities:

1. Overproduction of components and complete systems
2. Overproduction with relaxation of manufacturing conditions
3. Deliberate omission of important elements of design during outsourcing
4. Insertion of malicious functionality in electronic components and systems
5. Introduction of malicious components via third party suppliers of general purpose elements, such as USB or Ethernet ports.

Some types of counterfeiting are very hard or impossible to detect with currently available technologies. Authenticity of components is an important part of assurance, and broadly applicable evaluation methods need to be created or improved.

2.2 The Role of Evaluation

Current methods for assuring the authenticity and trustworthiness of both hardware and software systems rely on the skills of an evaluator. The lack of standardized methodologies and automated tools that are as dynamic as the computing environment means that the evaluator needs to correctly identify and manually evaluate known risk areas. The evaluator knows only what was detected and described historically, but, in order to be more successful, he/she must be aware of all known attacks while also anticipating new forms of attacks and vulnerabilities. From defining systematic approaches to assurance to identifying tools to automate and improve assurance techniques, significant new research is required. Existing methods developed for high assurance hardware systems and components are not always applicable for COTS products from an economic perspective. A systematic and extensible approach with solid scientific basis is required to ensure the authenticity and correctness of implementation in hardware components, particularly when they are deployed as the security anchor for a device or a platform.

External evaluations, such as Common Criteria, permit us to test crucial security functionality through independent evaluation, streamline the development process, and establish common benchmarks to compare products. However, it is important to remember that these tests can only be applied to the general design of a product rather than the instance of the implementation. Therefore, this approach to evaluation cannot solve the problem of authenticity and trustworthiness for an instance of the product. New evaluation methodologies are necessary to address these issues, approaches that are capable of assessing both resistance to attacks and authenticity of a system. These methodologies are not limited to those relying on the third party evaluations only, but can be applied to systems and devices in a trustworthy fashion by those involved in production, delivery, and configuration of systems.

3 Addressing the Problem of Authenticity

From the previous sections it follows that there is an urgent need for developing new methodologies that increase assurance in all areas, including authenticity and correctness of implementation that take into consideration the fact that different devices have different levels of security capabilities. These new technologies need to be defined in such a way that the approaches are applicable to the other parts of the computing ecosystem.

Solutions addressing the issues of the active and passive counterfeiting need novel techniques at various levels. They can rely on novel cryptographic building blocks exploiting unique physical properties of underlying hardware, such as sub-micron physical security primitives. A recent promising development in this context concerns Physically Unclonable Functions (PUFs) that are believed to offer a viable approach to assurance.

3.1 Physical Unclonable Functions

A Physical Unclonable Function (PUFs) [PRTG02] is a primitive that maps challenges to responses, which are highly dependent on the physical properties of the device, in which the PUF is contained or embedded. PUFs consist of two parts: a physical part and an operational part. The physical part is a physical system that is very difficult to clone. It inherits its unclonability from uncontrollable process variations during manufacturing. In the case of PUFs on an IC, such process variations are typically deep-submicron variations such as doping variations in transistors. The operational part corresponds to the function. In order to turn the physical system into a function, a set of challenges c_i (stimuli) has to be available to which the system responds with a set of sufficiently different responses r_i. Examples of PUFs include optical PUFs [PAPP02], silicon PUFs [GCDD02], coating PUFs [TSS+06], Intrinsic-PUFs [GKST07], and LC-PUFs [SBJ+08]. Regardless of their particular instantiation, their unclonability and tamper evidence properties have made PUFs very useful tools in IP protection and secure key storage applications[LIM05].

Note that PUF responses are noisy by nature. In other words, two calls to the PUF with the same challenge c will produce two different but closely related responses, where the measure of closeness can be defined via a distance function. Intuitively, the distance function should be small among responses originating from the same device and very large for PUF responses originating from different devices. Nevertheless, it is clear that the plain PUF response cannot be used as the key, since this would mean that the data encrypted under response could not be decrypted with noisy response, even if both responses originate from the same PUF embedded in the same device. In order to derive reliable and uniform strings from (imperfect) sources of randomness, such as a PUF, the concept of a fuzzy extractor or helper data algorithm were introduced in [LT03, DRS04] that employs an additional parameter called helper data that is specific for each PUF and the corresponding challenge.

Because of their properties, PUFs are more resilient to physical and side channel attacks and suitable for lightweight protocols [MAES09]. PUFs are also very hard to clone or predict [PAPP02]. As such, PUFs are a potentially useful mechanism to improve security assurance in various types of hardware, including protection of authenticity.

4 Unsolved Problems in Assurance

Targets of security attacks are moving up the stack to applications and downwards into the firmware, supporting a growing need for a coherent technology response that can span across all the security layers. At the same time as the security environment becomes more dynamic and harder to address, with new threats appearing every day, the issue of authenticity of systems and components leads to additional unsolved problems for hardware assurance.

Surveys consistently demonstrate that it is the opportunity for economic gain that is driving most attackers. These motivations are even stronger for those producing counterfeit hardware. Although serious thought has been given to the best practices that best guarantee assurance, the situation will improve only when new technologies and new approaches to assurance that can be applied to all elements of the ecosystem are developed. The propagation of consistent levels of assurance beyond hardware to build higher levels of assurance in the ecosystem is of paramount importance. We need to trust the whole computing environment that is becoming increasingly complex, not only the hardware elements.

The definition of new robust and pragmatic methods that can establish trustworthiness, validity, and authenticity of hardware devices and systems is of vital importance to ensure a safe computing environment for all levels of operations.

Security evaluation is an area of paramount importance to improve assurance. Some issues in currently used approaches to security evaluations have already been mentioned. There are additional difficulties associated with evaluation of proprietary technologies. For a variety of reasons, it is not always possible to disclose all the details of architectures or source to external entities, and it is therefore necessary to create methodologies for evaluation as well as security technologies that could confirm trustworthiness of hardware elements without the need to access sensitive components of information. These methodologies could then be reused in other areas where trustworthiness of custom made hardware elements, such as plane instrumentation, need to be determined and maintained. This approach can be extended to areas where it is imperative to ensure the genuine nature of an asset, for example, in pharmaceutical inventories.

At the same time, since serious security flaws may require replacement of hardware systems, it is necessary to devise new approaches to hardware security that is applicable to a wide range of devices and environments. Trust establishment is necessarily associated with sharing information among participants and users of trusted systems and networks, and therefore it is also important to ensure that privacy is safeguarded as assurance is improved, to guarantee users' and society's acceptance of trustworthy systems. In today's interconnected environment, a connected device or a component of a connected platform can potentially become a proxy for a user of such a device or platform. Therefore, devising privacy solutions that are compatible with a high level of assurance is an important part of the big picture.

To summarize, the following issues in security assurance need to be resolved in the near future:

1. Approach that covers all aspects of assurance, from resistance to attacks to authenticity.
2. Adherence to best practices is very important in improving security assurance, but significant steps forward are only possible with the help of new technologies and approaches that cover a wide range of devices.
3. Evaluation methods supplementing those currently available (e.g. through certification schemes), comprising a high level of automation and adequate tools, and addressing instances of products as well as general implementation issues need to be introduced.
4. Broadly applicable security assurance techniques are necessary to significantly improve the end-to-end security and reliability of the computing environment.

5 Conclusions

Building trustworthy devices and systems by increasing security assurance is a very difficult task. Current assurance technologies and evaluation methodologies target the general design of a product rather than instances of its implementation. They are not universally applicable and focus on a limited number of aspects of assurance. New research in security assurance needs to address the totality of issues in this area, devising solutions for all aspects of security assurance. The development of new approaches to broadly applicable hardware assurance and improving automation of the evaluation techniques can lead the way to improving the levels of assurance in the ecosystem and, consequently, the levels of trust in digital processes.

References

[AUST00] Austin, T. DIVA: A Dynamic Approach to Microprocessor Verification, May 2000.

[ALVE06] Alves-Foss, J., Oman, P. W., Taylor, C., nad Harrison, S. The MILS architecture for high-assurance embedded systems. *IJES* 2(3/4): 239-247 (2006)

[BENZ05] Benzel, T., Irvine, C., Levin, T., Bhaskara, G., . Nguyen, T., and Clark, P. *Design principles for security*. ISI-TR-605, Information Sciences Institute, Santa Monica, California, and NPS-CS-05-010, Naval Postgraduate School, Monterey, California, 2005.

[BEZN04] Beznosov, K. and Kruchten, P. 2004. Towards agile security assurance. In *Proceedings of the 2004 Workshop on New Security Paradigms* (Nova Scotia, Canada, September 20 – 23, 2004). NSPW '04. ACM, New York, NY, 47-54.

[DRS04] Dodis, Y., Reyzin, M., Smith, A.: Fuzzy extractors: How to generate strong keys from biometrics and other noisy data. In Cachin, C., Camenisch, J., eds.: Advances in Cryptology – EUROCRYPT 2004. Volume 3027 of LNCS., Springer-Verlag (2004) 523-540

[GCDD02] Gassend, B., Clarke, D.E., van Dijk, M., Devadas, S.: Silicon physical unknown functions. In Atluri, V., ed.: ACM Conference on Computer and Communications Security – CCS 2002, ACM (November 2002) 148-160

[GKST07] Guajardo, J., Kumar, S.S., Schrijen, G.J., Tuyls, P.: FPGA Intrinsic PUFs and Their Use for IP Protection. In Paillier, P., Verbauwhede, I., eds.: Cryptographic Hardware and Embedded Systems – CHES 2007. Volume 4727 of LNCS., Springer (September 10-13, 2007) 63-80

[GREV03] Greve, D. and M. Wilding and W.M. Vanfleet.. A Separation Kernel Formal Scurity Policy, In *Proceeding of the ACL2 Workshop 2003*, July 2003.

[HARD08] Hardin, D. S. 2008. Considerations in the design and verification of microprocessors for safety-critical and security-critical applications: invited tutorial. In *Proceedings of the 2008 international Conference on Formal Methods in Computer-Aided Design* (Portland, Oregon, November 17 – 20, 2008). A. Cimatti and R. B. Jones, Eds. Formal Methods in Computer Aided Design. IEEE Press, Piscataway, NJ, 1-8.

[ICC05] International Chamber of Commerce, Business Action to stop Counterfeiting and Piracy, United States Trade Representative, 2005, Special Report

[IRVI08] Irvine, C. and Leavitt, K. Trusted Hardware: Can It Be Trustworthy?

[KOUS07] Koushanfar, F. AND Potkonjak, M. 2007. CAD-based security, cryptography, and digital rights management. In Proceedings of the Design Automation Conference (DAC).

[LIM05] Lim, W., Lee, J., Gassend, B., Suh, E. G., van Dijk, M., and Devadas, S. Extracting Secret Keys from Integrated Circuits. *IEEE Transactions on Very Large Scale Integration (VLSI) Systems*, Volume 13, Issue 10, p.1200-1205, October 2005.

[KON03] Hopkins, D., Kontnik, L, and Turnage, T. *Counterfeiting exposed: Protecting your Brand and Customers*, New York: Wiley, 2003.[LT03] Linnartz, J.P.M.G., Tuyls, P.: New Shielding Functions to Enhance Privacy and Prevent Misuse of Biometric Templates. In Kittler, J., Nixon, M.S., eds.: Audioand

Video-Based Biometrie Person Authentication – AVBPA 2003. Volume 2688 of LNCS, Springer (June 9-11, 2003) 393-402

[MAES09] Maes,R., Schellekens, D, Tuyls, P., and Verbauwhede, I. Analysis and Design of Active IC Metering Schemes. In *Proc. of the 2nd IEEE International workshop on Hardware-Oriented Security and Trust*, San Francisco, CA, July 2009.

[MOJZ08] Majzoobi, M., Koushanfar, F., and Potkonjak, M. 2008. Lightweight secure PUFs. In *Proceedings of the 2008 IEEE/ACM international Conference on Computer-Aided Design* (San Jose, California, November 10 – 13, 2008). International Conference on Computer Aided Design. IEEE Press, Piscataway, NJ, 670-673.

[MYER08] Myers, J. P. and Riela, S. 2008. Taming the diversity of information assurance & security. *J. Comput. Small Coll.* 23, 4 (Apr. 2008), 173-179.

[OECD07] *The economic impact of counterfeiting and piracy, executive summary*, The OECD 2007, ICC, International Chamber of Commerce

[PAPP02] Pappu, R., Recht, B., Taylor, J., and Gershenfeld, N. 2002. Physical one-way functions. Science 297, 2026–2030.

[PFLE07] Pfleeger, C.P. & Pfleeger, S.L., *Security in Computing (4th ed.)*, Prentice Hall (Upper Saddle River, NJ), 2007.

[PHAM07] Pham, N. and Riguidel, M. 2007. Security Assurance Aggregation for IT Infrastructures. In *Proceedings of the Second international Conference on Systems and Networks Communications* (August 25 – 31, 2007). ICSNC. IEEE Computer Society, Washington, DC, 72.

[PIEP03] Pieprzyk, J., Hardjono, T., & Seberry, J., *Fundamentals of Computer Security*, Springer (New York), 2003.

[SBJ+08] Skoric, B., Bel, T., Blom, A., de Jong, B., Kretschman, H., Nellissen, A.: Randomized resonators as uniquely identifiable anti-counterfeiting tags. Technical report, Philips Research Laboratories (January 28th, 2008)

[SMIT05] Smith, Sean. *Trusted Computing Platforms: Design and Applications*. Springer-Verlag New York: Seacaucus, NJ, 2005

[TSS+06] Tuyls, P., Schrijen, G.J., Skoric, B., van Geloven, J., Verhaegh, N., Wolters, R.: Read-Proof Hardware from Protective Coatings. In Goubin, L., Matsui, M., eds.: Cryptographic Hardware and Embedded Systems – CHES 2006. Volume 4249 of LNCS., Springer (October 10-13, 2006) 369-383

[WAGN07] Wagner, I. and Bertacco, V. Engineering Trust with Semantic Guardians. *Design Automation and Test in Europe (DATE)*, Nice, France, April 2007

A Taxonomy of Cryptographic Techniques for Securing Electronic Identity Documents

Klaus Schmeh

cv cryptovision
klaus.schmeh@cryptovision.com

Abstract

There is a wide range of cryptographic techniques that may serve to prevent attacks on electronic identity documents (e-IDs). Many e-ID systems – including the ICAO ePass and virtually all national electronic identity cards – make intensive use of these methods. The first purpose of this work is to identify all cryptographic techniques that make an electronic identity document secure. As a second step, these techniques are grouped into several distinct classes. And third, they are evaluated according to their application areas and according to their advantages and disadvantages. In the fourth part of the paper, the ICAO ePass and the German electronic identity card (ePA) are examined with a view on the cryptographic techniques they use.

1 Introduction

More than 20 countries in the world are issuing electronic identity cards or have concrete plans to do so in the near future [Schmeh09a]. Other states use electronic health cards or other chip-card-based identity documents. In addition, about 60 countries in the world issue electronic passports according to the ICAO MRTD standard, and the number is growing rapidly. Electronic identity documents ranging from electronic identity cards to electronic travel documents are referred to as *e-IDs* in this paper.

The benefit an e-ID system provides is twofold: On the one side a microchip makes an identity document more secure; on the other side e-IDs can be used for additional applications, which are not possible with conventional documents. This paper will focus on the additional security e-IDs provide.

2 Attacks on e-IDs

Non-electronic identity documents and e-IDs can be the target of different kinds of attacks. The following list names the most important ones:

- *Complete fraud*: An attacker can try to create an identity document without altering or copying an existing one. This is referred to as complete fraud. Complete fraud is possible for both non-electronic identity documents and e-IDs. For an e-ID, complete fraud means that the attacker can freely choose the content of the fake document without being bound to the content of an existing one.

- *Cloning*: If an attacker copies an existing identity document, this is referred to as cloning. Cloning digital data is generally easier than cloning physical material. Therefore, cloning protection

N. Pohlmann, H. Reimer, W. Schneider (Editors): Securing Electronic Business Processes, Vieweg (2009), 349-356

is always a major issue for the design of an e-ID. As opposed to complete fraud, a cloning attack (by definition) always results in a document, which has the same content as an already existing genuine one.

- *Alteration*: An attacker might try to change the content of an identity document. While the physical part of an identity document may be very difficult to change, alteration of digital data is usually easy (as long as there is no special protection against it). In any case, an alteration attack does not result in a new identity document, but changes the appearance of an existing one.
- *Unauthorized reading*: The content of an identity document should not be accessible without the owner's acceptance. In the case of an e-ID, an attack like this is referred to as skimming. Skimming is especially a problem, when a wireless interface is used.
- *Eavesdropping*: Closely related to skimming is eavesdropping the communication between the e-ID and the terminal unit. This attack is not relevant for non-electronic identity documents, but it plays an important role for e-IDs with a wireless interface.
- *Man-in-the-middle*: When an e-ID chip communicates with a terminal unit, an attacker might conduct a man-in-the-middle-attack. This means that the attacker makes the chip believe that he is the terminal and the terminal that he is the chip. A man-in-the-middle-attack is only relevant for e-IDs. It is especially dangerous, when a wireless interface is used.
- *Usage by wrong person*: The use of an identity document by a different person than its owner is probably the most common attack. Both non-electronic identity documents and e-IDs can be attacked this way.
- *Illegal obtaining*: Non-electronic identity cards as well as e-IDs may be issued to the wrong person.
- *Denial of service*: Identity documents are targets for denial-of-service attacks. Both non-electronic identity cards and e-IDs can be attacked this way. However, the methods and implications are very different. In the case of an e-ID, the attacker may delete the microchip without the owner noticing it.
- *Marking*: It is possible to secretly mark an identity document. There are many ways to abuse these marks. Both non-electronic identity cards and e-IDs can be attacked this way. The methods and implications are very different.

There is a wide range of cryptographic techniques that may serve to inhibit or hinder some of these attacks. The purpose of this paper is to discuss and classify these techniques.

3 Classification

There are several technologies, which can be used to prevent attacks on e-IDs. The most important ones are cryptography, biometry, secure storage, and PIN query. In this work, only cryptography is covered. Cryptography provides for a broad range of methods to improve the security of an e-ID. Among the attacks mentioned above, complete fraud, cloning, alteration, unauthorized reading, eavesdropping, and man-in-the-middle can be prevented with cryptography. Usage by the wrong person should be addressed with biometry, while illegal obtaining is prevented not with technical but with organisational means.

For preventing denial-of-service and marking, cryptography is also not the major technology. However, it is possible to abuse cryptographic tools to start denial-of service or marking attacks. Especially the question of marking is very interesting, because it is possible to use covert channels in cryptographic protocols for this purpose. However this (important) question is out of scope in this work.

The first purpose of this paper is to classify the cryptographic techniques that make an e-ID secure. These cryptographic techniques can be divided into three groups: authentication of the chip unit, authentication of the terminal unit, and secure data exchange.

3.1 Authentication of the chip unit

Among the most important cryptographic tools used for securing e-IDs are the ones that are used for authenticating the card chip itself (chip authentication) or the content of the card chip (content authentication) or a statement about the e-ID (statement authentication). These tools are summarised under *authentication of the chip unit*. Authentication of the chip unit can prevent complete fraud, cloning, and alteration. It can be achieved with both asymmetric and symmetric cryptography.

3.1.1 Chip authentication

Chip authentication is accomplished with a challenge-response protocol. The terminal unit sends a challenge, and the chip replies with a response. Chip authentication can prevent complete fraud and cloning, but cannot prevent alteration. The challenge-response protocol is performed with either a secret or a private key. In both cases, the key must be stored on the chip in a secure way. In addition, the chip must be capable of computing a challenge out of a response, which means that a memory chip is not suitable (in other words, a microcontroller is necessary).

3.1.1.1 Symmetric chip authentication

In the symmetric case, the chip has stored a secret key (e.g. an AES key), which is used for the challenge-response protocol. Both the card and the verifier need to know this key. Symmetric card authentication is mainly recommendable in environments, where there are only few terminal units. In case of a large number of checking units, the management of the secret keys gets complicated. Nevertheless, there are card systems, where a large number of cards and checking units only use symmetric keys. E.g. bank cards are often realised this way.

3.1.1.2 Asymmetric chip authentication

In the case of asymmetric chip authentication, the chip uses a private key (e.g. RSA key) for the challenge-response protocol. The terminal unit needs the public key (usually provided as a digital certificate) of the chip in order to verify the correctness of the response. There are two ways to conduct an asymmetric challenge-response protocol [Schmeh09b]:

- The verifier sends a value (challenge); the proofer signs it and sends it back (response).
- The verifier encrypts a value and sends it to the proofer (challenge). The proofer decrypts it and sends the value back (response).

The two challenge-response approaches are quite similar. However, the first one is considered slightly better, because the value need not be kept secret. Therefore, all major network protocols use a digitally signed challenge. e-ID systems usually do the same. Asymmetric card authentication works well even in large user groups. The key management is easier than in the symmetric case, because the checking units only need to work with public keys. Most e-ID systems use this approach.

3.1.2 Content authentication

Apart from the chip itself, the digital content of the chip (i.e. the personal data of the owner) can be authenticated. Content authentication prevents alternation and complete fraud, but doesn't prevent cloning. It requires no microcontroller; it can also be applied on a memory card. Content authentication can be realized with both symmetric and asymmetric cryptography.

3.1.2.1 Symmetric content authentication (MAC)

In this case, the content of a chip is protected with a cryptographic hash value (usually referred to as MAC). The MAC is generated with a secret key as a part of the card personalisation. The terminal unit needs to know this secret key, while the card itself need not know it. Symmetric content authentication is mainly recommendable in environments, where there are few terminal units, because the key management is not feasible in large systems.

3.1.2.2 Asymmetric content authentication (digital signature)

Instead of a MAC, a digital signature can be used for securing the content of an e-ID. The checking unit uses a public key (usually provided by a digital certificate) to verify the signature. Asymmetric card authentication works well even in large environments. The key management is easier than in the symmetric case, because the checking units only need to work with public keys.

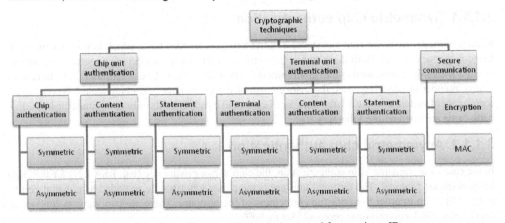

Fig. 1: Taxonomy of cryptographic techniques used for securing e-IDs

3.1.3 Statement authentication

Apart from authenticating the chip or the chip content, it is also possible to authenticate a statement, which is made about the chip (or the e-ID owner). The most obvious variant of such a statement authentication is a digital certificate that contains not only the public key of the owner but also additional information. E.g., a digital certificate may contain the owner's birth date. Apart from this, signed assertions (e.g. made with SAML) and attribute certificates can be used for statement authentication.

3.2 Authentication of the terminal unit

Terminal unit authentication uses similar cryptographic tools as card authentication. The purpose of these tools is mainly to prevent unauthorized reading.

3.2.1 Terminal authentication

Terminal authentication is realised with a similar challenge-response protocol as chip authentication. However, in this case not the chip computes the response out of the challenge, but the terminal. The chip needs to verify the response, which is only possible, when the chip has computation ability (i.e. it must be a microcontroller).

3.2.1.1 Symmetric terminal authentication

For terminal authentication, two approaches can be used. Both consist of a challenge-response protocol with symmetric keys. The difference lies in the way this key is obtained:

- *PIN-based symmetric challenge-response*: In this case, the secret key is derived from a PIN or some information printed on the card.

- *Key-based symmetric challenge-response*: In this case, the key is pre-installed on the chip.

The PIN-based symmetric challenge-response is less secure than the second option, but it still serves its purpose as a means against unauthorized reading.

3.2.1.2 Asymmetric terminal authentication

Asymmetric terminal authentication also provides for a challenge-response protocol. Yet, in this case, the terminal uses a private key. The chip must be capable of verifying the response, which is very often done with a digital certificate. However, not X.509 certificates are the most popular ones for this purpose, but CV certificates.

3.2.2 Content authentication

Like an e-ID, a terminal may store information that is signed or hashed. This information may tell the chip, if the terminal is authorized to access certain data on the chip.

3.2.2.1 Symmetric content authentication (MAC)

In this case, content stored by the terminal is protected with a cryptographic hash value (MAC). The MAC is generated with a secret key that must be known to the card. Symmetric content authentication is not very popular, as the key management is complicated.

3.2.2.2 Asymmetric content authentication (digital signature)

Instead of a MAC, a digital signature can be used for securing the content of a terminal unit. The chip uses a public key (usually provided by a CV certificate) to verify the signature. Asymmetric card authentication works well even in large environments. The key management is easier than in the symmetric case, because the checking units only need to work with public keys.

3.2.3 Terminal statement authentication

It is possible to issue digital certificates to terminals. These digital certificates may contain additional information, e.g. about their access rights. If this is the case, it can be regarded as terminal statement authentication. Apart from this, SAML assertions or attribute certificates may be used for this purpose.

3.3 Secure communication

An obvious approach to apply cryptography in e-ID systems is to encrypt, hash or sign the data exchange between the card chip and the checking system. This approach is called secure messaging or secure communication.

3.3.1 Encrypted communication

In this case all data exchanged by the chip and the terminal unit are encrypted. When data are exchanged this way, it is assumed that the card chip and the terminal unit share a secret key, which has been established as a part of the card authentication and terminal authentication.

3.3.2 Hashed communication

In this case all data exchanged by the chip and the terminal unit are hashed with a MAC function. When data are exchanged this way, it is assumed that the chip and the terminal unit share a secret key, which has been established as a part of the card authentication or terminal authentication. Hashed communication needs to be contrasted from symmetric card content authentication. In the latter case, the hash value is created as a part of the card initialisation process, while hashed communication assumes that the hash value is created dynamically before sending the data. Hashed communication is therefore more flexible, but it requires a microcontroller chip.

3.3.3 Signed communication

In this case, the data exchanged by the chip and the terminal unit are signed. No secret key needs to be exchanged. Signed communication needs to be contrasted from asymmetric card content authentication. In the latter case, the signature is created as a part of the card initialisation process, while signed communication assumes that the signature is created dynamically before sending the data. Signed communication is therefore more flexible, but it requires a microcontroller chip.

4 Evaluation

In this chapter, the previously introduced techniques are evaluated according to their advantages and disadvantages. In addition, it is discussed, which techniques can be omitted in certain circumstances.

4.1 Authentication of the chip unit

If possible, an e-ID should be protected with both chip authentication and content authentication. In both cases, the asymmetric version is clearly better, especially in large systems. If both techniques are applied properly, complete fraud, cloning and alteration attacks are nearly impossible. However, some e-ID implementations don't use chip authentication, others don't use content authentication, and some don't use either. The following two sub-chapters will look at this in more detail.

4.1.1 No chip authentication

There are the following reasons, why some e-ID systems don't support chip authentication:

- The e-ID chip used for chip authentication must be a microcontroller. However, many e-IDs only use memory chips.

- The public key (which is usually provided as a part of a digital certificate) or the secret authentication key must be available to all terminal units. In both cases, revocation checking must be possible. Some designers of e-ID systems omit chip authentication, because these requirements cause higher costs.

If chip authentication is not used, cloning is possible. This has to be prevented with physical security measures (e.g. security holograms on the card).

4.1.2 No content authentication

There are the following reasons, why some e-ID systems don't support content authentication:

- The private signing key or the hashing key must be available at the issuing station. This is the more complicated the more issuing stations exist.
- The public key (which is usually provided as a part of a digital certificate) or the secret hashing key must be available to all terminal units. In both cases, revocation checking must be possible. These requirements cause additional costs.

If content authentication is not used, alteration is possible. This has to be prevented with physical security measures (e.g. secure storage).

4.2 Authentication of the terminal unit

In an e-ID system, terminal authentication should be applied to avoid unauthorized reading. The following choices exist:

- *PIN based authentication*: This choice provides the lowest security level, but is sufficient, if all terminal units have the same access rights.
- *Secret key based authentication*: This choice is more secure than the PIN based variant, but the key management is more complicated. However, no distinguishing between different terminal systems is possible.
- *Public key based authentication*: This choice provides a high security. The access rights of a terminal unit can be noted in the digital certificate, which makes it possible to grant different terminal units different access rights.
- If access rights are noted in a digital certificate, this is a case of terminal statement authentication. Terminal content authentication is not necessary in this case.

4.3 Secure data exchange

Secure data exchange should be applied in order to avoid eavesdropping and man-in-the-middle. The following choices make sense:

- *Encrypted data exchange*: No integrity protection is used in this choice. In many cases, this is sufficient, because it is difficult for an attacker to manipulate encrypted data.
- *Encrypted and hashed data exchange*: Encryption and hashing can be combined, like it is done in many protocols. This is the most common choice.
- *Encrypted and signed data exchange*: If non-repudiation is an additional requirement, digital signatures should be used instead of hashing.

It usually doesn't make sense to combine hashing and signing.

5 A view on real systems

In the third part of the paper the techniques covered are compared with the specifications of the ICAO ePass and the German electronic identity card (ePA).

5.1 ICAO ePass

The ICAO ePass supports the following cryptographic techniques (in brackets the name that is given in the ePass specification) [DOC9303]:

- Asymmetric chip authentication (Active Authentication)
- Asymmetric chip content authentication (Passive Authentication)
- Symmetric terminal authentication, PIN-based (Basic Access Control)
- Secure communication, encrypted and hashed (Secure Messaging)

5.2 German ePA

The German ePA supports the following cryptographic techniques (only the identity card function of this document is covered, in brackets the name that is given in the ePA specification) [ePA08]:

- Symmetric chip authentication is supported (PACE)
- Asymmetric chip authentication is supported (Chip Authentication)Asymmetric chip content authentication (Passive Authentication)
- Symmetric terminal authentication, key-based (PACE)
- Asymmetric terminal authentication (Terminal Authentication)
- Asymmetric terminal statement authentication (Terminal Authentication)
- Secure communication, encrypted and hashed (Secure Messaging)
- Chip content authentication is not used for the identity card function of the ePA.

6 Conclusion

Cryptography provides for a wide range of techniques for securing e-IDs. Complete fraud, cloning, alteration, eavesdropping, and man-in-the-middle can be prevented with cryptographic techniques. However, the use of cryptography always causes additional costs. Therefore, the designer of an e-ID system always has to make a decision, whether he wants to use a certain technique or not. Even prominent e-ID systems like the ICAO ePass or the German ePA don't use all cryptographic techniques that seem appropriate. This paper states the basics for what might become a formal scheme to find out the most appropriate cryptographic techniques for a certain e-ID system.

References

[DOC9303] Part 1 – Machine Readable Passport – Volume 2. Specifications for Electronically Enabled Passports with Biometric Identification Capabilities. Sixth Edition 2006

[ePA08] Einführung des elektronischen Personalausweises in Deutschland. Grobkonzept – Version 2.0. Bundesministerium des Innern, Berlin 2008

[Schm09a] Schmeh, Klaus: Elektronische Ausweisdokumente. Carl Hanser Verlag, München 2009

[Schm09b] Schmeh, Klaus: Kryptografie; Verfahren, Protokolle, Infrastrukturen. Dpunkt Verlag, Heidelberg 2009

Index

A

access control
2, 3, 6, 11, 12, 29, 31, 46, 64, 71, 87, 92, 105, 116, 124, 140, 145, 146, 153, 154, 208, 230, 237, 241, 285, 294, 356

access control models
145

access management
27, 31, 35, 97–102, 105, 107, 119–121

accountability
18, 71, 232, 234, 236, 237, 239, 304

Advanced Electronic Signature
85, 320, 321, 327

analogous world
169, 171–173

anonymity
197–205

anonymizer
212

anonymous
162, 171, 184, 197–204, 210, 232, 236, 296, 301

Architectural Risk Assessment
281, 282, 284–286, 288, 289

auditing
268, 269, 304, 306, 309, 312

audit trail
236, 272

authenticated
12, 28, 32, 101, 138, 151, 217, 232–234, 237, 330, 337, 351

authentication
3–7, 10, 30, 32, 43, 44, 64–66, 68, 74, 91–93, 98, 99, 101, 105, 109–113, 119, 121, 133, 137, 138, 141, 142, 144, 149–151, 153, 154, 165, 174, 206, 209–216, 224, 226–228, 230, 232, 234, 236, 237, 247, 252, 257, 294–296, 304, 309, 329, 331, 334, 336, 348, 351–356

authorization
5, 7, 10, 12, 34, 43, 110, 116, 117, 119–121, 123, 124, 199, 232, 234, 236, 237, 304

authorisation management
28

awareness
22, 35, 52, 54, 62, 158–160, 170, 177, 178, 181, 182, 184–186, 189, 190, 192, 194, 204, 230, 270, 271, 273–278, 293, 307

B

backup
45, 238–240, 250

banking
108, 110, 112, 113, 115, 140, 157, 158, 171, 175, 216–219, 238, 263, 275, 292, 328, 331, 332

best practices   12, 17, 25, 26, 36, 57, 63, 70, 71, 109, 110, 118, 119, 235,
                                  281, 308, 311, 339, 342, 346

biometric   87–89, 92, 99, 137–142, 144, 206, 207, 309, 347, 356

Biometric Identification   356

biometric passport   206, 207

buffer overflow   236

Business Integration   28, 42

Business Process Modelling   145, 146

C

certificate   30, 64, 65, 73, 75–80, 82, 84, 85, 99, 101, 109, 111, 112,
                                  114, 126–132, 134–136, 158, 165, 237, 244, 255–261, 266,
                                  267, 322–327, 351–353, 355

classification   21, 43, 72, 73, 77–79, 81–84, 217, 230, 232, 240, 296, 309,
                                  350

Common Criteria   34, 53, 60, 298, 301, 341, 344

compliance   18, 27, 28, 31, 33, 37, 41, 46, 47, 66, 79–82, 109, 113, 116,
                                  117, 119, 120, 124, 133, 138, 150, 191, 192, 194, 238, 250,
                                  252, 256, 258, 263, 265, 274, 281, 283, 286, 288, 290, 304,
                                  306, 309

confidentiality   21, 109, 125, 149, 150, 152, 153, 198, 205, 230, 232, 237,
                                  240, 241, 255, 304, 309, 339

contactless chip   89, 91

credentials   3–5, 63, 64, 66, 67, 92, 101, 106, 108, 109, 111–113, 204,
                                  216, 238, 239

criminal   49–52, 62

critical infrastructures   48–50, 55–62

cryptographic   3, 4, 31, 51, 72, 73, 75, 76, 78, 84, 207, 209–213, 225, 257,
                                  265, 268, 291–296, 298–301, 327, 330–334, 339, 345,
                                  347–353, 356

cryptography   4, 30, 31, 56, 77, 82, 175, 207, 215, 265, 291–293, 295,
                                  296, 298, 300, 301, 333, 334, 336, 338, 347, 350–352, 354,
                                  356

D

data center	1, 234, 241
data flow	100, 230, 241
data privacy	255
data protection	52, 97, 99, 100, 103, 105, 125, 142, 187, 190, 192–194, 197, 198, 220, 258, 275
digital certificates	110, 111, 113, 125–127, 133–135, 353
digital identity	147, 149, 204
digital natives	172, 173, 175
digital signature	86, 88, 111–113, 265, 266, 268, 269, 298, 320, 322, 352, 353
disclosure	43, 91, 125, 308, 309, 312
diversity	160, 231, 259, 333, 343, 348

E

early adopters	90, 116, 117
eavesdropping	209, 350, 355, 356
economics	52, 123, 270
Economics	90, 175, 265, 269
e-government	97, 99, 100, 105, 108, 109, 112, 114, 194
ehealth	102
electronic commerce	170, 171, 174, 340
Electronic Commerce	46, 175
electronic identity card	97, 100, 101, 105, 349, 356
electronic invoice	320
electronic passports	349
electronic signature	27, 66, 74, 85, 92, 101, 109, 244, 245, 247, 265, 320, 321, 327
e-mail	65, 125–127, 129–132, 135, 136, 138, 164, 171, 176, 177, 230, 242–246, 250, 254, 257, 272
e-mail encryption	125–127, 129, 135, 136

encryption | 4, 109, 111, 112, 125–130, 132, 133, 135, 136, 150, 165, 166, 179, 199, 206, 223–228, 230, 235–238, 241, 257, 294, 295, 309, 333, 334, 339

Encryption | 111, 126, 129, 130, 132, 164, 165, 301, 337, 355

enterprise | 2, 8, 9, 17, 25–28, 31, 33, 35, 40, 41, 43, 49, 63–71, 100, 116–122, 129, 130, 137, 144, 145, 150, 187, 188, 193, 206, 224, 241, 285, 312

entitlement | 116–124

ethics | 169, 172, 173, 175, 176, 179

European Citizen Card | 91, 92

European Commission | 27, 89, 92, 189, 195, 196, 207, 242, 250, 337

F

file system encryption | 238

fingerprint | 87–89, 92, 138, 139, 144

firewall | 21, 56, 163, 179, 211, 230, 234, 235, 241, 288

fraud | 45, 66, 98, 107, 111–113, 125, 169, 171, 173, 175, 216, 218, 219, 262–264, 269, 275, 349–351, 354, 356

fundamental rights | 189, 194

fuzzing | 312–319

G

governance | 2, 31, 37–41, 43, 45, 47, 52, 54–57, 60, 62, 64, 71, 121, 144, 195, 275, 309

guidelines | 17, 26, 40, 53, 55, 85, 119, 182, 185, 190, 192, 232, 233, 258, 271, 281, 290

H

hacking | 313

hardening | 33, 230, 235, 281, 289

hardware assurance | 340, 341, 343, 346, 347

hash | 73, 78, 82–85, 214, 265, 269, 293, 295, 327, 330, 332, 333, 352–354 hash algorithm   78, 82, 265

hierarchical protection domains   231, 241

home network   158, 160, 163, 166, 167

I

identification   44, 55, 57–60, 62, 64, 66, 67, 85, 87, 91–93, 97, 98, 100,
                                   101, 104, 111, 112, 114, 149, 151, 198–202, 206, 213–215,
                                   236, 237, 258, 260, 266, 298, 309, 356

identity   1–3, 5, 7, 8, 10–13, 26, 27, 31, 32, 36, 49, 52, 63, 68, 70,
                                   88, 90, 91, 97–101, 105, 107–116, 118, 119, 121, 124, 138,
                                   139, 143, 146–150, 153, 154, 166, 171, 176, 183, 198, 200,
                                   201, 203, 204, 209, 213, 216, 255, 256, 259, 272, 296, 349,
                                   350, 356

identity card   90, 91, 97, 100, 101, 105, 108, 138, 349, 356

identity document   349, 350

identity federation   32, 116

identity management   1, 8, 11, 13, 26, 31, 32, 52, 68, 116, 118, 143, 146, 147,
                                   154, 204, 213, 296

Identity Theft   176

information assurance   348

information security   17–19, 21–26, 33, 37–47, 61, 71, 102, 104, 175, 186, 213,
                                   215, 230, 245, 252, 253, 270, 271, 273, 274, 276–278, 283,
                                   307, 337, 338

information security management   24, 26, 37, 42, 43, 61

integrity   32, 38, 51, 66, 109, 113, 125, 149, 150, 161, 232, 243, 247,
                                   251, 255, 259, 266, 304, 309, 320, 322, 324, 327–336, 338,
                                   339, 342, 355

interconnectivity   238, 239

internet safety   177–182, 184–186

interoperability   50, 53, 55, 57, 58, 62, 72–76, 87, 92, 103, 107, 109, 110,
                                   112–115, 117, 119, 124, 126, 129, 136, 242, 243, 246, 253,
                                   254, 256, 261

intrusion   22, 44, 230, 237

investigation   93, 100, 244, 246, 274

isolation   49, 51, 54

J

jump station   233, 238, 239

K

key management   32, 86, 208, 226, 227, 289, 351–353, 355

L

law   80, 81, 97, 105, 113, 138, 189, 191–193, 203, 204, 223,
                              243, 256, 263–265, 269, 275

law enforcement   113, 189

legal   28, 43, 71, 77, 79, 80, 85, 99–101, 103, 109, 110, 125, 133,
                              145, 170, 174, 187, 190–194, 197, 199, 203, 213, 242, 243,
                              250, 252, 257, 304, 306

Liberty Alliance   99

lifetime   89, 322, 324, 326

location privacy   204, 206, 214

logging   2, 33, 150, 234, 236, 239, 309

M

malware   21, 230

man-in-the-middle   208–211, 350, 355, 356

manipulation protection   264

maturity   17, 18, 23, 26, 50, 53, 54, 75, 123, 144, 316, 317, 319

methods   25, 26, 42, 51, 59, 61, 98, 101, 137–140, 144, 150, 151,
                              163, 173, 177–181, 184, 185, 198, 202, 204, 213, 216, 220,
                              264, 298, 339, 340, 342–344, 346, 347, 349, 350

metrics   17–26, 150, 202, 204, 316, 318, 333, 336

migration   30, 61, 230, 240

model-based testing   312, 317

model-driven security   119, 153, 154

monitoring   43, 102, 180, 216, 306, 309, 316, 329, 335, 336

N

national security	189, 194, 342
networks	2, 44, 49–52, 55–57, 62, 64, 66, 104, 116, 119, 122, 125, 157–160, 164, 182–185, 197–199, 201–204, 206–210, 212, 214, 215, 220, 223, 230–233, 239, 240, 262, 296, 301, 328, 331, 342, 346, 348
network security	29, 30, 56, 160, 215

O

| obfuscation | 333, 336 |
| online banking | 238 |

P

password policy	137
password reset	21, 31, 137–144
password synchronization	137, 138, 143
patching	1, 281
payment	31, 74, 148, 149, 151, 171, 172, 175, 201, 203, 206, 305
pdf	31, 46, 76, 92, 101, 107, 136, 154, 168, 186, 192, 198, 213, 229, 261, 283, 290, 301, 320–327
penetration testing	22, 59, 306, 310, 314
performance measurement	21, 26
personal data	90, 99, 101, 102, 104, 105, 174, 179, 187, 192, 197, 198, 206, 207, 273, 351
Phishing	179, 216, 220
pitfalls	27, 63, 69, 71, 240
policy enforcement	21, 106, 117, 118, 120, 123
policy management	9, 118, 123
portal	28, 30, 31, 52, 97, 98, 102, 107, 109, 110, 122, 138, 172, 178, 185, 186, 242
privacy	21, 49, 52, 55, 97–105, 113, 119, 124, 145, 158, 167, 175, 182–184, 187, 189–200, 202–215, 220, 255, 292, 295, 296, 299, 301, 303, 304, 309, 337, 343, 346, 347

privacy policy   211, 212

proactive security   62, 312, 318

processing   4, 8, 9, 12, 24, 53, 55, 76, 89, 90, 98, 101, 102, 104, 105,
                                      112, 116, 117, 119–121, 124, 139, 142, 163, 192, 193, 197,
                                      198, 200, 207, 220, 255, 264, 305, 320, 339

product security   314, 316

project management   54, 102

pseudonyms   204, 210, 212

public key algorithm   73, 78, 82

Public Key Infrastructure (PKI)   31, 33, 63, 64, 66, 68, 77, 81, 85, 86, 91, 93, 108–115,
                                      126–136, 255–258, 261, 266, 309, 327

public procurement   72–74, 76, 85, 86, 107, 113, 194

Q

qualified signatures   73, 74, 77, 79, 80, 260

R

regulation   43, 75, 87, 89, 90, 92, 190, 194, 198, 263

reliability   140, 204, 242, 243, 245, 252, 315, 346

remote access   63, 66, 67, 138, 158

remote attestation   331, 334, 338

renewal   65, 334

residence permit   87–92

responsibility   49, 59, 70, 76, 103, 163, 170, 188, 192, 194, 244

RFID   206–215, 294

risk management   18, 19, 21, 25, 37, 42, 43, 45, 77, 84, 86

risks   19, 36, 37, 39, 42, 44, 45, 51, 57, 61, 62, 146, 150, 151,
                                      158, 159, 161–163, 166, 168, 177–185, 189, 198, 231, 271,
                                      272, 282–286, 288

robustness   312, 315, 316, 329, 334, 339

Return on Investment (ROI)   38, 63–69, 71, 194

role management   31, 117, 118

S

safeguard	33, 34, 259
SAML	4, 32, 36, 116, 148, 150, 352, 353
secure channel	90, 333
security analysis	198, 210, 265, 313, 329, 336, 337
security assurance	278, 339–343, 345–348
security by design	290
security concept	189, 194, 223, 226–228, 239, 256, 258, 263
security controls	290,303, 19–23, 25, 26, 61, 271, 282–288, 307–310
security evaluation	301, 341
security infrastructure	125
security management	24, 26, 36, 37, 42, 43, 61, 175, 308
security measures	19, 52, 54, 56, 58, 130, 138, 150, 163, 166, 230, 231, 234, 258, 277, 339, 355
security mindset	169, 170, 311
security policy	44, 46, 55, 70, 121, 148, 153, 188, 189, 195, 241, 245, 252, 254, 271
security requirements	38, 44, 45, 58, 61, 109, 145, 146, 148–154, 223, 231, 255, 256, 281–284, 286–288, 290, 295, 303–307, 311
security research	188, 194–196, 318
security technology	189–192, 196
sensitivity	237, 289, 309
sensors	138, 198
single sign-on	30, 63–70, 137, 138, 237
skimming	262, 350
smart card	30, 63–71, 90, 91, 112, 132, 137, 138, 207, 263, 265–267, 269, 294, 335
Service-Oriented Architecture (SOA)	98, 118, 123, 145, 146, 148–150, 152, 153, 237
social commerce	169–173
social engineering	138, 169, 173, 175

Software Architect   282

Software Assurance   311

software security   53, 281–283, 309–312, 314, 319, 328

SPAM   21, 162, 163

speech recognition   139, 140

strong authentication   237

survey   46, 52, 60, 144, 164, 184, 204, 220, 242, 245, 258, 337

system administration   238, 239

T

telematics infrastructure   255, 256, 259, 260

testing   18, 22, 33, 35, 42, 58, 59, 61, 103, 119, 120, 124, 129, 163,
                                         228, 247, 258, 259, 264, 265, 298, 300, 304–306, 310,
                                         312–319

threats   50, 57–59, 61, 100, 150, 158, 167, 187–189, 213, 231, 263,
                                         264, 282–286, 289, 305, 308, 310, 341, 342, 346

transfer   30, 76, 114, 130, 132, 149, 152, 171, 172, 202, 214, 219,
                                         224, 228, 233, 235, 236, 239, 241, 263, 267, 286, 322, 333

travel documents   87, 88, 92, 113, 349

trojans   66, 216

Trust Center   127, 133

trust domains   255, 257, 259

trusted computing   204, 205, 296, 301, 330, 331, 337, 340, 348

Trusted Environment   205

Trusted Platform Module (TPM)   296, 300, 301, 330, 334–336

trust management   10, 11, 129

trust model   258

U

usability 21, 40, 42, 126, 157, 167, 262, 268, 314

USB 225, 227, 228, 270, 271, 335, 336, 343, 344

user 4, 5, 21, 23, 28, 29, 31, 34–36, 44, 58, 59, 61, 64, 67–70, 78, 92, 97–103, 105–107, 110, 111, 119, 126, 127, 130–132, 137–143, 147–150, 157–168, 187, 197–201, 203, 206, 208–213, 216–218, 220, 223, 227, 228, 230, 233, 234, 236–239, 241, 243, 247, 254–256, 271, 275, 296, 316, 320, 323, 331, 340, 346, 351

user acceptance 58, 59, 143, 158, 163, 165, 166

User Acceptance 61

user experience 157–159, 166, 168

user helpdesk 137, 138, 140

user perception 158–160, 166, 167

V

validation 61, 72, 73, 75–77, 84, 86, 106, 126–129, 132, 135, 259–261, 300, 320, 322–326, 333

validity 84, 88, 89, 132, 219, 242, 243, 259, 260, 269, 298, 320, 322–326, 346

values 6, 7, 19, 22, 28, 35, 36, 40, 84, 150, 162, 170, 191, 264, 294, 295, 320, 329, 335

verification 4, 11, 51, 84, 98, 99, 101, 105, 135, 139, 140, 204, 256, 257, 259, 260, 266–268, 293, 297, 298, 300, 321–324, 326, 328–335, 343, 347

Virtual Private Network (VPN) 56, 103, 164, 233, 259, 276, 295

virus scanner 236

Voice Biometrics 137, 141, 142, 144

voice recognition 139–141

vulnerability 21, 41, 42, 44, 50, 51, 53, 58–60, 62, 132, 161, 208, 214, 231, 281–286, 288, 289, 291–294, 298, 300, 306, 310, 312–314, 341, 344

W

Web 2.0   169

web service   146–148, 150, 163, 164

wireless   158, 199, 204, 206, 209, 211, 215, 303, 331, 350

X

XML   3, 31, 32, 76, 84–86, 102, 148, 189, 218, 252, 256, 258,
                                 266, 268, 282, 283, 290, 314, 321, 326, 327